# DISCOVERING
# Microsoft Office 2010

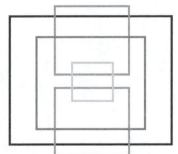

## WORD
## EXCEL
## ACCESS
## POWERPOINT

## Edward G. Martin

### City University of New York

WILEY *Custom*
LEARNING SOLUTIONS

JOHN WILEY & SONS, INC.

To my daughters,

Elissa and Andrea,

born in the years of the Apple II and IBM-PC

To order books or for customer service, please call 1(800)-CALL-WILEY (225-5945).

Printed in the United States of America.

ISBN 978-0-470-76928-7

Printed and bound by Walsworth Publishing Company.

10 9 8 7 6 5 4 3 2 1

# PREFACE

Microcomputers are wonderful tools that can save time and energy when used correctly. This book is designed to help you learn firsthand just how easy these tools are to use. The individual modules present an introduction to microcomputer hardware, Microsoft Windows 7, and the software applications of Microsoft Office 2010: Word, Excel, Access, and PowerPoint. Each is a powerful program with its own capabilities. A concluding appendix presents techniques for sharing data among these programs.

*Discovering Microsoft Office 2010* provides insight into the basics of these programs, but it does not examine all of their intricacies. There are many more techniques that you can master once you understand how each program works. I hope that once you complete this introduction, you'll experiment on your own, using the help features that come with each program. Don't worry about hurting the computer; just try learning a new technique each time you use the program. That's how I learned and, in fact, that's how I've taught thousands of students, educators, and administrators. Each skill was carefully worked out step by step to make sure it will work for you.

## Using the Modules

This book works best if you sit at a computer and try each command. Because gaining access to a computer is difficult at times, you should make the most of your computer sessions as follows:

1. Prepare for each computer session. A day or two before you sit at the keyboard, read through the next few lessons of the module. Pay attention to new vocabulary and explanations. Review new commands and note where you will have to save your files. Depending on your preparation and speed, you might easily cover several lessons in one lab session.

2. When you're using the computer, follow the module's directions unless your instructor or lab assistant tells you to modify them. It is a good idea to write any changes in the margins for future reference.

3. As you work, don't just press keys or move the mouse as you read. Instead, look at your computer screen after each action to see what has happened. Ask yourself what each action has done and how the screen has changed. Using this technique, you will learn the software quickly.

_____11/7/10

4.  Remember to save your work on diskette, flash drive, or in a folder, before you exit a program. Each lesson will cue you when to do this. You should also get into the habit of marking the point in the module where you stopped, so that you can resume the next time with ease. A line drawn across the margin with the date works fine as a place marker (such as the one in the margin here).

5.  Try the Quick Reviews (there are two in each module) and Practice Sheets as you encounter them. You may also want to refer to the Command Summary sections (located at the end of each module) as you work through the lessons. When you're done, try the projects at the end of each module to test your skills.

## About the Author

Dr. Edward Martin is a Business Professor and Department Chairman in the City University of New York. He teaches introductory computer concepts and advanced microcomputer applications, and has been a systems administrator, faculty trainer, and consultant. He has written more than seventy-five books on computer use including the _Mastering Today's Software_ series and _Discovering_ series (now in its 16th edition).

## Acknowledgments

The author wishes to thank Ryan Steffen, Beth Golub, and Lenore Belton of Wiley Publishing as well as Asif Hussain and Seth Kaye of Kingsborough Community College for their assistance in the development of this edition of Discovering Microsoft Office 2010. Thanks are also due to the careful typesetting, attention to detail, and layout skills of Rocky and Kim Buckley of Black Diamond Graphics.

Ed Martin
New York City, 2010

# CONTENTS IN BRIEF

# DETAILED CONTENTS

## SPREADSHEET MODULE: EXCEL 2010    **E-1**

# INTRODUCTORY MODULE

## INTRODUCING WINDOWS 7

## INTRODUCTION: WHY THIS MANUAL?

As silly as it may sound, computers are useful only if you use them! This manual gives you direct experience with Microsoft Windows 7 and four useful applications found in the Microsoft Office 2010 "suite" program: word processing, spreadsheets, database management, and presentation graphics. By following the step-by-step tutorials, you'll develop the skills you need to successfully use microcomputers.

*Discovering Microsoft Office 2010* provides the link between textbook theory and the harsh reality of trying to muddle through software manuals. From starting the computer to printing a document, you'll work through the directions and screens, even if you've never used a computer before. Here's how.

First, you will learn about microcomputer equipment and startup techniques. Next, you will practice the basics of Microsoft Windows 7. Windows is a graphical user interface or "GUI" (pronounced "gooey") that lets you communicate with the computer by using pictures (called icons) instead of words. Once you understand how to use Windows, you can then learn other software that share Windows' common commands. For each application, follow the tutorials in the appropriate module. When you're finished, feel free to experiment on your own. Try the projects at the end of each module to test your understanding. Remember, the more you practice, the easier it will be to use the microcomputer.

This manual can be used by itself with the appropriate software. However, you may also want to use it with a concepts text that provides more detailed discussions about computer hardware and software. Once you are familiar with the software, you may want to consult the software's own help screens to learn more about the capabilities each package has to offer.

## LESSON 1: HARDWARE

Figure I-1 shows a typical microcomputer setup with one disk drive (called "drive A") and a hard disk drive (called "drive C") housed in a system unit. A screen, keyboard, mouse, and printer are attached.

Your computer may have a different disk drive setup. As shown in Figure I-2, your computer may have disk drives arranged in other ways. The drives may be stacked above each other or positioned side by side. You may have a CD-ROM or DVD-ROM, CD-RW or DVD-RW ("burners").

In addition, all modern computers have Universal Serial Bus ("USB") ports that allow you to easily connect other peripherals or memory to your computer simply by plugging them in. USB ports are typically located in the back of the computer but are often found on the front as well. USB ports are identified by a standard icon (as shown in the margin).

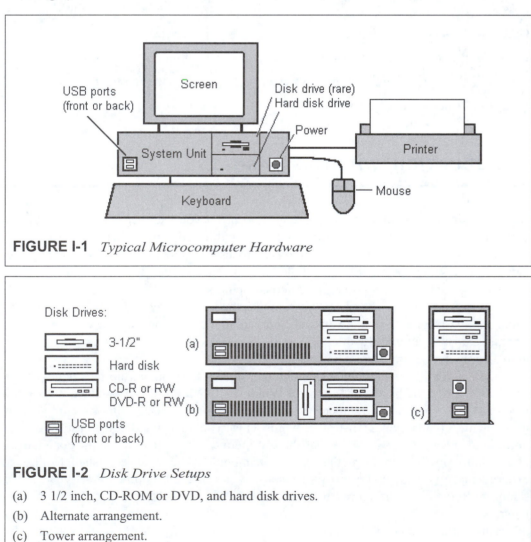

**FIGURE I-1**  *Typical Microcomputer Hardware*

**FIGURE I-2**  *Disk Drive Setups*

(a)   3 1/2 inch, CD-ROM or DVD, and hard disk drives.

(b)   Alternate arrangement.

(c)   Tower arrangement.

If you have a 3 1/2-inch floppy diskette drive, it is usually called drive A. A hard-disk drive is usually called drive C. CD-ROM (or DVD) drives are typically called drive D (or E). USB ports use letters that follow these drives (E, F, or G). Your computer may also be connected to a local area network (LAN). If so, the network is typically identified with an F, although your network may differ.

The following short summary may be helpful to you. Computers have four components, each with a specific task. *Input* components let you put instructions, or data, into the computer. The *processor*, which is inside the system unit, performs all the required logic and math. *Storage* retains data and programs needed for processing in a format the computer can interpret. *Output* components communicate back to you in a form you can understand.

## Input Components

Input is typically provided through the keyboard, which has alphabetic and symbol keys, a numeric keypad, function keys, and other special keys (see Figure I-3) whose functions vary with the software in use. The following section takes you on a quick tour of some of them, starting at the upper-left corner of the keyboard, as shown in Figure I-3.

> **NOTE:** Your keyboard layout may differ from the current standard shown in Figure I-3. While the keys may be placed elsewhere, they have the same functions.

Locate each key on your keyboard as it is presented and discussed here. Become familiar with each key's location (but do not press it).

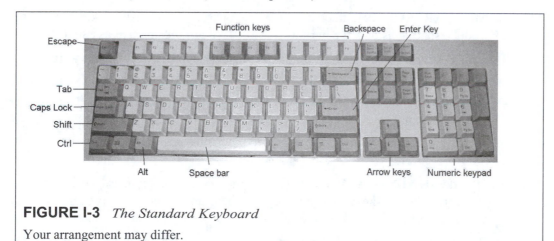

**FIGURE I-3** *The Standard Keyboard*
Your arrangement may differ.

a. **ESCAPE** key: Labeled "Esc," this key is located in the upper-left corner of the keyboard. Many programs use it to return to a previous menu, or to cancel an action. It is shown as ⌞ESC⌟ in this manual.

b. **FUNCTION** keys: Typically found across the top of the keyboard, function keys are labeled F1 through F12. (The action that occurs when each of these keys is pressed is defined by each program. Function keys are shown as ⌞F1⌟ through ⌞F12⌟ in this manual.)

c. **TAB** key: Found two keys below ⌞ESC⌟, the ⌞TAB⌟ key usually works like a typewriter's ⌞TAB⌟, but can be used with the ⌞SHIFT⌟ key (see item "e" below) to tab backward at times. It is also used by some programs to move among screen items. It is shown as ⌞TAB⌟ in this manual.

**d.** **CAPS LOCK** key: Located below the [TAB] key, this key is a *toggle* switch. This means that you press it once to turn it on, and press it again to shut it off. [CAPS LOCK] "locks in" capital letters only. It does not affect any other key. It is shown as [CAPS LOCK] in this manual.

**e.** **SHIFT** key: Beneath the [CAPS LOCK] key is one of two [SHIFT] keys. (There is another one on the right side of the keyboard.) The [SHIFT] key is used to select uppercase letters (when [CAPS LOCK] is off), or to produce the symbols shown at the top of each key. For instance, to type a dollar sign, you would press and hold [SHIFT] with one finger, press the **4** key (typically with your other hand), and then release both. This manual lists that sequence as [SHIFT] + **4**. (If CAPS LOCK is toggled on, pressing [SHIFT] will select lowercase letters.)

**f.** **CONTROL** key: Under [SHIFT] is the [CTRL] (Control) key, which, like SHIFT, also lets you use a key for another purpose. For example, pressing [CTRL] and [END] in some programs will move to the end of a document. You'll see it in this manual as [CTRL] + [END], which means "hold the [CTRL] key and press the [END] key." A second [CTRL] key is located on the other side of the keyboard. It works exactly the same way.

**g.** **ALTERNATE** key: The [ALT] (Alternate) key is found next to the [CTRL] key on both sides of the keyboard. Like [CTRL], it expands each key's use and is always used with another key; for example, [ALT] + **X**, which means "hold down the [ALT] key and press the X key."

**h.** **SPACE BAR**: At the bottom center of the keyboard is a long narrow key that is used to produce spaces, as on a typewriter. It is displayed in this manual as [SPACE].

**i.** **DELETE** key: In most cases, it removes whatever symbol is currently at the insertion point. It is displayed in this manual as [DELETE].

**j.** **POINTER CONTROL** (or **ARROW**) keys: To the right of the [CTRL] key are four keys labeled with arrows pointing left [←], down [↓], right [→], and up [↑]. These arrow keys are used to move the screen pointer one position in the corresponding direction.

**k.** **PLUS** and **MINUS** keys: At the extreme right side of the keyboard, in the numeric keypad, are + and − keys that are used for math and some word processing functions. Your keyboard may also have division (/) and multiplication (*) keys here.

**l.** **NUM LOCK** key: Found on the top row of the numeric keypad, this toggle key lets you choose between using the keypad to control the screen position of the insertion point or to enter numbers. For example, with NUM LOCK off, the **4** key can be used to move the insertion point to the left; with NUM LOCK on, the **4** key will enter a **4**. If you ever find your numeric keys acting strangely, you probably pressed [NUM LOCK] by mistake. If so, press it again to toggle it off.

**m.** **BACKSPACE** key: This key displays a left-pointing arrow and the word Backspace, and is located in the upper-right corner of the keyboard's typewriter section. [BACKSPACE] moves the insertion point one space to the left, usually erasing any character that might be in its path. It is listed as [BACKSPACE] in this manual.

n.  **ENTER** (or **RETURN**) key: Located below ⌷BACKSPACE⌷ , this large key displaying a bent arrow ⌷↵⌷ and the word Enter, is used most commonly to signal the completion of an action. It is listed as ⌷↵⌷ in this manual.

> **NOTE:** Most keys will repeat if you do not release them quickly. Try to develop a light touch on the keyboard.

### The Mouse

Input can also be supplied through a pointing device such as a mouse that lets you select menu choices directly from the screen. As you move the mouse on a flat surface (as in Figure I-4), a pointer moves in a similar manner on your screen. You can then "click" (press) a mouse button to invoke the desired action. A mouse greatly simplifies using Windows and other applications. In fact, this book assumes that you will be using a mouse or some other pointing device (such as a trackball or touchpad). You will learn more about the mouse shortly.

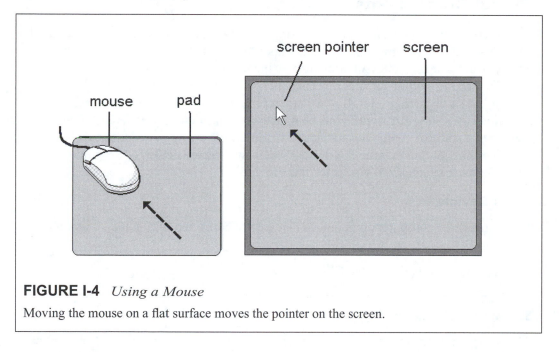

**FIGURE I-4**  *Using a Mouse*

Moving the mouse on a flat surface moves the pointer on the screen.

## Processing

Processing converts the raw data you enter into a more meaningful form called information. Processing is performed by the central processing unit (or CPU) hidden inside the computer's system unit. Programs (sets of instructions) and data are entered into the CPU from either the keyboard, mouse, or a disk drive. The CPU, the "brain" of your computer, follows the instructions to process the data into a new form.

## Storage

Storage can be primary or secondary. Most primary storage (kept on integrated circuits or "chips" inside the system unit) is used to retain data and instructions temporarily while they are being processed. It is erased when the computer is turned off. Disks and "flash" drives are secondary storage (see Lesson 2). Simply put, secondary storage provides a more permanent way to store programs and data outside the computer's primary storage. This way, you can easily load new instructions into the CPU and copy information before the computer is turned off. You can save material and have the computer retrieve it without ever having to type it again. Disks require the use of a disk drive, which can send data to, or read data from, the disk. Your computer system may have one or more disk drives. They may be "floppy" diskette drives, hard disk drives, or even optical disk drives (CD-ROM, CD-RW, or DVD). They are typically installed within the system unit or may remain outside the computer, connected by a cable. Flash drives (also called jump-, pocket-, pen-, or thumb-drives) are convenient hardware items, about the size of a pack of gum, that plug directly into a computer's USB port and store considerable amounts of data.

## Output Components

Output comes in three basic forms. The first is the screen, or monitor, which resembles a TV. This is the major form of communication between the CPU and you. It shows you what you are entering and will often display the results of computer activity.

The second output form is a printer used to produce printed "hardcopy." You may have an inkjet or laser printer. If you share a printer with other computers, make sure that the printer is ready to receive your computer's output before you send it. This is often done with a selector switch located near the printer.

The third output is sound. Your computer may have speakers that produce sounds, music, or even synthesized voices to "talk" to you.

### Quick Review #1

1. Name three computer components that are not contained within the system unit.

    _____

2. What is the function of the CPU?

    _____

3. What is a flash drive?

    _____

4. What action should you take when you see a command such as "$\boxed{\text{CTRL}}$ + **B**" in this book?

    _____

5. Name three forms of output.

    _____

## LESSON 2: PRIMARY AND SECONDARY STORAGE

As you have learned, there are two types of computer memory or storage: primary and secondary. Primary storage plays the same role for the computer that your own memory does for you. Any data or program that the computer uses must be entered into primary storage. Secondary storage (such as a disk or flash drive) provides an additional storage area, in much the same way as your notebook functions for you. On disk, you can keep many different programs or data for computer use. A collection of disks can contain unlimited storage, even though your computer's primary memory is limited (see Figure I-5).

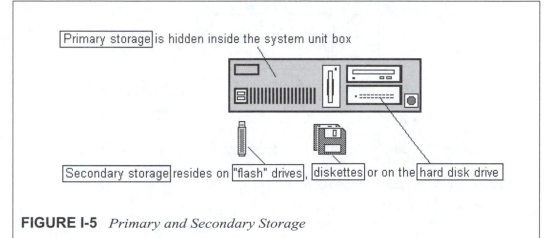

Primary storage is hidden inside the system unit box

Secondary storage resides on "flash" drives, diskettes or on the hard disk drive

**FIGURE I-5**  *Primary and Secondary Storage*

Primary storage is kept within the system unit, whereas secondary storage is kept on disk.

**NOTE:**  Most primary memory is composed of RAM—random access memory—that is available for your use but is erased when the computer is turned off. A smaller portion of primary memory called ROM—read only memory—is used to permanently store a small set of instructions that tell the computer what to do when it is turned on. These instructions include loading from secondary storage into RAM the programs the computer needs to begin to process applications.

The capacity of both primary and secondary storage is measured by how many characters they can hold. One byte (pronounced "bite") is the amount of memory needed to hold one typed character—a letter, number, symbol, or even a blank space. A byte is a very small amount, so larger units were developed to define computer storage. A kilobyte (abbreviated K or KB) is approximately one thousand bytes of storage. A megabyte (M, MB, or Meg) is about one million bytes of storage. A gigabyte (G, GB, or Gig) is just over one billion bytes of storage.

Knowing how much memory is available in your computer's primary and secondary storage helps you ascertain whether your programs and data will fit. In today's microcomputers, typical primary storage (RAM) ranges from a low of 512 Meg (512 million characters) to a more usable 1 or 2 Gig. Secondary storage, almost 1.5 (actually 1.44) Meg in standard diskettes, can reach about 2 Gig in flash drives and more than 160 Gig in microcomputer hard disk drives.

**NOTE:**  One K is actually 2 to the 10th power, or 1024. One Meg is actually 2 to the 20th power, or 1,048,576. It is convenient, though, to use the approximations of 1,000 and 1,000,000 when working with memory.

When you use application software, you place data and instructions into primary memory (RAM) for the computer's use. Software is usually kept on the hard disk (as in

Figure I-6). You then give the computer a command to start and the software takes over. If your computer is connected to a network, programs are typically kept in a main computer and brought into your primary storage when needed. Your computer's hard disk drive contains special programs to start your computer and access the network.

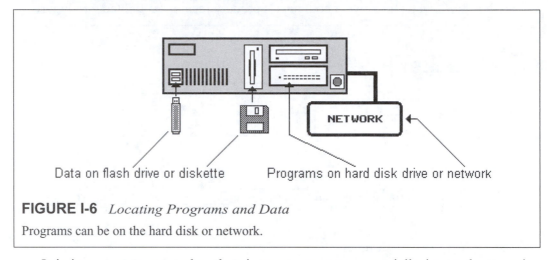

Data on flash drive or diskette          Programs on hard disk drive or network

**FIGURE I-6**  *Locating Programs and Data*

Programs can be on the hard disk or network.

It is important to remember that, in most programs, especially in word processing and spreadsheets, all the additions and changes you make to your data are kept in the computer's primary memory while the software is in use. Before leaving the program, you must copy the data that is in primary storage onto a disk (secondary storage); otherwise, your new work will be lost.

Each software program has an easy way to accomplish this task. Data, such as those found in a document or spreadsheet, can be stored on disk (or flash drive) in a separate unit known as a file. At some point in any program you are using, you can save your work on secondary storage and assign it a filename so that the program can find it again. Filenames can be up to 255 characters long, but it is up to you to pick meaningful names. For example, a budget for June 2010 might be named MONTH BUDGET 0610, while the year's budget might be 2010 YEAR BUDGET. Some programs also allow you to use up to four characters as an extension (such as .DOCX in Word documents or .LTR, as in EGM1101.LTR). Part of the skill in effectively using programs is creating meaningful filenames. It involves careful thought, but you can always change the names later.

## Care of Diskettes

Although this is rare, the standard diskette that your computer may use is a 3-1/2 inch high-density (HD) "floppy" diskette (the term "floppy" refers to the very thin medium used in the diskette). This diskette can hold about 1.4 Meg, or a little more than 1.4 million typewritten characters—enough to hold almost 700 single-spaced pages. Not bad for a flimsy piece of magnetic material that costs less than ten cents! Typical HD diskettes in use today are encased in plastic and have a metal protective cover.

**NOTE:** Other disk formats include high-capacity "zip" disks that can hold in excess of 100 Meg!

The recording medium used in all diskettes is thin and magnetic, making them susceptible to a number of problems. Even though diskettes are a relatively durable means of storing data, a little care goes a long way in protecting work contained on them.

**NOTE:** To help avoid confusion, the term "diskette" in this manual refers to the 3-1/2 inch variety; the term "disk" refers to the hard disk drive. Both disks and diskettes are secondary storage and serve the same purpose.

### Some Suggestions for Handling Your Diskettes

1. Store diskettes vertically, away from heat and moisture.

2. It is best to hold diskettes gently between thumb and forefinger in the area covered by the label.

3. When you place a label on a diskette, be sure that the label does not touch its metal cover. (See Figure I-7.)

4. Do not bend or attempt to open diskettes.

5. Keep diskettes away from magnets and magnetic fields, which can destroy the information on them. Keeping diskettes at least a foot away from monitors is a good idea. It is also a good idea to store diskettes in a plastic box for safekeeping.

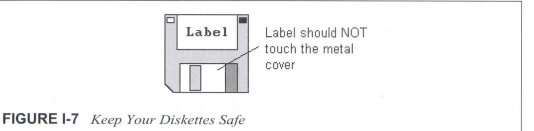

**FIGURE I-7** *Keep Your Diskettes Safe*

The protective metal covers on 3-1/2 inch diskettes should not be impeded by labels.

### Inserting Diskettes into the Computer's Disk Drive

1. Select the proper diskette. This is not as easy as it sounds because most diskettes look alike! Make sure you label all your diskettes and read the labels correctly.

2. Hold 3-1/2 inch diskettes with the metal cover pointed away from you. Then simply slide it into the disk drive. Do not force the diskette. If it does not slide in easily, you may be holding it upside down. As in Figure I-8a, the metal cover should go into the drive first, label side toward you. If the disk drive is positioned horizontally, keep the label uppermost; if the drive is vertical, keep the bottom of the diskette, as in Figure I-8b, closer to the drive's eject button.

3. To remove a 3-1/2 inch diskette, simply press the eject button located on the disk drive. The diskette will pop out for easy removal.

4. Do not leave diskettes lying on tables, or worse, on top of the monitor. Dust, smoke (especially cigarette smoke), and liquids are a diskette's natural enemies, as are electromagnetic waves that come from TVs, VCRs, and other electronic equipment.

### Flash Drives

It is more likely that you will use a flash drive instead of floppy diskettes. A flash drive, typically the size of a pack of chewing gum, offers an inexpensive and convenient way to store much larger amounts of data, ranging from 32 Meg to several Gig—the equivalent of hundreds of floppy diskettes. Unlike disks, flash drives are composed of a type of EEP-ROM ("Electrically Erasable Programmable Read-Only Memory") that can store and erase blocks of data easily. As shown in Figure I-8c, once its protective plastic cover is removed, a flash drive is simply plugged into any USB port on a computer. (To remove a flash drive, click the "Safely Remove Hardware" icon on the Windows taskbar and follow the dialog boxes.)

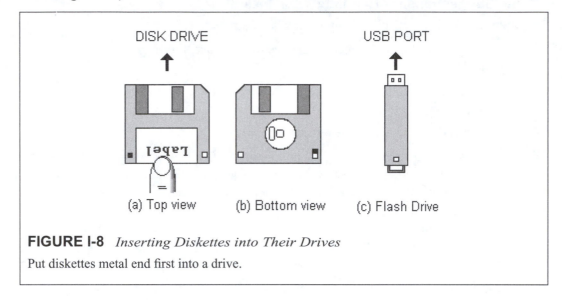

**FIGURE I-8**   *Inserting Diskettes into Their Drives*

Put diskettes metal end first into a drive.

## LESSON 3: UNDERSTANDING THE WINDOWS SCREEN

Before you can use a program, you must first load the computer with the basic instructions it needs to work. These instructions are contained in a set of programs called the operating system ("OS"), which is part of Windows. This process is known as "booting." Startup procedures differ greatly from one computer lab to the next. Some labs require computers to be left on. Others allow individual computers to be turned on as needed. Check with your instructor or lab technician for your specific startup procedure.

You may want to write the specific commands for your computer system in the allotted spaces for future reference. In a short time, this routine will become second nature to you, and you will not need to use the startup reference at all.

### Computer Startup Procedure

1.  Make sure there is no diskette in drive A. The hard disk typically contains the startup programs needed to boot the system.

2.  Turn on your computer's system unit and monitor.

3.  Wait while the computer performs self-tests of its circuits and memory. The message "Starting Windows" may appear briefly.

**NOTE:**  If you started with a diskette in drive A, you may see a "Non-system disk" message. No harm done. Remove your diskette and press any key to start again.

4. Your goal now is to start Windows. This may happen automatically, or you may have to enter some commands. Check with your instructor for your computer's specific procedure, and circle the letter of the appropriate step for future reference.

   a. Automatic: If Windows appears automatically, skip to step 5 now.

   A Welcome screen may appear, as shown in Figure I-9. Take a quick look at this screen.

   - At the lower left is an "Ease of Access" button that opens a menu of accessibility adjustments to the Windows program, such as Narrator, Magnifier, High Contrast, Onscreen Keyboard, Sticky Keys, and Filter Keys. (You may read about any of these in Windows' Help screen.)

   - The lower right button accesses additional logoff options.

   b. Figure I-9 displays one user name. If other user names appear, click the appropriate user name to select it. Next, if asked, type your password and press the Enter key ⏎. Continue with step 5.

   c. Other messages/steps (supplied by your instructor if needed):

   _____

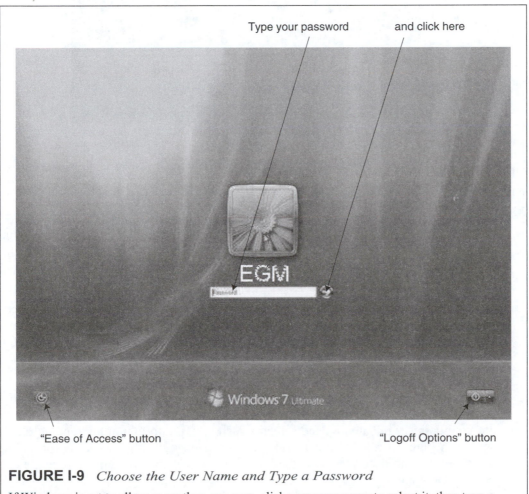

Type your password          and click here

EGM

"Ease of Access" button                    "Logoff Options" button

**FIGURE I-9**   *Choose the User Name and Type a Password*

If Windows is set to allow more than one user, click your user name to select it, then type a password and press ⏎.

5. You are now in Windows.

## THE WINDOWS DESKTOP

> **NOTE:**   Once you are in Windows, you must always exit properly before turning off your computer. If you want to stop before you learn how to use the mouse, you can always quit by using the keyboard: Press CTRL + ESC , then press **U** twice.

Your screen should resemble Figure I-10. Don't worry if your screen differs slightly for now. Examine your screen to identify each component as it is introduced.

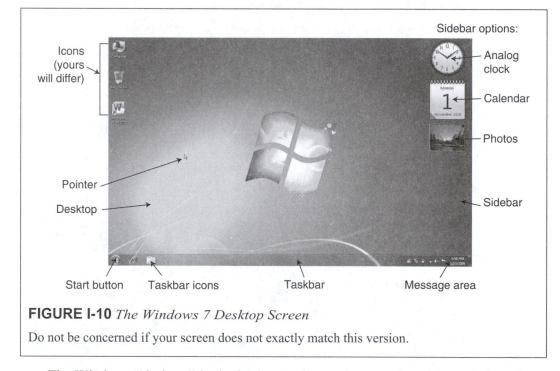

**FIGURE I-10** *The Windows 7 Desktop Screen*

Do not be concerned if your screen does not exactly match this version.

a.  The Windows "desktop" is the background area that contains objects such as icons and windows (more on these in a moment). It is one of the two main sections of the Windows screen. Like your own desktop, you can arrange objects on it to suit your needs and change them anytime you like.

b.  One or more icons may occupy the desktop (often at the upper-left corner). An *icon* is a graphic symbol that represents a program, a document, or some other Windows feature. A title beneath the icon identifies the item represented by the icon. Figure I-10 shows three icons: "Computer," "Recycle Bin" and "Word 2010." Programs or documents can be opened by double-clicking the icon with a mouse.

c.  Windows may also display a "Sidebar" on the right side of the desktop. The *Sidebar* is a desktop area that contains additional icons for *gadgets* (mini-programs), which are continuously updated on the screen—such as a photo album and analog clock, shown in Figure I-10b. You can add (or remove) gadgets such as *feeds* (providing news, sports, and headlines from the Internet), *launchers* (program shortcuts), a calculator, CPU meter, notes, and others.

d.  A "taskbar" appears across the bottom of the screen. At the moment, only a *Start* button (at the lower left), perhaps some icons, and a time indicator (at the right) appear on the taskbar.

- The *Start* button accesses Windows' menu, from which you can launch (start) programs or turn off Windows entirely.

- The time indicator not only displays the system time, but may include icons that provide additional information about your system. For example, the loudspeaker icon contains volume controls for the computer.

- Each time you launch a program, a corresponding program button will be placed on the taskbar. You can then click the desired button to quickly switch among open programs, as you will see.

- Windows may display additional icons on the taskbar. They are not important for our current discussion.

e.　One additional item found on the screen is the pointer, which displays your current screen location. Although the pointer most often resembles an arrow, its shape will change as you alter its function (see Figure I-11). You control the position of the pointer by using a pointing device, typically a mouse, although your system might use a trackball or touch pad.

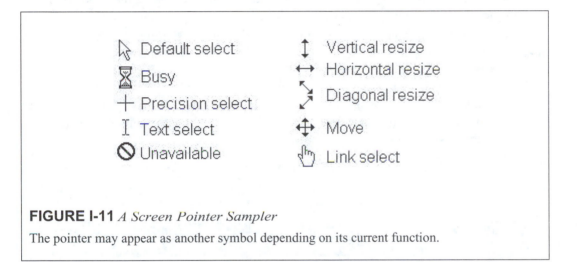

**FIGURE I-11** *A Screen Pointer Sampler*

The pointer may appear as another symbol depending on its current function.

Moving your mouse changes the position of the pointer. Try this:

1.　Move the mouse so that the pointer moves to the upper-left corner of the screen. Notice that the pointer reflects your movements on the screen.

**NOTE:**　If your mouse runs out of space on the desk, simply lift it and replace it where there is more room in the direction you want to move. As long as the mouse is lifted, the screen pointer will not be affected.

2.　Move the mouse diagonally to the lower right of the screen. Note that the pointer reflects the movement.

3.　Using the mouse, point to the *Recycle Bin* icon, and then point to the *Start* button in the taskbar. Practice pointing to various locations on the desktop until you feel comfortable moving the mouse pointer. The proper positioning of a mouse is an important skill when using Windows.

## Selecting Items with the Mouse

Some commands are invoked by pointing to them. For most, however, once you position the mouse pointer, you must then press a mouse button in one of four ways:

- *Click:* Tap (press and release) the left mouse button once.
- *Right-click:* Tap the right mouse button once.
- *Double-click:* Quickly tap the left mouse button twice.
- *Drag and drop:* Press and hold the left mouse button down. Move ("drag") the mouse to a new location and then release it ("drop").

These mouse techniques are common to all Windows programs and should be mastered quickly. You will now practice two of them as you learn more about the Windows screen:

1. As shown in Figure I-12a, point to the *Recycle Bin* icon on the desktop (as shown, use the *tip* of the arrow to point).

2. Double-click the icon. This may take some practice. (You may find it easier to hold the mouse steady with one hand while double-clicking it with the other until you master the technique.)

The Recycle Bin icon opens to a window, as shown in Figure I-12b. Notice, too, that its program button appears on the taskbar. You can now examine the remaining Windows components.

A window, such as the Recycle Bin, is a rectangular area on the desktop, enclosed by a frame that contains programs, documents, or folders (groups of files). The window that you are currently using is called the active window. Although many windows can be opened on the desktop, there can only be one active window at a time.

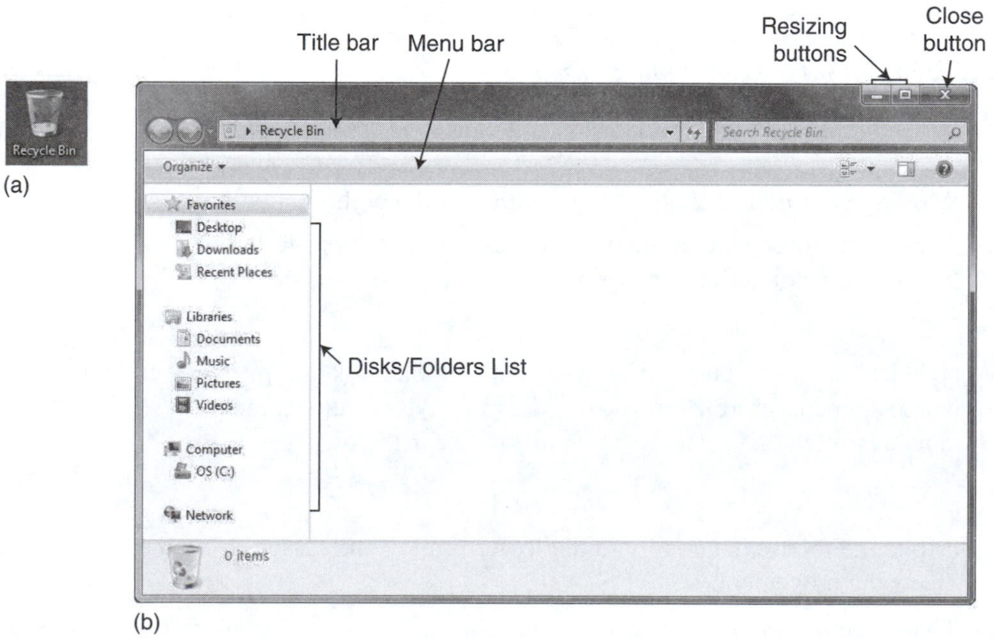

**FIGURE I-12** *The Recycle Bin Window*

Double-clicking a desktop icon (a) opens its window on the desktop as seen in (b).
Note: Your window may differ in content or size.

3. Examine the Recycle Bin window starting in the upper-left corner. Most of the components here are common to all windows that you use.

   a. A *title bar* appears across the top of the window. It contains an identifying title. The title bar will change color when the window is active to distinguish it from other windows on the desktop. The active window is also indicated by its taskbar button, which will appear "pressed."

   b. Two *resizing buttons* appear to the right of the title bar. The first button (with an underline) is the *minimize button*. It reduces the window to a taskbar button or desktop icon when clicked. The second button that appears depends on the current size of the window. If the window is not yet at full size, a *maximize button* (with a large rectangle) will appear. When clicked, it will enlarge the window to fill the screen. If the window is already at full size, a *restore button* (with two smaller rectangles) will appear instead. This button restores a window to its original size and position.

   c. A *close button*, containing an X, appears to the right of the two resizing buttons. When clicked, it closes the window and exits the program.

   d. A *menu bar* appears below the title bar in all application windows. (Document windows, as you will see, have no menu bar.) The menu bar contains a set of pull-down menus that let you perform various functions, such as saving and opening files, editing, and getting help.

   e. *Scroll bars* may appear along the right side and/or bottom of any window that is too small to display its entire contents. The scroll bar end arrows can be clicked, or the center "elevator" box can be dragged, to view other portions of the window.

## Using the Menu Bar to Close a Window

While you are in this window, try the following exercise to acquaint yourself with the operation of the menu bar.

1. Point to the word *Organize* in the Recycle Bin menu bar, as shown in Figure I-13a, and click the mouse (press and release the left mouse button).

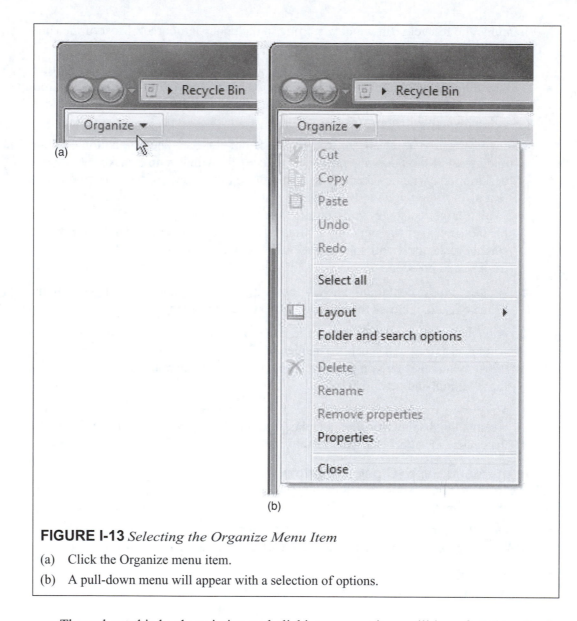

**FIGURE I-13** *Selecting the Organize Menu Item*

(a)   Click the Organize menu item.

(b)   A pull-down menu will appear with a selection of options.

   Throughout this book, pointing and clicking a menu item will be referred to simply as "click," as in "Click File in the menu bar." Clicking a menu item causes a pull-down menu to appear. In this case, the File (or Organize) submenu should appear as in Figure I-13b. If not, press ESC to cancel the command and repeat step 1.

   Examine the pull-down menu for a moment. Items can be selected by simply clicking the appropriate line. Although there are none in this particular menu, items with an ellipsis (...) will invoke another menu if selected. Items with keys displayed to their right can be invoked by pressing the shortcut keys shown. You can also select a menu item by pressing its underlined letter on the keyboard.

> **NOTE:** In general, if the wrong menu appears, you can cancel it by pressing $\boxed{\text{ESC}}$ or pointing outside the menu area and clicking the mouse.

2. Click *Close* at the bottom of the menu, as shown in Figure I-13b. The Recycle Bin window closes.

> **NOTE:** You can also close a window by clicking its close (X) button at the extreme right of its title bar.

### Exiting Windows

The last skill you must master in this section is how to exit Windows properly. This will guarantee that all your files are saved correctly. Do not simply shut off the computer when you are through. In Windows, the exit process is known as "logging off" or "turning off." Most typically, it is called "shutting down."

> **NOTE:** There is a difference between logging off and turning off. When you *log* off, you simply close your user account but the computer remains on for easy access by you or another user. When you *turn* off, you actually shut down Windows so that you can safely turn off the computer (some computers turn off automatically).

1. Click the *Start* button on the taskbar, as in Figure I-14a. (You can also press $\boxed{\text{CTRL}}$ + $\boxed{\text{ESC}}$ .)

2. Click the *Shut Down* button (as shown in Figure I-14b). If you click the arrow (as shown in Figure I-14c), a menu pops up offering other shut down options.

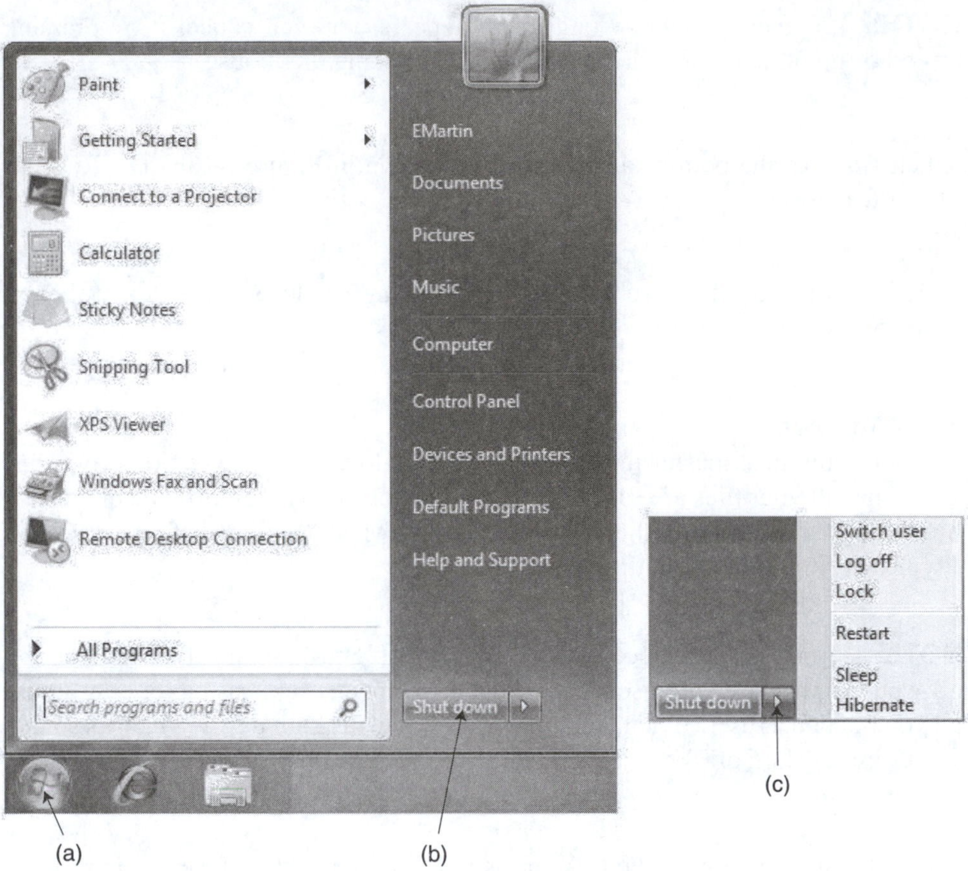

**FIGURE I-14** *Turning Off Windows*

To exit:

(a)  Click Start.

(b)  Click Shut Down.

(c)  Click this arrow to access other options.

**3.**  After a brief wait, the computer should turn itself off. This is a good place to stop for now. Follow your lab procedure for shutting off your computer.

## LESSON 4: WINDOW FUNDAMENTALS

Windows' powerful multitasking feature allows you to work with more than one window at a time. Here, you will practice the fundamentals of launching programs and adjusting their windows for best effect.

### Launching Programs

In Windows, launch means "start." Programs may be launched through a desktop icon or through the *Start* button. In the following exercise, you will locate and launch two standard Windows programs: Paint and Notepad, both located in the Accessories submenu of "All Programs."

**1.** Start Windows.

**2.** Click the *Start* button to access the Windows menu, as shown in Figure I-15a.

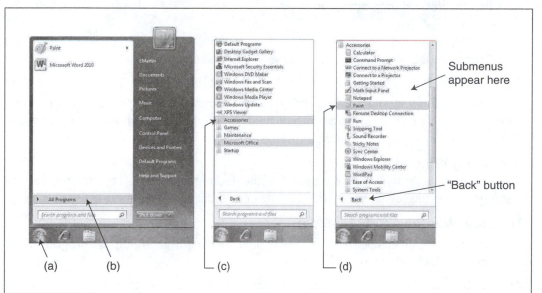

**FIGURE I-15** *Launching a Program*

(a)  Click the Start button to access the Windows menu.

(b)  Point to the All Programs menu item to invoke its submenu.

(c)  Point to the next menu item in the sequence until you reach the submenu that contains the desired program. (Your list may differ.)

(d)  Click the desired program to launch it.

Examine the menu for a moment. Note that the "All Programs" menu item displays an arrow symbol to its left. The arrow indicates that the item will open to a submenu when you point to it.

**3.** Point to *All Programs* on the Windows menu to access its submenu, as shown in Figure I-15b.

> **NOTE:** The submenu actually *replaces* the current list, so there is no need to move right, just continue to select choices.

**4.** Point to *Accessories* to access its submenu, as shown in Figure I-15c.

**5.** Now that you have found the desired submenu, click the Paint program item in the rightmost list to launch it, as shown in Figure I-15d. Note that a scroll bar allows you to look at the entire menu. In addition, a *Back* button has replaced the *All Programs* option, allowing you to return to a previous menu if needed by clicking it.

Note that the Paint window appears on the desktop and that a corresponding icon is placed on the taskbar. The program has been launched and is now available for use.

> **NOTE:** This procedure can be followed to launch any program: Click the *Start* button, point to All Programs and then each submenu in succession, and then click the desired program to launch it.

**6.** Repeat steps 2–4 to access the *Accessories* submenu again.

**7.** Click the Notepad program item in the rightmost list to launch it.

Two windows should now appear on the desktop, with corresponding program icons on the taskbar. The active program is indicated by a highlighted window title bar and by a taskbar icon that appears "brighter."

### Arranging Windows

Windows can be arranged and/or resized on the desktop as needed. Try the following two techniques—arranging windows side by side and cascade—to see these effects:

### To Show Windows Side by Side:

**1.** Right-click any blank space on the taskbar between the rightmost program button and the time, as shown in Figure I-16.

**2.** Click *Show Windows Side by Side* in the shortcut menu that appears.

**3.** Click anywhere in the Notepad window to make it active for now.

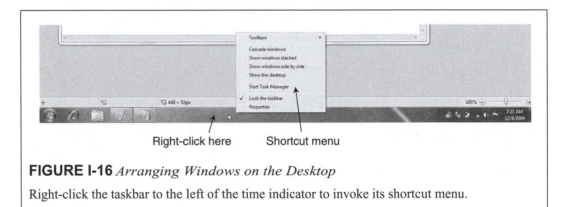

Right-click here     Shortcut menu

**FIGURE I-16** *Arranging Windows on the Desktop*

Right-click the taskbar to the left of the time indicator to invoke its shortcut menu.

As shown in Figure I-17, windows now appear next to each other on the desktop without overlap. The active window is shown by its highlighted title bar and frame.

Highlighted title bar (Close button is red)

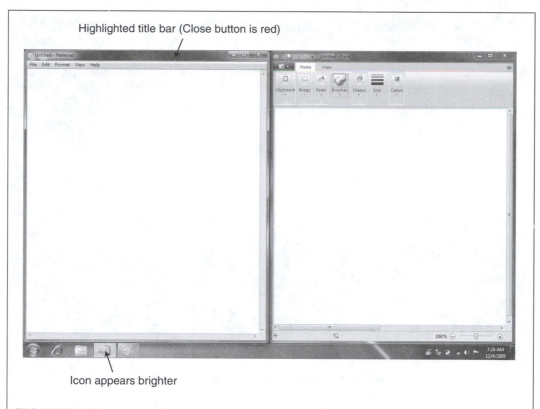

Icon appears brighter

**FIGURE I-17** *Side by Side Windows*

Windows are displayed next to each other with no overlap. A highlighted title bar and a taskbar icon that appears "brighter" show the active window.

**NOTE:** To show windows stacked, repeat Steps 1 and 2 but select the "Show Windows Stacked" option.

### To Cascade Windows:

1. Right-click the empty space on the taskbar, as you did in step 2 of the Side by Side procedure.

2. Click *Cascade Windows* in the shortcut menu.

3. Click anywhere in the Notepad window to make it active for now.

   As shown in Figure I-18, cascading windows appear in an overlapping stack on the desktop with the active window uppermost.

**FIGURE I-18** *Cascading Windows*

Cascaded windows appear in a stack with the active window uppermost.

## Switching Between Programs

Although both programs are now available for use, only one can be active at a time. You can easily switch the active window using the taskbar.

### Using the Taskbar to Switch Programs

**1.** Click the Paint button on the taskbar, as shown in Figure I-19a (or press [ALT] + [TAB]).

Note that its taskbar icon now appears "brighter" and its highlighted window moves to the foreground, in front of the Notepad window.

> **NOTE:** Point to a taskbar icon to see a small image of its window, as shown in Figure I-19b.

**2.** Click the Notepad icon on the taskbar (or press [ALT] + [TAB]). Note the taskbar button and window changes.

### Using a Window to Switch Programs

You can also switch programs by directly clicking any portion of the desired window on the desktop. Try this:

**1.** Click the Paint window's title bar (as shown in Figure I-19c) to make it active.

**2.** Click the portion of the Notepad window that sticks out beneath the Paint window's frame (as in Figure I-19d).

**3.** For now, make the Paint window active by clicking its taskbar button.

**4.** Now close the Paint window by clicking its close button.

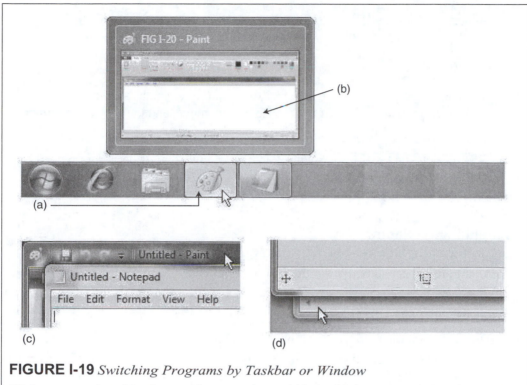

**FIGURE I-19** *Switching Programs by Taskbar or Window*

Click a program's taskbar button (a), or anywhere within its title bar (c) or window frame (d) to make its window active. Pointing to an icon displays its window (b).

## Custom Resizing Windows

You can also change the size of any window to better suit your needs.

1.  Point to the bottom edge of the Notepad window, as shown in Figure I-20a.

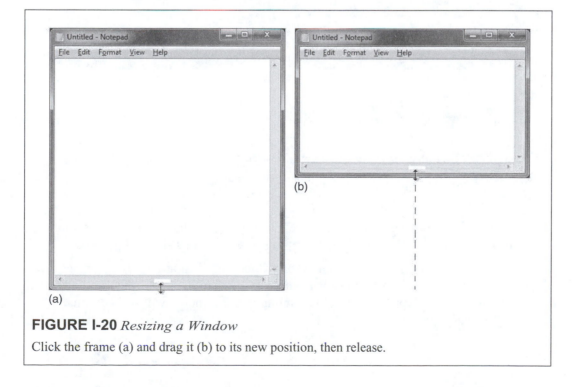

**FIGURE I-20** *Resizing a Window*

Click the frame (a) and drag it (b) to its new position, then release.

> **NOTE:** The pointer is correctly positioned when its shape changes to a vertical double arrow.

**2.** Drag the bottom window edge about halfway up the screen, as shown in Figure I-20b. Remember, press and hold the left mouse button, move, and then release the button.

> **NOTE:** You can "grab" and then drag any window edge or corner as needed to resize a window.

### Repositioning Windows

You can also change the location of a window by dragging it with your mouse.

**1.** Point to the Notepad window's title bar, then press and hold the left mouse button.

**2.** Move the mouse, in this case, down and to the right. As you move, the window moves with you to the new location.

**3.** Release the mouse button to position the window.

The window has been moved to its new position on the screen. Note that moving a window does not alter its size.

### Changing to Standard Window Sizes

Although items in an open window can be accessed regardless of the window's size, it is easier to use a window when it is maximized.

**1.** To maximize a window, click its *maximize* button (rectangle) at the upper right, as shown in Figure I-21a. The Notepad window increases to its maximum size.

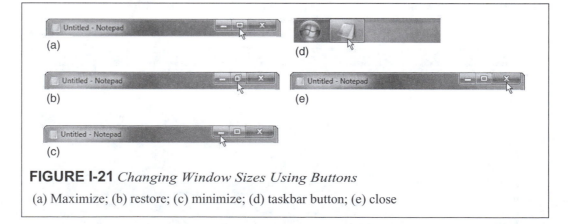

**FIGURE I-21** *Changing Window Sizes Using Buttons*

(a) Maximize; (b) restore; (c) minimize; (d) taskbar button; (e) close

**2.** To return the window to its former size, click its *restore* button (double rectangle), as shown in Figure I-21b. The window returns to its previous size and position.

When the desktop gets too cluttered, or you do not need access to a particular window, you can reduce it to a taskbar button. Note that this is not the same as closing the window. Any application that is running in this window will still continue.

3. To reduce a window to its taskbar button, click its *minimize* button, as shown in Figure I-21c. The taskbar button can remain in this form until you need to enlarge or open the window again.

   When you want to use a window that has been reduced to the taskbar, you must first re-open it.

4. To re-open the window, click Notepad's taskbar button, as shown in Figure I-21d. The window returns to its previous size and position.

### Closing a Window

You can also close a window that is not currently needed. For example, to close the Notepad window, perform this step:

1. Click its *close* button, as shown in Figure I-21e.

2. If you want to exit Windows for now, click *Start*, *Turn Off Computer*, and then *Turn Off*. Otherwise, continue to the next lesson.

### Quick Review #2

1. Name three safety tips for handling diskettes.

   _____

2. What happens when you double-click an icon on the Windows desktop?

   _____

3. What is the difference between *maximize* and *restore*?

   _____

4. What do the underlined letters in Windows menu items signify?

   _____

5. Name three ways to arrange windows on the desktop.

   _____

## USING THE HELP PROGRAM

Windows provides a useful help program to which you can refer at any time. The following exercise demonstrates some of its features:

1. Start Windows if needed.

2. To open the Help dialog box, click the *Start* button on the taskbar and then click *Help and Support* on the Windows menu.

   A Help and Support Center window appears. A set of topics lets you access various types of help simply by clicking one. A search option (at the top) lets you find any additional help.

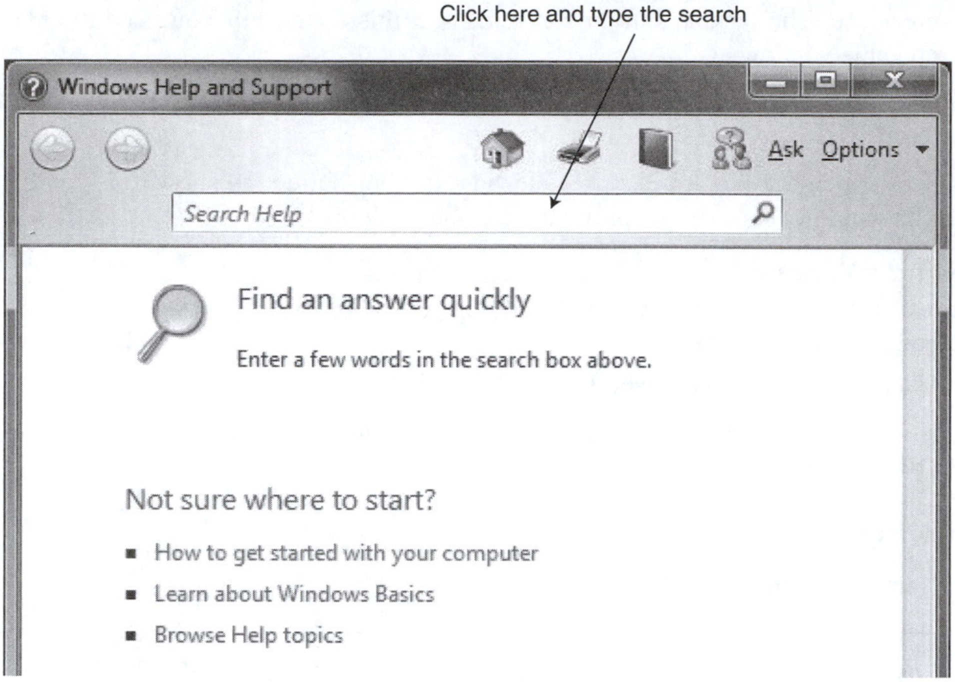

Click here and type the search

Windows Help and Support

Ask Options ▼

Search Help

Find an answer quickly

Enter a few words in the search box above.

Not sure where to start?

- How to get started with your computer
- Learn about Windows Basics
- Browse Help topics

**FIGURE I-22** *The Help and Support Window*

You will now try using the search feature for practice.

**To Use the Search Feature**

To access the search feature, just click the *Search* box, enter the desired topic, and then read the information that appears on the screen. For example, to review how to close a window, complete the following steps:

1. Click the *Search* box, as shown in Figure I-22.

2. Type **close** and then click the magnifying glass icon to the right of your entry.

    A number of topics will be suggested that match your search word. If no topic is displayed, try another word.

3. When you're done, click the Help window's close button to end Help.

4. Turn off Windows if you want to stop, or continue on to the next lesson.

    Windows returns to the point at which you invoked Help, and you can continue with your work.

## LESSON 5: FORMATTING A DISKETTE

**NOTE:** If you are not using a floppy diskette, just read through this section for information but do not format.

It is likely that your diskette has already been prepared for use with your computer, but there will be times when you may want to prepare a diskette on which to save files. Before a new diskette can be used, you must format it. Formatting places magnetic markings on the diskette so that the computer can find specific locations later to store or retrieve files.

You format a new diskette only once—not each time you use it. Otherwise, you'd erase everything you had previously stored! You can also purchase preformatted diskettes, which eliminates the need to format your own. WARNING! If your diskette has already been prepared for use with your computer system, DO NOT format it again. Instead, read this section to learn how to prepare diskettes, but do not perform the instructions.

## Formatting a Diskette in Windows

Remember, do not perform these steps unless your instructor directs you to do so.

1. If needed, start Windows.

2. If your desktop contains a *Computer* icon, double-click it now to open its window. If there is no icon, click *Start*, and then click the *Computer* menu item in the right column.

3. Put an unformatted diskette in drive A.

4. Right-click the "Floppy Disk Drive A:" icon to access its shortcut menu.

5. Click the *Format* option.
   The Format dialog box allows you to specify various format instructions.

6. The listing in the Capacity box should match the diskette to be formatted. If it does not, click its down arrow and select the proper capacity.

> **NOTE:** Most diskettes (although rarely used today) are 1.44 MB 3-1/2 inch (high-density).

7. Make sure that the quick format is not selected. If needed, click it to remove the check mark.

8. There is another option of interest in this dialog box: volume labels. You may want to identify each new diskette with a unique volume name. You are allowed up to eleven characters. If you want to add a label to your diskette, press ⌐ALT¬ + **L** to access the volume label text box (or click it), and then type a label. It is a good idea to use your name or ID number as a label to help identify the diskette should you lose it.

9. When you're ready to proceed, click *Start*. (To cancel, click *Close*.)

10. A warning box will appear. Click *OK* to continue.
    WARNING: When you format a disk (or diskette), anything currently on that disk will be erased. It's up to you to be careful. Computers are useful, but they are not foolproof.

11. Wait. A bar will appear in the Formatting line at the bottom of the dialog box displaying the computer's progress. You will hear noise in the drive as the computer marks the diskette.
    When done, a Format Complete dialog box will appear.

12. Click *OK* to return to the Format dialog box.

    You could now format another diskette. If you put another diskette in the drive and click *Start*, the format routine will start again. If you select *Close*, you will end the format procedure.

13. For now, click *Close* to close the Format dialog box.

14. Click the *Close* button on the *Computer* window.

15. You can exit from Windows or continue to the next lesson.

### Applying an External Label to Your Diskette

It is a good practice to place an external label on your diskette so that you will be able to identify it. You can print or type a label before placing it on a diskette. As you've seen in Figure I-7, place the label on a 3-1/2 inch diskette in the disk's center above the metal protective cover so as not to impede its movement. The cover must be able to slide open when the diskette is inserted into the disk drive. Fold any extra label up and over the back.

### LESSON 6: MANAGING FILES WITH MY COMPUTER

Windows' Computer program provides a graphical interface that lets you organize objects: files or folders (groups of files) on your flash drives or disks. You can list, copy, move, rename, delete, and print files. You can also prepare new diskettes for use on your computer. The following exercises demonstrate some of its basic features.

1. Start Windows if needed.

    For this exercise, you will need to create a small file to use for practice. Try the following:

2. Open the Notepad program as you did earlier (click *Start*, then point to All Programs, Accessories, and then click *Notepad*).

3. Type your first name in the Notepad window. You will now save this as a file.

4. If appropriate for your system, make sure your flash drive is in a USB port, or place a formatted diskette in drive A. If you plan to save this file elsewhere, skip this step (check with your instructor).

5. Click *File* in the menu bar.

6. Click *Save* in the drop-down list.

7. In the Save As dialog box, as shown in Figure I-23a, click and drag the vertical scroll bar until you see its desired location (as shown in Figure I-23b).

8. Click the desired location (removable disk or diskette) and then click *File Name* and type **TEST**.

9. Click *Save*.

10. Close the Notepad window.

    You have now saved a small file on your diskette (or in a folder) and can continue with the remaining exercises.

11. Open the Computer window, as shown in Figure I-24 (double-click its desktop icon or, if that is not available, click Start and then Computer).

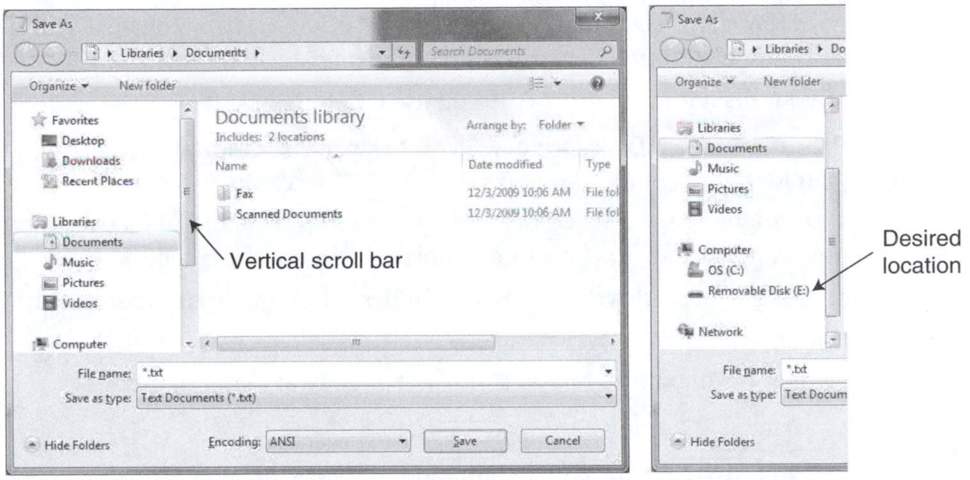

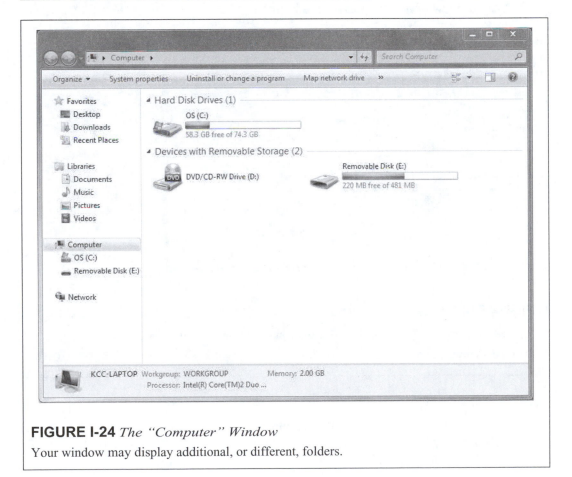

(a)                                                                    (b)

**FIGURE I-23** *Saving a File*

Drag the vertical scroll bar (a) down to find the desired location (b).

**FIGURE I-24** *The "Computer" Window*

Your window may display additional, or different, folders.

In this example, the Computer window displays three icon objects: a hard disk (OS (C:)), a DVD/CD-RW drive (D:), and a Removable Disk drive (E:). Your list will differ. To examine the contents of drive A, perform the following steps:

1. Make sure your diskette is in drive A if you use a floppy diskette.

   Double-click the Floppy Disk Drive A: icon to open its window. Of course, if you are using a folder, you could examine that as well. Go to Step 3.

   This window might be maximized or it might appear as a smaller window. Although any open window can be used, it is best to maximize it while you practice.

2. If you are using a flash drive, or network folder, click the appropriate location as needed.

3. Click the window's maximize button if it is not already at maximum size.

### Viewing Files

Windows allows you to view your files in a number of ways: as icons, details, lists, tiles, or content. It doesn't matter which view you use as long as you understand its contents. First, set "icons" view:

1. Click the "More Options" drop-down arrow of the "Change Your View" option, as shown in Figure I-25a.

   A list of view options appears, as in Figure I-25b.

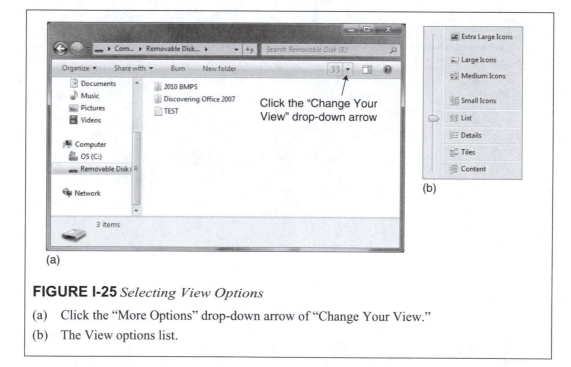

(a)

**FIGURE I-25** *Selecting View Options*

(a)    Click the "More Options" drop-down arrow of "Change Your View."

(b)    The View options list.

2. Click the *Large Icons* option.

   The TEST file in your list of files should resemble Figure I-26a, although your disk or folder may have other files as well. The Icons view displays an icon for each file or folder, with its name beneath it.

3. Click the *View More Options* arrow and then *Details*.

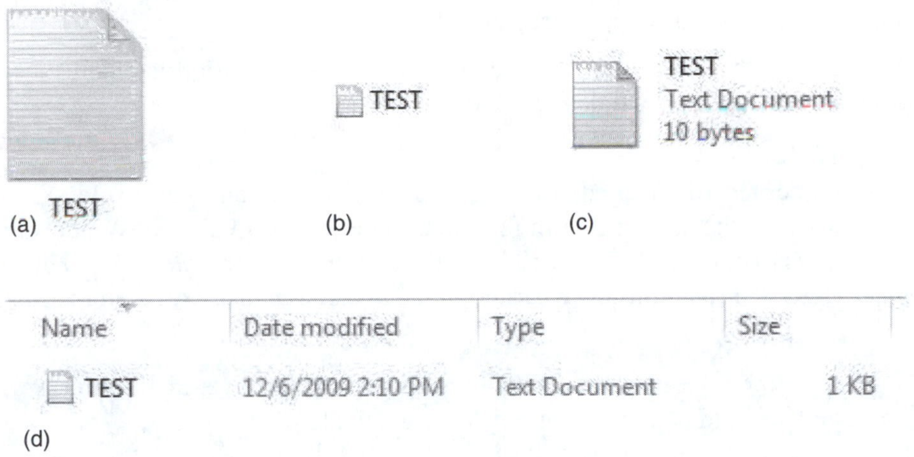

**FIGURE I-26** *Changing the View*

(a)  Icons (Large Icons) view.

(b)  List (Small Icons) view.

(c)  Tiles view.

(d)  Details view.

As shown in Figure I-26d, the Details view displays a small icon for each file or folder, followed by a name and related details: size, type, and date last modified. (If you had more than one file, clicking a column title would arrange the list in that order.)

4.  Click *View More Options* and then *List*.

The List view, as shown in Figure I-26b, displays small icons and filenames only.

5.  Click *View More Options* and then *Tiles*.

The Tiles view, as shown in Figure I-26c, displays a large icon for each file with its name, file type, and approximate size to the right. Although any view can be used to manipulate files, remain in the Tiles view for the following exercises.

**NOTE:**  The Extra Large Icons view is useful when you have image files. In this view, miniature images of each file are displayed for easier recognition.

## Exiting from the Computer Window

When you no longer need Computer, you can close it just like any other window, by clicking its close button. Try this:

1.  Click the window's close button.

## Manipulating Files in the "Computer" Window

At times, you will want to copy a file, change its name or location, or erase it when it is no longer needed. The Computer window allows you to do all these things with ease. To prepare for these exercises, complete the following steps as you did in the previous exercise:

1. Open the Computer window and, if appropriate, make sure your flash drive is in a USB port or your diskette is in the disk drive.

2. Double-click the Flash Drive or Floppy Drive (A:) (or appropriate path) icon in the window, maximize its window, and select the Tiles view.

**Copying a File**

A file can be copied (duplicated) for safekeeping. There is one basic rule: You cannot have two files with the same name in the same folder, as you will see. Windows offers a number of ways to copy a file; you will learn the one that uses the menu bar. This exercise copies the TEST file that you saved earlier on the diskette in drive A (or in a folder).

> **NOTE:** If you do not have the TEST file on your flash drive, diskette, or in your folder, go back and create it, or use any file available.

1. Click the *TEST* file in the window to highlight it, as shown in Figure I-27a. Note the file's size appears at the bottom "Details" section of the window.

2. Click *Organize* in the menu bar and then *Copy* in the list that appears.

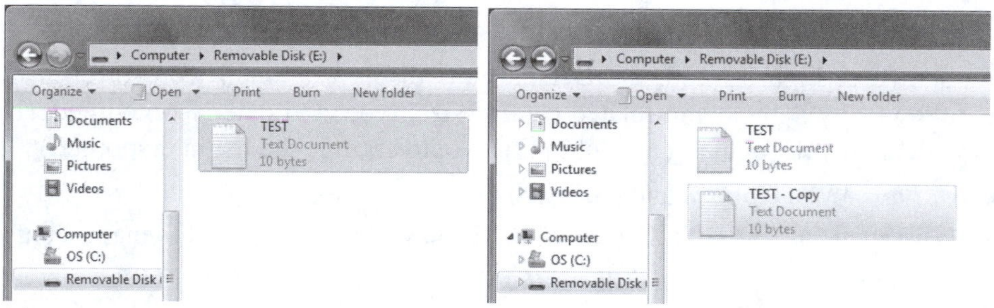

**FIGURE I-27** *Copying a File*

(a)    Click the desired object to select it.

(b)    After pasting into the same folder, a Copy entry appears in the list.

The file has been copied to Windows' clipboard—a temporary holding area in RAM memory. At this point, you could specify a new destination for the copy by closing this window and opening another disk icon, such as drive C. For now, however, you will simply copy it back onto your diskette or folder.

3. Click *Organize* in the menu bar and then *Paste* in the list that appears.

After a moment, a new file labeled "TEST - Copy" will appear at the end of the file list, as shown in Figure I-27b. This technique can be used to copy any file. Simply select the file, invoke *Organize*, *Copy* and then *Organize*, *Paste*. (If you copy a file to a different folder, it will retain its original name, without the addition of a "Copy" notation.)

**NOTE:** You can copy more than one file at a time. After clicking the first file, press and hold CTRL while clicking additional filenames. Each will be highlighted. (To deselect a file, repeat the CTRL + click procedure.) When all the files to be copied have been selected, invoke the *Organize, Copy, Organize, Paste* commands.

### A Word to the Wise—Save Your Files!

You can save a file any time—either as you work on it or after you have finished. Those of us who have seen hours of work disappear in the twinkling of an eye have learned to save often! Get into the habit of stopping every ten minutes or so to save your work to a folder or diskette. With most programs (as you will see), it takes only seconds to copy your file. DO IT!!! Your mental health will stay intact, especially when the unexpected happens (as it inevitably will) and you'll be thankful that all you lost were the last ten minutes of work.

When you're working on an important project, it is much safer to copy your file onto another folder on your hard disk or better yet, a flash drive or external hard drive. Disks and flash drives do not last forever, and the one that fails is usually the one you didn't copy. Of course, any copy command should be used ONLY where it does not violate copyright laws. Just because you *can* copy a file doesn't mean you should.

**NOTE:** You can move a file by selecting *Organize, Cut* instead of *Organize, Copy*. Then switch to another folder and complete the *Organize, Paste* routine.

### Renaming a File

You can change the name of a file whenever it suits your needs. As an example, assume you want to rename the "TEST - Copy" file to "Silly." To do this, follow these steps:

1. Open Computer and the appropriate folder if it is not already open.

2. Right-click the "TEST - Copy" file in the list. A shortcut menu appears.

3. Click *Rename* in the shortcut menu. A rectangle appears around the filename, as shown in Figure I-28a. You can now type the new filename.

4. Type **Silly** in the box, as shown in Figure I-28b.

5. Press ↵ to complete the renaming.

**FIGURE I-28** *Renaming a File*

(a)　To rename, right-click the object, then click Rename.

(b)　Type the new filename and press ⏎ .

**NOTE:** Your file may display a ".txt" extension, which identifies the file type as a text file. Many programs automatically add an extension to the filename. It is important, when renaming files, that you include the extension in the new filename if it appears in the original filename.

### Deleting a File

A file can be deleted when it is no longer needed. For example, to delete the file named "Silly," do the following:

**1.** Make sure the window displays the flash drive or appropriate folder that contains the file.

**2.** Right-click the "Silly" file in the list.

**3.** Click *Delete* in the shortcut menu.

A Delete File dialog box should appear, asking you to confirm the delete. Make sure it is set to delete the proper file. If not, click *No* to cancel the procedure and repeat steps 1–3.

**4.** If the file shown is correct, click *Yes* to confirm. The file is gone.

**5.** Also, delete the TEST file, using the procedure in steps 2-4.

**6.** Close the window.

**NOTE:** When you delete a file from the *hard* disk drive (C:), it is actually sent to Windows' Recycle Bin. You can restore it later (and thus cancel the deletion), or empty the Recycle Bin to truly erase the file. To empty the Recycle Bin, right-click its icon, then click E*mpty Recycle Bin*, *Yes*. However, when you delete a file from a flash drive or diskette, it is not sent to the Recycle Bin; it is simply deleted.

### A Note about Undeleting a File

Deleting a file does not really remove it, but replaces the first character in its filename with a symbol that hides it from view. The file will remain in this hidden state until another file is saved on this specific flash drive, disk, or diskette. Only then will it actually be overwritten with the new material and lost for good. This opens up the possibility of undeleting files (as long as no new files have been saved). If you inadvertently delete a file, do not save anything else. Instead, see your instructor or lab technician to learn how to undelete a file using your specific system.

## Using Folders

As you have learned, a folder (a disk "subdirectory") is a holder for files or other folders. Disks contain a root directory, or a main folder, that keeps track of all the files on the disk. This one main folder is usually sufficient for diskettes. However, as disk capacity increases (as in a flash drive, hard disk, CD, DVD, or network), it is wiser to subdivide the storage area into folders. Each folder contains a group of related files. In turn, these folders can be divided into other folders as the need arises. Knowledge of creating and using folders will allow you to use secondary storage more efficiently. For now, you can practice on your own diskette or flash drive.

### Creating a Folder

To create a new folder on your diskette or flash drive, follow these steps:

1. Open the Computer window.

2. Make sure your diskette is in the disk drive (or flash drive in the USB port).

3. Double-click the appropriate flash drive or diskette icon in the window.

4. As shown in Figure I-29a, click the *New Folder* option in the menu bar.

    A "New Folder" icon appears in the object list, awaiting a new name as in Figure I-29b.

5. Type **Letters** and press ⏎.

6. Click outside the folder name, as in Figure I-29c.

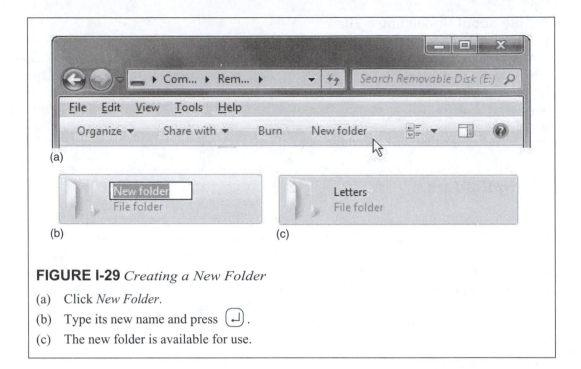

**FIGURE I-29** *Creating a New Folder*

(a)   Click *New Folder*.

(b)   Type its new name and press ⏎ .

(c)   The new folder is available for use.

The Letters folder is now available for use. You can save files in it, copy or move files to it, or delete files from it, just as you would any other object, by double-clicking it to open its window. For example, to copy a file into it, you would double-click the folder just before invoking the final *Edit* (or *Organize*), *Paste* command. You can also copy, rename, or delete folders using the file techniques you've learned. However, remember that folders can contain groups of files or other folders. When you copy a folder, everything in it is copied. When you delete a folder, everything in it is erased!

**NOTE:** Although you should leave the Letters folder on your diskette or flash drive, to delete a folder in general, follow the procedure to delete any object: right-click it, click *Delete*, and then click *Yes*.

8.   When done, close the window.

You're finished with the Windows introduction. Test your understanding by trying a few of the exercises that follow.

## EXERCISES

**Exercise 1.** List and describe the four basic components of a computer system. Give an example of each.

**Exercise 2.** Describe the difference between primary and secondary storage. List and describe the basic units of capacity.

**Exercise 3.** List the steps required to start your computer and access the Windows desktop.

**Exercise 4.** Identify these basic Windows desktop components: (a) desktop, (b) icons, (c) taskbar, (d) Start button, (e) Recycle Bin.

**Exercise 5.** Identify and describe the four basic mouse techniques.

**Exercise 6.** Identify the purpose and describe the location of these window components: (a) program icon, (b) title bar, (c) resizing buttons, (d) close button, (e) menu bar, (f) scroll bar.

**Exercise 7.** Describe multitasking, tiling and cascading windows, and switching the active window on the desktop.

**Exercise 8.** Describe techniques for resizing a window.

**Exercise 9.** Explain the process of accessing Windows' Help screen.

**Exercise 10.** Describe the differences between these views: large icon, small icon, list, details.

**Exercise 11.** Describe the procedure to copy a file using the Computer window.

**Exercise 12.** Describe the procedure to rename a file using the Computer window.

**Exercise 13.** Describe the procedure to delete a file using the Computer window.

**Exercise 14.** Describe the procedure to create a new folder using the Computer window.

**Exercise 15.** Describe the procedure to format a diskette if you use one.

## CONTINUING ON YOUR OWN

This module has introduced you to the most basic concepts in using a microcomputer with Windows. You have learned how to start Windows and how to perform a few simple window and file maintenance chores. You have learned some of the common screen components and commands used by all Windows programs. This is sufficient for now to enable you to continue on to study the application software in the remaining modules. After all, the purpose of this manual is to get you to use applications. Windows is just the vehicle that allows you to drive them.

However, Windows itself is an impressive collection of thousands of commands that have been integrated into the simple GUI environment you have been learning. You could spend an entire semester studying Windows alone and still not learn all of its hidden treasures. When you get a chance, you might want to explore some of the following menus:

• In *Accessories*, you'll find an on-screen calculator, calendar, word processors (WordPad and Notepad), and a paint program.

• In *System Tools*, found within the *Accessories* submenu, you can prepare backups of all your files and access backup programs—such as System Restore.

• In the *Control Panel*, found within the *Systems tools* menu or the *Start* menu, you can manage all the hardware settings for your computer, add new equipment, and change colors or formats of Windows.

These are just a few items to look at when you have time. Good luck with the remaining modules and with your new skills!

## WINDOWS 7 COMMAND SUMMARY

| | |
|---|---|
| CASCADE WINDOWS: | Right-click taskbar, then click Cascade Windows. |
| CLOSE A WINDOW: | Click the close ("X") button on the title bar, or click File, Close. |
| COPY A FILE: | Open My Computer, open disk/folder, click file icon, click *Organize, Copy*, move to new folder, click *Organize, Paste*. |
| CREATE A FOLDER: | Open My Computer, open disk/folder, click *File, New, New Folder*, type name and press ⏎. |
| DELETE A FILE: | Open My Computer, open disk/folder, click file icon, press DELETE. |
| FORMAT A DISK: | Open My Computer, right-click desired disk drive icon, click *Format*. |
| HELP: | Click *Start* and then *Help*. |
| LAUNCH A PROGRAM: | Click *Start*, point to *All Programs*, continue to point to menus until desired item appears. Click icon. |
| MAXIMIZE A WINDOW: | Click the maximize (rectangle) button on the title bar. |
| MINIMIZE A WINDOW: | Click the minimize (underscore) button on the title bar. |
| MOUSE ACTIONS: | *Click:* Tap (press and release) the left mouse button. |
| | *Right-click:* Tap the right mouse button. |
| | *Double-click:* Quickly tap the left mouse button twice. |
| | *Drag:* Press and hold the left mouse button, then move. |
| | *Drop:* Release the mouse button. |
| OPEN A WINDOW: | Double-click its icon or use Start menu. |
| RENAME A FILE: | Open My Computer, open disk/folder icon, click file icon, click Edit, *Rename*, type new name and press ⏎. |
| REPOSITION A WINDOW: | Click and drag title bar (on nonmaximized window). |
| RESIZE A WINDOW: | Click and drag window frame as needed. |
| RESTORE A WINDOW: | Click the restore (two rectangles) button on the title bar. |
| START THE COMPUTER: | Without a diskette in drive A, turn on power and wait. |
| SWITCH AMONG MULTITASKED PROGRAMS: | Click icon on taskbar, click window, or press ALT + TAB. |
| TILE WINDOWS: | Right-click taskbar, then click *Show Windows Side by Sid* or *Show Windows Stacked*. |
| TURN OFF WINDOWS: | Click *Start* button, right-most arrow, *Shut Down*. |

# WORD PROCESSING MODULE

## WORD 2010

**W**

## LESSON 1: LAUNCHING WORD

In this module, you will learn the basics of Microsoft Office 2010's word processor, Word—one of the most popular word processing programs in the world. The skills you will learn in this module are sufficient for most general writing needs. Once you master the basic techniques presented in this module, you may want to explore the many advanced features of Word by invoking the Help screens offered in the program.

Remember to watch your screen as you invoke commands. Do not just press keys or click the mouse, but examine the effect of each step before you continue to the next. In this way, you will understand each command and master them more quickly.

The startup instructions for your computer were presented in the Introductory module. Refer back to them as needed to remind you how to start your computer.

1. If needed, start Windows. Your screen should display the Windows desktop and taskbar.

2. If appropriate for your system, make sure that a formatted diskette—on which you'll save your work—is in drive A (this is unnecessary if you are using a flash drive, or a folder on your hard disk or network).

   The easiest way to launch a program is to use a desktop or taskbar icon (if one exists).

Microsoft
Word 2010

3. If your desktop (or taskbar) displays a Word icon, double-click it now and continue with step 9.

   If there is no icon, you can always launch Word through the Start menu. Try this approach, using Figure W-1 as a guide:

4. Click the *Start* button to access the Windows menu.

5. Point to *All Programs* to access its menu.

6. If a Microsoft Word item appears in the list, continue with step 8.

7. Point to the menu group item that contains Microsoft Word. This is often "Microsoft Office." If a different menu item contains Word in your computer system, write its title here for future reference: _____.

8. Click the Microsoft Word menu item to launch (start) it.

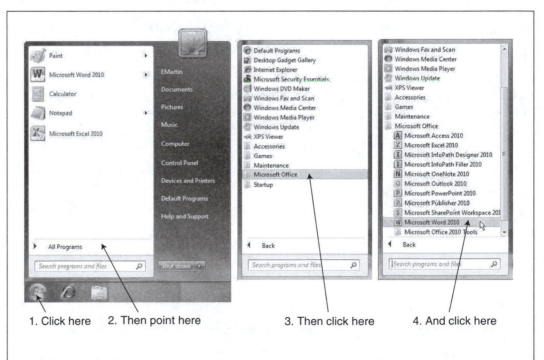

1. Click here     2. Then point here          3. Then click here          4. And click here

**FIGURE W-1**   *Launching Word*
Click Start, All Programs, Microsoft Office, and then the Word menu item to launch Word.
(Your list may differ.)

After some copyright information, a blank work screen should appear.

9. If an error message or question appears on your screen, check with your instructor or lab technician for the proper response.

## THE WORD WINDOW

Congratulations! You've opened the Word program window, as shown in Figure W-2. This window contains the Word program and a document window through which you can see your document as you work on it.

Use the next few paragraphs to identify the important parts of the Word window as you locate each on your own screen. Figure W-2 shows the information that currently appears on the screen. Your screen may differ slightly. Many items may already be familiar to you, since they are common to all Windows screens. Examine the screen from the top-left corner to the bottom right.

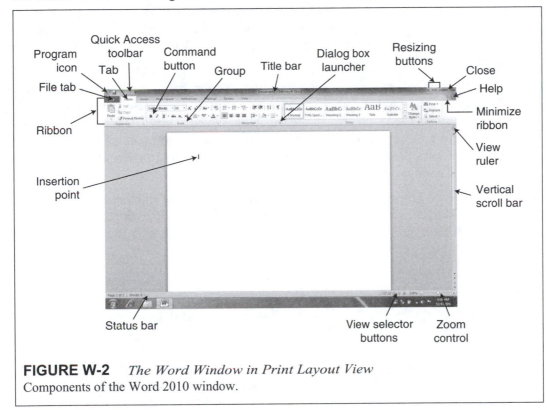

**FIGURE W-2**   *The Word Window in Print Layout View*
Components of the Word 2010 window.

a.  **Title bar:** At the top of the screen is Word's title bar. At the extreme left is the Program Icon and a Quick Access Toolbar (more on these in a moment). A document number (no name has been assigned as yet) appears in the center. Resizing buttons and the close button (labeled "X") appear at the right. (Although Word can handle many documents at the same time, you will only be concerned with one document at a time in this module.)

b.  **The Program Icon:** Clicking the program icon opens a submenu to resize or close the window.

c.  **Quick Access Toolbar:** Word's Quick Access toolbar ("QAT")—to the right of the Microsoft Office Button—contains often-used command buttons such as save, undo, and redo. You can customize this toolbar to include any other commands you wish to add.

d.  **Ribbon:** Beneath the title bar is the heart of Word's menu system—the ribbon. The *ribbon* is a collection of *tabs*, *groups*, and *command buttons* that can be clicked by mouse to perform needed tasks. (More on this shortly.) Clicking the Minimize Ribbon button, or CTRL + F1 will reduce the ribbon to display only tabs.

e.  **File tab:** The blue file tab appears first in the ribbon. Clicking it opens a file menu with commands for saving, printing, closing a file, and exiting the program. It also provides access to many Word options settings.

> **NOTE:**  The title bar, File Tab, Quick Access Toolbar, and ribbon are standard features found in every Microsoft Office 2010 program.

f.  **Insertion point:** A blinking vertical line, called the *insertion point*, appears near the upper left. It displays your exact typing position on the screen. As you type, or as you press arrow keys, the insertion point will move around the screen. Word starts with margins of 1 inch, so the insertion point is currently 1 inch from the left and top of the page.

g.  **Mouse pointer:** Somewhere on the screen, a pointer that resembles a capital I or an arrow may appear (as shown in the margin). This is the mouse pointer, which displays the current location of your mouse on the screen. The "I" symbol is used to position the mouse within your text; the arrow pointer is for command buttons. As in other Windows programs, other symbols may replace the I or arrow as you use the mouse for various purposes.

h.  **Task pane:** At times, a task pane may appear on the left or right side of the screen to provide additional information or commands as need arises. Task panes do not interfere with your view of the document—you can leave a task pane open or, if you wish, close it by clicking its close ("X") button.

> **NOTE:**  The arrow keys ($\leftarrow$ $\uparrow$ $\rightarrow$ $\downarrow$) can move you around text that has already been typed, but they will not move past the end of a document.

i.  **Text area** or **Workspace***:* The white space in the rest of the window is available for typing. As you type, it will fill up with characters, words, and sentences. When you reach the bottom of the workspace, the text will move up, or "scroll," to provide more space below. There may be hundreds of lines in your document, but the workspace can display about twenty lines at a time (depending on the type size and toolbar rows on the screen), or about half of a standard page of typing paper. *Don't worry* if your typing disappears off the workspace top as you work. It is not lost. There is simply no room to show it. (If you move the insertion point back up, you will see it again.) In addition, the WYSIWYG (for "What You See Is What You Get") screen displays text in a size and type style that match its printed image.

j.  **Scroll bars:** The right and lower edges of the workspace may be framed by vertical and horizontal scroll bars that let you use the mouse to view different portions of your document. In addition, two page icons located at the bottom of the vertical scroll bar enable you to move forward or backward through your document, one page at a time, by clicking the appropriate icon.

k.  **View Ruler button:** Just above the vertical scroll bar is the View Ruler button. (You will click this in a moment to activate this feature.)

**l.**    **Status bar:** The line at the bottom of the Word window is called the *status bar*. It displays messages about your document. Items **m–r** introduce some of these status bar components.

**m.**   **Page** indicates the current page number of your document that is displayed on the screen. As shown by the message *Page 1 of 1*, you are now on the first page of your document, which is one page long.

**n.**    **Word Count:** As you type, a word count appears on the status bar to the right of the page number. It displays the total number of words in your document.

**o.**    When text has been typed, a **Proofing Error** icon will appear to the right of the Word Count indicating the status of automatic spelling and grammar checks. The icon will either have a green check for "no errors" or a red "X" for "potential errors found." More on this later.

**p.**    **View selector:** To the right of the status bar are five small command buttons that allow you to change how the document appears on your screen. The views include: print layout, full screen reading, web layout, outline, and draft views.

**q.**    **Zoom:** The right-most section of the status bar contains a zoom control (currently at 100%) that allows you to change the magnification of screen text from 10% to 500%. You can drag the center indicator to any magnification you wish, or click the + and – icons to change the magnification in steps of 10.

**r.**    Windows' **taskbar** appears on the bottom of the screen, beneath Word's window. You can click its Start button to launch other programs or Windows features, as you have seen in the Introductory module.

## The Ruler Bar

A horizontal ruler bar, as shown in Figure W-3, is another helpful part of the screen. It displays the document's current margins, tabs, and indents. It can also be accessed by mouse to change these settings.

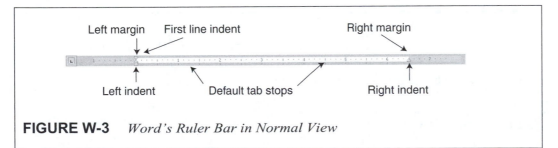

**FIGURE W-3**    *Word's Ruler Bar in Normal View*

By default, the ruler bar is not displayed in Word when you begin. If yours is not, display it now by completing the following steps:

**1.**    Click the *View Ruler* button (just below the ribbon on the right side of the window).

> **NOTE:** The ribbon can also activate the ruler bar: Click the View tab, then Ruler in the Show group. Then, click the Home tab again.

The ruler bar displays pointers and symbols superimposed on a numbered line. The position of these symbols may differ on your screen, but examine what the bar tells you about your document:

Left  Right

- The straight lines at the 0" and 6 1/2" marks show the left and right margins respectively. You can set the margins wherever you need them. Currently, there are six and a half inches of text area between the left and right margins (which are one inch each).

- The triangle shapes display indent settings. You can indent text from the left or right margin and create first line or hanging indents as well. By default, all indents are set to zero. (You will learn more about indents later.)

- The tick marks beneath the numbers show any default tabs that are set. Currently, tabs are set every half-inch. Each time you press ⎡TAB⎤, the insertion point moves to the next tab position. Other symbols, as shown in the margin, may appear on your ruler. The first four shapes show additional tabs that you set; the last two markers are used to adjust text indents (as you will see).

2. If you want to stop for now, click the blue File tab and then the red *Exit* button (at the lower left of the menu).

### Quick Review #1

1. List all the steps or commands needed in your system to launch Word:

   _____

   _____

2. In the Word window, where would you look to find the document number or title?

   _____

3. Which items do you click to activate the ruler if it is not already on the screen?

   _____


## LESSON 2: THE KEYBOARD

Briefly examine some of the keys you'll be using. In time, you'll find that there are many insertion point movements and techniques that will increase your typing speed. Find each key on your keyboard as each is introduced in the following section.

## Using the Keys

1. Basic keys:

   a. Alphabetic keys (A-Z and a-z).

   b. Numeric keys (0-9).

   c. ⎡SHIFT⎤ generates the upper symbol (or uppercase) of a key when held while that key is pressed.

   d. ⎡TAB⎤ moves the insertion point to the next tab setting.

   e. ⎡SPACE⎤ generates a blank space.

   **f.** [CAPS LOCK] "locks in" capital letters with one press and returns (toggles back) to normal when pressed again. It affects only letter keys.

   **g.** [BACKSPACE] moves one space to the left and erases the character at that position.

   **h.** Enter ([↵]) ends a paragraph or inserts a blank line.

**2.** Special keys: Word uses the keyboard's special keys to make word processing functions easier. The [CTRL], [ALT], and [SHIFT] keys are used with other keys to produce powerful effects (as you will see). Find each of the following keys on your keyboard:

   **a.** [CTRL] (Control) and [ALT],(Alternate)

   **b.** [DELETE]

   **c.** [ESC] (Escape)

   **d.** Arrow keys ([→], [↓], [←], [↑])

   **e.** [PGUP] and [PGDN] (Page Up and Page Down)

   **f.** [HOME] and [END]

## The Word Ribbon

Most of the commands you will use in Word are contained in the Microsoft Office *ribbon*—the four-line band across the top of the window. The ribbon is divided into core tasks, each represented by a tab. For example, the "Home" tab (as shown in Figure W-4a) contains most of the writing commands you will need; the "Insert" tab (as in Figure W-4b) contains most of the commands for inserting shapes, tables, pages, and illustrations into your document; and so on.

### Ribbon-Group-Command

Each tab is divided into *groups*—smaller sets of related commands arranged by function. In the Home tab, for example, the groups are Clipboard, Font, Paragraph, Styles, and Editing. Each group contains command buttons that you can click to activate an appropriate action. The command buttons remain in view and are always available for immediate use. (By default, the Home tab appears when you open a new document, since it is the one you will use most often.)

> **NOTE:** The bottom right corner of each group typically contains a *Dialog Box Launcher* icon that, when clicked, activates a dialog box containing a variety of additional commands and settings. (You'll try this later.)

In addition to the File tab, Word's ribbon includes seven "standard" tabs. At times, based on your actions, "contextual" tools will be added as temporary tabs (shown in a different color accent). When you finish your task, the contextual tab will disappear from the ribbon.

> **NOTE:** Although you can leave any ribbon tab active, it is a good idea to click the "Home" tab when you are finished using a set of commands, so it is always available.

### Using the Ribbon

Word's ribbon provides an easy way to invoke commands. Most often, you simply click the desired command button. If the command is contained in another tab, first click the desired tab to make it active and then click the command button. You can choose a command from the ribbon using either of these methods:

- By mouse: If needed, click the desired tab to make it active. Click the desired command to select it (the preferred method).

- By keyboard: Press ALT to see mnemonic *tab* letters (as shown in Figure W-4c). Press the desired letter of the needed tab, then press the letter of the command (as shown in Figure W-4d).

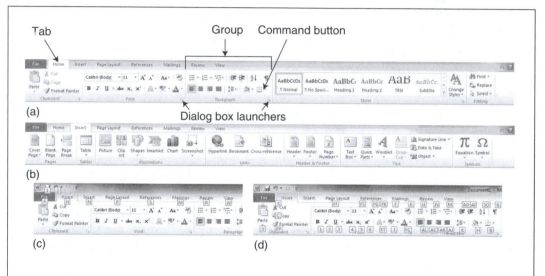

(a)

(b)

(c)     (d)

**FIGURE W-4**    *Using Word's Ribbon*

Word's Ribbon is divided into tabs, groups, and command buttons.

(a)   The Home tab.

(b)   The Insert tab.

(c)   Pressing ALT displays letters that can be pressed to access a tab (not recommended).

(d)   Pressing a tab letter (such as "H" for "Home") opens that tab with additional letters that can be pressed to invoke a command.

Try the following exercise. Let's say you wanted to set bold text:

1. Launch Word if necessary.

2. Click the *Home* tab if it is not already active.

3. Click the Bold command button.
   Note that the Bold command button is now highlighted indicating that it is active.

### Function Keys and Shortcut Commands

Word lets you use CTRL, ALT, or SHIFT in combination with function keys and other alphabetic keys to provide shortcuts to many of its commands, such as CTRL + B for "Bold." At times, you may prefer these keys to using the ribbon commands.

4. Point to the Bold button. A tool tip appears, indicating its function and any shortcut that might be available.

## The File Menu

Commands that relate to opening, saving, and printing files are stored in a separate "File" menu, accessed through the File tab. Try this:

**1.**   Click the File tab, located at the left of the ribbon.

A file menu appears, as shown in Figure W-5. The left side presents twelve file options. If no document is currently open, as shown in Figure W-5a, the right side lists recently opened documents (if any) that can be clicked to open for use. If a document is open, information about it will appear to the right, as shown in Figure W-5b. You can switch these screens by clicking the "Info" or "Recent" menu options as needed. The "Options" item accesses a dialog box that allows you to adjust most options in Word to better suit your needs. (For now, leave them alone.) At the extreme lower right, an "Exit" item allows you to leave the Word program when you are done.

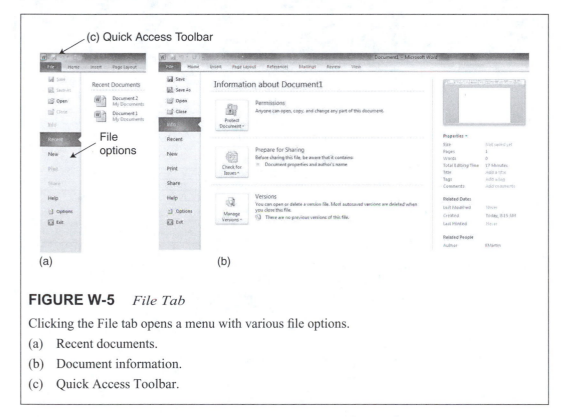

**FIGURE W-5**   *File Tab*

Clicking the File tab opens a menu with various file options.

(a)   Recent documents.

(b)   Document information.

(c)   Quick Access Toolbar.

**2.**   For now, click the Home tab to close this menu.

## The Quick Access Toolbar

Word also offers a fast way to access a number of useful commands in its Quick Access Toolbar ("QAT"), located to the right of the Program icon, as shown in Figure W-5c. You can click buttons to save, undo, or redo easily.

> **NOTE:**   You can add any command you want to the QAT by clicking the customize button at the end of the toolbar and following the directions. This allows you to place your often-used commands in an easily-accessible, one-click, location.

### Getting On-Screen Help

Word offers a help feature that provides easy access to information about the program and its commands. To get on-screen help at any time,

1.   Click the *Help* button, located at the extreme right of the ribbon (or press F1).

A Word Help dialog box and question area will appear as shown in Figure W-6. You can type keywords of interest. Try the following example:

2.   Type **ribbon** and press ⏎ (or click the *Search* button).

A list of options appears. You could pick one topic by clicking it, but for now,

3.   Click the dialog box's *Close* button.

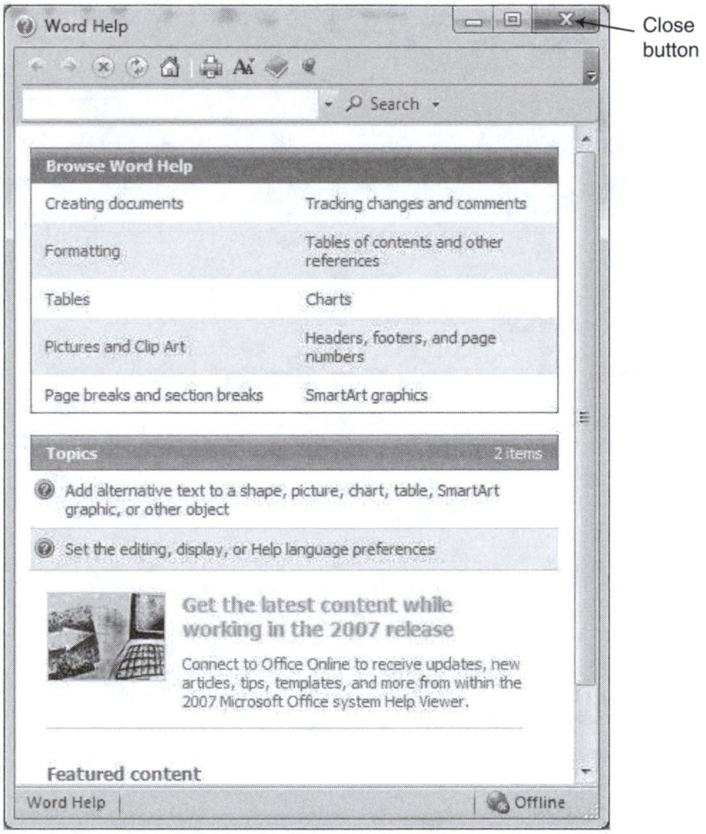

**FIGURE W-6**   *Word's Help Feature*

Type a question (or keyword) and then click Search to obtain information.

## Working with the Word Window

First, practice clearing the screen to start again. Here's how to erase the contents of the window and start a new document.

### To Erase the Screen

To erase a screen in Word, you simply close the current window. Try this:

1.   Click the File tab and then *Close* (or press ALT + **F**, **C**).

2.   A dialog box with the message "Do you want to save changes to Document 1?" may appear. If so, click the "Don't Save" button.

The document window will disappear, and you can start a new document.

**To Open a Fresh Window**

You now need to open a blank, or fresh, document window to begin your work. To open a fresh document window, complete the following steps:

1.   Click the File tab and then *New*.

     A New Document dialog box appears, offering various document style templates that you can use for general writing, letters and faxes, memos, reports, and Web pages. Although you may want to explore these styles in the future, for now, select the Blank Document style as follows:

2.   Click the *Blank document* option in the "Home" category (if necessary).

3.   Click the *Create* button (at the lower right of the dialog box).

## Setting the Screen View

Word offers screen views of varying detail. "Draft" view displays text and graphic material for quick and easy editing. "Print Layout" view (the default in Word) adds margins, headers and footers, footnotes, and page numbering to the display. The "Web Layout" and "Full Screen Reading" views adjust the display for easier onscreen viewing with larger text that wraps to fit the window. To switch the view, use the View tab on the ribbon, or click the view buttons at the lower-right corner of the status bar, as follows:

1.   To switch to Draft view, click the *Draft View* button (the last button).

2.   To switch to Print Layout view, click the *Print Layout View* button (the first button).

     Although you can use whichever view you prefer, the Print Layout view is appropriate for most typing needs.

> **NOTE:** You can also set views by clicking the *Views* tab on the ribbon, then clicking the desired view.

## Stopping Without Saving

If you want to stop for now, complete the following steps:

1.   Click the Close ("X") button in the upper-right corner of the window. (You could also click the File tab and then the *Exit* option at the end of the menu.)

2.   If asked, click *No*. You will learn more about exiting Word at the end of Lesson 4.

3.   You should now be in Windows and can shut down normally.

4.   If you are using a LAN, you may be required to leave your computer on. Check with your instructor as to the procedure to follow in your lab. Otherwise, shut off the computer and monitor.

## LESSON 3: ENTERING TEXT

> **NOTE:** Once you start this lesson, you must continue through the end of Lesson 4 before stopping so you'll know how to save your work (on a diskette, flash drive, or in a folder) and exit Word properly. From then on, save your work before you exit from Word.

## Word Wrap and Defaults

Unlike typewriters, word processors do not use "ENTERs" at the end of each line because of the way documents are stored in memory. Imagine a train with each car representing one word. As you type, each new "car" is added to the train. When you reach the right margin, the program sees if the last "car" fits into the remaining space. If not, it moves the word to the next line and continues. This is called "word wrap"—where words are "wrapped" around to the next line automatically. Whenever you change the text or margins, Word automatically readjusts the text "cars" to fit again. Therefore, **NEVER** press the Enter key just because you've reached the margin. Only use the Enter key when you want to end a line early (as when you finish a paragraph) or to create a blank line. Pressing the Enter key (shown as ↵) inserts a hidden character, called a "hard" return, which ends the line at that point. As you type the example below, watch your screen to see how word wrap works.

**1.** Launch Word if needed, or simply obtain a fresh screen.

A word about defaults. *Default* settings are those used by Word unless you specify other values. For example, by default, Word 2010 uses a Calibri font (typestyle) of 11 pt. size, margins of 1 inch and line spacing of 1.15 lines. For now, you will use these default settings. Later, you will learn how to change them.

> **NOTE:** Examine the Font group on the Home tab. If Word does not display "Calibri" or "11" in the top two boxes (as shown in Figure W-7), click the drop-down arrow next to each and then click the appropriate item in the list to change them to these values.

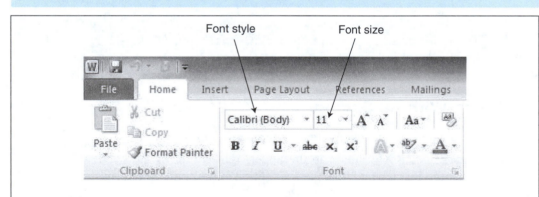

**FIGURE W-7**   *Using the default Font and Size*

Change these values if they do not display Calibri and 11 (click the drop-down arrow and then the desired option).

**2.** First, put a heading on this document. Here's how:

**a.** Type your name, then press ↵.

**b.** Type your class title (or course number) and then press ↵.

**c.** Type the date and then press ↵.

**d.** Press ↵ once more to move to the next line. For example, if I did it, it might look like Figure W-8 on my screen:

Edward Martin

Introduction to Computers

November 1, 2010

|← ——— The insertion point is here

**FIGURE W-8**   *The Completed Heading*

Your screen should display your name, class, and today's date.

You are now going to practice entering text, purposely including some errors that will be corrected by Word's automatic spellcheck and by you, later.

3.  Type the text shown in Figure W-9, including its errors! Don't worry about where each line ends; just keep typing and let word wrap adjust the text. If you make an un-planned mistake, press BACKSPACE to remove it before continuing. Press TAB only where you see it marked at the beginning of the example. Press ↵ only at the end where you see the "[ENTER]" key. Leave one space after the period ending each sentence. Your text lines may end in different places based on the margins and type size in your program. Don't worry about it for now.

TAB Using a word proccessor like Word 2010 is not as hard as it seemed to be beefore I began to use this manual. I am typping all ready and can't wait to try out other functions. As I type, the words appear o my screen. This is preety easy. Soon I will learn how to save this document on a disk or flash drive. I hope I can learn how to use this porgram. ↵ENTER

**FIGURE W-9**   *Entering Text*

Press the Tab key as shown and then type the text with all its "mistakes." Do not press the Enter key after each line, but only at the end as shown.

**NOTE:** Typists often leave two spaces at the end of a sentence. Although this is appropriate for a *monospaced* typestyle, such as Courier, it is better to leave one space when using a *proportional* typestyle, such as Calibri, the default in Word.

As you type, Word's automatic spell program ("AutoCorrect") may identify com-monly misspelled words and correct them (such as beefore). In addition, a red or blue wavy underline may appear beneath some words. This is part of Word's Spellcheck pro-gram. It automatically marks words that are potentially misspelled. Do not worry about it for now. Shortly, you will learn how to use this feature to fix some of your mistakes. Wavy, green underlines may also appear. This is Word's grammar check at work. You can ignore them for now.

Note, too, that a "word count" and "proofing" icon (with a red "X" indicating that you have some mistakes) appear in the status bar. Figure W-10 shows how the text might appear. Compare it to your screen. Your name should appear at the upper left of the screen, but your lines might end at different places than the example here.

> **NOTE:**  If the screen text is difficult to see, you can magnify it. Click the *Zoom* slider control on the status bar and then drag it to a desired zoom setting (or click the "+" or "-" button on either side as needed. This does not alter the final printed text size; it just makes it easier to see on the screen.

Before continuing, be sure that you have the same five mistakes that remain in your document, as shown in Figure W-7 (proccessor, typping, all ready, o, and preety). If they are correct, make them "wrong" by moving the insertion point back to each and then typing or deleting as needed. In Lesson 5, you will return to this text to learn how to correct these mistakes.

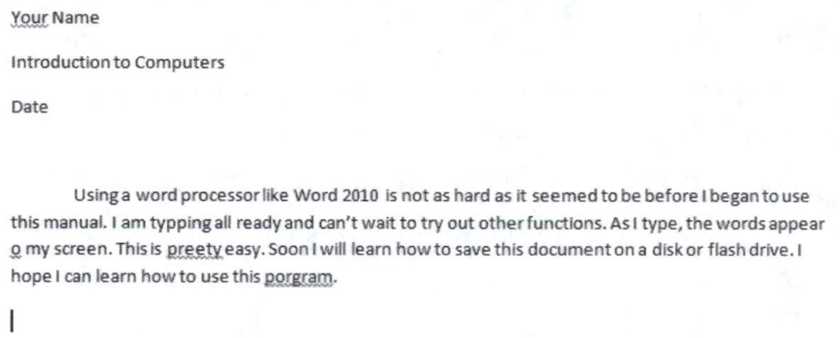

---

Your Name

Introduction to Computers

Date

Using a word processor like Word 2010 is not as hard as it seemed to be before I began to use this manual. I am typping all ready and can't wait to try out other functions. As I type, the words appear o my screen. This is preety easy. Soon I will learn how to save this document on a disk or flash drive. I hope I can learn how to use this porgram.

**FIGURE W-10**　*Word Screen after Typing the Example*

Ignore Spellcheck's wavy lines (if they appear) for now.

---

## LESSON 4: SAVING AND OPENING A DOCUMENT AND EXITING WORD

The document on your screen is currently in your computer's primary memory (RAM), but not yet saved on secondary storage (disk or flash drive). If you were to exit Word or shut off the computer now, your document would be lost!

It is important, then, to copy the document to disk (or flash drive) with a SAVE command. Most users save every ten minutes or so as they work. This way, if anything happens (power failure, forgetfulness, a mix-up), they've lost only a small part of their work. It's a good habit for you to develop; don't wait for a major loss to convince you!

It is a fairly simple process to save a document:

1. Click the File tab and then Save to begin the save process. (You could also click the Save button on the Quick Access toolbar or press Ctrl+S.)

A Save As dialog box appears, as shown in Figure W-11. Although your computer may be set to save your file in the correct location, it is a good idea to always check. Otherwise, your file may end up somewhere where you can't find it easily.

2.   Examine the entry shown in the Save in box (as shown in Figure W-11a). It should display the diskette, flash drive, or folder in which you plan to save your document. (Check with your instructor or lab personnel if needed.) If it is not correct, you can change it as follows:

   a.   Click the vertical scroll bar, as shown in Figure W-11b, until you see the desired drive or folder.

   b.   Click the drive or the path you want to use, as in Figure W-11c. (Typically, a flash drive will appear as (E:) or (F:) depending on your system.) A list of available folders and files appears. Your list may differ, but it will always appear alphabetically, displaying folders first, followed by files.

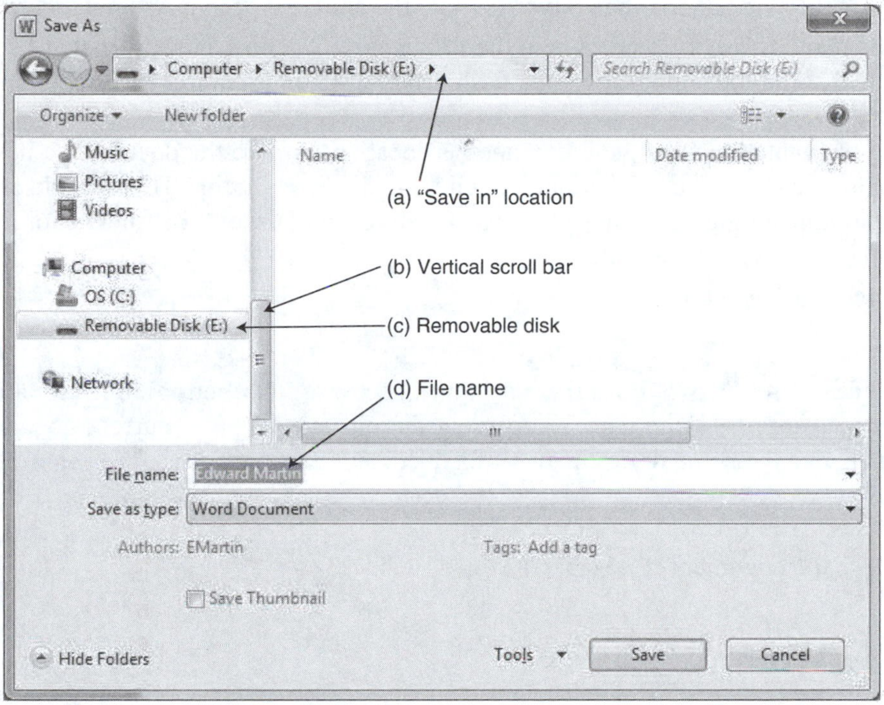

**FIGURE W-11**   *The Save As Dialog Box*

(a)+(b)+(c)  Check and set the destination (Save in) drive or folder before naming the file.

(d)   Give the file a name.

Because this is the first time you're saving the document, you must enter a filename under which it will be saved. A document's name should convey some meaning that will make it easy to remember in the future. For example:

BUDGET10JAN might contain the January 2010 budget.

LTR OCT0710 might be a letter written on October 7, 2010.

LETTER 05 EGM might be letter #5 written by author EGM.

3.   Click the *File name* box (near the bottom of the dialog box—as shown in Figure W-11d) to access it.

By default, Word lists the first few words in your document as the file's name. You can easily change it as follows:

4.   Delete its current contents (press BACKSPACE).

5.   Type SAMPLE1 and then click *Save*.

**NOTE:** Although you may not see it in the file list, Word adds a .DOCX extension to each filename to identify it as a Word 2010 document. (Releases of Word prior to 2007 used a .DOC extension.)

After you name your document and save it, Word will use the name automatically whenever you issue the File, Save command again. Note that its name now appears in the title bar, identifying the saved document. If you wanted to change the name of the document, you could save it in a slightly different manner, called Save As. For example, try this Save As routine:

**6.** Click the File tab and then Save As (note the choice is "Save As" *not* "Save").

The name SAMPLE1 appears in the *File name* entry box. Note, too, that the *Save in* entry box (at the top) now shows the flash drive, diskette (or folder) that contains SAMPLE1.

If you wanted to save the file in another location, or give the document a new name, you could make the changes here before clicking the Save button. This would save a new file without changing or erasing the one already on the diskette or folder. For now, just exit without resaving it, as follows:

**7.** Click the *Cancel* button.

**NOTE:** Use *Save* (or click the *Save* quick access toolbar button) to resave a document using the same name—replacing the old one with the current document. To change the name or destination of a document, use *Save As*.

**8.** Close the document (File tab, *Close*).

## Exiting Word

When you finish working in Word, you should exit from it. If you have already saved your document, you will simply return to the Windows desktop. However, if you've made any changes to your document since last saving it, Word will ask you if you want to save the changes before actually exiting.

**NOTE:** If you do not want to exit at this time, simply read through the procedure and then continue with the next lesson.

**1.** Click the File tab and then *Exit* (at the end of the menu) to begin the Exit command. (You could also click the Close-"X" button at the upper-right corner of the window.)

**2.** If you are asked to save changes, click "Don't Save" or press **N**. You should now be returned to Windows' desktop.

**NOTE:** In typical use, you would want to save your changes by selecting "Save." However, in this example, you have already saved your document, and there is no reason to go through the save procedure again.

3. If you want to stop for now, turn off Windows, and if appropriate, remove your diskette (or flash drive). Otherwise, continue with "Opening a Document."

## Opening a Document

Once you save a document, it is available for additional viewing, editing, or printing. You can type part of a document, save it, exit from Word, and then return another time to continue where you left off. To prepare for these exercises, complete the following steps:

1. If necessary, start Windows and launch Word (review the Introductory module if you need help).

> **NOTE:** A fresh document window is displayed when Word is launched.

## Opening a Document Window

"Opening" a document retrieves a previously stored file from secondary storage (your diskette, flash drive, or folder) and copies it into a fresh document window for your use.

1. Click the File tab.

   The File menu appears (as you've seen earlier in Figure W-5). If the document you want to open is listed in the right "Recent Documents" list, you could click its name to open it. (Let's assume it is not listed for purposes of this exercise.) If not, you can open it by continuing as follows:

2. Click the *Open* option in the menu.

   An Open dialog box appears, waiting for you to type in a filename, as shown in Figure W-12.

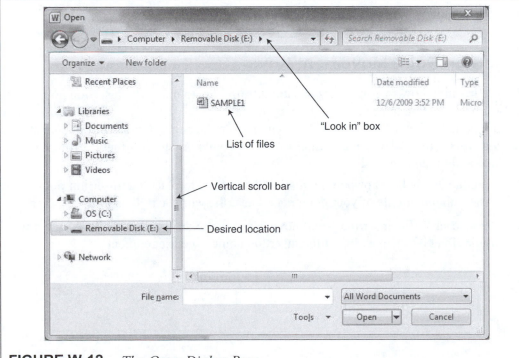

**FIGURE W-12**   *The Open Dialog Box*

The File name entry box awaits a file to open. (The "Look in" entry and files listed in the box may differ on your screen.)

2.  If needed, change the "Look in" entry to the location that has your file. (As you did when saving, drag the vertical scroll bar to view the desired disk, drive, or folder, and then click it.)

3.  In the list of available files, click *SAMPLE1* to select it.

4.  Click the *Open* button to open the file. (You can also just double-click the filename directly to open it.)

    The SAMPLE1 document is opened for use. You'll see the document's name in the title bar at the top of the screen.

> **NOTE:**   When you are done with a document, you should close it (use the File tab and *Close*) before opening another document.

## LESSON 5: FIXING MISTAKES WITH SPELLCHECK

Because your Word document is not yet on paper, corrections can be made easily with simple adjustments to the text on the screen. Although Word's AutoCorrect program will fix many common misspellings and typing errors as you type, there may be others that you must correct yourself. In the next few lessons, you will practice using Spellcheck, inserting and deleting text, and having the computer find and replace text automatically. Remember, when you want to stop, first save your document and then exit from Word (refer to Lesson 4 if necessary).

1.  If needed, start Windows and launch Word.

2.  Open SAMPLE1 if it is not already on your screen.

### Insertion Point Movement Keys

Before learning how to edit text, you should learn how to move the insertion point within a document. As you have seen, the four arrow keys ($\rightarrow$, $\downarrow$, $\leftarrow$, $\uparrow$) will move the insertion point one character at a time anywhere from the beginning of your document until its end. Using the CTRL and HOME keys, in combination with these arrow keys, can provide additional controls.

1.  Use the arrow keys, or point and click the mouse, to place the insertion point somewhere in the middle of your document—near the word "can't" is fine.

2.  Press each of the insertion point movement keystrokes listed in Table W-1 and watch their effect on the position of the insertion point in your document.

| Keystroke: | Insertion point moves: |
|---|---|
| → | One character right |
| ← | One character left |
| ↑ | One line up |
| ↓ | One line down |
| CTRL + → | One word right |
| CTRL + ← | One word left |
| HOME | To the start of the current line |
| END | To the end of the current line |
| CTRL + END | To the document's end |
| CTRL + HOME | To the document's start |

**TABLE W-1**     *Basic Insertion Point Movements*

**W**

**NOTE:**   Note that the insertion point moves over text *without* changing it. Remember, though, that it cannot move past the end of the document.

## Using Spellcheck

If your screen displays red or blue wavy underlines beneath some words (or if the status bar displays the "Proofing Errors" icon), then Spellcheck is active. Spellcheck is a Word feature that checks text entries for errors in spelling and capitalization as you type. (As you have seen earlier, a related feature—AutoCorrect—automatically corrects common typing errors and completes abbreviations.) You can activate Spellcheck by clicking the File tab, *Options*, *Proofing*, then the *Check spelling as you type* option (to place a checkmark in its box) and then *OK*. (If Spellcheck cannot be made active on your system, do not make these changes now, but wait until later to correct them manually.)

1.   If the SAMPLE1 document is not on your screen, open it now.

2.   Point anywhere within the word "typping," as shown in Figure W-13a.

3.   While pointing to the word, right-click the mouse (press its right button) to access Spellcheck's shortcut menu, as shown in Figure W-13b.

     A shortcut menu appears with a list of possible corrections.

4.   Click *typing* in the shortcut menu to select it as the replacement.

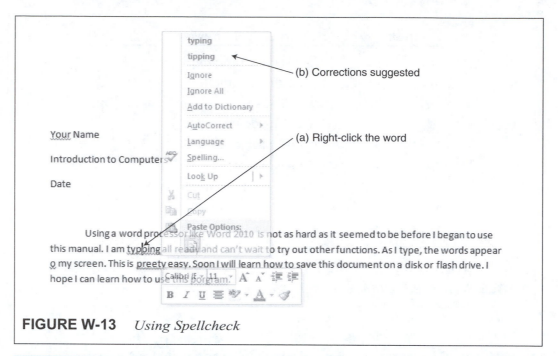

**FIGURE W-13**     *Using Spellcheck*

**NOTE:**  To cancel the Spellcheck shortcut menu *without* making any changes, simply click the document outside the shortcut menu.

Although you could continue to right-click each potential misspelling in your document one-by-one, there's a simple way to locate each spelling error using the status bar's Proofing icon. Try this:

**5.**  Click the Proofing Errors found icon on the status bar.

This icon should display a red "X" indicating there are potential errors in the document. (If it displays a green checkmark, there are no errors found.)

The program locates the first red-underlined word—in this case, perhaps, "proccessor"—and offers corrections in the shortcut list. (Sometimes, the program will identify *your name* as "wrong" if it does not recognize the spelling. If this occurs, simply click *Ignore*, and repeat Step 5.)

**6.**  Click "processor" in the shortcut list to correct it.

**7.**  Using either the right-click method or the Proofing icon, locate and fix the words "o" (on), "preety" and "porgram."

**8.**  Resave the SAMPLE1 document (click the *Save quick access toolbar button* or click the File tab, and then *Save*).

## LESSON 6: INSERTING AND DELETING TEXT

Often, you will want to add new material to a document. To add text to the end, just move the insertion point there and start typing. But what about adding something—a word or sentence—in the middle of the document? Or maybe you notice a missing space or misspelled word that requires more space than before. Being able to insert new text wherever you want is another important advantage of using a word processor.

## Insert Mode

By default, Word is set to *insert text*. This means that it will push "old" text (text already on the screen) over to make space for new letters as you type.

You will now correct another error, and add a few more words, to practice using the insert technique.

1.   If needed, open SAMPLE1.

2.   If you did not correct "on" previously, do it now by following Step 3. Otherwise, skip to the "Another Insert Example" below.

3.   Click the location or use the arrow keys to move the insertion point to the space just *after* the o in "appear o my screen" (on the third line).

4.   Type an **n** and see the "o" become the word "on." The rest of the line moved over to make space for the "n" that you inserted.

> **NOTE:** If the line did *not* move over (that is, there is no space after the "n" you typed) then Word's Insert may not be active. To check: Click the *Microsoft Office* button, *Word Options*, and *Advanced*. If the "Use Overtype mode" is checked, click it to remove the check mark, and then click *OK*. (If it is not clicked, just click OK.) If needed, press the Spacebar to insert the missing space before continuing.

## Another Insert Example

Say you want to add the words "every one of the" to your document in the second sentence:

1.   To start, move the insertion point so it is in the same place as the letter "o" in "other" (in the second line) as shown in Figure W-14a.

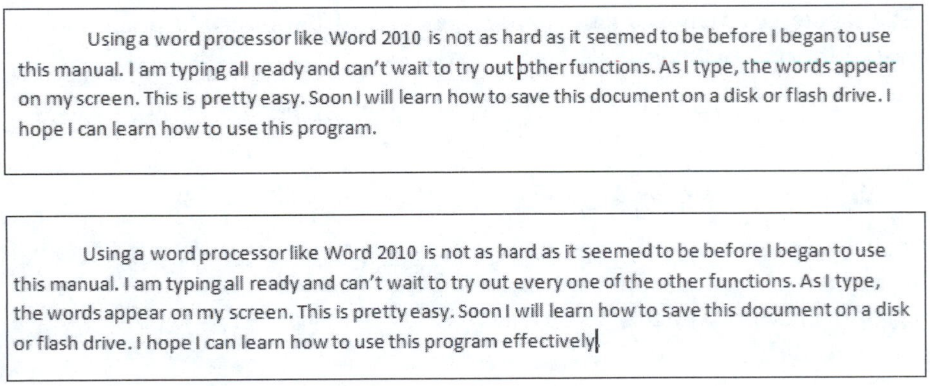

Using a word processor like Word 2010 is not as hard as it seemed to be before I began to use this manual. I am typing all ready and can't wait to try out other functions. As I type, the words appear on my screen. This is pretty easy. Soon I will learn how to save this document on a disk or flash drive. I hope I can learn how to use this program.

(a)

Using a word processor like Word 2010 is not as hard as it seemed to be before I began to use this manual. I am typing all ready and can't wait to try out every one of the other functions. As I type, the words appear on my screen. This is pretty easy. Soon I will learn how to save this document on a disk or flash drive. I hope I can learn how to use this program effectively

(b)

**FIGURE W-14**   *Inserting New Words*

(a)   Preparing to insert text.
(b)   Both insertions have been completed.

2.   With the insertion point to the immediate left of the letter "o," type **every one of the** (with a space at the end).

Watch the "old" text move over to make room. As you type, the words will be automatically reformatted to fit the margins. Try one last insert:

3.  Move the insertion point to the period after the word "program."

4.  Type a space and then the word **effectively**.

    As you type, the period moves. Your screen should resemble Figure W-14b. You've now corrected almost all of the original mistakes!

5.  Save your document with a new name. Click the *Microsoft Office* button, and then *Save As*, verify that the Save In drive is still set to the proper destination, then type **SAMPLE2** and press ⏎.

    (The document's name should appear in the title bar when you're done.)

### Quick Review #2

1.  Why is a space needed after the added phrase "every one of the"?

    _____

2.  What does the Insert mode do to existing text as you type?

    _____

3.  What did you gain by saving your file with a new name?

    _____


## DELETING TEXT

Deleting characters or words is as easy as inserting. To prepare for this exercise:

1.  Open the SAMPLE2 document if it is not already on your screen.

    With practice, you can remove a character, a word, or any block of text. Try fixing the remaining errors using the *Delete* key.

2.  Move the insertion point to the second "l" in the word "all" (in the second line *between* the two "ll"s).

3.  Press ⸢DELETE⸥ once. Notice that the final "l" is erased and "ready" moves closer. The delete key removes letters at the position of the insertion point and moves the rest of the text to the left.

4.  Press ⸢DELETE⸥ again to remove the space, creating the new word "already."

> **NOTE:**   In this example, "all" and "ready" are acceptable words on their own. Spellcheck would not be appropriate. (Delete removes characters to the *right* of the insertion point. You could also use the Backspace key to remove letters to the *left* of the insertion point.)

Word's Undo feature can cancel your last deletion—a handy tool if you deleted too far. Try this now:

5.  Click the <u>*Undo Clear*</u> button in the Quick Access toolbar (or press ⸢CTRL⸥ + **Z**). The deletion has been cancelled; the character has returned.

6.  Press ⸢DELETE⸥ to remove the "l" again.

7.  If you did not use Spellcheck earlier, delete the extra letters in "typping" now.

8.  Save the file with its current name—SAMPLE2 (use the Save quick access button or the File tab and *Save*).

**W**

## Fixing an Accidental ENTER by Revealing Hidden Codes

The Delete key can be used to remove an unwanted ENTER (a "hard return") that you might have pressed by mistake. A hard return entered in the wrong place in your document can break up a sentence before reaching the right margin. The following steps demonstrate this point:

**1.** Move your insertion point to the space after "processor like Word."

**2.** Press ⏎ to force a hard return.

Notice that the sentence now breaks at this point, as shown in Figure W-15a.

(a)

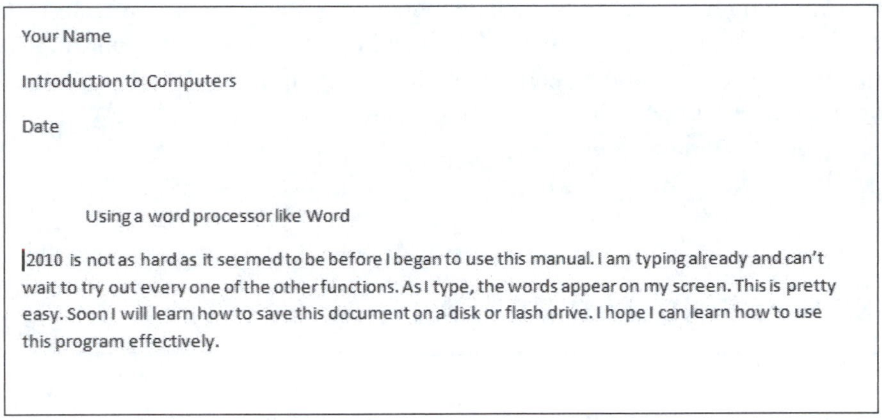

Your Name

Introduction to Computers

Date


          Using a word processor like Word

2010 is not as hard as it seemed to be before I began to use this manual. I am typing already and can't wait to try out every one of the other functions. As I type, the words appear on my screen. This is pretty easy. Soon I will learn how to save this document on a disk or flash drive. I hope I can learn how to use this program effectively.

(b)

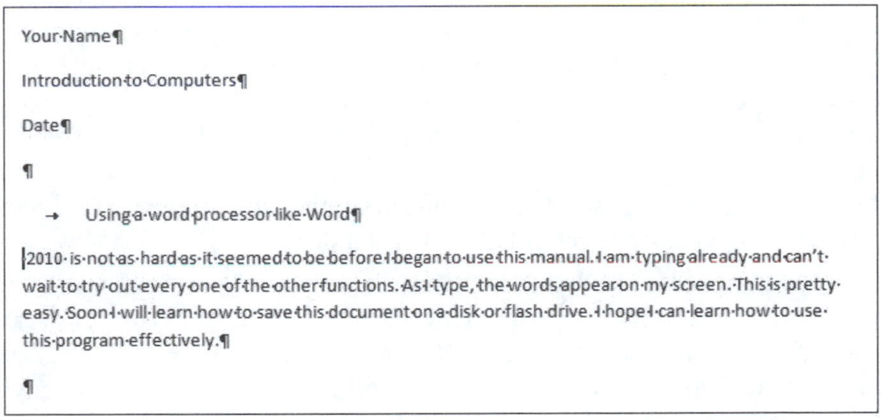

Your·Name¶

Introduction·to·Computers¶

Date¶

¶

    →    Using·a·word·processor·like·Word¶

2010·is·not·as·hard·as·it·seemed·to·be·before·I·began·to·use·this·manual.·I·am·typing·already·and·can't· wait·to·try·out·every·one·of·the·other·functions.·As·I·type,·the·words·appear·on·my·screen.·This·is·pretty· easy.·Soon·I·will·learn·how·to·save·this·document·on·a·disk·or·flash·drive.·I·hope·I·can·learn·how·to·use· this·program·effectively.¶

¶

**FIGURE W-15**   *Revealing Hidden Codes*

(a)   An "invisible" hard return has been placed in the first line.

(b)   The screen displays the hidden code markers for hard returns (¶), tabs (→), and spaces (·).

Although you will not see it on your screen, there is a hard return after "processor like Word " that causes the line to break. Word keeps some formatting symbols "hidden" so that they will not interfere with the appearance of your work on the screen. However, you can view them when needed. Here's an easy way to see an "invisible" hard return and remove it:

**3.** Click the *Show/Hide* button—located in the Paragraph group on the Home tab (or press Ctrl+Shift+8).   ¶

As shown in Figure W-15b, your document now displays codes for any hard return, space, or tab that you have typed into your document.

4. To remove the unwanted hard return, use the arrow keys (or click the mouse) to position the insertion point to the immediate left of the hard return (in this case, after "Word").

5. Press DELETE to remove it.

The words on the next line jump back to where they belong. When you are done, you can shut off the Show/Hide view option as follows:

6. Turn off the view option by clicking the *Show/Hide* icon.

7. Close the document but do not save the document.

> **NOTE:** You may use the Show/Hide view option whenever you want to see the "hidden" codes in your document. You can also leave the option on the screen as you work. As your understanding of the screen improves, you can delete unwanted codes without using the option at all. Just move to where you know the hidden code is, and delete it.

## LESSON 7: FIND AND REPLACE

There may be times when you want to locate a word or phrase somewhere in your document. You might even want to replace it with something else. It would be nice to be able to change all occurrences of a word or phrase without having to find each one, delete it, and insert its replacement. For example, what if you wrote a story about Mr. Smith, and then decided to change the name to Jones? Imagine trying to find every occurrence of Smith in a long document. Fortunately, Word has a special function, called "replace," which does this with ease.

First, let's examine a few potential problems. Otherwise, you may find some surprising results after replacing one set of letters with another.

- Words within words can cause problems. When you type a word for the program to find, you create a "string," or pattern, of characters. Word compares this string character-by-character to others throughout the document to find matches. For example, if you type "the" as the word to find, Word will not only find "the," but anything with the letter sequence "t-h-e" in it, such as "theory," "bathe," and "father." If you replace "his" with "her," you might create words like "hertory" ("history") and "whertle" ("whistle")! The good news is that you can protect against this happening by selecting the *Whole Words* option offered in the Find and Replace menu (more on this later).

- Capital letters can cause another problem. Some may need to be fixed after replacement. For example, replacing "I" with "we" may cause some sentences to start with "we" instead of "We." In other cases, the search may ignore words that only differ in case. For example, the search for "Apple" may not find "apple" or "APPLE."

- Grammar and verbs might also need adjustment. If you replace a word like "energetic" with "lively," you might end up with "an lively person." Changing singular to plural might result in "we was" or "they enjoys." Including a noun and verb when you replace might help. For example, you might find "he was" and replace it with "we were." It is difficult, however, to figure out all combinations of nouns and verbs that may occur in your document.

The moral is, "Be careful when you replace, for the computer will do exactly what it is told." Some replacements may require you to examine each change individually and decide whether the replacement is correct.

> **NOTE:** You must always proofread your document to check for grammatical and typing errors. After all, your work reflects upon you, not the computer.

## Word's Replace Function

Now that you understand some of the pitfalls of replacing text, try using the replace function to change every "word" in the SAMPLE2 document to "text." To do this, complete the following steps:

1. Start Windows and launch Word or, if you have an open document, close its window and open SAMPLE2.

   You are now ready to try the replace technique.

   Word starts a search at the current location of your insertion point. Usually, you will want the search to include the entire document from its start, so you should move the insertion point to the beginning of your document.

2. Use CTRL + HOME to move to the start of the document quickly.

> **NOTE:** Proper insertion point position is essential to using Word because almost every command *takes place at the current insertion point position*. This is true whether you find, delete, insert, move, copy, underline, or change margins or tabs. Make sure that your insertion point is positioned correctly before invoking a Word command or edit.

3. Click *Replace* (in the Editing group of the Home tab as shown in Figure W-16a) to start the Replace function.

   A Find and Replace dialog box appears on your screen, resembling Figure W-16b.

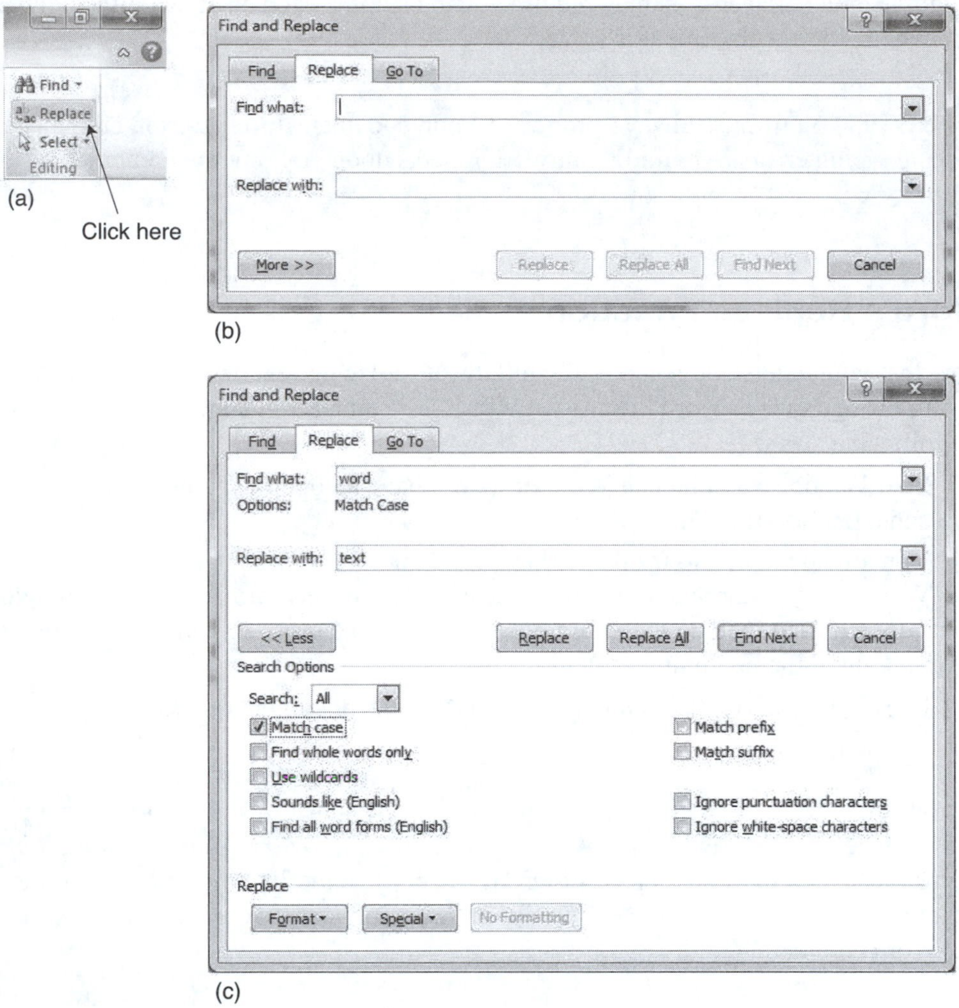

**FIGURE W-16**   *The Replace Dialog Box*

(a)   Invoking the Replace function.

(b)   The standard box.

(c)   The expanded box provides access to additional search settings.

Word can replace one item at a time, or all at once. If you select the "Replace" button, Word will replace only the current match. The "Replace All" button will replace all matches. You'll try both methods in this exercise.

4.   Click the *Find what* entry box if you're not already there.

5.   Type **word** (the text string to be found) in the Find what entry box.

6.   Click the *Replace with* entry box (or press TAB) to move there.

7.   Type **text** (this is the replacement string).

Because you want only words with lowercase letters to be replaced (that is, "word" but not "Word"), you must perform one more step before continuing with the replace:

8.   Click the *More* button (at the bottom left) to expand the Find and Replace dialog box.

9.   Now, click the *Match Case* check box, as in Figure W-16c.

This will ensure that only words that match the letters you typed in lowercase will be found. Note that the option is now checked and the words "Match Case" appears in the Options list under "Find." You can now continue.

10.  Click the *Replace All* button to invoke the replacement.

A message will appear, advising you when the replacements are complete.

11.  Click *OK* to acknowledge the message and continue.

12.  Click the *Close* button to close the dialog box.

The two occurrences of "word" have been changed to "text!" Compare your screen to Figure W-17. Note that the capitalized "Word" was *not* replaced, since it did not match the case as required. (Note, too, that the "s" from "words" has remained to form the new word "texts." Also, the word "text" in the third line doesn't really make sense. Although it doesn't matter for this exercise, remember that a computer will only do what you tell it to, whether it makes sense or not!

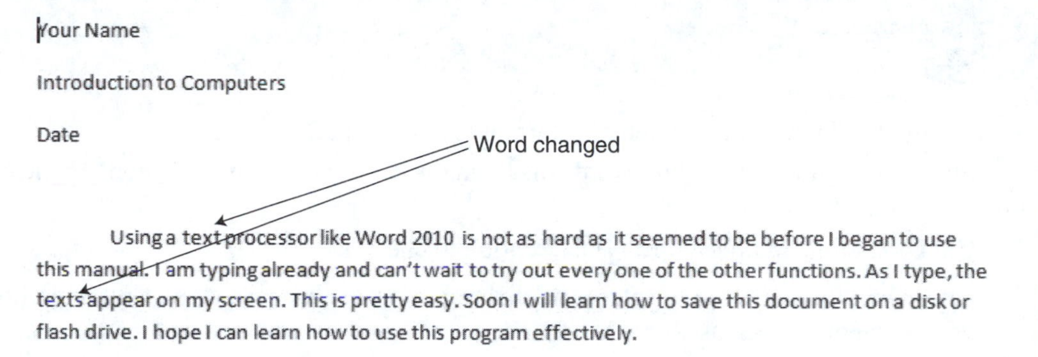

Your Name

Introduction to Computers

Date

Word changed

Using a text processor like Word 2010 is not as hard as it seemed to be before I began to use this manual. I am typing already and can't wait to try out every one of the other functions. As I type, the texts appear on my screen. This is pretty easy. Soon I will learn how to save this document on a disk or flash drive. I hope I can learn how to use this program effectively.

**FIGURE W-17**     *The Screen after Replacement*

**NOTE:**   If your screen does not show all changes, you may have started with your insertion point in the wrong place. If necessary, you can click the *Undo* Quick Access toolbar button (or press CTRL + **Z**) to undo a faulty (or unexpected) replacement.

13.  Save the document as SAMPLE3 (use the *Microsoft Office* button, *Save As*).

**NOTE:**   You can also *locate* text in a document without having to replace it. Just use the *Find* button instead of *Replace*. For example, you might type **XXX** to mark a place in your document and then search for it later to continue your work.

## Exercises in Replace

Now, you'll practice using the "Replace option" (rather than "Replace All") to individually control which text is replaced. In this example, you'll change a few "I"s (as shown in Figure W-18) to "we" as follows:

1.  Move to the start of SAMPLE3 (press CTRL + HOME ).

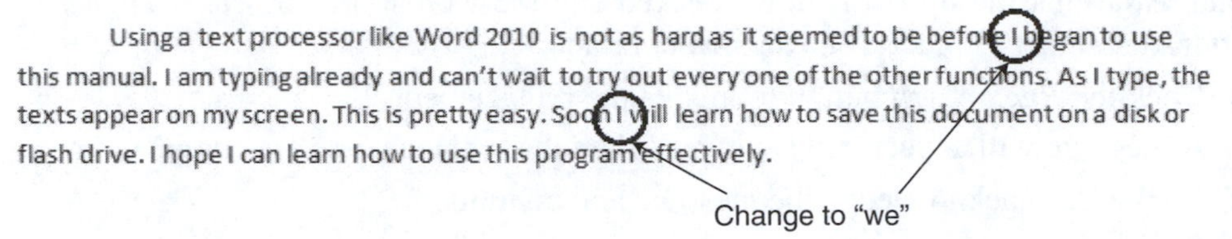

Using a text processor like Word 2010 is not as hard as it seemed to be before I began to use this manual. I am typing already and can't wait to try out every one of the other functions. As I type, the texts appear on my screen. This is pretty easy. Soon I will learn how to save this document on a disk or flash drive. I hope I can learn how to use this program effectively.

Change to "we"

**FIGURE W-18**     *The SAMPLE3 Document is Ready for the Replace Option*

**2.**   Click the *Replace* button (in the Editing group of the Home tab).

**NOTE:**   When you activate a new Find or Replace, the Find entry might contain the last "Find what" text you used. Simply delete the old text and then type the new characters.

**3.**   For the Find what entry, delete the current text and type **I**.

Since we do not want to find words that contain "I" (such as "Introduction" in the example), set one more option:

**4.**   Click the "Find Whole Words Only" option to check it.

**5.**   Click the "Less" button to return the dialog box to its standard size. This will allow you to see the screen as words are found.

**6.**   For the Replace with entry, delete the current text and type **we**.

**7.**   Click *Find Next* to find the next match for the word "I."

Word finds the first "I" and, instead of changing it, highlights it (typically in blue) and awaits your command, as shown in Figure W-19. You want to change this "I" so:

**8.**   Click *Replace* to replace this word.

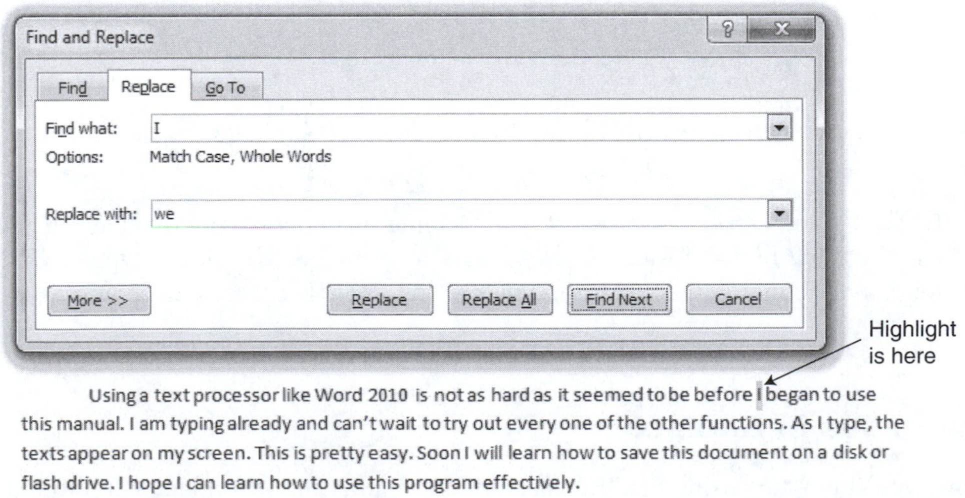

| Find and Replace |
| --- |

Find    Replace    Go To

Find what:    I

Options:    Match Case, Whole Words

Replace with:    we

More >>          Replace    Replace All    Find Next    Cancel

Highlight is here

Using a text processor like Word 2010 is not as hard as it seemed to be before I began to use this manual. I am typing already and can't wait to try out every one of the other functions. As I type, the texts appear on my screen. This is pretty easy. Soon I will learn how to save this document on a disk or flash drive. I hope I can learn how to use this program effectively.

**FIGURE W-19**   *Finding a Search Word*

Word has located the first "I" and awaits your command to continue (Find Next) or replace.

The program will replace this "I" with "we" and then find the next occurrence of the word "I." You do *not* want to replace this "I" so,

9. Click *Find Next* to skip this word without changing it. The program will move on to the next.

10. Click *Find Next* again to skip the next "I."

11. Click *Replace* for the next match.

Since there are no more changes we wish to make, you can close the dialog box, but let's clean up some of the options before we do so they do not affect a future search.

> **NOTE:** As long as an entry remains in the Find What entry box of the Find and Replace dialog box, the Page buttons beneath the vertical scroll bar in the Word window appear "blue" and can be clicked to locate the next (or previous) "Find" match. While they are blue, they do not function as Page Down or Page Up buttons. By using Replace instead of Replace All, you were able to control which "I" was changed by clicking the *Find Next* or *Replace* button as desired. In general, it is safer to use the Replace option to find each word and then replace it, controlling each change.

12. To remove the options, click *More*, *Match Case*, *Find Whole Words Only*, *Less*, and then *Close*.

13. Save the document again as SAMPLE3. Close the document.

> **NOTE:** You might want to experiment with other Find and Replace options in the future, such as "sounds like," wildcards, format, and special.

## LESSON 8: CENTERING, UNDERLINING, AND BOLDING TEXT

Word can easily make changes to text. Centering text is an example of an easy change. Complete the following steps to practice centering text:

1. Open SAMPLE2.

2. Move to the end of the document ( CTRL + END ).

3. Press ↵ to start a new line.

Although you could invoke centering through the menu, it is much easier to use the toolbar button or shortcut key. Try this:

4. Click the *Center* button (*Home* tab, *Paragraph* Group) or press CTRL + **E**.

Note how the insertion point automatically moves to the middle of the line. Once the center setting is active, each line you enter after the centered line will automatically be centered as well, until you select another alignment.

5. Type **Word Exercises** and press ↵. It's centered!

6. Now, return to left alignment by clicking the *Align Left* command button (or by pressing CTRL + **L**).

## Uncentering Text

To uncenter text, simply replace the center code as follows:

1.  Click anywhere within "Word Exercises."

2.  Click the Align Left command button (or press [CTRL] + **L**). The centering should be removed.

## Centering Previously Typed Words

You can also center words you've already typed.

1.  With the insertion point on the same line, click the Center button (or press [CTRL] + **E**).

> **NOTE:**   You can center before you start typing or after you finish. Use the command buttons or press the appropriate shortcut keys.

2.  Move down to the next line (press the ↓ key). Then center the words "Centering Example."

3.  Press [↵] to start a new line and then set left alignment.

4.  Save the document as SAMPLE4.

## Changing Text Appearance—Underline and Bold

Until now, you have been typing text without any enhancements. However, you can use Word to change the appearance of text to add emphasis where you decide it is appropriate. Some of Word's text enhancements are shown in Table W-2. The following exercises will demonstrate two of the most common enhancements—underline and bold. Once you master these, try some of the other enhancements using the same techniques that you learn here.

| Regular | Underline | Superscript | Emboss |
|---------|-----------|-------------|--------|
| *Italic* | Double Underline | Subscript | Engrave |
| **Bold** | Dotted Underline | Shadow | Color |
| ***Bold Italic*** | SMALL CAPS | Outline | Strikethrough |

**TABLE W-2**    *A Text Sampler*

Some text enhancements in Word.

## Underlining

1.  Open SAMPLE4 if it is not already on the screen.

2.  Move to the end of the document ([CTRL] + [END]).

3.  Press [↵] once to start a new line if needed.
    You will now type a sentence with one underlined word to practice the technique.

4.  Type **This is one example of an** with a space after the last word.

Word can underline as you type if you invoke the underline feature, type the desired text, and then shut off the underline feature. First you will learn the "long" way to invoke any text enhancement. Then, you'll use the command buttons and keyboard shortcuts.

**5.** Click the *Font* dialog box launcher, as shown in Figure W-20a.

> **NOTE:** Dialog box launch buttons are located in the lower-right corner of each group on the ribbon.

A Font dialog box appears as in Figure W-20b. A *font* is a typestyle that determines the appearance of text. The Font dialog box allows you to control all text enhancements. You can change font style, font size, and text appearance from this menu.

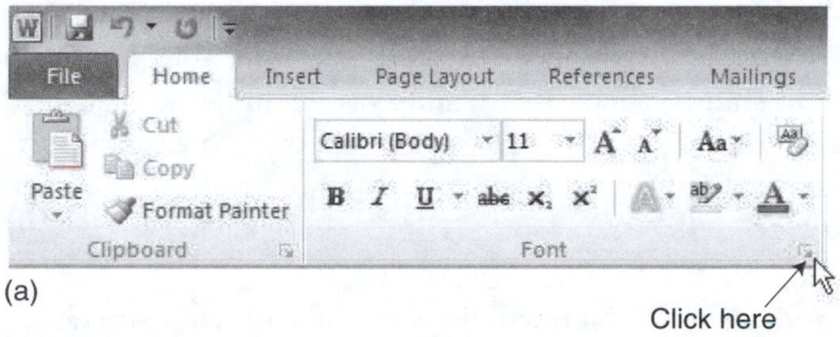

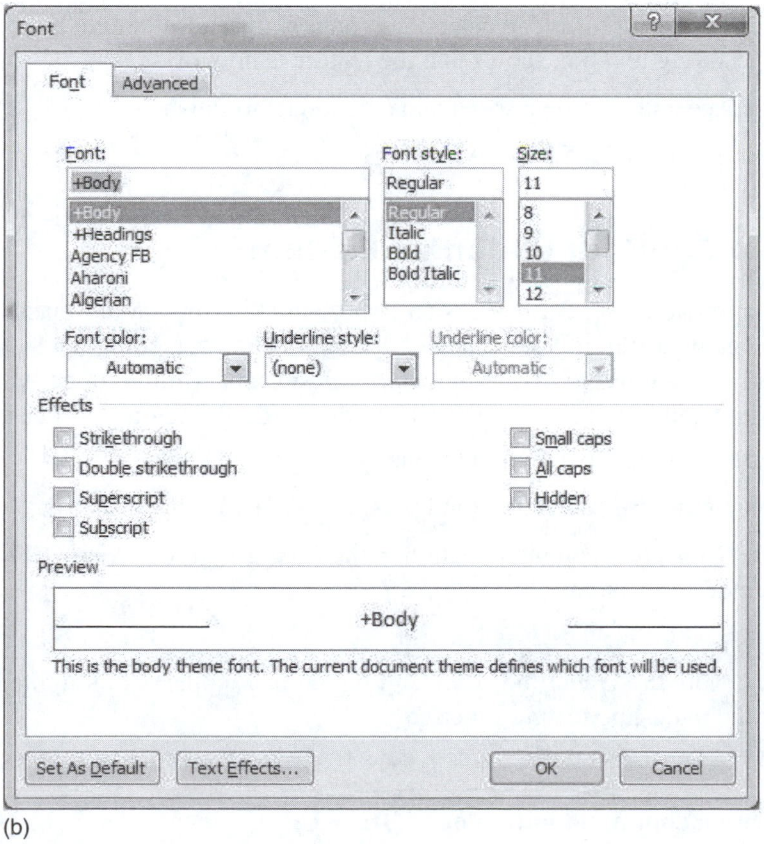

**FIGURE W-20**   *Opening the Font Dialog Box*

(a)   Click the Font Dialog Box launcher.

(b)   The Font Dialog Box.

Note that the Underline style (located in the center of the box) currently shows "(none)." Select *Underline* as follows:

**6.** Click the drop-down arrow at the right of the Underline style box. A list of options appears.

**7.** Click the single line option (just under "Words Only").

> **NOTE:** Note that the Underline box now displays a "single line" and that the resulting text box at the lower right reflects the change.

**8.** Click OK to close the dialog box.

> **NOTE:** As with centering, any text you type from this point on will be underlined until you shut the underline feature off again. Note that the "U" command button (in the *Font* group of the *Home* tab) appears "pressed"—a visual indicator that the underline feature is active.

**9.** Now type **underlined** (which will be underlined on your screen).

**10.** When done, repeat steps 5-8 selecting "(none)" instead of single underlining in step 7. The resulting text box shows that the feature is now off.

**11.** Type a space and then type **word** and a period (.) to finish.

**12.** Save this document again as SAMPLE4.

## Using the Shortcut Underline Feature

The "long" approach to underlining is an important skill you should master because you can invoke many different font changes—font, style, size, color, and other effects—through the Font dialog box. However, if you desire underlining alone, you can use the underline command button, or CTRL + U, to turn underlining on or off easily. Try this:

**1.** Type a space after the period in the last sentence.

**2.** Type **You can also underline** (and press SPACE after the last "e").

**3.** Click the *Underline* command button in the *Font* group (or press CTRL + U) to turn on the underline feature.

> **NOTE:** Note the Underline command button now appears highlighted, indicating that the underline feature is active.

**4.** Type **with a command button or CTRL + U.**

> **NOTE:** Note that all words typed in step 4 are underlined.

5.  Click the *Underline* command button (or press CTRL + **U**) to shut off the underline  function. (The command button returns to normal as expected.)

6.  Type a period to complete the sentence.

> **NOTE:**   Clicking the drop-down arrow in the *Underline* command button opens a list of underline options from which a selection can be made.

## Selecting a Block of Text for Underlining

At times, you may want to underline a word or sentence that has already been typed. This is easily done with the *select* command. You simply identify (or select) the text with the keyboard or mouse, and then invoke the underline command as follows:

•   By mouse, click at the start of the text you want to select. Press the left mouse button, drag the pointer to the end of the text block to highlight it, and then release the mouse button.

•   By keyboard, move the insertion point to the start of the text you want to select. Press and hold SHIFT. Then press the appropriate arrow key(s) to move the insertion point to the end of the text block.

Complete the following steps using the *mouse* approach:

1.  Click just to the left of "o" in "one." This is the start of the text block.

2.  Press and hold the left mouse button.

3.  Now, while still pressing, move the mouse pointer to the space past the last letter you want underlined—in this case, the last "e" in "example."

The text will now be highlighted as shown in Figure W-21a. Note, too, that a collection of Font command buttons appears in a box above your selection. This collection offers the most common text changes and can be used in lieu of the ribbon. (However, the *Underline* button is not included.)

4.  Release the mouse button.

5.  Click the *Underline* command button in the Font group (or press CTRL + **U**) to invoke the underline feature.

The highlighted text is now underlined, as shown in Figure W-21b.

6.  Click the mouse to deselect the text block.

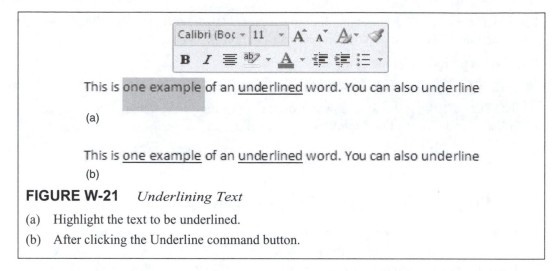

**FIGURE W-21**   *Underlining Text*

(a)   Highlight the text to be underlined.

(b)   After clicking the Underline command button.

To underline a *single* word, simply click anywhere within the word and then click the *Underline* command button. Try this:

**7.**   Click anywhere within the word "also."

**8.**   Click the *Underline* command button.

## Removing Underlining

You can remove underlining by selecting a block of text (or clicking one word) and then invoking the underline command again. Try this:

**1.**   Click the word "command."

**2.**   Click the *Underline* command button. The underline has been removed from the word.

> **NOTE:**   To remove underline from more than one word, select the text first and then click the *Underline* command button.

## Bolding Text

Bold type (which appears darker than regular type when printed) can be produced using techniques identical to the ones you used to underline. Simply click the Bold command button or press CTRL + **B** instead of the Underline command. In this example, you'll practice the "one word" approach to bold the text "word":

**1.**   Click anywhere within the word "word" in the last line of text.

**2.**   Invoke the bold command by clicking the *Bold* command button or pressing CTRL + **B**.

The word will appear in bold print.

**3.**   Save this document again as SAMPLE4.

> **NOTE:**   As in underlining, you can bold as you type by simply invoking the bold command, typing the desired text, and then shutting off bold.

## Format Painter

Word also enables you to copy the *format* of existing text (not the text itself) and apply it to any other text. You simply select the text with the format you desire, click the *Format Painter* command button and then click the text to which you want the format applied. Its size, style, color, and enhancements will be applied to the new text. (This is especially useful when you have applied multiple font changes to specific text. Here's the technique:

**1.** Click the word "word" (which is currently bold).

**2.** Click the *Format Painter* command button (*Home* tab, *Clipboard* group) to "copy" the format.

**3.** Drag the mouse pointer (which now displays a paintbrush icon) over the words "This is" and release the mouse. The format has been copied to this selection.

**4.** Close the document *without* saving the changes.

> **NOTE:** In step 2, you could double-click the Format Painter command button if you wanted to apply the format to more than one text selection in your document. Then click and drag each selection. When done, click the Format Painter button one more time to deselect it.

## LESSON 9: CHANGING THE FORMAT—MARGINS, TABS, AND LINE SPACING

Word uses preset (default) margins and tabs that are fine for most typing needs. However, at times, you may want to change these settings. Word presets the margins 1 inch vertically and horizontally from each page edge, and tabs every one-half inch, but the settings are easily changed. This exercise will change the left margin to 1.5 inches, the right to 2 inches, and then set tabs at .75 inches and 1.25 inches from the left margin.

**1.** Launch Word if needed.

**2.** Open SAMPLE2.

### Setting New Margins

**1.** Click the *Page Layout* tab in the ribbon, as in Figure W-22a.

> **NOTE:** To select a "standard" set of margins, you could click the Margins option button and then select one from the list that appears.

**2.** Click the *Page Setup* dialog launcher (as shown in Figure W-22b).
A Page Setup dialog box appears on your screen as shown in Figure W-22d.

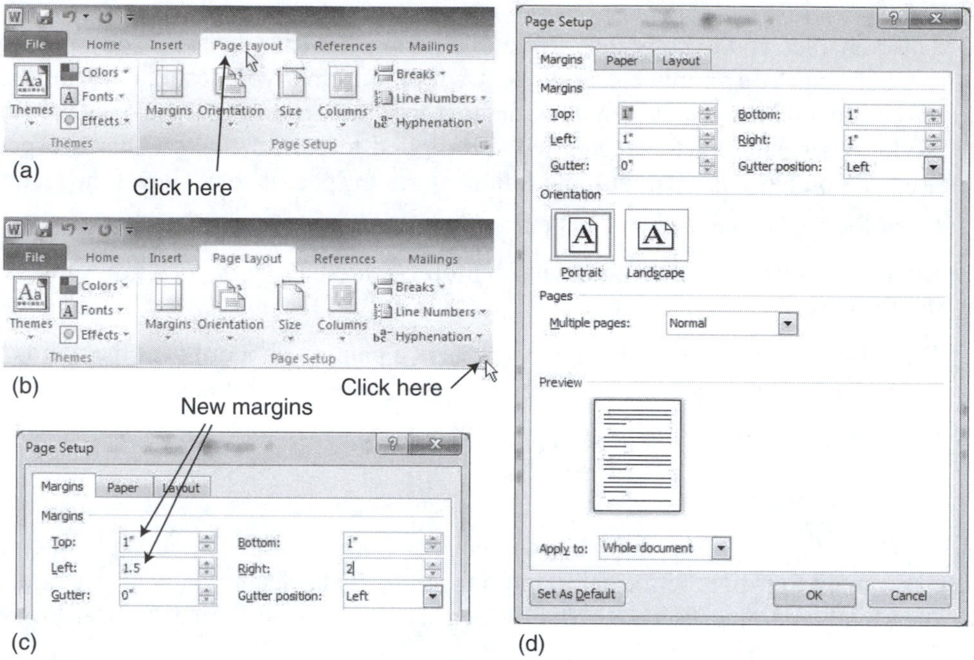

**FIGURE W-22**   *Margins Screen of the Page Setup Dialog Box*

(a)   Click the Page Layout tab.

(b)   Click the *Page Setup* dialog launcher.

(c)   The new margins have been set.

(d)   The Page Setup dialog box.

3.   Click within the *Left* entry box to move to the *Left margin* entry (currently 1").

4.   Delete the current margin and type **1.5** to set the new left margin.

5.   Click the *Right* entry box to move to the *Right margin* entry.

6.   Delete the current margin and type **2** to set the new right margin. (The top of your screen should resemble Figure W-22c.)

To make sure that the new margins are set for the whole document, perform the following step:

7.   Examine the *Apply To* entry box (at the lower left). If "Whole document" is displayed, continue to step 8. If it is not, click the drop-down arrow to the right of the *Apply To* box, and then click the *Whole document* choice.

**NOTE:**   The preview page image in the menu has changed to display your new margin choices.

You could continue to specify new top or bottom margins, but for now, finish with the following step:

8.   Click *OK* (or press ⏎) to accept the changes.

9.   Click the *Home* tab to reset it.

The document window will return. As you see in your ruler, the margins in the document have changed to the new settings—1 1/2" left margin, 2" right margin, leaving 5" for text.

## Setting New Tabs

There are two ways to set tab stops in a document—by menu or by ruler. The menu approach provides many options for customizing tabs; the ruler just a few basic ones. You'll try both. (Remember that changes affect only the current paragraph or selected text.) First, try the menu approach:

1. Move to the document's start.

2. Select the entire document (press CTRL + **A** or click *Select*—in the *Editing* group—and then *Select All*) so that the new tab settings will be applied throughout the document, instead of only to the first paragraph.

   To access the Tabs dialog box:

3. Click the Home tab in the ribbon if needed.

4. Click the *Paragraph* dialog box launcher (in the *Paragraph* group).

5. Click the *Tabs* button (at the lower left).

   A Tabs dialog box appears as in Figure W-23. In this example, every one-half inch has a default tab indicated by tick marks on the ruler bar and the 0.5" that appears in the Default Tab Stops entry box.

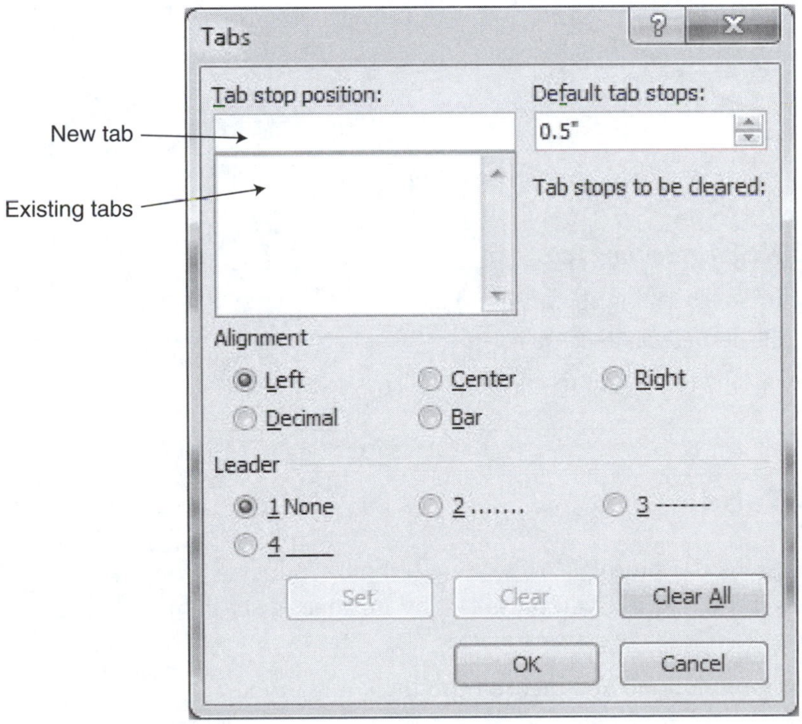

**FIGURE  W-23**   *The Tabs Dialog Box*

Word measures tabs *relative* to the left margin. That way, if you change the left margin, all the tabs are reset appropriately. When typing relative tabs, 0 represents the left margin, 1 is 1 inch to the right, 2 is 2 inches, and so on. You can set a new tab by typing its relative distance from the left margin and then selecting *Set* as in the following exercise:

6.  If needed, click the Tab stop position entry box to move to it.

7.  To set a 1.25 inch left tab, type **1.25** and click the *Set* button (do not press ⏎).
    The desired tab appears in the Tab list, as shown in Figure W-24a.

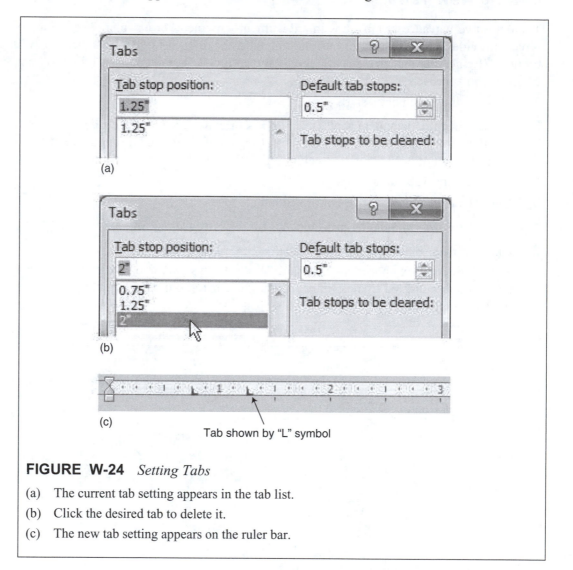

(a)

(b)

(c)

Tab shown by "L" symbol

**FIGURE  W-24**    *Setting Tabs*

(a)    The current tab setting appears in the tab list.

(b)    Click the desired tab to delete it.

(c)    The new tab setting appears on the ruler bar.

## Setting Tabs

8.  Repeat steps 6-7 but type **.75** to set a left tab .75 inches from the left margin. It, too,
    appears in the list. (If you press ⏎ by mistake, reset the tab dialog box with Steps
    4–5.)

9.  Set one more left tab at 2 inches from the left margin.

**NOTE:**   There are four types of tabs you can set: left, right, center, and decimal.
In brief, text *begins* at a left tab, *ends* at a right tab, and is centered *around* a center tab. Numeric data are placed so that their decimal points (if any) *align* at a
decimal tab position.

To clear a tab setting, you follow the same procedure as in step 7 but select *Clear* instead of *Set*. For example, to delete the 2-inch tab, complete the following steps:

**10.** Click the **2"** in the *Tab stop list* to select it, as shown in Figure W-24b.

**11.** Click *Clear* to clear the selected tab stop from the list.

> **NOTE:** You can delete all tabs by selecting *Clear All* in the dialog box.

**12.** When you're finished setting or clearing tabs, click *OK* (or press ⏎) to accept the changes.

**13.** Click anywhere to deselect the text (remove the highlight).

The text should now reflect the new tab settings. As shown in Figure W-24c, the "L" markers on the ruler bar indicate where left tabs have been set.

**14.** Click the Home tab to reset it.

**15.** Save this document as SAMPLE5.

## Setting Tabs with the Ruler Bar

A faster way to set or delete tabs is to use the ruler bar directly. Let's say you want to place a left tab at the 3-inch mark. Follow these steps:

**1.** Move to the start of the document and select the entire document (press CTRL + **A**).

In this way, the new tab setting will be applied throughout the document, not just to the first paragraph.

**2.** Point to the 3-inch mark on the ruler bar, as shown in Figure W-25a.

**3.** Click the mouse.

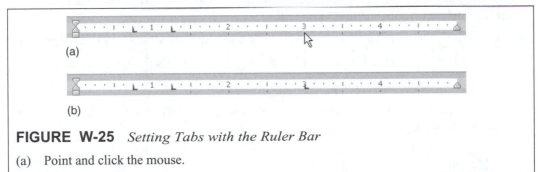

(a)

(b)

**FIGURE W-25**   *Setting Tabs with the Ruler Bar*

(a)  Point and click the mouse.

(b)  The new tab is set.

The tab is set, as shown by the new "L" marker seen in Figure W-25b.
To remove a tab from the ruler bar, complete the following steps:

**4.** Point to the tab (in this example, the "L" marker at the 3-inch mark).

**5.** Press and hold the left mouse button, then drag the "L" marker beneath the ruler bar onto the text area.

**6.** Now release the mouse button (drop the "L"). The tab is gone.

**7.** Click anywhere to deselect the text.

**8.** Close the document without saving it.

ㄴㅗㅗ↓ㅣ♡☐

> **NOTE:** To set a center, right, or decimal tab, first click the button at the extreme left of the ruler bar (which currently displays an "L" marker") until it displays the marker you desire (left, center, right, decimal, bar, first line indent, hanging indent, as shown in the margin), then click the mouse at the desired spot on the ruler bar. The selected marker will appear.

## Changing Line Spacing

By default, Word uses 1.15 line spacing, but you can change to single or double spacing (or other settings) easily. In this exercise, you will set double-spaced text.

1.    Open SAMPLE4 and click anywhere within the first paragraph.

      First, the quick way:

2.    Click the *Line and Paragraph Spacing* command button (*Home* tab, *Paragraph* group).

      A drop-down list appears, as shown in Figure W-26a. Note that the "1.15" option is checked—showing that it is active.

3.    Click the "2.0" spacing option.

      The paragraph's line spacing has been changed to 2.

      Using the Paragraph dialog box gives you much more control over spacing and many other paragraph settings. Try this:

4.    Click the *Paragraph* dialog box launcher (*Home* tab, *Paragraph* group). A Paragraph dialog box appears.

5.    Click the *Indents* and *Spacing* tab if needed.

      Your screen should now resemble Figure W-26b.

      Examine the Spacing section (mid-box). Note that Line Spacing is set to "Double." Also note that an extra 10 pts. of space is added after each paragraph by default. You will often want to remove this setting. You will practice changing both:

6.    Click the "After" down arrow twice (as shown in Figure W-26c) to set this value to zero.

7.    Click the drop-down arrow in the *Line spacing* box to access the spacing pull-down list.

8.    Click *1.5 lines* to select one-and-a-half line spacing.

9.    Click OK. The first paragraph will now be one-and-a-half-spaced (with no additional space after each paragraph).

> **NOTE:** The text in the current paragraph (or in the selected text block) will conform to the new spacing until you change it back. To change an entire document, select all ( CTRL + **A**) before invoking the spacing change.

## Using the Keyboard to Set Spacing

Spacing is a great example of one setting that is easier to invoke by keyboard rather than mouse. Try this:

1.    Click somewhere within the paragraph.

2.    Press CTRL + **1** to set single spacing.

3.    Press CTRL + **2** to set double spacing.

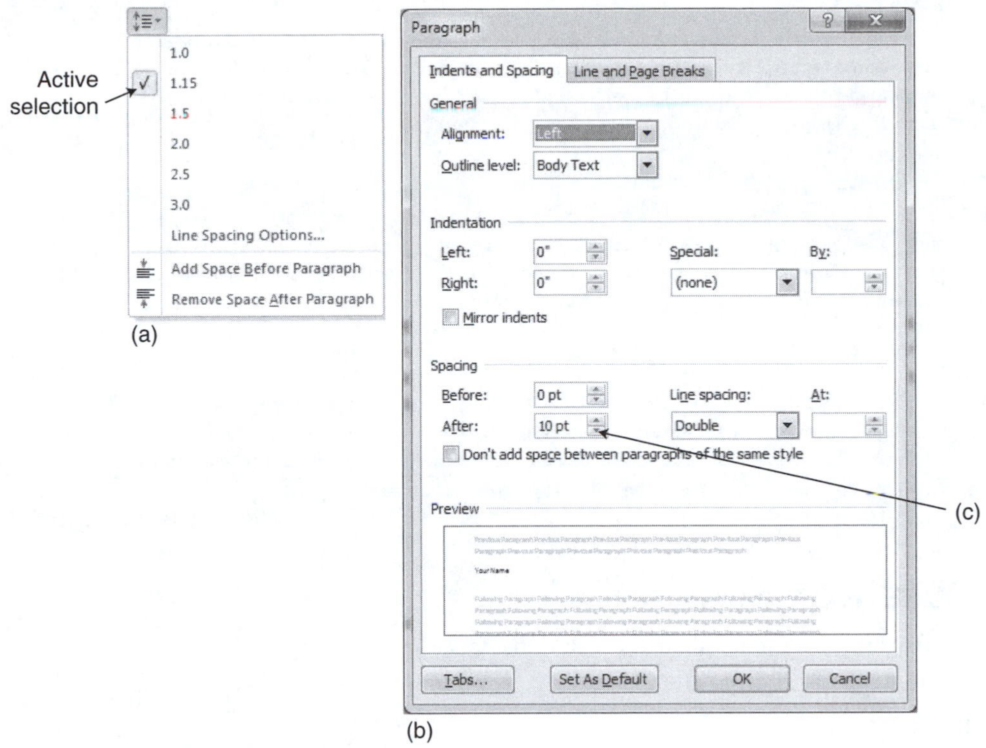

**FIGURE  W-26**   *Changing Line Spacing*

(a)   Clicking the Line Spacing button opens its drop-down list.

(b)   The Indents and Spacing tab of the Paragraph dialog box.

(c)   The "After" down arrow button.

**4.**   Press ⌈CTRL⌋ + **5** to set line-and-a-half spacing.

**5.**   Close the document without saving the changes.

## LESSON 10: MOVING AND ALIGNING TEXT

You can move any text by "cutting" it from the document and then "pasting" it back somewhere else (even into another document). To do this, you must first identify the text to be moved (as you have done in underlining).

**1.**   Open SAMPLE4.

You'll practice the technique by moving the first sentence to the end of the paragraph.

**2.**   Click just to the left of the "U" in "Using a word processor," as in Figure W-27a.

Using a word processor like Word 2010 is not as hard as it seemed to be before I began to use this manual. I am typing already and can't wait to try out every one of the other functions. As I type, the words appear on my screen. This is pretty easy. Soon I will learn how to save this document on a disk or flash drive. I hope I can learn how to use this program effectively.

(a)

Using a word processor like Word 2010 is not as hard as it seemed to be before I began to use this manual. I am typing already and can't wait to try out every one of the other functions. As I type, the words appear on my screen. This is pretty easy. Soon I will learn how to save this document on a disk or flash drive. I hope I can learn how to use this program effectively.

(b)

I am typing already and can't wait to try out every one of the other functions. As I type, the words appear on my screen. This is pretty easy. Soon I will learn how to save this document on a disk or flash drive. I hope I can learn how to use this program effectively. Using a word processor like Word 2010 is not as hard as it seemed to be before I began to use this manual.

(c)     🗐 (Ctrl) ◀—— Paste options icon

**FIGURE W-27** *Moving Text*

(a)   Place the insertion point at the start of the text.

(b)   Highlight the desired text.

(c)   After the paste command.

## Moving Text

**3.** Click and drag the I-beam pointer to the space after the word "manual." on the next line (as shown in Figure W-27b). As you move, the text will be highlighted.

✂ Cut     **4.** Click the *Cut* command button (*Home* tab, *Clipboard* group) or press ⌨CTRL + **X**.

The text block disappears from the screen and is moved to the Clipboard, a temporary memory area, awaiting the next step. Now, position the insertion point where you want the text to "reappear."

**5.** Click the document at the end of the paragraph, past the space after the word "effectively." Press the SPACE BAR to leave a space after the paragraph.

 **6.** Click the *Paste* command button (or press CTRL + **V**) to paste the block back into the document, thus completing the move.

The text should resemble Figure W-27c. (You may note a "Paste Options" icon that appears on the screen near the pasted sentence. Clicking this allows you to control which formats are copied with the text.)

🗐 Copy    > **NOTE:** Copying is used less often than moving, but it can be a useful technique. You can copy text using the same procedures, but click *Copy* instead of *Cut* in the appropriate steps. You can also try block deletions. Select a block and press DELETE.

**7.** Close the window without saving the document again.

## Aligning Margins

Aligned means "arranged in a straight line." Text is typically aligned only at the left margin ("align left"), leaving the right margin nonaligned or "ragged," as in Figure W-28a. This is the default setting in Word. You can also align both margins at the same time (called "justified" in Word). To do this, the program places additional space between the words in each line to bring the end of the last word in line with the right margin. This resembles the text in a newspaper or book, where both margins are neatly lined up, as in Figure W-28b.

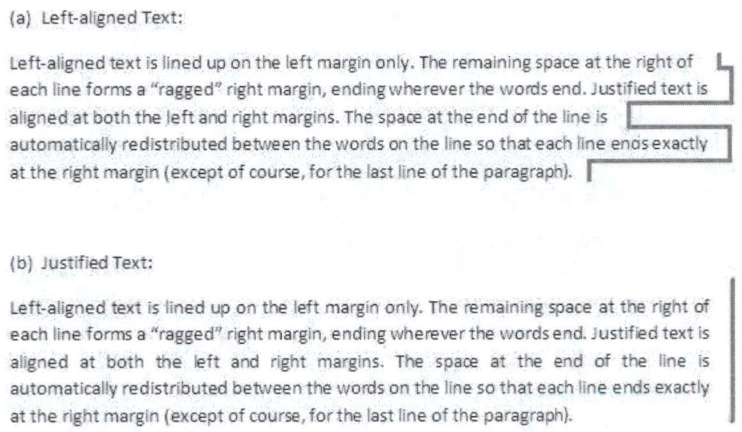

(a) Left-aligned Text:

Left-aligned text is lined up on the left margin only. The remaining space at the right of each line forms a "ragged" right margin, ending wherever the words end. Justified text is aligned at both the left and right margins. The space at the end of the line is automatically redistributed between the words on the line so that each line ends exactly at the right margin (except of course, for the last line of the paragraph).

(b) Justified Text:

Left-aligned text is lined up on the left margin only. The remaining space at the right of each line forms a "ragged" right margin, ending wherever the words end. Justified text is aligned at both the left and right margins. The space at the end of the line is automatically redistributed between the words on the line so that each line ends exactly at the right margin (except of course, for the last line of the paragraph).

**FIGURE W-28** *Alignment Samples*

You can alter text alignment through the *Paragraph* dialog box, or by using alignment command buttons. Like tabs, alignment changes the current paragraph or the selected text block. To prepare for this exercise, complete the following steps:

1. Launch Word (if needed) or close any open window.

2. Open the SAMPLE2 document.

3. Click anywhere in the first paragraph that begins "Using a word processor . . . ."

Notice how the left-aligned text currently forms a nonaligned, "ragged" right margin, much like the sample in Figure W-28a.

## Aligning by Dialog Box

You can use the Paragraph dialog box to change the alignment as follows:

1. Click the *Paragraph* dialog box launcher (Home tab, Paragraph group).

A Paragraph dialog box appears, as you saw earlier in Figure W-26. In the upper-left corner, the current alignment shows "Left."

2. To change the alignment, first click the drop-down arrow next to the *Alignment* entry box, as shown in Figure W-29a.

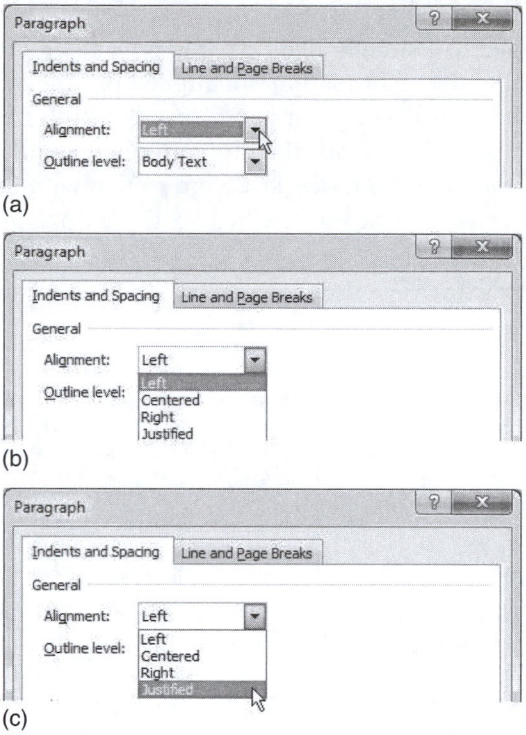

**FIGURE W-29** *Changing the Alignment*

(a) Click the alignment drop-down arrow.

(b) The drop-down list appears.

(c) Click the desired alignment.

A menu of alignment choices appears in a drop-down list, as shown in Figure W-29b. To set the alignment to fully justified, complete the following steps:

3. Click *Justified*, as shown in Figure W-29c.

4. Click *OK* to accept the change.

## Aligning by Command Button or Shortcut Keys

A faster way to change text alignment is to click one of the alignment command buttons, as shown in Figure W-30a, or to press the appropriate shortcut keys, as in Figure W-30b. Here's an example:

(a)

| Alignment: | Shortcut keys: |
|---|---|
| Left | Ctrl + L |
| Right | Ctrl + R |
| Center | Ctrl + E |
| Justified | Ctrl + J |

(b)

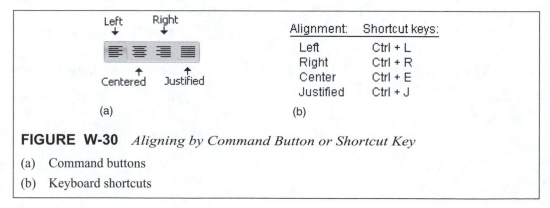

**FIGURE W-30** *Aligning by Command Button or Shortcut Key*

(a) Command buttons

(b) Keyboard shortcuts

1. Click within the first paragraph.

2. Click the *Align Left* command button. Note that the text returns to left alignment.  You can also use shortcut keys to align paragraphs of text. Try this:

3. Press CTRL + **R** to align right.

4. Press CTRL + **L** to align left.

5. Close the file *without* saving it.

> **NOTE:** Alignment can be changed as often as you want. Position the insertion point in the desired paragraph, or select a block of text, and then invoke the desired alignment by command button or shortcut key.

## LESSON 11: PRINTING A DOCUMENT

The final destination of most documents is paper. Although you work with documents on the screen and save them on disk for editing and future use, your goal is to produce a printed document ("hardcopy") of the finished document.

### Using Print Preview

Before you commit your work to print, however, it is a good idea to review the pages on the screen. This lets you see how the margins and tabs, type style (font), type size, and content all work together before you waste paper printing incorrect pages. Word's Print Preview lets you do this easily. Try the following:

1. Open SAMPLE2.

2. Click the File tab.

3. Click the Print option, as shown in Figure W-31a.

   Your screen should display a number of print options at the left and an image of your document on the right, as shown in Figure W-31b. Depending on the zoom (magnification) selected, the text of the document may be legible, or it may be "greeked" (represented by symbols or shades of gray instead of the actual letters). Word provides a "zoom" slide button that lets you examine your pages at varying levels of detail and display. Try this:

4. Drag the Zoom slide button (currently at 60%) at the lower right to 100%, as shown in Figure W-31c.

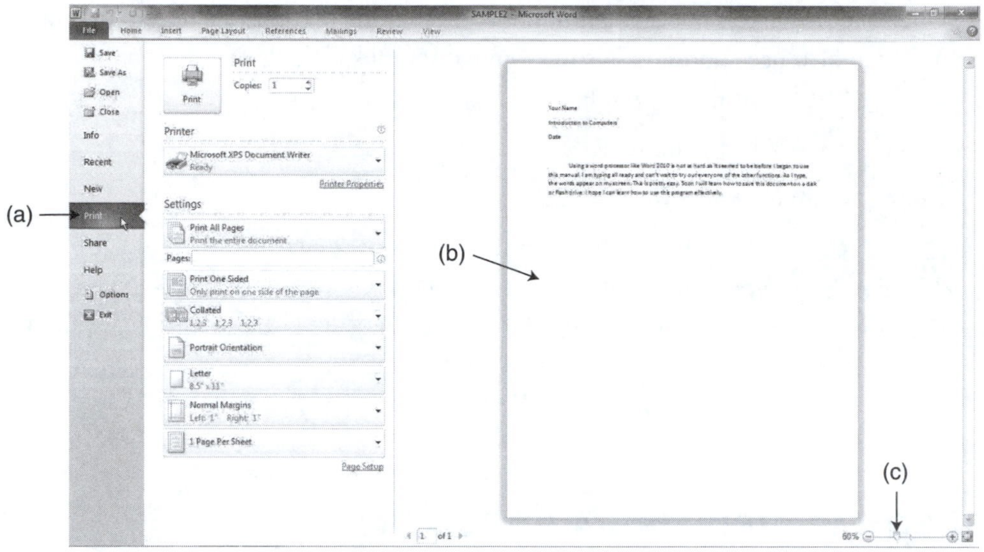

**FIGURE W-31**  *The Print Preview Screen*

(a)   Point to the right arrow in the Print Option.

(b)   The document image appears.

(c)   The Zoom control.

You can now clearly see the text in your document and how it fits the page.

### Printing a Document

Once you are satisfied that the document is ready for printing, you can invoke Word's Print command. Complete the following steps to master the basic technique:

Examine the settings portion of the screen, as shown in Figure W-32 (your printer name will differ). Although there are many options in this box, this discussion will focus on the following page range options:

1.  Click the drop-down arrow in the first settings box to see the options.

    •  *Print All Pages* prints the entire document.

    •  *Print Current Page* prints only the current page.

    •  *Print Custom Pages* allows you to select specific pages to be printed.

    •  *Print Selection* prints a previously selected text block.

2.  For now, click *Print All Pages* to print the entire document.

3.  This is a good place to verify that your printer is ready. Check its power, computer connection, and paper supply before you continue. Otherwise, nothing will print! See your instructor or lab technician if you require assistance. View the printer displayed above the settings; if necessary, use the drop-down arrow to change it to the appropriate printer.

4.  Click the Print button at the top to begin printing. Be patient as the document is sent to the printer.

5.  When done, click the Home tab and close the current document window.

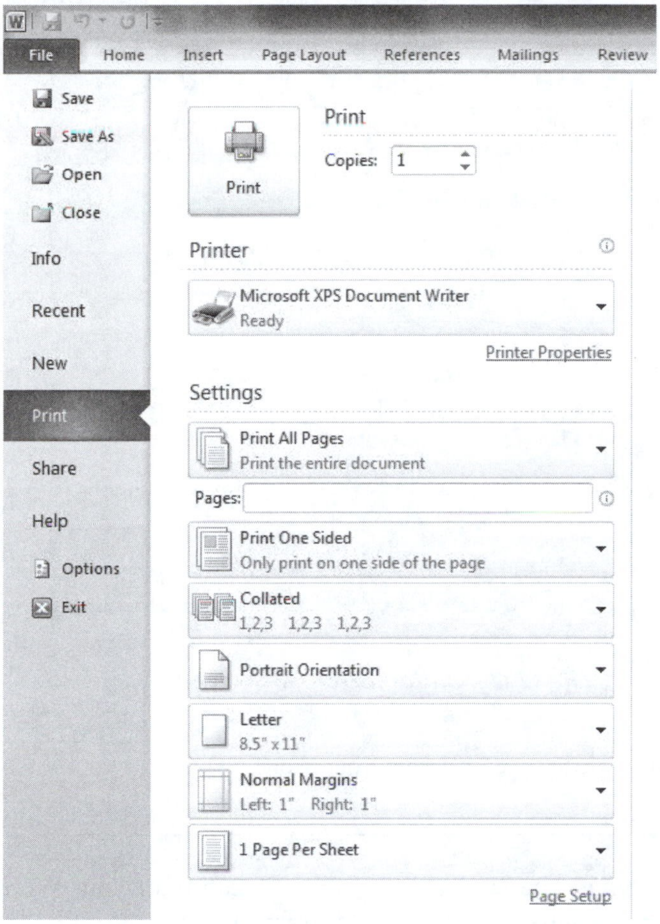

**FIGURE W-32**   *Print Settings*

**NOTE:**  You need not print an entire document. You can select a block of text to be printed, invoke the print command, click the *Print Selection* option in the Print Settings box, and then click *Print*. Word also lets you print as many documents as you want without first displaying them on the screen by using the Open dialog box. You will see this in the next lesson.

## LESSON 12: MANAGING FILES WITH THE OPEN DIALOG BOX

The Open dialog box can help you locate documents and perform many file functions typically carried out through Windows, such as displaying disk or folder contents, copying, renaming, printing, or deleting files. Complete the following steps to examine some of these options:

**1.** Click the File tab and then *Open*.

   An Open dialog box should now appear, as shown in Figure W-33a. (Your list of files may differ.)

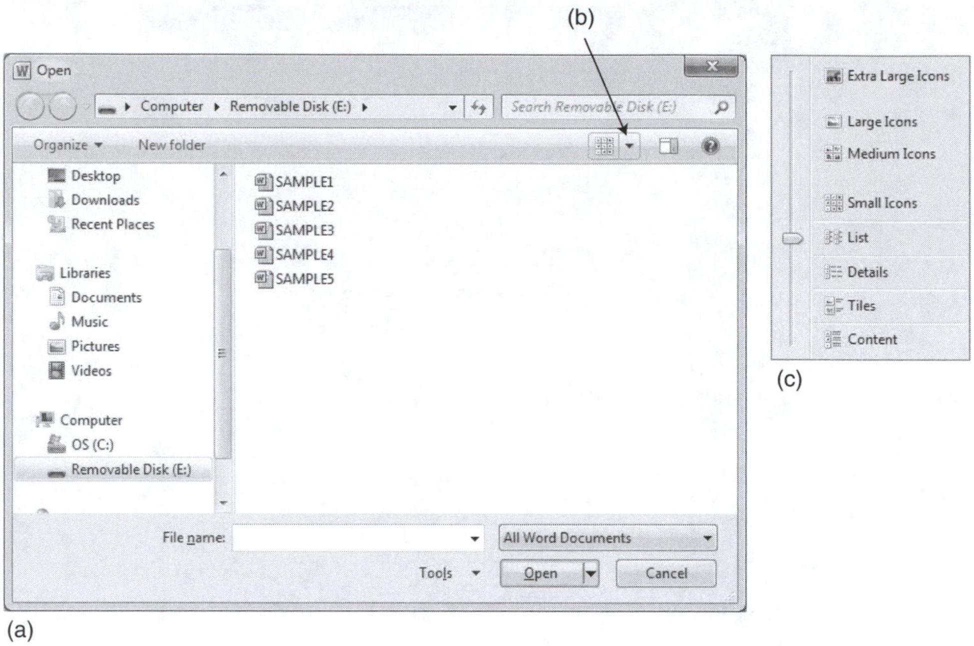

**FIGURE  W-33**   *The Open Dialog Box*

(a)   Open dialog box

(b)   View drop-down arrow of "Change Your View"

(c)   Views list

2.   If needed, change the *Look in* entry to the location of your Word document files—drag the vertical scroll bar and select it from the list.

The dialog box lists objects—first folders and then files—alphabetically by name. If the list is extensive, you can use the scroll bar to see more objects.

3.   Click the *SAMPLE4* file in the list to select it.

You will first examine a few ways of viewing your files.

4.   Click the *More Options* drop-down arrow in the "Change Your View" option (as in Figure W-33b) to see the view options.

A list appears, as shown in Figure W-33c. The active view ("List") is highlighted. (Feel free to explore them later on.)

5.   Click the *Details* option to change the view.

6.   Repeat Step 4, and then click the *List* option.

## File Management

Try each of the following examples to see how the Open dialog box can be used to perform basic file management. As you invoke each option, watch what happens in the dialog box.

**Cop**y duplicates a file. This exercise copies the SAMPLE4 file:

1.   Right-click SAMPLE4 in the object list, as shown in Figure W-34a. A shortcut menu will appear, as shown in Figure W-34b.

2.   Click *Copy*. The file has been copied to the Windows Clipboard.

3.   Right-click anywhere inside the blank portion of the object list, below the last object, as shown in Figure W-34c.

**4.**   Click _Paste_ in the new shortcut list that appears, as in Figure W-34d.

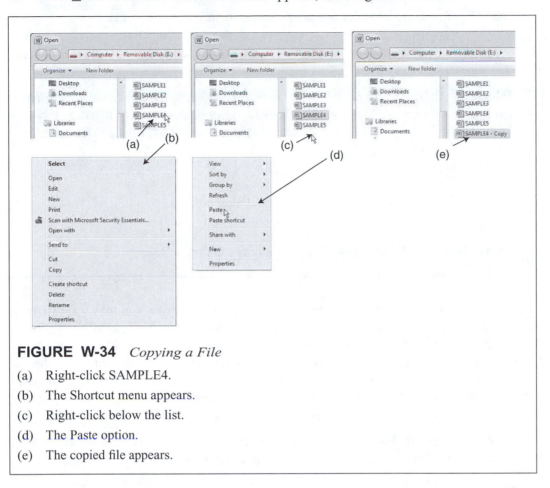

**FIGURE W-34**   _Copying a File_

(a)   Right-click SAMPLE4.

(b)   The Shortcut menu appears.

(c)   Right-click below the list.

(d)   The Paste option.

(e)   The copied file appears.

A new file, "SAMPLE4-Copy," appears alphabetically in the list, as in Figure W-34e. You have successfully copied your file.

**NOTE:** Copying within the same folder (as you have done here) results in a new file whose name ends with "Copy." If you were to copy into a different folder or disk, the filename would match the original—in this case, SAMPLE4.

**Rename** allows you to change the name of a file. This exercise will change "SAMPLE4-Copy" to "DOUBLE."

**1.**   Right-click _SAMPLE4-Copy_ in the object list for its shortcut menu.

**2.**   Click _Rename_. A rectangle appears around the filename.

**3.**   Type **DOUBLE** and then click outside the name. The new name appears in the list.

**Delete** erases a file. This exercise will delete the file named DOUBLE:

**1.**   Right-click the _DOUBLE_ file for its shortcut menu.

**2.**   Click _Delete_. A Delete File dialog box appears.

**3.**   Click _Yes_. The file will be removed from the list. (You could have selected _No_ if you did not want to delete the file.)

**NOTE:** You can also delete a file by clicking it and pressing (DELETE).

**NOTE:** Although it is not presented here, the Open dialog box can also be used to search for specific files. By default, only Word documents are listed, but you can use the *Files of type* drop-down box at the bottom of the dialog box to adjust the files that are displayed.

4.   Click the *Cancel* button to close the Open dialog box.

## LESSON 13: INDENTING PARAGRAPHS

Margin settings determine the overall document layout. At times, you may want to indent a specific paragraph (or text block) beyond the margin settings without affecting the rest of the document. This feature is useful for preparing numbered lists, blocking quotes, or designing résumés. You can indent a paragraph many ways: using the ruler bar, the Formatting command button or the Paragraph dialog box. First, you'll try Word's automatic numbering feature to create numbered, indented paragraphs.

1.   Launch Word if needed and obtain a fresh work screen.

2.   Type the text shown in Figure W-35. (Start with "1. This is" and continue to "is added." pressing (↵) only when you see the Enter icon.)

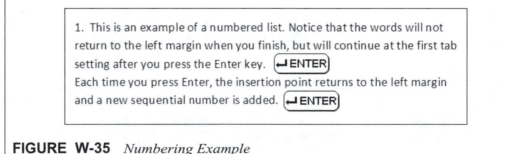

1. This is an example of a numbered list. Notice that the words will not return to the left margin when you finish, but will continue at the first tab setting after you press the Enter key. (↵ENTER)
Each time you press Enter, the insertion point returns to the left margin and a new sequential number is added. (↵ENTER)

**FIGURE W-35**   *Numbering Example*

**NOTE:** Note that Word has automatically added the next number in sequence ("2.") and indented the text to the first tab setting.

After pressing (↵) after the second sentence, note that Word adds a "3." to the list. Because you have completed the list and need no additional number:

3.   Click the *Numbering* command button (*Home* tab, *Paragraph* group) to toggle off the numbered list feature.

4.   Click within the text and compare your screen to Figure W-36.

5.   Save this document as SAMPLE6.

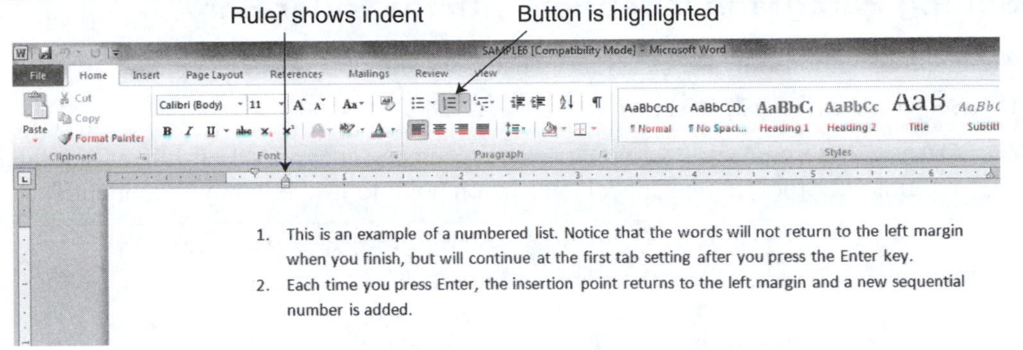

Ruler shows indent
Button is highlighted
1. This is an example of a numbered list. Notice that the words will not return to the left margin when you finish, but will continue at the first tab setting after you press the Enter key.
2. Each time you press Enter, the insertion point returns to the left margin and a new sequential number is added.

**FIGURE W-36** *The Numbered List*

**NOTE:** Note that the Numbering command button now appears highlighted, indicating that the numbering feature is active within this portion of the text. Note, too, that the ruler bar displays a paragraph indent. Once you create a numbered list in this manner, pressing ↵ additional times within the list or deleting numbered paragraphs will automatically adjust the remaining numbers.

The Formatting command buttons, shown in Figure W-37, can change the appearance of your list. Try this:

6. Select the entire list (drag the mouse or use CTRL + **A**).
7. Click the *Bullets* command button.

Bullets
Numbering
Multilevel List
Decrease Indent
Increase Indent

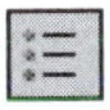

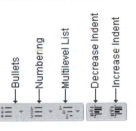

**FIGURE W-37** *List and Indent Buttons*

**NOTE:** Note that the numbered paragraphs have changed to bulleted items. The increase/decrease indent command buttons enable you to change the level of indentation of the items.

8. Click the *Increase Indent* button to increase the amount of indention.
9. Click the *Decrease Indent* button to return the indent to its former position.
10. Click the *Bullets* button again.

With both buttons off, the paragraphs return to "normal"—unnumbered and unbulleted—text. You can always reset numbers or bullets by selecting the text and clicking the appropriate command button.

## Setting Paragraph Indention with the Ruler Bar

Paragraph indention can also be achieved using the ruler bar. For example,

1.   Select the entire list, as shown in Figure W-38a.

2.   As shown in Figure W-38a, point to the rectangular marker ("Left Indent") at the left margin. (The tool tip that appears when you point to it will help you to identify it.)

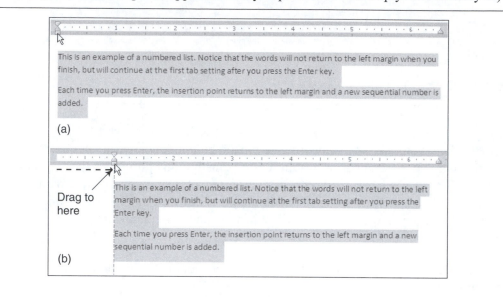

**FIGURE  W-38**   *Indenting a Paragraph*

(a)   After selecting text, click the rectangular left indent marker.

(b)   Drag the marker 1 inch to the right and release.

This marker controls the amount of indent that will be added to the document's left margin for the selected text block. It is currently set to zero by default. (It is important to drag the rectangular marker so that all three markers move as one.)

3.   Click and drag the marker to the 1-inch mark on the ruler bar, then release it, as in Figure W-38b.

4.   Click away from the text.

(If you dragged a triangular marker by mistake, click the *Undo* Quick Access toolbar button [or press CTRL + **Z**] and repeat steps 1-3.)

The text has been indented (shifted) an additional one inch from the left margin.

> **NOTE:**  Dragging the right indent marker will increase the indent at the right margin as well. Dragging the left top triangle marker ("First Line Indent") only indents the first line of the paragraph.

## Creating Page Breaks

Word begins a new page each time it reaches a set position (with 1" margins, usually 9 inches or 48 lines). At times, however, you need to control where a new page will start. For example, you might have a title page with a few lines and then want to start the actual report on a new page. Page breaks that you create yourself are called hard page breaks, much like the hard returns that you create each time you press the Enter key.

1. Press CTRL + END to jump to the end of the document.

2. To force a hard page break, move to the left margin and press CTRL + ↵ . You could also use the ribbon: *Insert tab*, *Page Break* (*Page* group), but this is slower. As shown in Figure W-39a, a page break appears.

3. Scroll to the top of the document (or click CTRL + HOME ). Note that the text is still on page 1.

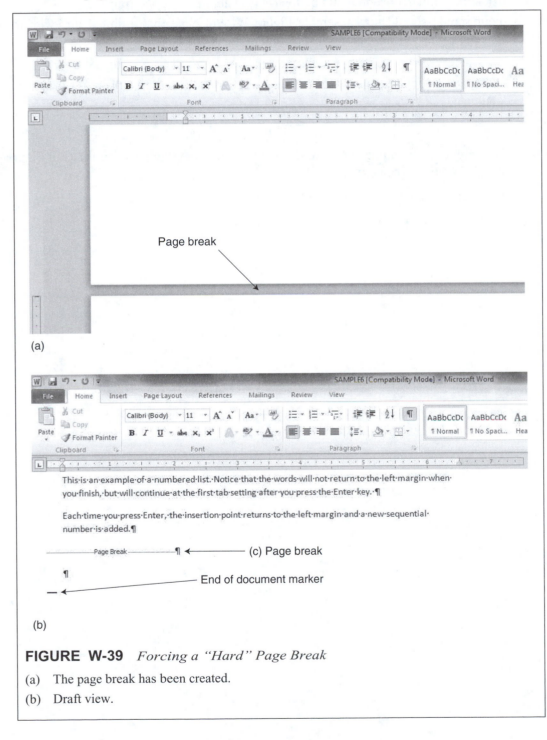

(a)

(b)

**FIGURE W-39** *Forcing a "Hard" Page Break*

(a) The page break has been created.

(b) Draft view.

## Removing Page Breaks

To remove a hard page break, you must locate it first. This is easier to do in Draft view. Try this:

1. Click the *Draft* view button (located at the lower right of the window).

2. Press CTRL + HOME to move to the start of the document.

3. Click the *Show/Hide* command button (*Home* tab, *Paragraph* group).

   Your screen should now resemble Figure W-39b. Note that a dotted line with the words "Page Break" clearly shows its position in the document.

> **NOTE:** An added bonus in *Draft* view, a horizontal bar marks the end of your document.

4. To remove the hard page break, click on the dotted line (the page break) as in Figure W-39c and press DELETE.

5. Now. Click the Print Layout view button to return your screen to "normal" view.

6. Close the document without saving it again.

**Word Practice Sheet—Screen Exercises**

Your Name:_____

Class: _____ Date: _____

1.  Name two ways that you can add a left tab setting to a paragraph:

    (a) _____

    (b) _____.

2.  Fill in the names of the items shown in the screen below. (You may refer to your screen.)

    (a) _____      (i) _____

    (b) _____      (j) _____

    (c) _____      (k) _____

    (d) _____      (l) _____

    (e) _____      (m) _____

    (f) _____      (n) _____

    (g) _____      (o) _____

    (h) _____      (p) _____

3.  Name three methods that you can use to align a text block:

    (a) _____ (b) _____ (c) _____.

4.  Open the Tabs dialog box (Home tab, Paragraph dialog box launcher, Tabs). Referring to the dialog box, list the four types of leader that can be set:

    (a) _____ (b) _____ (c) _____ (d) _____.
    Then, close the dialog box.

5.  Drag the top triangle on the left margin of the ruler bar a half-inch to the right and release. Type at least two lines of text.

    (a) What happened to the text? _____. Highlight the text, drag the top triangle back to the left margin and drag the lower triangle a half-inch to the right and release.

    (b) How did the text change?_____

    _____

    Drag the marker back to the left margin and erase the added text.

## LESSON 14: FOOTNOTES AND PAGE NUMBERS

Another useful feature of Word is its ability to create footnotes or endnotes. These notes allow you to provide references or comments without interrupting text flow. The procedures for creating footnotes and endnotes are identical—only their placement in the document differs. Footnotes appear at the end of each *page*, whereas endnotes are placed at the end of the *document*. If you select footnotes, Word will automatically adjust text so that the footnotes and proper margins are maintained on each page. This brief exercise demonstrates how to create, edit, and delete footnotes.

## Creating Footnotes

Assume you want to place a footnote at the end of the first paragraph of your SAMPLE2 document. When your document is printed, a numbered marker will be placed in the text and the footnote will appear at the bottom of the page, as in Figure W-40. In this exercise, the footnote reads "This is an example of a footnote." Of course, in your real work, you will type text in a format appropriate for your research papers.

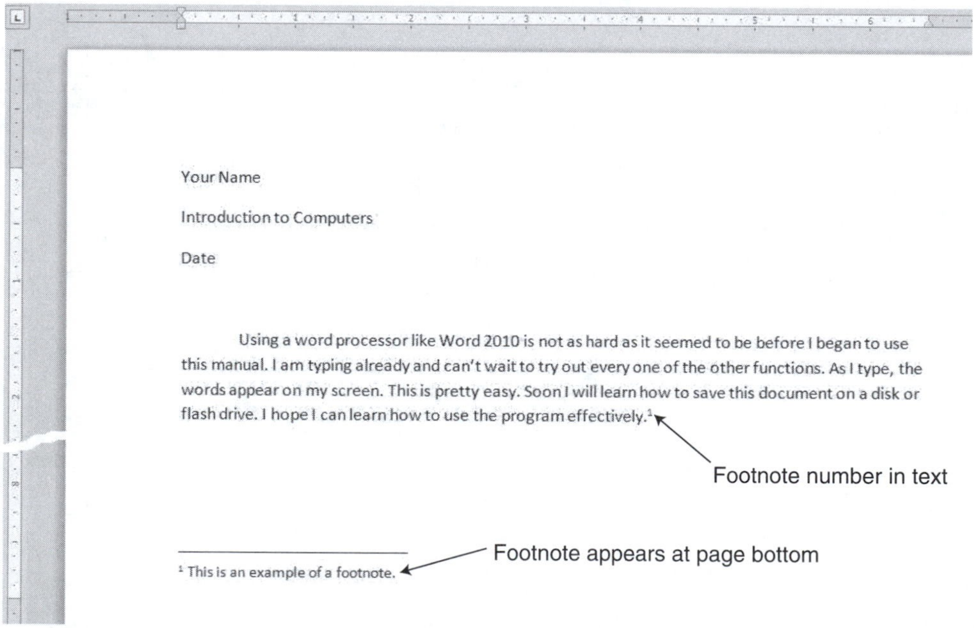

Your Name

Introduction to Computers

Date

Using a word processor like Word 2010 is not as hard as it seemed to be before I began to use this manual. I am typing already and can't wait to try out every one of the other functions. As I type, the words appear on my screen. This is pretty easy. Soon I will learn how to save this document on a disk or flash drive. I hope I can learn how to use the program effectively.[1]

Footnote number in text

Footnote appears at page bottom

[1] This is an example of a footnote.

**FIGURE W-40**  *Creating a Footnote*

1.  Close any open document and then open SAMPLE2.

    Your screen should resemble the text in Figure W-40, except for the footnote and its marker.

2.  Position the insertion point where you want the numbered marker to appear. In this exercise, place the insertion point at the end of the paragraph, after the period that follows "effectively."

    Footnotes will not be shown on the screen when it is in Draft view, so you should change the screen to Print Layout view if it is not already set that way.

3.  Click the *Print Layout* view button if needed.

4.  To invoke the footnotes feature, click the *References* tab in the ribbon, and then *Insert Footnote* (in the *Footnotes* group).

**NOTE:** If you wanted an endnote, you could click the *Insert Endnotes* command button instead in step 4.

A blank numbered footnote appears at the bottom of the screen.

**5.**   Type **This is an example of a footnote**.

Note that the footnote uses Calibri 10 point by default. (If desired in the future, you could select the footnote text and then change the font style or size.)

**NOTE:**  Note that the footnote appears beneath a separator line created by Word, as shown in Figure W-40.

**6.**   Move to the start of the document (CTRL + HOME). Note that a numbered footnote marker appears in the text.

**7.**   Save the document as SAMPLE7.

## Inserting Additional Footnotes

Footnotes can be inserted anywhere in your document using the same procedure. Word will automatically renumber any footnotes that come after the newly added one. For example, assume you want to add another footnote, as in Figure W-41.

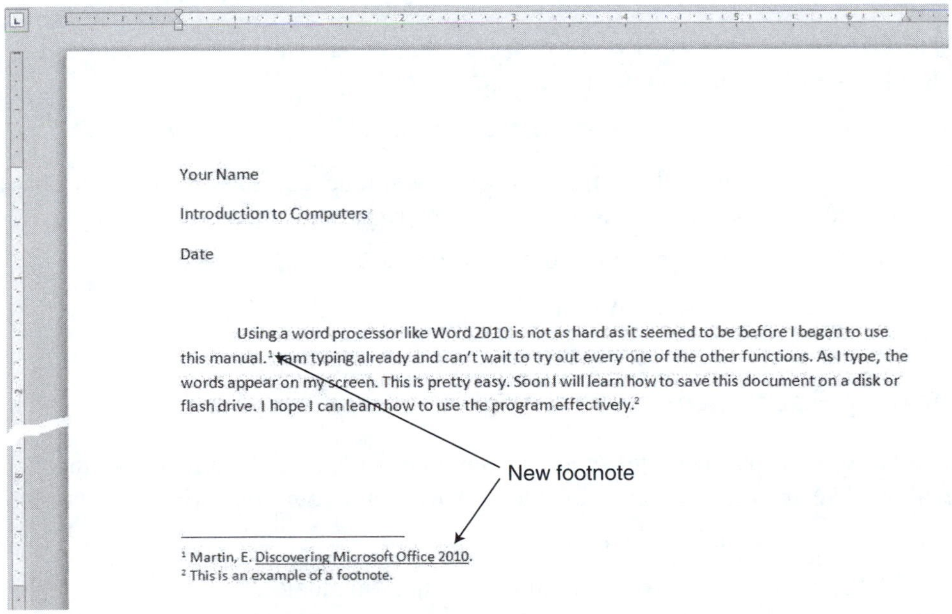

Your Name

Introduction to Computers

Date

Using a word processor like Word 2010 is not as hard as it seemed to be before I began to use this manual.¹ I am typing already and can't wait to try out every one of the other functions. As I type, the words appear on my screen. This is pretty easy. Soon I will learn how to save this document on a disk or flash drive. I hope I can learn how to use the program effectively.²

New footnote

¹ Martin, E. Discovering Microsoft Office 2010.
² This is an example of a footnote.

**FIGURE  W-41**   *Inserting a Second Footnote*

**1.**   Open SAMPLE7 if it is not already on the screen.

**2.**   Position the insertion point after the period at the end of the word "manual" on the second line of the paragraph.

**3.**   As before, click the *Insert Footnote* command button (*References* tab, *Footnotes* group).

> **NOTE:** Note that the new footnote is listed as number 1 because it occurs first in the document.

4. Type the following footnote: **Martin, E. <u>Discovering Microsoft Office 2010</u>**. (Underline the title.)

5. Move to the start of the document ([CTRL] + [HOME]).

> **NOTE:** Note that a new number 1 footnote marker appears in the text (because you placed this footnote earlier in the document) and the former footnote 1 has been renumbered as number 2.

6. Save the document again as SAMPLE7.

7. Compare the top and bottom of your document page to Figure W-41.

## Editing Footnotes

Editing footnote content is as easy as editing text.

1. Open SAMPLE7 if it is not already on the screen.

2. Scroll to the bottom of the page until you can see your footnotes.

> **NOTE:** In this case, [CTRL] + [END] would not be helpful, since it moves to the last line of text, not to the footnotes.

At this point, you could use any editing technique you have learned to change the text of the footnote as needed (insert, delete, underline, and so on). For example,

3. Click after "2010" in the first footnote. Press [SPACE] and type (**Wiley**).

4. Resave the document as SAMPLE7.

## Deleting Footnotes

Occasionally, you may need to remove a footnote from your document. Footnotes can be deleted just like any other selected text block. This exercise will remove the second footnote.

1. Move to the start of the document.

2. Click to the immediate left of footnote 1 (after "manual").
   Here's an interesting Word feature that enables you to identify footnotes using a tool tip:

3. Point to the footnote number with your mouse and wait a moment.
   As shown in Figure W-42a, a box (the "tool tip") appears displaying the complete footnote reference. This is a useful feature that lets you see the footnote without having to view the bottom of the page.

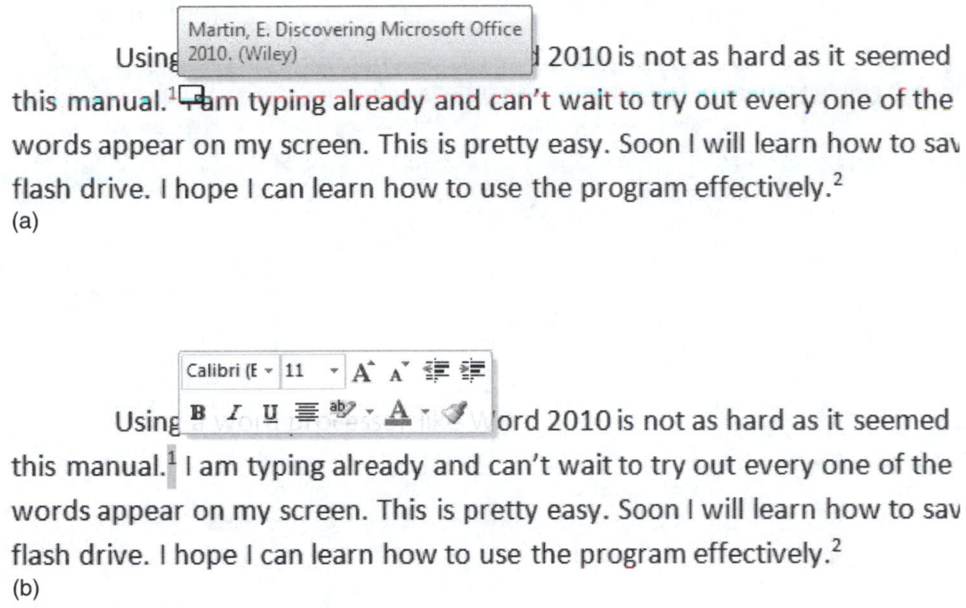

Martin, E. Discovering Microsoft Office 2010. (Wiley)

Using [ ] 2010 is not as hard as it seemed this manual.[1] I am typing already and can't wait to try out every one of the words appear on my screen. This is pretty easy. Soon I will learn how to sav flash drive. I hope I can learn how to use the program effectively.[2]

(a)

Calibri (E ▾ 11  ▾ A˄ A˅ 譚 譚
B I U ≡ ᵃᵇᵧ ▾ A ▾ ✂

Using [ ]ord 2010 is not as hard as it seemed this manual.[1] I am typing already and can't wait to try out every one of the words appear on my screen. This is pretty easy. Soon I will learn how to sav flash drive. I hope I can learn how to use the program effectively.[2]

(b)

**FIGURE  W-42**    *Deleting a Footnote*

(a)   Point to the footnote number.

(b)   Drag over the number to select it.

**4.**   Select the footnote number as in Figure W-42b (drag the mouse to highlight it).

**5.**   Press ⌈DELETE⌋.

The footnote number and its note at the bottom of the page have been deleted. Also note that the numbering of the footnote that comes after it (the "old" #2) has been automatically renumbered by Word.

**6.**   Close the document but do *not* save these changes.

## Numbering Pages

When you print a document that exceeds one page, you might want to have sequential numbers added to each page automatically. This is easily accomplished.

**1.**   Open SAMPLE7.

**2.**   Position your insertion point on the page where you want page numbers to begin. In this case, move to the start of the document.

**3.**   As shown in Figure W-43a, click the *Insert* tab and then the *Page Number command button* (*Header & Footer* group).

A Page Number drop-down list appears, as shown in Figure W-43b. From this list, you can select the position of the printed page number—top or bottom—as well as its horizontal position. Complete the following example to see how the procedure works:

**4.**   Point to the *Top of page* option.

An options box appears listing fifty-eight style and position options for your number. (The first four options are shown in Figure W-43c.) You can scroll to see all the options before selecting one.

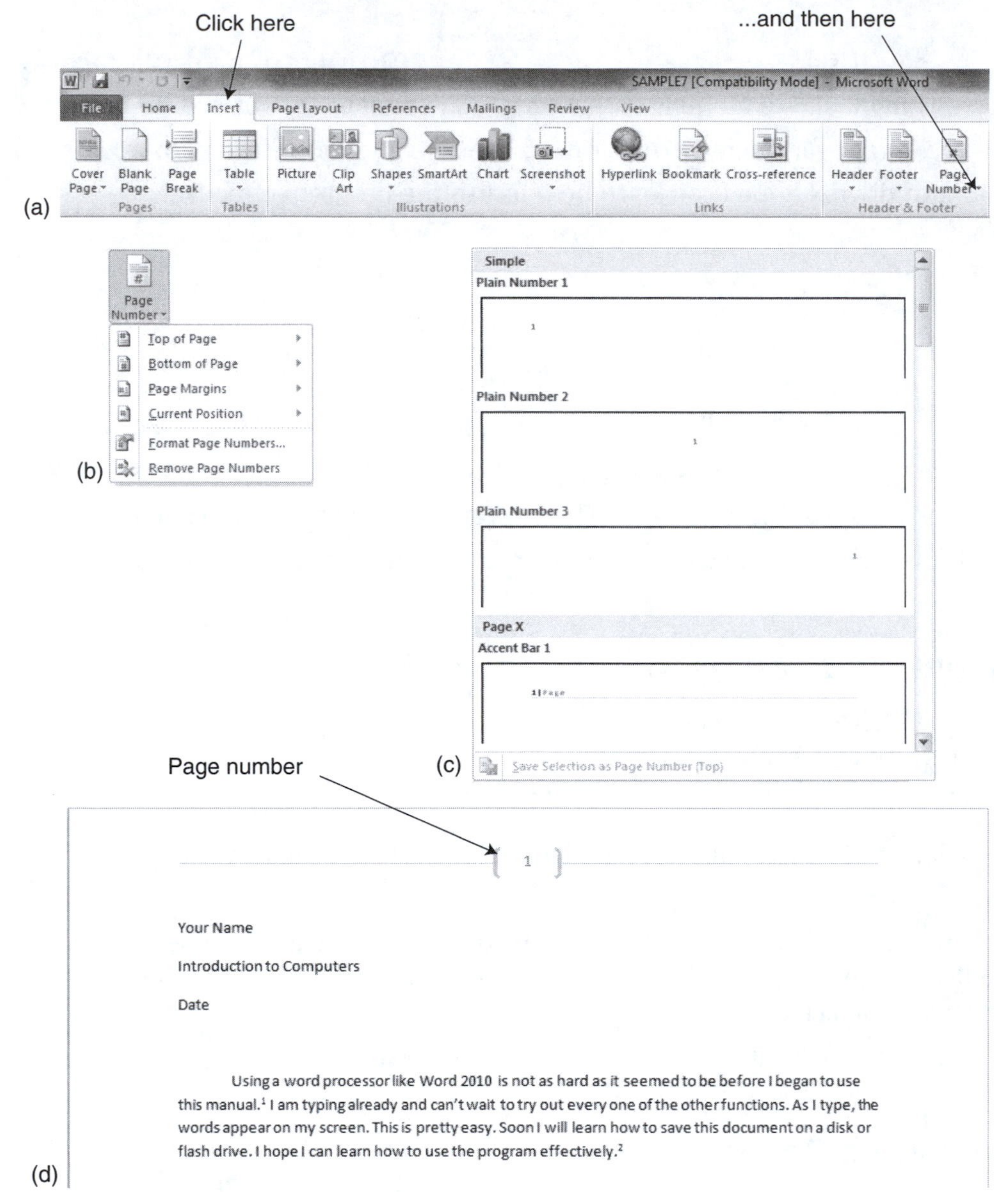

**FIGURE W-43** *The Page Number Drop-Down List*

(a)   Click the Page Number command button on the Insert tab.

(b)   The Position drop-down list.

(c)   The Style Options box.

(d)   The Page Number appears.

Now, set the horizontal alignment as follows:

5.   Scroll down to the *Brackets 2* option (approximately 10th in the list).

6.   Click the *Brackets 2* option to apply it.

When this document is printed or viewed, a page number will appear in the selected style and position on every page (as shown in Figure W-43d).

7.   Save the document again as SAMPLE7 and then close it.

## LESSON 15: TOOLS–SPELLING, GRAMMAR, AND THESAURUS

Word offers separate tools that can assist you in your writing. These include a spelling and grammar-checking program and a thesaurus. Careful use of these tools can help you improve your writing skills and detect the typical errors that most writers make.

### Using Word's Spelling and Grammar Tool

Word's spelling and grammar tool checks your document for typing and spelling errors. It will also identify common errors in grammar and punctuation. However, it will not check the proper usage or meaning of words—that's up to you. For example, if you type "I herd the sound," the program will not correct "herd," because it is spelled correctly, even though it is used *incorrectly* in this sentence. The following example demonstrates the use of this tool.

1.   Open a new document and CAREFULLY type the following sentences (with all mistakes): **Is this as exampul of of cheking speling. Letmesee if it works.**

> **NOTE:** Spellcheck underlines potential errors with red wavy lines. Grammar check uses green wavy lines. You can disregard them for now. Also note that the "Proofing Errors" icon on the status bar shows a red "X"—indicating that potential errors have been found in the document.

2.   Move to the start of the document.

3.   Click the Review tab and then the *Spelling and Grammar* button (Proofing group) to access the spelling and grammar tools.

The program will begin to check your writing for spelling and grammatical errors. It will search for each of the words in its spelling list. If it cannot find a particular word, it will highlight the word in context and may present some suggestions in its dialog box, as in Figure W-44.

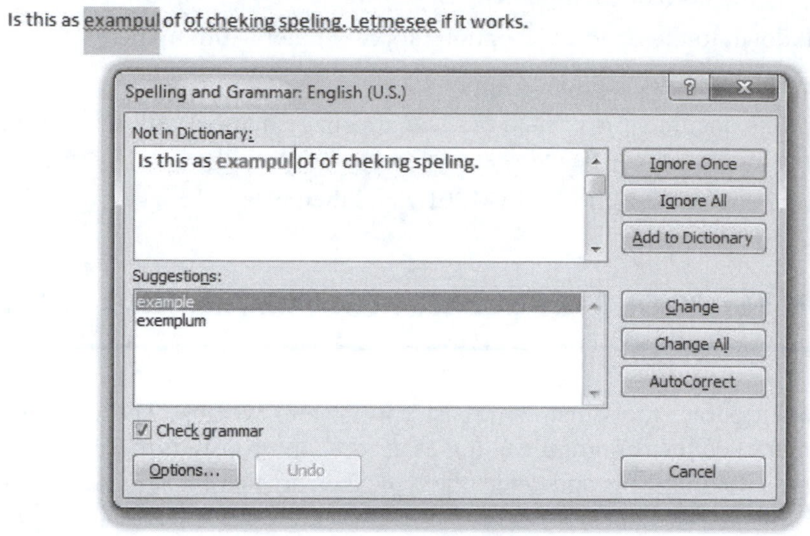

**FIGURE W-44**   *Word's Spelling Tool in Action*

**NOTE:** Notice that the program did not stop at the word "as." This is because "as" is spelled *correctly* although it is used *incorrectly* in the sentence. As long as a word is spelled correctly, the Spelling tool does not identify it as a spelling mistake.

The first misspelled word that the spelling and grammar tool locates is "exampul." The program suggests that you meant to type "example," which it lists as the first choice, (as you've seen in Figure W-44).

4. The highlighted choice is correct, so click the *Change* button to accept the suggested change.

The word "example" replaces the misspelled word and the program continues.

The spelling and grammar tool now finds the repeated words ("of of") and suggests that you replace them with one single "of." Although this is not technically a spelling error, it is such a common typing mistake that the developers of Word included it in the spelling tool.

5. Click the *Delete* button to delete the extra "of."

The program now finds "cheking" misspelled and offers a number of possible replacements.

6. If necessary, scroll to and click the proper replacement, "checking," then click *Change*.

Next, the program will find "speling" and offer the correct word, probably as the first choice. (If not, scroll to and click the desired replacement.)

7. Click *Change*.

The grammar check portion of the spelling and grammar tool now suggests that you add a question mark to the end of the sentence.

8. Click *Change* to accept this suggestion.

The word "Letmesee" should be identified next, as shown in Figure W-45. It is a typographical error—text that was typed incorrectly. When typographical errors are made (as in this case), or a word is badly misspelled, Word may not suggest the correct replacement or may, in fact, be unable to offer any suggestions at all. When this occurs, you can correct it yourself.

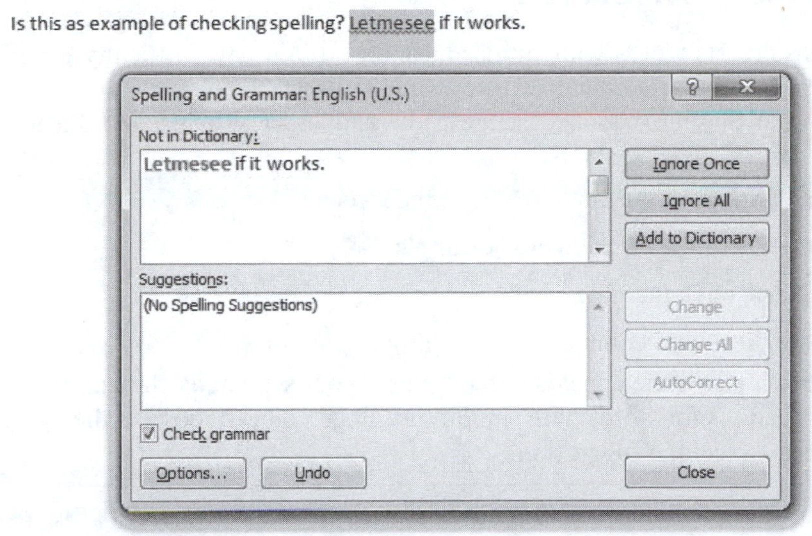

Is this as example of checking spelling? Letmesee if it works.

| Spelling and Grammar: English (U.S.) | ? X |
| --- | --- |

**Not in Dictionary:**

Letmesee if it works.

- Ignore Once
- Ignore All
- Add to Dictionary

**Suggestions:**

(No Spelling Suggestions)

- Change
- Change All
- AutoCorrect

☑ Check grammar

Options...    Undo                              Close

**FIGURE W-45**  *Finding a Typographical Error*

9. To correct an error, click within the error in the dialog box and then type the correction. In this case, add spaces to create the phrase "Let me see" as three words.

**NOTE:** You can also correct errors using normal Word editing techniques. In this case, you could click to position the insertion point between the two words and insert a space.

10. Once you make the corrections, click *Change* to fix the error and continue.

**NOTE:** Of course, you can make note of the error and fix it through regular editing when you return to the document.

When the entire document has been checked for spelling errors (and repeated words), a dialog box indicates that the spelling and grammar check is complete.

11. Click *OK* to return to your document.

12. Now manually fix the word "as" so that it correctly reads "an."

**NOTE:** You can stop the spelling and grammar tool at any time by clicking its *Cancel* button.

Like other document changes, you must now save the document or the spelling corrections will be lost.

13. Save this document as SAMPLE8.

## Using Word's Thesaurus

A thesaurus suggests words with similar meaning. If you have difficulty finding just the right word in your writing, simply type a word similar to the one you are trying to recall, then invoke the thesaurus tool to suggest alternatives. Try using Word's thesaurus by completing the following steps:

1.  Open SAMPLE8 if it is not already on the screen.

2.  Click anywhere within the word "example."

3.  If necessary, click the *Review* tab.

4.  Click the *Thesaurus* command button (Proofing group).

    A Research task pane appears at the right of your screen, as shown in Figure W-46, offering suggestions for words with similar meaning. You can move to the one you prefer and select it or cancel the suggestion.

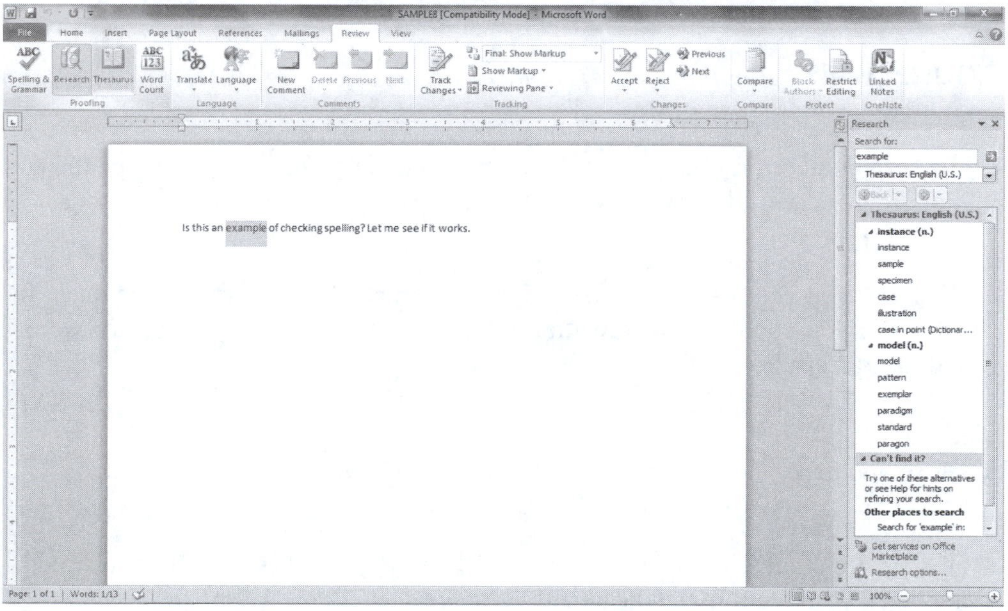

**FIGURE  W-46**   *Word's Thesaurus*

5.  Point to the word *model* in the Thesaurus list to highlight it. (If you click it by mistake, click the *Back* button and repeat step 5.)

6.  Click the drop-down arrow next to *model*.

7.  Click the *Insert* option to replace "example" with this synonym.

> **NOTE:** If you want to investigate words further, highlight a choice, click its drop-down arrow, and then select "Look Up" to see other synonyms. You can then highlight the one you want.

7.  Close the document without saving it.

8.  Click the "X" button in the *Research* task pane to close it.

> **NOTE:** Warning! Changing a word to its synonym does not change other words in your document. You still have to check word agreement, such as changing "a" to "an."

## LESSON 16: ENHANCING THE DOCUMENT—FONTS AND CLIP ART

As you have learned, a font is a type style that determines the appearance of text. The size and style of the font can be changed easily. Word's default font is typically Calibri 11 pt ("pt" is an abbreviation of "point," a measure of type size), a font that is useful for most applications. However, you can select other fonts to improve the look of the text in your document. The following exercise will demonstrate a few basic techniques to get you started:

1. Launch Word or close the current window.

2. Obtain a fresh (blank) screen (File tab, *New*, *Blank Document, Create*).

### Changing the Font

A font change, like most other Word commands, affects the text in the current paragraph or selected text block, or new text typed after the insertion point position. For example, to change the font for the whole document, complete the following steps:

1. Click the *Font* dialog box launcher (*Home* tab, *Font* group).

   A Font dialog box appears as you've seen earlier in Figure W-20. This dialog box displays information about the current font and allows you to adjust the font, style, size, appearance, and color. A printed sample of the current font, with all chosen enhancements, can be seen at the bottom of the box.

   A list of other available fonts appears in a font list at the upper left of your screen. The fonts in your list may differ. A highlight indicates the current font, "+Body."

> **NOTE:** In the future, you can set any font style and size to be Word's default using this dialog box. Just select the desired options and click the Default button at the lower left.

2. Press ⬇ or ⬆ to see other available fonts in the list.

### Selecting a New Font

To select a new font, complete the following steps:

3. Press an **A** to move quickly to the top of the list.

> **NOTE:** Pressing an alphabetic key will "jump" to fonts that start with that letter in the font list. You can then use the arrow keys to view other fonts.

4. Move the highlight bar to the desired font, in this case "Arial," and then scroll and click it to select it. (If you do not have Arial, pick a different font.)

The new font is chosen. You should see a sample of the font at the bottom of the dialog box. Although you could leave the dialog box now, try one more font adjustment before accepting the new font.

### Changing the Font Size

If you want, you can also adjust the font's point size. A point is a typesetting measure of height (just about 1/72 inch). A typical font size is 12 points or about 1/6 inch high. Larger point sizes produce bigger text. Here's how to change the font point size:

5. Click the down arrow in the size box to scroll to and click the *18* option. Note that the sample text changes to the new size.

Your screen should resemble Figure W-47. You can change other font characteristics, such as font style or appearance, by marking the appropriate box(es) on this screen, but for now, you can exit the dialog box as follows:

6. Click *OK* to accept the new font and size.

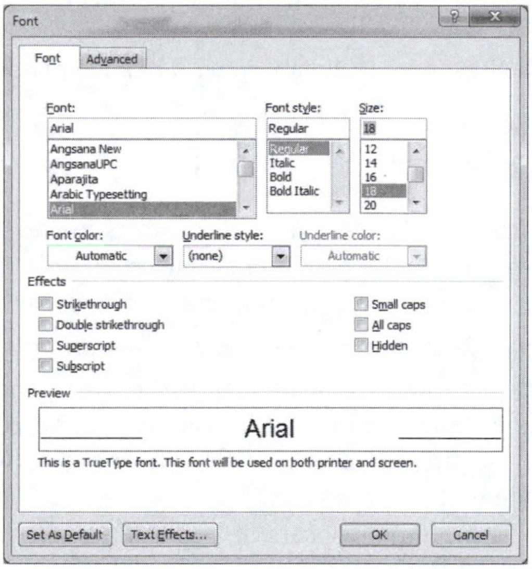

**FIGURE  W-47**   *Changing Font Characteristics*

Its name and size should appear at the top of the Font group, as shown in Figure W-48a.

7. Type **This is a sample of the new font**. and press ⏎ .

**NOTE:**   Note that the text now appears in its new style and size. Any text you type after making a font change will appear in the new style and size. You can make as many font changes as you desire; simply position the insertion point and invoke the change.

### Adjusting Fonts with Text Blocks

As with other text enhancements, you can also change a font by selecting a block of text and then invoking the change. Although you can use the menu approach as you did in the previous section, you can also change font style and size directly using the Font group on the *Home* tab. Try the following example to see this technique in action:

1.  Click and drag over the word "sample," as shown in Figure W-48b.

    You will first change the font itself.

2.  Click the drop-down arrow next to the font name in the Font group (as in Figure W-48c).

3.  Scroll down to, and then click, the desired font, in this case, *Times New Roman*.

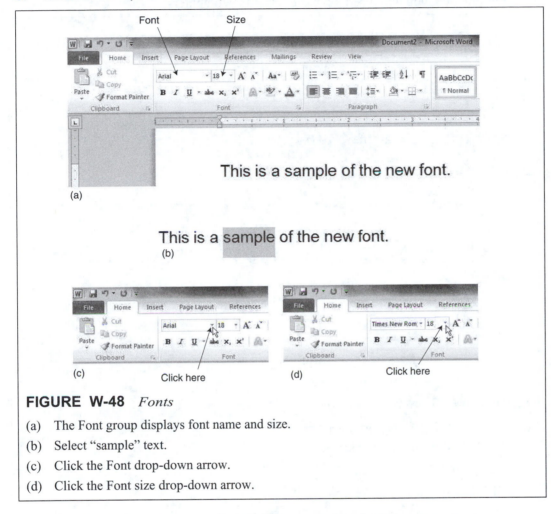

**FIGURE W-48**  *Fonts*

(a)  The Font group displays font name and size.

(b)  Select "sample" text.

(c)  Click the Font drop-down arrow.

(d)  Click the Font size drop-down arrow.

Note that the text has been adjusted. Now, try a size change:

4.  Click the drop-down arrow next to the Font size in the Font group (as in Figure W-48d).

5.  Click the desired font size, in this case, 36 point. The selected text has again been modified.

> **NOTE:** You could also click the *Grow Font* or *Shrink Font* command buttons in the *Font* group to incrementally adjust the size of selected text.

6.  Click outside the text to deselect it.

7.  Save the document again as SAMPLE9.

## Adding Clip Art

You can also enhance your documents by adding *clip art*, professionally created graphics that can be copied into your document. Here's a brief introduction to the technique.

1.    Open the SAMPLE9 document.

2.    Click the *Insert* tab, and then the *Clip Art* command button (*Illustrations* group).

     A Clip Art task pane appears on the right side of the window, as shown in Figure W-49a. For practice, you will insert a picture related to computers.

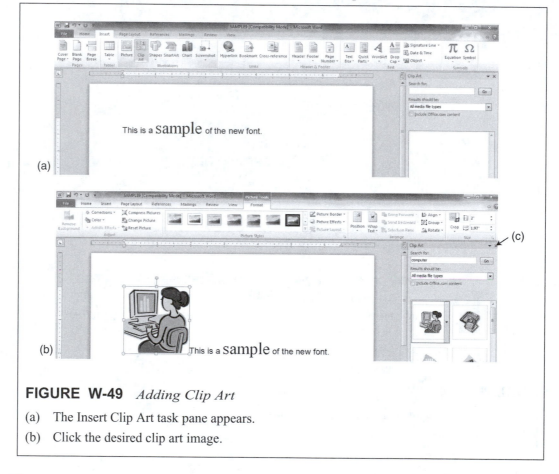

**FIGURE W-49**   *Adding Clip Art*

(a)    The Insert Clip Art task pane appears.

(b)    Click the desired clip art image.

3.    Click in the "Search for" entry box.

4.    Type **computer** in the entry box and click the Go button to its right.

5.    If a "Microsoft Clip Organizer" box appears referring to online images, click *No*.

     A set of images appears that matches your search. You could scroll through them, but for now,

6.    Click the first one to select it. It appears in your document, as shown in Figure W-49b.

7.    Click the *Clip Art* task pane Close button "X" (at the extreme right side of the screen as in Figure W-49c) to remove it from the window.

**NOTE:** Make sure the image is selected (surrounded by a rectangle). If it is not, click the image to select it.

There are many ways you can modify this image—apply a style, resize it, move it, align it with text, and so on. Note that a contextual tab named "Picture Tools—Format" has been added to the ribbon, providing many picture options. Try the following to see how they work:

**Picture Styles**

There are twenty-eight picture styles that can be applied to the image—the first few of which are displayed in the *Picture Styles* group.

**8.** Point to *Picture Style 1*.

Note how the image temporarily changes in your document to show you how it will appear if you were to select this style. (If you wanted to apply a style, you could just click it.)

**9.** In succession, point to the next four picture styles to see their effect on the image.

> **NOTE:** To see the remaining picture styles, click the down arrow at the right of the Picture Styles group to see other rows of style options. (Note, too, that the right side of the *Picture Styles* group contains additional command buttons for shapes, borders, and other effects that you may want to explore in the future.)

**Arranging Images and Text**

The *Arrange* group provides controls for positioning the image and forming text around it. For example,

**10.** Click the *Position* command button (*Arrange* group as shown in Figure W-50a).

**11.** Point to the first option (top left) in the "With Text Wrapping" list, as shown in Figure W-50b. Note how the image and text are adjusted appropriately.

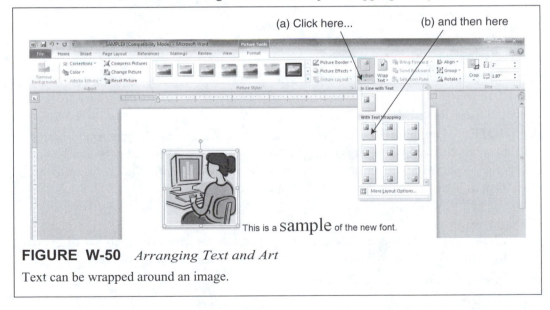

**FIGURE W-50**   *Arranging Text and Art*

Text can be wrapped around an image.

**12.** Click this option to apply it to the image.

**Resizing an Image**

You can also adjust the image by using the circle shapes at its corners (called "handles"). For example,

**13.** Point to the lower right-hand corner handle, as shown in Figure W-51a. (When the pointer is correctly positioned, it will appear as a diagonal line with arrows.)

**14.** Click the corner handle and drag the pointer (now resembling a "+" sign) close to the center of the image (as shown in Figure W-51b).

**15.** Release the mouse. The picture has been re-sized, as shown in Figure W-51c.

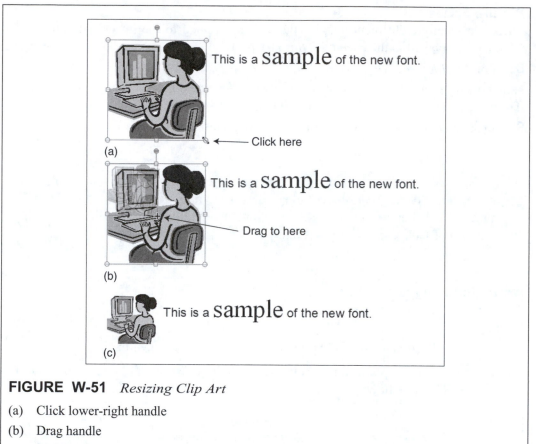

**FIGURE W-51**  *Resizing Clip Art*

(a) Click lower-right handle

(b) Drag handle

(c) Resized image

**NOTE:** Dragging a corner handle ensures that the image's height and width ratio remains constant. That is, the picture looks the same but just gets smaller (or larger)—depending on whether you drag the pointer towards the center or away from it. Dragging an *edge* does not maintain the ratio.

**16.** Click outside the image to deselect it. Notice that the contextual tab has disappeared from the ribbon. (It will reappear whenever you click an image to select it.)

**17.** Resave the document as SAMPLE9.

**18.** Close the document.

CONGRATULATIONS! You have completed this module! Try the projects that follow to see how well you understand the basics of Microsoft Word 2010.

## WORD PROCESSING PROJECTS

Complete these projects to see how well you've mastered basic word processing techniques. Try each first without looking back into the module. If you need help, refer to the Command Summary at the end of this module.

**Project 1** *Memo:* Center the heading and then, using a left-aligned text setting, type the following memo. Remember to press the Enter key only where needed. Replace the bold words with your name and today's date. Save the memo as WORD1 and print it.

---

**COMPUTER PRACTICE COMPANY**
12345 Main Street
ANYPLACE, USA 12345-6789

TO:          Office Managers

FROM:       **Your Name,** Computer Services

DATE:        **Today's date**

SUBJECT:   Use of Word 2010

You are invited to attend an executive review of Word 2010 to be held next Tuesday from 3:00-5:00 p.m. in our computer conference room.

It is hoped that this brief session will help acquaint you with its newer capabilities, including graphics and integration with Office 2010. Because we are expanding our desktop publishing, you might want to see how this new program can help your office produce memos, newsletters, and reports.

Please reserve your space now by contacting me no later than Friday afternoon. As usual, refreshments will be served.

---

**Project 2** *Poem:* Select a poem that you enjoy. Type your name and class at the top, followed by the title and author of the poem, centered. Then, type the poem exactly the way it appears in print, spaced and tabbed as needed. Save it as WORD2 and print it.

**Project 3** *Spelling Project:* Create a spelling sample as follows: (1) Set the left and right margins at 2" from each edge. Now type the following (errors and all): Using a werd procesor is much easyer than using a typwriter beacuse you can korrect al the erorrs withuot haveing to retype it it. (2) Save this file as WORD3A. (3) Save the file again as WORD3B. (4) Edit WORD3B to find and correct all the errors that AutoCorrect did not fix. You may use Word's Spellcheck or spelling tool, but you must review the document yourself to find all the errors. (5) Resave the file and then print WORD3A and WORD3B.

**Project 4** *Title Page:* Create a title page for a paper to include the title WORD 2010 PRACTICE centered and near the middle of the paper top to bottom. Then, in the lower-right corner, type your name, class, and date. On the second page, type a paragraph selected from any book of your choice. Using a format used in your school for research papers, place a footnote at the end of the paragraph, identifying the source by author, title, and page. Add a page number. Save the document as WORD4 and print it.

**Project 5** *Creating a List:* Create a list by following these steps: (1) Set the left margin at 1.5", and tabs at .9" and 2.3" from the left margin. (2) Type the following list, using TAB to align as needed.

USING COMPUTERS IN BUSINESS
HARDWARE:
    Keyboard
    Screen
    Printer
    Disk Drive
    Mouse

SOFTWARE:
    Word Processing: Word
    Spreadsheets: Excel
    Database Management:  Access
    Presentation Graphics: PowerPoint

(3) Save the list as WORD5A. (4) Cut and paste the appropriate lines so that the SOFTWARE list comes before the HARDWARE and save this modified list as WORD5B. (5) Print WORD5A and WORD5B.

**Project 6** *Letter I:* Type, save, and print the letter below as WORD6. (Do NOT try to match the margins, just use the default settings and type.) Set a JUSTIFIED alignment. Center the heading, use tabs where needed, and leave blank lines as shown.

---

GREED-R-US COLLECTION AGENCY
123 Money Avenue
Anytown, USA 12345-6789

**Today's Date**

Mr. I. O. Yoo
Fly-By-Night Corporation
Anyplace, USA 98765-4321

Dear Mr. Yoo:

According to our records, you still owe $67,070 for computer equipment purchased last year from our client, the Gigantic Computer Company.

Unless this amount is paid in full by April 15th, we will be forced to take drastic action. If this office does not receive a bank or cashier's check for $67,070 within the next two weeks, we will send our trained attack hamsters to chew through all your computer wires, thus making all your computer equipment inoperative.

We look forward to hearing from you at your earliest convenience. Our hamsters are getting impatient, and we don't know how long we can keep them caged.

Sincerely,

**Your Name**
Collection Manager

---

**Project 7** *Letter II:* Open WORD6 and make these changes: (1) Change $67,070 to $75,460 in the two places where it appears. (2) Add the words "and extremely vicious" after "trained" in paragraph two, so it now reads "trained and extremely vicious attack hamsters." (3) Move one space after the period at the end of the last paragraph and add this sentence:

**Your payment will allow us to buy fresh food for our hungry hamsters, thus averting this potential tragedy.** (4) Add a new paragraph as follows: **Please consider the consequences of not responding to this letter. Our hamsters have very sharp teeth and love to gnaw on things—especially computer equipment.** (5) Save this edited letter as WORD7 and print it.

**Project 8** *Letter III:* (1) Using a technique of your choice, copy WORD7 into a new file called WORD8. (2) Open WORD8 and use the find and replace procedure to change every "hamster" to "parakeet." Use editing techniques as needed to fix any problems. (3) Use find and replace to change the word "computer" to "microcomputer" in these two locations only: the first line of the first paragraph and the second "computer" in the last line of the second paragraph. Do not change the word "computer" in any other location! (4) Save this letter with the same name, WORD8, and then print it.

**Project 9** *Business Letter:* Write a letter in proper business form (you can use the form in Project 6) to me, Dr. Edward Martin, c/o John Wiley and Sons, Inc., 111 River Street, Hoboken, NJ 07030. Mention this book (underlined or italicized, of course) and tell me what you like and dislike about it, and how you feel about the course you're taking. Show off your skills (bold, underline, center, fonts, footnotes, and so on)! Save the letter as WORD9 and print it. You might actually mail a copy to me, too!

**Project 10** *Book Section:* In a new window, use the Numbered List or Indent command and bold where needed to copy, as closely as possible, Lesson 6, Inserting and Deleting Text. Include the opening paragraph and the first two steps. Save this document as WORD10 and print it. You may have to adjust margins, tabs, and justification to get a close match.

**Project 11** *Résumé:* Prepare a résumé with your name and a list of education, work experience, skills, and references, neatly typed in a format useful to you. Check with your instructor, library, or career center for samples of effective résumés. Save the file as WORD11 and print it.

**Project 12** *Class Notes:* Select a page of handwritten class notes in any course you are currently taking and prepare a typed copy of the page. Identify the source in a footnote. Save the document as WORD12 and print it. Photocopy the original page of notes and attach it to the printed copy of the project.

**Project 13** *Article:* Select a short newspaper or magazine article (or a portion of a larger one). Setting your margins and tabs appropriately, copy the article as closely as you can. Bold the headline for emphasis. At the bottom, type the name of the publication, date, and page on which you found the article. Type your name and class underneath. Save the document as WORD13 and print it. If possible, attach the original article (or a photocopy) to your printed copy.

**Project 14** *Phone List:* Setting your tabs appropriately, create a phone list in three columns: Last Name, First Name, and Phone Number. The top of your page should resemble the display below.

Your Name
Your Class
Today's Date

Phone List

Last Name          First Name          Phone Number

The list should include at least ten names and phone numbers. You can use real names and numbers, or be creative and make them up. Save this document as WORD14 and print it.

**Project 15** *Thesaurus Sample:* Type your name, class, and date at the top of a blank screen. Select and type at least two famous sayings onto the screen (e.g., "Fourscore and seven years ago . . ." or "A rolling stone gathers no moss"). Create a page break and copy your name and both sayings onto page two. Now, on the second page, replace as many words as you can in the sayings with other words of similar meaning. Use the thesaurus to help change as many of the words as possible. Save the document as WORD15 and print out both pages. For example, the second saying above may become "A gyrating rock acquires no fungus."

**EXTRA** Design, save, and print other projects that interest you. See how many other ways you can apply word processing. For example: a term paper for another course (double-spaced), a newsletter, an advertisement, travel directions, recipes, a letter to a friend, an original poem or short story.

## CONTINUING ON YOUR OWN—THINGS TO CONSIDER

This module has presented all the basic word processing functions sufficient for almost every purpose. However, there are other topics beyond the scope of this manual that will greatly expand your word processing power. You have gained enough experience and confidence to continue on your own using the on-screen Help menus or the reference manual that came with your program. Good luck!

Remember, you cannot harm the program or the computer by experimenting. If you're worried about your data disk, make a backup copy for safekeeping. Here are some topics you might like to explore:

1. Jumping to different pages.
2. Working with more than one document on the screen.
3. Copying parts of one document into another.
4. Using headers and footers.
5. Changing, placing, or omitting page numbers.
6. Saving portions (blocks) of documents to disk.
7. Doing math calculations.
8. Creating form letters from address lists (mail merge).
9. Printing mailing labels.
10. Creating and editing tables.
11. Drawing art.
12. Using columns for newsletters.
13. Sharing text with other programs.
14. Using styles and templates.
15. Developing and using macros.

## COMMAND SUMMARY—WORD 2010

**NOTE:** Ribbon command button is shown in BOLD CAPS followed by its location in parentheses—Tab (in italics) and Group—as in "**BOLD** (*Home*, Font)."

| | |
|---|---|
| ALIGN TEXT: | Any **ALIGN** button (*Home*, Paragraph) |
| BEGIN WORD: | Double-click desktop icon, or click *Start*, *All Programs*, Word |
| BOLD: | **BOLD** (*Home*, Font) or [CTRL] + **B** to start and end |
| CANCEL A COMMAND: | [ESC], click outside box, or select *Cancel* |
| CENTER: | **CENTER** (*Home*, Paragraph) or [CTRL] + **E** |
| CLEAR SCREEN: | MS Office Button, *Close*, then *No* if needed |
| COPY A FILE: | MS Office Button, *Open*, right-click file, *Copy*, type name |
| COPY TEXT: | Same as MOVE, but select *Copy* ([CTRL] + **C**) |
| DELETE A FILE: | MS Office Button, *Open*, right-click file, press [DELETE] |
| DELETE TEXT: | [BACKSPACE] erases left of insertion point; [DELETE] erases right |
| EXIT WORD: | Close button (X) or MS Office Button, E_xit Word |
| FONT: | Any **FONT** button (*Home*, Font) |
| FOOTNOTE: | **INSERT FOOTNOTE** (*References*, Footnote) |
| GO TO END/START: | [CTRL] + [END]  or  [CTRL] + [HOME] |
| HELP: | **HELP** button (upper-right corner of window) |
| LINE SPACING: | **LINE SPACING** (*Home*, Paragraph) |
| MARGINS: | **Page Setup Dialog Box Launcher** (*Page Layout*, Page Setup) |
| MOVE TEXT BLOCK: | Click start of block, drag mouse to end, |
| | **CUT** (*Home*, Clipboard) or [CTRL] + **X**, move to new spot, |
| | **PASTE** (*Home*, Clipboard) or [CTRL] + **Y** |
| OPEN A FILE: | MS Office Button, *Open*, click filename, *OK* |
| PAGE BREAK: | [CTRL] + [↵] or **PAGE BREAK** (*Insert*, Pages) |
| PAGE NUMBERING: | **PAGE NUMBER** (*Insert*, Header & Footer) |
| PARAGRAPH INDENT: | **INDENT** (Page *Layout*, Paragraph) or drag markers on ruler |
| PRINT: | MS Office Button, *Print*, select options, then *Print* |
| REPLACE: | **REPLACE** (*Home*, Editing) to start. Complete items. |
| REVEAL HIDDEN CODES: | **Show/Hide** (*Home*, Paragraph) |
| RULER BAR: | **View Ruler** (above vertical scroll bar on right side of window) |
| SAVE: | MS Office Button, *Save* or *Save As*, type filename [↵] |
| SCREEN MODE: | Any **VIEW** button at lower-right corner of window, next to zoom |

**W**

SELECT TEXT:                    Drag mouse, or [SHIFT] + arrow

SPELLING & GRAMMAR:             **SPELLING & GRAMMAR** (*Review*, Proofing)

TAB SET:                        Click ruler bar or Tabs button, **Paragraph dialog box launcher** (Home, Paragraph)

THESAURUS:                      **Thesaurus** (*Review*, Proofing)

UNDERLINE:                      **UNDERLINE** (*Home*, Font) or [CTRL] + **U**

ZOOM:                           Drag Zoom slide (lower-right corner of screen) or click its + or -

# SPREADSHEET MODULE

## EXCEL 2010

**E**

## LESSON 1: LAUNCHING EXCEL

In this module, you'll examine Microsoft Office 2010's spreadsheet program: Excel. Electronic spreadsheets (or "worksheets") are extremely useful tools. They can present data in columns quickly and easily and their math capabilities eliminate the need for you to do time-consuming calculations. Once a worksheet is created, you can change its contents, add or delete data, or alter columns or rows and the results will be recalculated automatically!

All modern spreadsheets were developed from the original VisiCalc program created in 1979, and so, their screens and capabilities are remarkably similar. If you learn the techniques of one spreadsheet program, it is fairly easy to use most others. Remember to watch your screen as you invoke the commands in this module. Do not just press keys or click the mouse; examine the effect of each step before you go on to the next. This way, you'll learn each command and understand its use.

As you saw in the introductory module, your computer needs special startup programs. If you have a hard disk system, the programs are contained on the hard disk, which is used to boot the computer. The startup instructions were presented in the introductory module. Refer to the appropriate instructions as needed to remind you how to start your computer system.

**1.** Start Windows.

**2.** If appropriate for your system, make sure that your diskette is in drive A (this is unnecessary if you are using a flash drive, or a folder on your hard disk or network).

The easiest way to launch a program is to use a desktop or taskbar icon (if one exists).

**3.** If your desktop (or taskbar) displays an Excel icon, double-click it now and continue after step 8.

If there is no icon, or if you prefer, you can always launch Excel through the Start menu. Try this approach, using Figure E-1 as a guide:

**4.** Click the *Start* button to access the Windows menu.

**5.** Point to *All Programs* to access its menu.

**6.** If the Microsoft Excel menu item appears in the resultant menu list, skip to step 8.

**7.** Point to the menu item that contains Microsoft Excel. This is often *Microsoft Office*. If a different menu item contains Excel, write its title here for future reference: _____.

**8.** Click the *Microsoft Excel* menu item (as in Figure E-1) to launch it.

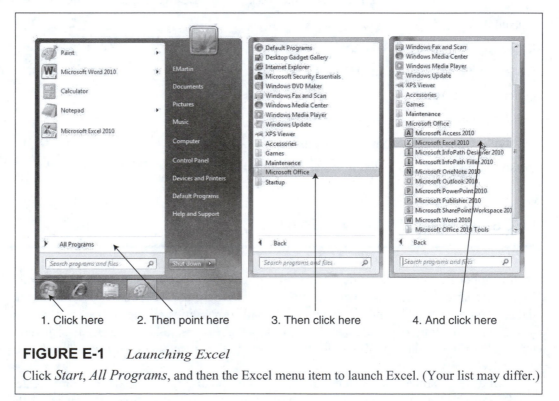

1. Click here    2. Then point here    3. Then click here    4. And click here

**FIGURE E-1**    *Launching Excel*

Click *Start*, *All Programs*, and then the Excel menu item to launch Excel. (Your list may differ.)

A copyright notice appears on the screen. This notice will be quickly replaced with a screen that resembles Figure E-2.

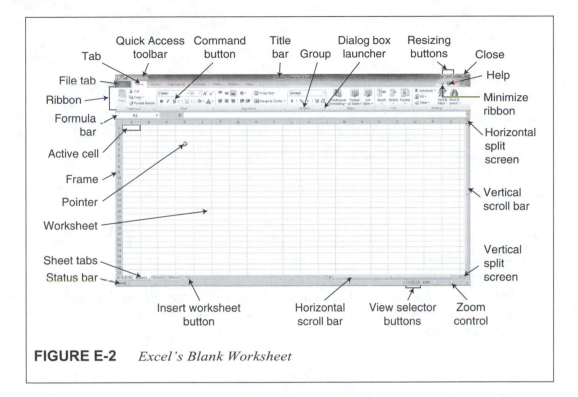

**FIGURE E-2**    *Excel's Blank Worksheet*

## The Excel Window

Congratulations! You've reached an empty workbook window, which is always displayed when you start Excel. The term "workbook" is used by Excel to describe the file in which you work and store your data. You can save as many workbook files as you want on your diskette, flash drive, or folder by giving each a unique name. A workbook is like a binder that can contain separate worksheets, charts, and other material. In this module, you will develop one worksheet and one chart.

The screen itself is a window that lets you see a portion of your worksheet. Each worksheet is like a gigantic sheet of paper in the computer's memory, divided into columns and rows for easy reference. Although Excel allows a staggering 16,384 columns and 1,048,576 rows (over 17 billion cells), you will not need this massive amount of space.

When you start a new worksheet, imagine that you are viewing the upper-left corner of the entire sheet. You can see a number of *vertical* columns and *horizontal* rows on the screen. Each column is identified with a letter placed in the top border above the worksheet; the first twenty-six columns use the letters A-Z, the next twenty-six use AA-AZ, then BA-BZ, and so on to ZA-ZZ, and then AAA-AAZ, until column XFD, for a total of 16,384 columns. Each row is identified with a number (1 to 1,048,576) in the left border of the worksheet. The intersection of each column and row forms a cell into which you can place values, text, formulas, or functions as needed, as shown in Figure E-3. A cell is identified by a *cell address*, which specifies its column and row. For example, the first cell's address is A1 and the last cell is XFD1048576.

**E**

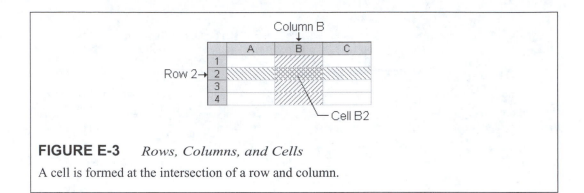

**FIGURE E-3**   *Rows, Columns, and Cells*

A cell is formed at the intersection of a row and column.

A few other items appear on the worksheet to assist in using the program. Find each on your screen as you refer back to Figure E-2. Note that your screen may not display all the features listed below.

a.   **Title bar:** The top line of the screen (the *title* bar) displays the typical window items: the title (Book1 - Microsoft Excel) in the center, and two resizing buttons and a close button at the right. If you are not sure of the functions of these items, review the introductory module.

**NOTE:**  If this window is not yet at full size, click the maximize button at the upper-right corner of the screen. Also maximize the document window by clicking its maximize button.

b.   **Program Icon:** The icon at the upper left can be clicked to access a resizing and close submenu.

c.   **Quick Access Toolbar:** Excel's Quick Access toolbar ("QAT")—to the right of the Program icon—contains often-used command buttons such as save, undo, and redo. You can customize this toolbar to include any other commands you wish to add.

d.   **Ribbon:** Beneath the title bar is the heart of Excel's menu system—the ribbon. The ribbon is a collection of *tabs*, *groups*, and *command buttons* that can be clicked by mouse to perform needed tasks. (More on this shortly.)

e.   **File tab:** The first tab in the ribbon is the green File tab. Clicking it opens a menu with commands for saving, printing and closing a file. It also provides access to many Excel options.

**NOTE:**  The title bar, Microsoft Office button, quick access toolbar, and ribbon are standard features found in every Microsoft Office 2010 program.

f.   **The formula bar:** Directly beneath the ribbon is Excel's formula bar. The formula bar displays the active cell's address at the left in a Name box, and its contents at the right. In this example, the active cell is A1 and it is currently empty. The right side of the bar also serves as an entry area, much like a one-line word processor. Whatever you type is displayed on this line, allowing you to edit the entry before placing it into the active cell on the worksheet.

**g.**   **The frame (or *border*):** Located beneath the formula bar and down the left side of the window, the frame consists of a horizontal row of letters and a vertical column of numbers. The frame provides a set of reference coordinates (much like a map) to help identify cell locations in the worksheet. The frame itself can also be used to select entire rows or columns (as you will see).

**h.**   **The worksheet:** The worksheet comprises most of the rest of the screen. It can be found below, and to the right of, the frame. Grid lines in the worksheet help define its rows, columns, and cells. The typical screen displays columns A-L and rows 1-25 although this may vary depending on the size and resolution of the your current window.

**i.**   **Task pane:** At times, a *task pane* (a portion of the window) will appear on the right side to provide additional information or commands when needed. You can leave the task pane open or close it by clicking its Close button. (There is no task pane currently displayed.)

**j.**   **Sheet tabs:** A set of tab markers at the bottom of the worksheet identifies the current worksheet in bold type (**Sheet1**) and allows you to move to other sheets as needed by simply clicking the appropriate tab. By default, three sheets (and thus, three tabs) are set in an initial worksheet. This can be changed as needed. The last tab is the "Insert Worksheet" button that allows you to insert more worksheet pages as needed. The four buttons to the left of the sheet tabs are "scrolling buttons" that let you access other worksheets (if more tabs are used than will fit in this space).

> **NOTE:** You can change the name of a sheet tab by double-clicking it and typing a new name. Thus you might create sheet tabs that read JAN or FEB (and so on) instead of the default names of Sheet1 or Sheet2. You can also right-click the tab scrolling button and then click the desired sheet.

**k.**   **Scroll bars:** Scroll bars are located to the right and beneath the worksheet. You can drag scroll bars to view other parts of the worksheet. The horizontal scroll bar shares the same line as the sheet tabs. The vertical scroll bar is at the extreme right of the window.

**l.**   **Split Screen buttons:** Just above and below the vertical scroll bar are two thin command buttons that can be dragged to split the image on the screen to show two portions of a worksheet. The Horizontal Split Screen button is at the top, the Vertical Split Screen button is at the bottom.

**m.**   **The status bar:** The status bar is the last line in the Excel window. It contains a *mode indicator*, currently showing Ready, at the left. This indicator will change to reflect the current status of the program's operation. The center and right side of the status bar provide areas for messages about errors and various keyboard toggles that have been set.

**n.**   **View selector:** To the right of the status bar are three small command buttons that allow you to change how the workbook appears on your screen. The Excel views include: normal, print layout, and page break preview.

**o.**   **Zoom:** The right-most section of the status bar contains a zoom control (currently at 100%) that allows you to change the magnification of screen text from 10% to 400%. You can drag the center indicator to any magnification you wish, or click the [+] and [–] icons to change the magnification in steps of 10.

**p.** **The active cell:** The active cell is the cell currently in use on the worksheet (indicated by a cell pointer—a highlighting rectangle around the cell). Entries from the formula bar are automatically placed into the active cell when you move to another cell (using the arrow keys) or press the ⏎ key.

**q.** A **mouse pointer** will appear somewhere on the screen, looking like a plus sign when in the worksheet area and an arrow almost everywhere else. You can point and click items in the menu bar, or on the ribbon, to invoke commands. Clicking a specific cell will make it the active cell.

**r.** The Windows **taskbar** appears at the bottom of the screen. You can click its *Start* button to launch other programs or Windows features, as you have seen in the introductory module.

Examine the screen a little more closely. As shown in Figure E-2, the left side of the formula bar identifies the active cell as A1—the cell formed by the intersection of column A and row 1. Whenever you start a new worksheet, the active cell will be A1. The rest of the formula bar is blank, indicating that the active cell is currently empty. The mode indicator at the left of the status bar displays the Ready message, showing that Excel is ready for a command.

The first nineteen columns (labeled A through S) and twenty-seven rows of the Sheet1 worksheet (labeled 1 through 27) can be seen in the workbook window. (This may vary depending on your screen resolution.) As expected, Cell A1 is highlighted by a rectangle, graphically identifying it as the active cell, along with the address A1 in the formula bar.

> **NOTE:** You can identify the *active cell* three ways: (1) the cell address in the name box of formula bar, (2) the highlighted cell in the worksheet itself, and (3) highlighted row and column identifiers (typically orange) in the frame.

**Excel Practice Sheet—Screen Exercises**

Your Name:_____

Class: _____ Date: _____

1. Name two ways that you can identify the active cell in the screen below:

    (a) _____

    (b) _____

2. Fill in the names of the items shown in the screen below.

    (a) _____    (g) _____

    (b) _____    (h) _____

    (c) _____    (i) _____

    (d) _____    (j) _____

    (e) _____    (k) _____

    (f) _____    (l) _____

      Watch the screen as you press each key below. Note the highlighted cell and frame and changes in the active line or cell contents.

3. Press →  three times. What is the active cell? _____.

4. Press →  twelve times! What cell are you in now? What happened to the screen as you moved there?

5. Press CTRL + HOME—the highlight moves to Cell A1. Now, type **12** but do *not* press ↵. What appears in the formula bar?

6. Press ↵. What appears in the active cell?

      To clear your screen for now, click Microsoft Office Button, *Close, No*. If you want to stop for now, click Microsoft Office Button, *Exit, No*, then (if appropriate for your system) shut down Windows and any LAN or hard disk menus. Remove your diskette if appropriate. If you are using a LAN, you may be told to leave the computer on. Otherwise, shut off the computer and monitor.

## LESSON 2: ENTERING DATA AND ISSUING COMMANDS

### Using the Keyboard

Alphabetic keys, number keys, [SHIFT], and [SPACE] have the same use as in typing. Many other important keys are used extensively in spreadsheet work as shown in Table E-1. Note that some require [SHIFT] to be pressed at the same time, such as *, +, ( , ), <, and > if entered from the keyboard ([SHIFT] is not required if you use the numeric keypad).

| KEY | APPLICATION |
| --- | --- |
| [CAPS LOCK] | Locks or unlocks capital letters with a press |
| [ESC] | Cancels the current operation, or backs up to the previous menu |
| [↵] (Enter) | Places entry into a cell or executes a formula |
| * + - / | Multiplication, addition, subtraction, division |
| = > < | Formulas: equal to, greater than, less than operators |
| ( ) = | Formulas and built-in functions |
| . | Decimal point or period |
| [↑] [↓] [←] [→] | Up, down, left, right cell moves and pointing |
| [INSERT] or [DELETE] | Editing |
| [CTRL]+[HOME] | Move to cell A1 |
| [CTRL]+[END] | Move to the last cell in the worksheet |
| [END] | Used with arrow keys to move to the last cell in any direction |
| [PgUp] or [PgDn] | Move one screen up or down |
| [ALT]+[PgDn] | Move one screen right |
| [ALT]+[PgUp] | Move one screen left |

**Table E-1**      *Excel Keys*

The numeric keypad is often used for *cell pointer* movement, reserving the typewriter number keys for *numeric* input. However, you can always press [NUM LOCK] to switch the numeric keypad to numeric entry, and then [NUM LOCK] again to switch back. This use of the keypad is confusing and not recommended until you have gained greater skill.

Keyboards that have separate numeric keypad and cursor controls are ideal for spreadsheet use. You can use the numeric pad for numeric entry and move the cell pointer with the separate arrow direction keys. (If your numeric keypad moves the pointer when a key is pressed, press [NUM LOCK] to switch its operation.)

### Entering Data Values

> **NOTE:** Read through the lesson to learn how to save and exit. Do not simply shut off the computer when finished with this lesson. Instead, save your work before you exit. This way, you can continue where you left off next time.

Cells can contain *formulas* or constant *values*. *Values* include text, numbers, dates, and logical values (such as T/F). Excel interprets most entries correctly as you enter them. However, entries that mix letters, symbols, and numbers will usually (with exceptions noted in the following list) be interpreted as text. This is fine for phone numbers or addresses but cannot be used for math calculations. Math must be handled by *formulas*, which will be discussed soon. Keep the following in mind as you place values in Excel:

*Text:* Contains alphabetic characters, numbers, or symbols; can also be specified by an initial apostrophe (').

*Numbers:* Contain numbers (0-9), decimal point, exponent symbols, or optional initial plus or minus sign.

*Dates:* Contain numbers and a slash or minus in the form m/d/yy or m-d-yy, as in 4/25/10.

You will now set up a simple payroll sheet that you will use to learn Excel.

1. First, obtain a new blank worksheet by starting again (see Lesson 1) or by erasing your current screen. Click the File tab, *Close, "Don't Save"* (if needed), and then the File tab, *New, Blank Workbook, Create.*

2. Move to cell C1 (click the cell or use the arrow keys to move there).

3. Now, type your name, two spaces, and then your class. (Don't worry if the text exceeds the size of the cell—it will appear anyway.)

4. Press ⏎.

5. For each step listed in Table E-2, *move* to the cell and then *type* the entry as shown. Press ⏎ after typing each entry or move to the next cell. Your entry will be placed into the active cell.

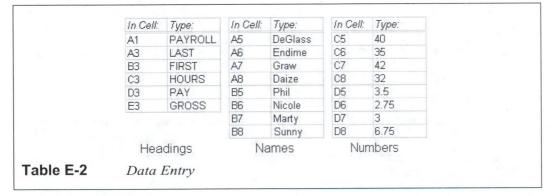

| In Cell: | Type: | In Cell: | Type: | In Cell: | Type: |
|----------|---------|----------|--------|----------|-------|
| A1 | PAYROLL | A5 | DeGlass | C5 | 40 |
| A3 | LAST | A6 | Endime | C6 | 35 |
| B3 | FIRST | A7 | Graw | C7 | 42 |
| C3 | HOURS | A8 | Daize | C8 | 32 |
| D3 | PAY | B5 | Phil | D5 | 3.5 |
| E3 | GROSS | B6 | Nicole | D6 | 2.75 |
|    |         | B7 | Marty | D7 | 3 |
|    |         | B8 | Sunny | D8 | 6.75 |
| | Headings | | Names | | Numbers |

**Table E-2**      *Data Entry*

**NOTE:** Excel automatically recognizes the entries in columns A and B as *text* because each contains only alphabetic characters. Entries in the other cells are treated as numbers because each contains only *numbers* or decimal points.

When you are done, compare your screen to Figure E-4. If you made an error, click that cell, retype it correctly, and press ⏎.

| | A | B | C | D | E |
|---|---------|-------|-------|------|-------|
| 1 | PAYROLL | | YOUR NAME & CLASS | | |
| 2 | | | | | |
| 3 | LAST | FIRST | HOURS | PAY | GROSS |
| 4 | | | | | |
| 5 | DeGlass | Phil | 40 | 3.5 | |
| 6 | Endime | Nicole | 35 | 2.75 | |
| 7 | Graw | Marty | 42 | 3 | |
| 8 | Daize | Sunny | 32 | 6.75 | |
| 9 | | | | | |

**FIGURE E-4**      *Sample Payroll Sheet*

Note that text is aligned left; numbers are aligned right in each cell.

## Issuing Commands

Text and numbers (and formulas, as you will see) can be typed directly into workbook cells, but much of Excel's power is hidden in the sets of commands found in the *ribbon*. As with other Windows programs, the ribbon offers choices that allow you to adjust the way the worksheet looks, insert or delete columns and rows, copy or move cell data, erase, and edit (to name a few). Because you will be using the ribbon often, you might as well become familiar with it now.

## The Excel Ribbon

Most of the commands you will use in Excel are contained in the Microsoft Office *ribbon*—the four-line band across the top of the window. The ribbon is divided into core tasks, each represented by a tab. For example, the "Home" tab (as shown in Figure E-5a) contains most of the basic entry commands you will need; the "Insert" tab (as in Figure E-5b) contains most of the commands for inserting shapes, illustrations, tables, charts, and text into your worksheet; and so on.

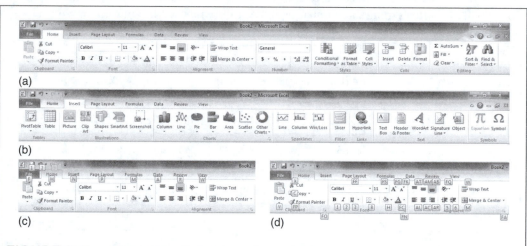

**FIGURE E-5**  *Using Excel's Ribbon*

Excel's ribbon is divided into tabs, groups, and command buttons.

(a)   The Home tab.

(b)   The Insert tab.

(c)   Pressing ⎡ALT⎤ displays letters that can be pressed to access a tab (not recommended).

(d)   Pressing a tab letter (such as "H" for "Home") opens that tab with additional letters that can be pressed to invoke a command.

### Ribbon-Group-Command

Each tab is divided into *groups*—smaller sets of related commands arranged by function. In the Home tab, for example, the groups are Clipboard, Font, Alignment, Number, Styles, Cells, and Editing. Each group contains command buttons that you can click to activate an appropriate action. The command buttons remain in view and are always available for immediate use. (By default, the Home tab appears when you open a new workbook, since it is the one you will use most often.)

**NOTE:** The bottom right corner of each group typically contains a *Dialog Box Launcher* icon that, when clicked, activates a dialog box containing a variety of additional commands and settings. (You'll try this later.)

Excel's ribbon includes the File tab and seven "standard" tabs. At times, based on your actions, "contextual" tools will be added as temporary tabs (shown in a different color accent). When you finish your task, the contextual tab will disappear from the ribbon.

**NOTE:** Although you can leave any ribbon tab active, it is a good idea to click the "Home" tab when you are finished using a set of commands, so it is always available.

## Using the Ribbon

Excel's ribbon provides an easy way to invoke commands. Most often, you simply click the desired command button. If the command is contained in another tab, first click the desired tab to make it active and then click the command button. You can choose a command from the ribbon using either of these methods:

- By mouse: If needed, click the desired tab to make it active. Click the desired command to select it (the preferred method).

- By keyboard: Press ⌐ALT⌐ to see mnemonic *tab* letters (as shown in Figure E-5c). Press the desired letter of the needed tab, then press the letter of the command (as shown in Figure E-5d).

  Try the following exercise. Let's say you wanted to set bold text:

1.  Launch Excel if necessary.

2.  Click the *Home* tab if it is not already active.

3.  Click the Bold command button.

    Note that the Bold command button is now highlighted, indicating that it is active.

## The File Menu

Commands that relate to opening, saving, and printing files are stored in a separate "File" menu, accessed through the green File tab. Try this:

1.  Click the File tab, located in the upper-left corner of the window.

A file menu appears, as shown in Figure E-6. The left side presents twelve file options. The right side lists various information depending on the option, such as recently opened documents (if any) that can be clicked to open for use. The "Options" button near the end of the list accesses a dialog box that allows you to adjust most options in Excel to better suit your needs. (For now, leave them alone.) At the extreme bottom, an "Exit" button allows you to leave the Excel program when you are done.

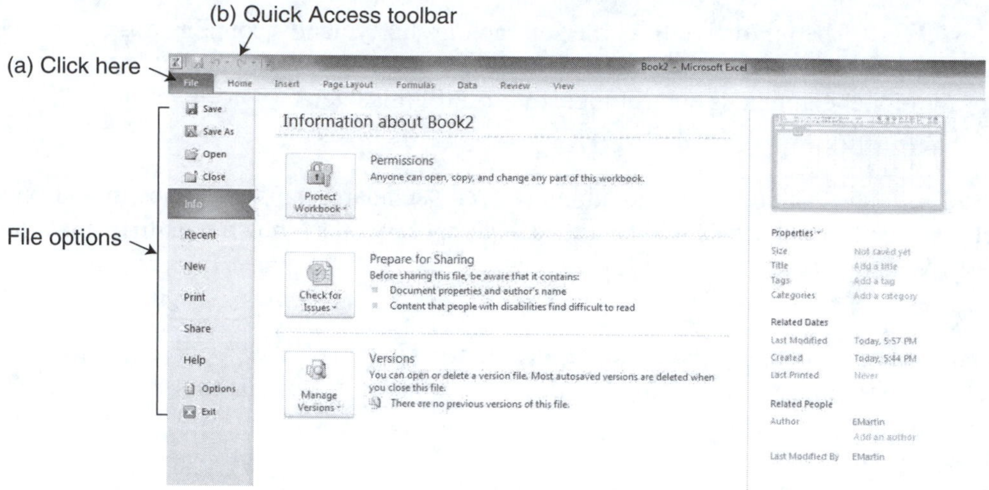

**FIGURE E-6**     *Additional Excel Commands*

(a)   Clicking the File tab opens a menu with various file options.

(b)   The Quick Access Toolbar.

**2.**   For now, click outside the menu to close it.

## The Quick Access Toolbar

Excel also offers a fast way to access a number of useful commands in its Quick Access Toolbar ("QAT"), located in the title bar, as shown in Figure E-6b. You can click buttons to save, undo, or redo easily.

> **NOTE:**  You can add any command you want to the QAT by clicking the customize button at the end of the toolbar and following the directions. This allows you to place your often-used commands in an easily-accessible, one-click, location.

### Getting On-Screen Help

Excel offers a help feature that provides easy access to information about the program and its commands. To get on-screen help at any time,

**1.**   Click the *Help* button, located at the extreme right of the ribbon (or press F1).

An Excel Help dialog box and question area will appear as shown in Figure E-7. You can type keywords of interest. Try the following example:

**2.**   Type **ribbon** and press ⏎ (or click the *Search* button).

A list of options appears. You could pick one topic by clicking it, but for now,

**3.**   Click the dialog box's Close button (as in Figure E-7).

> **NOTE:** If you are in doubt as to the use of a particular command button, point to it and wait a moment. Excel will display its name in a "tool tip" box that appears beneath the button.

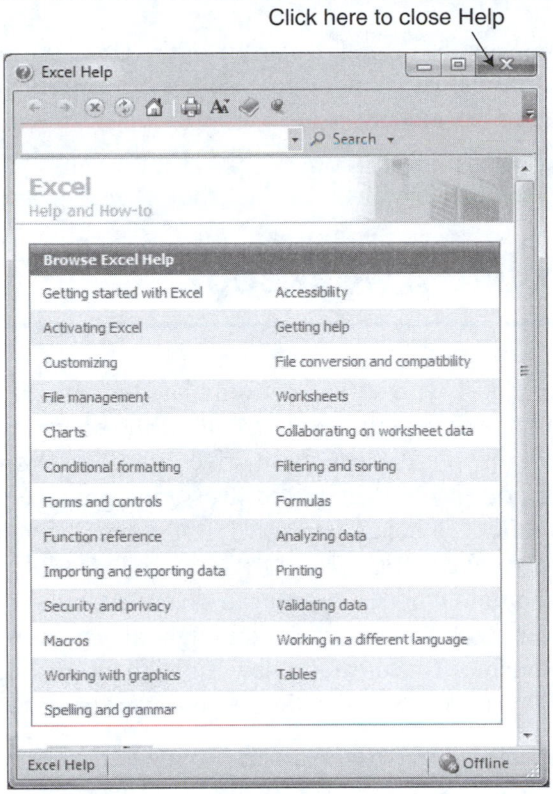

Click here to close Help

**FIGURE E-7**    *Excel's Help Feature*

Type a question (or keyword) and then click Search to obtain information.

## Shortcut Keys

Although it is easier to use a mouse for most tasks, Excel also provides an extensive set of shortcut keys. You can use keys (in combination with CTRL or ALT) to invoke many of Excel's commands. For example, pressing CTRL + **N** creates a new file; CTRL + **O** *opens* an existing file.

   If you are interested in these shortcut approaches, examine each command button as you use it. You will note that some shortcut keys are displayed in the "tool tip" that appears when you point to a command button. You can also learn more about these shortcut commands by searching for shortcuts in the help feature.

## The Undo Command

The *Undo* command cancels the last actions you issued. It is extremely useful when you make a mistake or when your actions produce unexpected results. When it is invoked, Undo returns your worksheet to its state prior to the last action taken. You can invoke the Undo command by clicking the Undo button on the Quick Access Toolbar, or pressing the shortcut keys CTRL + **Z**.

**NOTE:** You can click the drop-down arrow of the Undo button to access a list of the most recent actions. By pointing to each desired action, you can create a set that will be undone with one click.

## LESSON 3: SAVING A WORKBOOK

As you fill your worksheet with values or formulas, the entries are stored in the computer's primary memory. If you exit Excel or turn off the computer, all your work will be lost, unless you save it on your diskette, flash drive, or folder. Worksheets can be saved at any time, whether or not they are completed. It is good practice to save your worksheet every few minutes while it is being developed. (Of course, if you don't need the worksheet, you don't have to save it at all.)

If you're editing an old worksheet, you can save it again with the same name, which replaces the old version with the new one. You might also want to save a changed worksheet with a different name. This creates a new file without erasing the old one. You will try both methods. In this exercise, you will save your workbook with the name WORK1.

**NOTE:** Recall that Excel saves *workbooks*. Each workbook may contain more than one worksheet (or chart) page.

The *Save in* entry (or *Look in* when opening a file) directs Excel to the location in which your files are stored. It is usually set correctly and needs no adjustment. However, when you are using a computer for the first time, sharing a lab computer, or even when opening or saving files, you should get into the habit of glancing at the *Save in* or *Look in* entry to make sure it is set properly, and changing it if it is not. Do this now as follows:

1. Make sure that your diskette is in the correct drive or your flash drive is ready (if appropriate for your system) and that you have entered values into the worksheet as shown in Lesson 2. If not, do it now.

Now follow each direction, one step at a time, always watching your screen to see how your actions have altered it.

Although you can leave the cell pointer in any cell, you may want to move it back to cell A1 before saving. This way, your worksheet will look correct the next time you use it.

2. Press CTRL + HOME now to return the cell pointer to cell A1.

3. Click the File tab and then *Save*.

**NOTE:** Remember that the appropriate icon is displayed in the margin for easy reference.

Since this is the first time you are saving a worksheet, a Save As dialog box appears, as shown in Figure E-8.

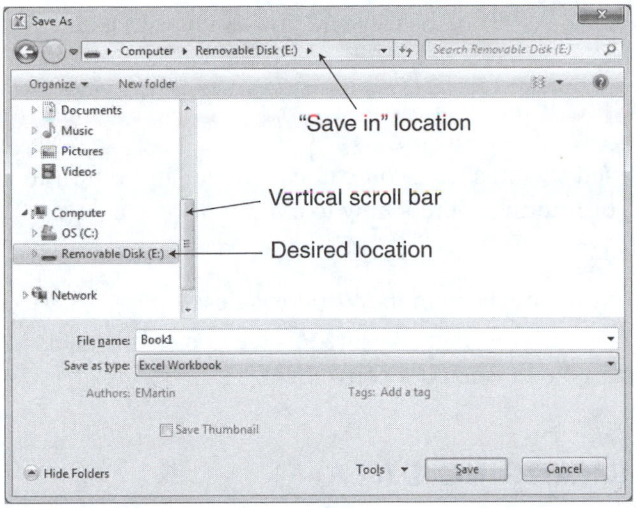

**FIGURE E-8**    *The Save As Dialog Box*

4. Examine the *Save in* entry line. If it displays the proper drive or folder, continue with step 5. If it does not, you must change it now by performing the following steps:

   a. Click and drag the vertical scroll bar until the desired drive or folder appears.

   b. Click the desired drive or folder from the drop-down list that appears.

5. Click the *File name* entry line and delete its contents.

6. Type the filename **WORK1** and then click *Save*.

7. If a Summary Info dialog box appears, click the *Save* button.

   A "Saving WORK1" message appears on the status bar briefly as a copy of your single worksheet is saved in a file called WORK1. When it is done, you will be returned to the screen to continue where you left off.

> **NOTE:** Although you may not see it, Excel saves all workbooks with the extension ".XLSX" to identify them as Excel 2010 workbooks.

Let's say you have made some changes to the worksheet and now want to save it again. To simulate saving a new version of a worksheet with the same name, try this:

8. Click the File tab and then *Save* (or click the *Save* quick access toolbar button).

   The worksheet is immediately saved again to your diskette, flash drive, or folder, in the same file and with the same filename. You then return to the screen where you can continue with your work.

## Using Save or Save As

In general, you can save a worksheet in one of two ways. You can use the *Save* command or the *Save As* command. Here's the difference:

- Use *Save* to save a new worksheet, or to easily save an "old" worksheet with the same name periodically as you work on it. Save is quick, but it does not check for duplicate filenames before it saves.

- Use *Save As* to give a worksheet a new filename. Unlike the Save command, Save As brings up the Save As dialog box, where you can type in a new filename or location.

## Exiting Excel

Once you have saved a worksheet, you can exit Excel and return to any worksheet later for further editing or printing. Here's how to exit:

1. Click the File tab.

2. Click *Exit*. You're now back in the Windows desktop.

    You can stop now if you want. Be sure to save your worksheets in each section. Then you can exit and start again when it's convenient.

## LESSON 4: CHANGING DATA

Before you can change the data in your worksheet, you must have the worksheet copied from its storage location and loaded into the computer's main memory (RAM).

## Launching Excel

To open a workbook that is on your diskette, flash drive, or folder, you first must be in the Excel program. To get there, follow the program launch procedure you learned in Lesson 1:

1. Start Windows if necessary.

2. Be sure your diskette is in drive A or your flash drive is ready (if appropriate).

3. Launch Excel using the directions in Lesson 1.

    You'll now open your WORK1 workbook.

## The Open Procedure

When you "open" a workbook, Excel locates the file in the location you specify and copies it into a new window on your screen. The actual *Open* procedure is almost identical to *Save*.

> **NOTE:** Opening a workbook creates a new document window. To ensure that you do not open more than one window at a time, for now, close any open workbook window before opening a new one.

1. Click the File tab.

    A list of recently-opened Excel workbooks appears on the right side of the menu. In the future, if one of these files is the one you wish to open, just click it. For now, though, use the more traditional approach:

2. Click *Open*.

    An *Open* dialog box will appear, as shown in Figure E-9. A list of the available workbooks is displayed at the left of the box. The file you saved earlier, WORK1, should appear in the list (see step 3 if it does not).

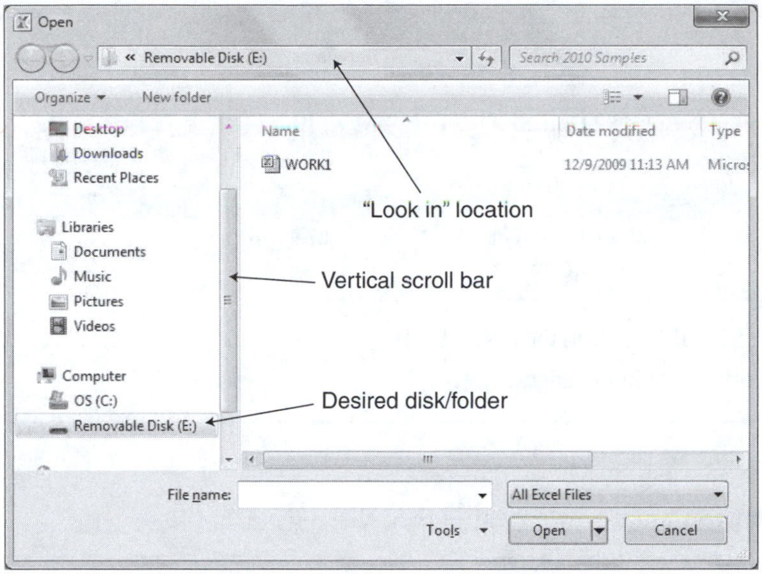

**FIGURE E-9**    *The Open Dialog Box*

3.  If the proper folder or drive appears in the *Look in* box, continue with step 4. If it does not, click and scroll the vertical scroll bar and then click the desired folder or drive from the list.

    Your list may display the WORK1 file with an extension of .XLSX. (Remember that this extension was automatically added to the filename when it was saved to identify it as an Excel 2010 workbook. Earlier versions of Excel used an .XLS extension.) Note, too, that only workbooks are listed, whether or not the extension is displayed.

> **NOTE:**  If your folder, flash drive, or diskette contains more workbooks than can be shown, use the scroll bar to view the additional workbook files.

4.  Click *WORK1* to highlight it.

5.  Click the *Open* button to open the file.

> **NOTE:**  You can also double-click the desired file in step 4 to open it immediately, without having to click the *Open* button.

## Changing Data with Typeover and Erase

Changing cell contents is easy. Suppose you typed an incorrect entry or just want to change it. Simply move the rectangular cell pointer to the cell and retype the entry the way you want it. Try this, as follows:

1.  Open WORK1 if it isn't already on the screen.

2.  Move the cell pointer to cell C5 where the number 40 appears (as shown in Figure E-10a). You can just click the cell to move there.

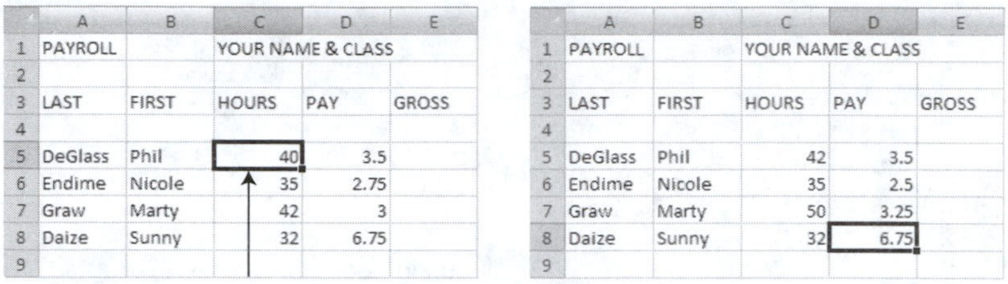

**FIGURE E-10**    *Preparing to Change Data*

(a)   Move the cell pointer to the desired cell.

(b)   The worksheet after changes.

3.   Type the number **42**.

   The change should now appear in the cell.

4.   Press ↵ to accept the change.

   Now, make these additional changes using the same technique as in steps 2-4:

5.   Change the contents of cell D6 from 2.75 to 2.5.

6.   Change the contents of cell C7 from 42 to 50.

7.   Change the contents of cell D7 from 3 to 3.25.

   Your screen should now look like Figure E-10b. If not, move to the appropriate cells and type over their contents to change your screen.

8.   Save this worksheet with the same name, WORK1, using the Save command.


## Clearing a Cell

Sometimes you want to remove a cell's contents and leave it empty. Although typing a space in a cell seems to do the job, it leads to other math problems. Keep in mind that a *blank cell* is not the same as an *empty* one! Let's say you wanted to erase the contents of cell D5 completely. Here's the correct way to do it:

1.   Move to cell D5.

   Now, how do you get rid of its contents without typing something else in the cell?

2.   Press (DELETE). The cell is clear.

3.   For now, click the *Undo* toolbar button to return the 3.5 to the cell.

   You can also erase a *range* of cells using this procedure. Click the first cell, then drag the pointer to the last cell, highlighting the range of cells to be erased. Once the range has been identified, press (DELETE).

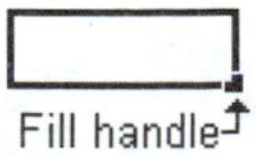

Fill handle

**NOTE**:  A faster mouse method is also available. After you identify the entire range to be erased (one or more cells), point to the small rectangle at the lower-right of the current cell pointer—this is called the "fill handle." Drag the pointer upward until the entire range is highlighted, and then release it. Try this sometime!

## LESSON 5: USING FORMULAS AND BUILT-IN FUNCTIONS

So far, worksheets are interesting but nothing spectacular. You've typed some labels and numbers and made some changes, but now you'll begin to see the power of Excel and why spreadsheet programs are so popular.

### Formulas

A major advantage of a spreadsheet program is its ability to perform math. For example, instead of manually calculating gross pay and totals, you will create formulas to do this. First, review the math symbols that are standard in computer use: addition +, subtraction -, multiplication *, division /, parentheses ( ) for indicating order of precedence (discussed below), and exponentiation ^ (raising to a power). Here are several examples of simple calculations:

| | |
|---|---|
| =A1 + A2 | Adds the value of cell A1 to the value of cell A2. |
| =A1 - A2 | Subtracts the value of cell A2 from the value of cell A1. |
| =A1 * A2 | Multiplies the value of cell A1 by the value of cell A2. |
| =A1 / A2 | Divides the value of cell A1 by the value of cell A2. |

> **NOTE:** Formulas in Excel typically begin with an = symbol, although a + or - symbol can also be used.

**E**

You can use any combination of math operators. However, remember that there is an order (or precedence) of operations in math: Operations in parentheses are performed first, followed by exponentiation, then by multiplication and division, and finally, addition and subtraction. The mnemonic "**P**lease **E**xcuse **M**y **D**ear **A**unt **S**ally" is an easy way to remember the order of precedence (with each first letter reminding you of an operation).

Review these more complicated examples for practice:

| | |
|---|---|
| =(A1 + A2) / A3 | Divides the sum of the values in cell A1 and A2 by the value in cell A3. |
| =A1 ^ 2 + A2 / A3 | Squares the value in cell A1, divides the value in cell A2 by the value in cell A3, then adds the two results together. |
| =A1 - A2 / A3 | Divides the value in cell A2 by the value in cell A3, then subtracts the result from the value in cell A1. |

To do worksheet math, first move to the cell where you want the answer to appear and then type a formula that refers to the cells that hold the values you need. This sounds harder than it is. For example, if you wanted to add the values in cells A1 and A2 and put the result in cell A3, you would first move the pointer to cell A3 and then type **=A1+A2**, which means "add the value in A1 to the value in A2." You must start with an equals symbol (=) so that Excel recognizes the cell contents as a formula, not a value.

In the simple payroll example in WORK1, you will multiply the *hours worked* by the *pay rate* to find the gross pay. You could conceptualize this as follows: GROSS = HOURS * PAY.

## Using Math Formulas

Now look at your worksheet. The first cell where you want to calculate gross pay is cell E5. Cells C5 and D5 contain the hours and pay values you need. So, you will enter a formula in E5 that says "multiply the value in C5 by the value in D5 and put the result in E5." Remember to start the formula with an "=" symbol to indicate you are entering a formula, not a value. Try this as follows.

**1.** Open the WORK1 workbook if it's not already on the screen.

**2.** Click cell E5 to move there.

**3.** Type =**C5*D5** and press ⏎.

**4.** Move back to cell E5.

Notice that the *formula* (=C5*D5) appears in the right side of the formula bar, but the *answer* (147) appears on the worksheet in cell E5, as shown in Figure E-11.

The formula is here... but the answer is

| | A | B | C | D | E |
|---|---|---|---|---|---|
| | E5 | | ▼ | fx | =C5*D5 |
| 1 | PAYROLL | | YOUR NAME & CLASS | | |
| 2 | | | | | |
| 3 | LAST | FIRST | HOURS | PAY | GROSS |
| 4 | | | | | |
| 5 | DeGlass | Phil | 42 | 3.5 | 147 |
| 6 | Endime | Nicole | 35 | 2.5 | |
| 7 | Graw | Marty | 50 | 3.25 | |
| 8 | Daize | Sunny | 32 | 6.75 | |
| 9 | | | | | |

**FIGURE E-11**   *Using a Formula*

The result of a calculation appears in the cell. The formula itself can be seen only in the formula bar of the active cell.

**NOTE:** Formulas do not appear in the worksheet—only the result of their calculation. To see a formula, click the desired cell and then view its formula in the formula bar. If a formula appears to be correct but produces a result that is clearly *not* correct, check that the cell references are correct and that the *contents* of those cells are numeric (not text)! A common error is to type text that looks like a number. (Excel assigns a value of zero to text in any formula.)

Now, further examine the power that formulas offer you:

**5.** Move to cell C5.

**6.** Type **25** and press ⏎.

Examine cell E5. Note that the display has changed to 87.5 (the result of the formula multiplying the new value 25 times the hourly pay). The formula has recalculated its result to reflect the contents contained in the cells referenced in the formula.

7.  Move back to cell C5, type **42** and press ⏎ . Note the result in cell E5 is 147 once again.

Now move to each cell listed below, one at a time, and type in the appropriate formula to calculate gross pay as follows (later you'll learn how to copy a formula without having to retype it):

8.  In cell E6, type =**C6\*D6** and press ⏎ .

9.  In cell E7, type =**C7\*D7** and press ⏎ .

10. In cell E8, type =**C8\*D8** and press ⏎ .

11. Compare your result to Figure E-12. If your screen does not yield the same results in Column E, move to the appropriate cells and retype the cell formulas as needed.

12. When your worksheet results match Figure E-12, save your workbook with the same name, WORK1.

| | A | B | C | D | E |
|---|---|---|---|---|---|
| 1 | PAYROLL | | YOUR NAME & CLASS | | |
| 2 | | | | | |
| 3 | LAST | FIRST | HOURS | PAY | GROSS |
| 4 | | | | | |
| 5 | DeGlass | Phil | 42 | 3.5 | 147 |
| 6 | Endime | Nicole | 35 | 2.5 | 87.5 |
| 7 | Graw | Marty | 50 | 3.25 | 162.5 |
| 8 | Daize | Sunny | 32 | 6.75 | 216 |

**FIGURE E-12**    *The Worksheet with GROSS Formulas Added*

## Adding a Total

You will now add another formula that will *total* the gross values in column E. An easy way to total a column or row of numbers is to use Excel's AutoSum feature. Try this:

1.  First, click cell E10, where you want the total to appear.

2.  Click the *AutoSum* command button (*Home* tab, *Editing* group).
    Excel suggests a range of cells. For now,

3.  Press ⏎ to accept. The answer appears in cell E10.

Now, if you change any employee's hours or pay, the cells that display the gross and total will both automatically change! Try it. Then change the hours or pay value back to what it was (so it will match the values in Figure E-12).

Now, provide a label for the total as follows:

4.  Move to cell A10, type **Total** and press ⏎ . The result appears as in Figure E-13.

| | A | B | C | D | E |
|---|---|---|---|---|---|
| 1 | PAYROLL | | YOUR NAME & CLASS | | |
| 2 | | | | | |
| 3 | LAST | FIRST | HOURS | PAY | GROSS |
| 4 | | | | | |
| 5 | DeGlass | Phil | 42 | 3.5 | 147 |
| 6 | Endime | Nicole | 35 | 2.5 | 87.5 |
| 7 | Graw | Marty | 50 | 3.25 | 162.5 |
| 8 | Daize | Sunny | 32 | 6.75 | 216 |
| 9 | | | | | |
| 10 | Total | | | | 613 |

**FIGURE E-13**     *TOTAL Formula and Label Added*

You can type any formula you need using *any* combination of math operators and cell references. Excel also offers *built-in functions* (a type of automatic formula) such as SUM, AVERAGE, and COUNT, which are much easier to use. As with other formulas, all these functions start with an equals symbol (=) to identify them. Many of these functions define a rectangular block of cells, called a *range*, upon which the function will operate. Ranges are shown by identifying the first cell and last cell, separated by a colon. Figure E-14 displays a few sample ranges.

As you have seen in the AutoSum feature, the SUM function has the form =SUM(first cell:last cell), which means "sum up all the values in the cells included in the range, from the first cell address to the last cell address." You could just as easily sum four cells or a thousand cells, just by changing the first and last cell addresses. You can type any function you need. You'll try using the AVERAGE function in the following exercise.

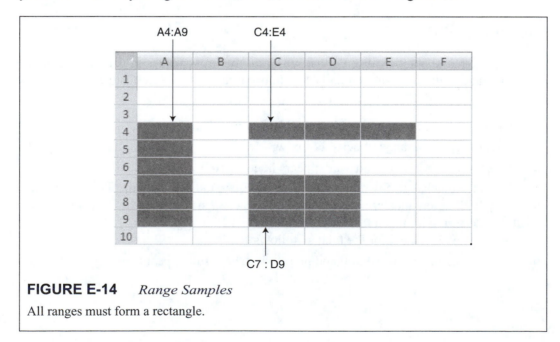

**FIGURE E-14**     *Range Samples*

All ranges must form a rectangle.

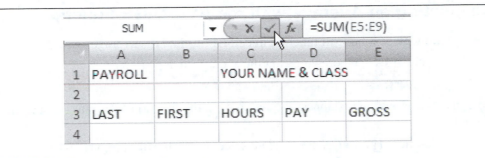

**FIGURE E-15**   *Using the Enter Button*

Clicking the checkmark (Enter) button on the formula bar will enter a formula without moving out of the active cell.

## More on Built-in Functions

Built-in functions let you add, average, find minimum or maximum values, and calculate standard deviations, as well as many other values. To use most of them, you type an = followed by the function name. Then type a parenthesis, the first cell address of the desired range, a colon, the last cell address of the range, and finally, a closing parenthesis, and press ↵ or click the check mark button (√) on the formula bar, as shown in Figure E-15. (Some functions do not require a range.)

**NOTE:**  You may want to access the Help feature to learn more about all the built-in functions offered in Excel.

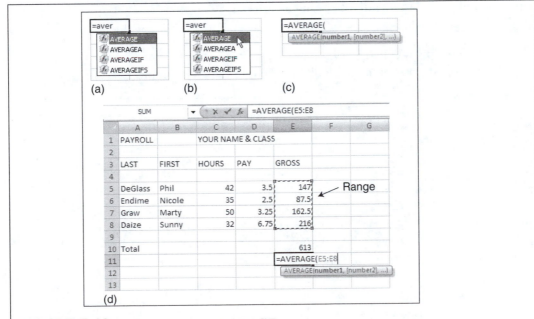

**FIGURE E-16**   *Creating an AVERAGE*

(a)   Typing the first four letters of a function invokes a box of function "guesses."

(b)   Click the function name you want.

(c)   The function name is completed, just awaiting a range to be specified.

(d)   Click the first cell and drag to the last.

## Calculating an Average with the AVERAGE Function

You will now place a built-in function in cell E11 to find the average gross pay.

1. Move to cell E11, where you want the average to appear.

2. Type **=AVER**

Note that a drop-down box appears, "guessing" at the function you want (as shown in Figure E-16a).

3. Double-click *AVERAGE* in the list to select it (as shown in Figure E-16b).

The function name is completed and an open parenthesis is added, awaiting a range (as shown in Figure E-16c).

4. Now click the first cell of the range to be averaged, in this case, E5.

5. Press and hold the left mouse button and drag the mouse pointer to the last cell in the range, E8, as shown in Figure E-16d.

6. Release the mouse.

   The range is typed into the function for you.

7. Type a closing parenthesis and then press ⏎.

> **NOTE:** If you omit the closing parenthesis, Excel will automatically insert it when you press ⏎.

   The result will appear. If you prefer, you could type a function entirely without pointing to the range. This is especially useful in large ranges where it would be difficult to point to the range. In this example, you could have typed **=AVERAGE(E5:E8)**. Now, you can add a label to identify the result as follows:

8. Click cell A11.

9. Type **Average** and press ⏎.

   Your worksheet should now look like the one shown in Figure E-17.

| | A | B | C | D | E |
|---|---|---|---|---|---|
| 1 | PAYROLL | | YOUR NAME & CLASS | | |
| 2 | | | | | |
| 3 | LAST | FIRST | HOURS | PAY | GROSS |
| 4 | | | | | |
| 5 | DeGlass | Phil | 42 | 3.5 | 147 |
| 6 | Endime | Nicole | 35 | 2.5 | 87.5 |
| 7 | Graw | Marty | 50 | 3.25 | 162.5 |
| 8 | Daize | Sunny | 32 | 6.75 | 216 |
| 9 | | | | | |
| 10 | Total | | | | 613 |
| 11 | Average | | | | 153.25 |

**FIGURE E-17** *The Worksheet with a Total and Average*

**10.** Click the File tab and then *Save As* to save this worksheet with the *new* name of WORK2.

> **NOTE:** Always put the cell pointer in the cell where you want the result to appear *before* you begin to type a formula or built-in function.

Figure E-18 displays some additional built-in functions that might be of interest. You can learn more about Excel's functions through its help feature.

| | A | B | C | FUNCTION |
|---|---|---|---|---|
| 1 | 11 | | 78.6 | =SUM(A1:A7) |
| 2 | 1 | | 13.1 | =AVERAGE(A1:A7) |
| 3 | 49 | | 49 | =MAX(A1:A7) |
| 4 | 0 | | -3 | =MIN(A1:A7) |
| 5 | -3 | | 6 | =COUNT(A1:A7) |
| 6 | | | 17.91972842 | =STDEVP(A1:A7) |
| 7 | 20.6 | | 21 | =ROUND(A7,0) |
| 8 | | | 7 | =SQRT(A3) |
| 9 | | | 3 | =ABS(A5) |
| 10 | | | 20 | =INT(A7) |
| 11 | | | 0.65077547 | =RAND() |
| 12 | SAMPLE | SAM | | =LEFT(A12,3) |
| 13 | | LE | | =RIGHT(A12,2) |
| 14 | | | 6 | =LEN(A12) |
| 15 | | sample | | =LOWER(A12) |
| 16 | | Sample | | =PROPER(A12) |
| 17 | | SAMPLESAMPLE | | =REPT(A12,2) |

**FIGURE E-18**    *Additional Built-in Functions*

A function sampler.

*Values and Formulas*—A Word of WARNING: If you erase a formula by mistake, *DO NOT* replace it by simply typing its value, even if the two results look the same. The value you type may look fine now, but it will not be able to change to reflect new results later. For example, the formula in cell E5 currently produces a result of 147. If you change Phil's hours, the formula in the cell will recalculate a new result. However, if you were to type the *value* 147 in cell E5, it will no longer be a formula, and cannot change even if Phil's hours change. If you erase a formula by mistake, retype the formula itself, *not its current value* (or use *Undo*).

## A Note about Ranges

When used with command buttons or dialog boxes, cell ranges must be identified *first*, before invoking the command. Here's how:

- *With a mouse:* Point to the first cell; while pressing the left mouse button, drag the pointer to the last cell; then release.

- *With the keyboard:* Move to the first cell, press *and hold* [SHIFT]; use the arrow keys to move to the last cell; then release the [SHIFT].

  The range will be highlighted on the screen. You can then invoke the command button or menu command in the normal manner. (If you want to cancel the range, simply move the cell pointer elsewhere outside the range.)

### Quick Review #1

Assume the following cell contents: A1=21, A2=35, A3=16, and B1=15.

1.  What result would the formula =A1+B1 generate? _____

2.  What would appear in cell C2 if its formula was =A2? _____

3.  Write the formula that would calculate the total of the three numbers in column A.

    _____

4.  Write the equivalent SUM function to the formula in number 3.

    _____

5.  Write the formula that would average the numbers in cells A2 and A3.

    _____


## LESSON 6: CHANGING CELL APPEARANCE

It's time to make your worksheet look better. To do this, you'll adjust column widths, format titles to line up with data, and change some numbers to dollars and cents. In Excel, as in most spreadsheet programs, you *do not* include commas or dollar signs when you type a value. Instead, you simply enter the numerals (and a negative sign and decimal point if appropriate), and then use the menu commands or buttons to adjust the appearance of the cell to display these symbols.

1.  Open the WORK2 workbook if it's not already on the screen. It should look like Figure E-17.

2.  Follow the exercises by moving the pointer when instructed and invoking each command listed. Pause after pressing *each command* and note the changes that occur on your screen.


### Changing the Column Width

1.  Click cell C5 (actually, any cell in column C will do).

2.  Click the *Format* command button (*Home* tab, *Cells* group).
    A drop-down list appears.

3.  Click the *Width* option.
    A Column Width dialog box will appear. The current default width set by Excel is 8.43 characters.

4.  Type **7** and click OK to set the new column width.

> **NOTE:** You can also change a *range* of column widths at the same time by identifying a range of columns before invoking the command.

## Changing Column Width with a Mouse

Try another column width change, this time using the mouse.

5.　Point to the vertical line between columns D and E in the worksheet frame, as shown in Figure E-19a.

6.　Press and hold the left mouse button.

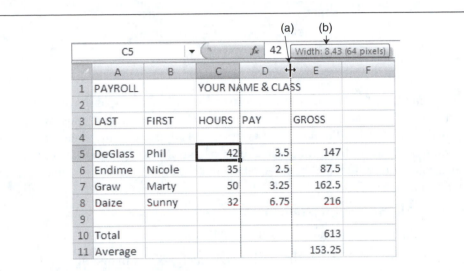

**FIGURE E-19**　*Changing Column Width by Mouse*

(a)　Point to the vertical frame line.

(b)　The current width appears in a box above the column.

As shown in Figure E-19b, the column is now outlined by a rectangular dotted frame and its current width appears in a box above the column.

7.　S-l-o-w-l-y drag the mouse pointer left until the width is displayed as *8.00* (61 pixels). This may take some practice, and you may have to move the mouse back and forth until the width is just right.

8.　Release the mouse button to accept your change. Column D is now eight characters wide.

**NOTE:** You can increase or decrease column width by dragging the mouse pointer right or left respectively in the column frame.

## Double-clicking a Column Width

You can also let Excel automatically set an appropriate column width, so that it best fits the widest data in the column. Let's say you wanted to apply this to Column B. Try this:

1.　Point to the column divider between the B and C column labels in the frame.

2.　Double-click the frame at this point.
　　Column B has been adjusted to display the widest name.

## Changing the Text Position in a Cell

Figure E-20 shows the three possible ways to orient text in a cell: aligned left, centered, or aligned right. Aligned-left text starts at the left side of the cell; aligned-right text ends at the right side. Centered text is equally spaced from both edges of the cell.

| TEXT ← | TEXT | → TEXT |
|--------|------|--------|
| Aligned Left | Centered | Aligned Right |

**FIGURE E-20**    *Text Alignments Within a Cell*

By default, text is aligned left when first entered into a cell, as in row 3 of your worksheet. (Numbers are aligned right, as in column C.) However, like most things in Excel, text position in a cell is flexible. That is, it can be adjusted at any time *after* the text has been entered. This can be accomplished by mouse or by using a format cell command. In this example, you will adjust the three labels in columns C, D, and E. First, you'll use the menu approach, as follows:

### Changing Alignment by Menu

1.  Move to cell C3, which displays the HOURS label.

2.  To select the range of cells from C3 to E3, click C3 and then drag to E3.
    The three cells are identified within a rectangle.

**NOTE:**  When a range is displayed, the current cell appears "normal," whereas the remaining cells in the range are highlighted.

3.  Click the Alignment Dialog Box Launcher (*Home* tab, *Alignment* group).

4.  Click the Alignment tab if needed, as shown in Figure E-21a.

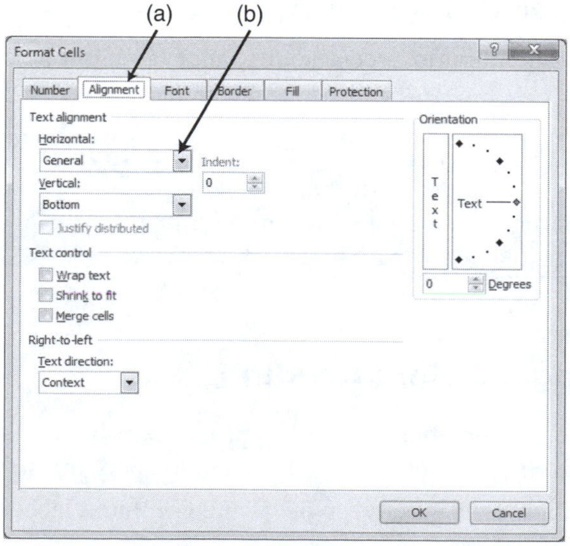

**FIGURE E-21**    *The Format Cells Dialog Box*

(a)   Click the Alignment tab.

(b)   Click the Horizontal drop-down arrow.

The Alignment section lets you adjust text position—horizontally, vertically, and even at an angle. You can now select the desired position.

5. Click the *Horizontal* drop-down arrow (as shown in Figure E-21b), then click *Right* (*Indent*) and press ⏎.

6. Click *OK* to accept the change.

7. Click anywhere to remove the highlight from the range.

The labels in cells C3, D3, and E3 are now aligned right.

### Changing Alignment by Command Button

The toolbar alignment buttons provide a much easier way to adjust text alignment in a cell by mouse. This exercise will change the text alignment in cells A10 and A11.

8. Click cell A10 to move there.

9. Drag the cell pointer down to cell A11 to identify the range (A10:A11).

10. Click the *Align Right* command button (*Home* tab, *Alignment* group).

11. Click anywhere to cancel the highlighted range.

The Total and Average text labels have been moved to the aligned-right position, as shown in Figure E-22. As you can see, the command button approach is much quicker, but the dialog box approach provides many additional options for you to explore and apply in the future.

|  | A | B | C | D | E |
|---|---|---|---|---|---|
| 1 | PAYROLL | | YOUR NAME & CLASS | | |
| 2 | | | | | |
| 3 | LAST | FIRST | HOURS | PAY | GROSS |
| 4 | | | | | |
| 5 | DeGlass | Phil | 42 | 3.5 | 147 |
| 6 | Endime | Nicole | 35 | 2.5 | 87.5 |
| 7 | Graw | Marty | 50 | 3.25 | 162.5 |
| 8 | Daize | Sunny | 32 | 6.75 | 216 |
| 9 | | | | | |
| 10 | Total | | | | 613 |
| 11 | Average | | | | 153.25 |

**FIGURE E-22** *The Worksheet with Right-Aligned Text*
The labels in Cells C3:E3 and A10:A11 have been right-aligned.

12. Save this amended worksheet as WORK3.

**NOTE:** You can orient text aligned right, aligned left, or centered using the same approach. Use the dialog box or command button technique as you prefer.

## Changing Value Format

Examine Figure E-23. When you enter values into cells, you type only numbers and decimal points. Once entered, there are many ways you can adjust a value's display to fit your needs. You may add dollar signs, commas, or fix the number of decimal places shown.

| A value typed as 1234.56 will look like: | # of Decimal Places | | |
|---|---|---|---|
| Default FORMAT type | 0 | 1 | 2 |
| Number (without separator) | 1235 | 1234.6 | 1234.56 |
| Comma | 1,235 | 1,234.6 | 1,234.56 |
| Accounting | $    1,235 | $    1,234.6 | $    1,234.56 |

**FIGURE E-23**   *A Few Value Formats*

For example, *number format* locks in a fixed number of decimal places; *comma format* will add commas if the value equals or exceeds 1,000; *accounting (currency) format* adds dollar signs. Negative numbers will appear with a minus sign in number format; comma or accounting formats show negative values in parentheses. Most often, accounting format and comma format will meet your needs and are included in Excel as command buttons.

**NOTE:** Accounting (currency format)—using the $ command button—places the dollar signs at the extreme left of the cell. It is customary to place dollar signs only in the top value and summary values in a column of numbers.

It is easy to change basic cell appearance and formatting using a mouse and toolbar button. The menu approach provides additional flexibility in assigning formats. (You can explore these features on your own. Here you will use the command button approach.)

### Command Button Approach to Formatting

1. Click cell D5 to set the upper-left corner of the range to be changed.

2. Click and drag the cell pointer to cell E11 to set the entire range, as in Figure E-24.

$  3. Click the *Accounting* button to select the format (*Home* tab, *Number* group).

4. Click anywhere to cancel the highlighted range.

|    | A | B | C | D | E | F |
|----|-----|-------|-------|------|--------|---|
| 1  | PAYROLL | | YOUR NAME & CLASS | | | |
| 2  | | | | | | |
| 3  | LAST | FIRST | HOURS | PAY | GROSS | |
| 4  | | | | | | |
| 5  | DeGlass | Phil | 42 | 3.5 | 147 | |
| 6  | Endime | Nicole | 35 | 2.5 | 87.5 | |
| 7  | Graw | Marty | 50 | 3.25 | 162.5 | |
| 8  | Daize | Sunny | 32 | 6.75 | 216 | |
| 9  | | | | | | |
| 10 | Total | | | | 613 | |
| 11 | Average | | | | 153.25 | |
| 12 | | | | | | |

Range set

**FIGURE E-24**   *Formatting by Command Button*

Set the range by clicking the upper-left cell (D5) and dragging to the lower-right (E11).

The *Accounting* style adds dollar signs and displays values with two decimal places.

**NOTE:** You can adjust the number of decimals displayed by setting the range and then clicking the *Increase Decimal* or *Decrease Decimal* command buttons (*Home* tab, *Number* group). Each click changes the display by one digit.

Now try changing the number format in the middle rows to remove the dollar signs. You do this by using the comma format instead of accounting.

5.  Click cell D6, then drag the pointer to cell E8, as in Figure E-25.

6.  Click the *Comma* command button (*Home* tab, *Number* group).

7.  Click outside the highlighted range to deselect it.

|  | A | B | C | D | E | F |
|---|---|---|---|---|---|---|
| 1 | PAYROLL | | YOUR NAME & CLASS | | | |
| 2 | | | | | | |
| 3 | LAST | FIRST | HOURS | PAY | GROSS | |
| 4 | | | | | | |
| 5 | DeGlass | Phil | 42 | $  3.50 | $ 147.00 | |
| 6 | Endime | Nicole | 35 | $  2.50 | $  87.50 | |
| 7 | Graw | Marty | 50 | $  3.25 | $ 162.50 | |
| 8 | Daize | Sunny | 32 | $  6.75 | $ 216.00 | |
| 9 | | | | | | |
| 10 | Total | | | | $ 613.00 | |
| 11 | Average | | | | $ 153.25 | |
| 12 | | | | | | |

**FIGURE E-25**   *Setting a Comma Format*

Select the range that does not include the top or summary rows (D6:E8).

Your worksheet now has dollar signs only in the top row, total, and average cells, as shown in Figure E-26.

|  | A | B | C | D | E |
|---|---|---|---|---|---|
| 1 | PAYROLL | | YOUR NAME & CLASS | | |
| 2 | | | | | |
| 3 | LAST | FIRST | HOURS | PAY | GROSS |
| 4 | | | | | |
| 5 | DeGlass | Phil | 42 | $  3.50 | $ 147.00 |
| 6 | Endime | Nicole | 35 | 2.50 | 87.50 |
| 7 | Graw | Marty | 50 | 3.25 | 162.50 |
| 8 | Daize | Sunny | 32 | 6.75 | 216.00 |
| 9 | | | | | |
| 10 | Total | | | | $ 613.00 |
| 11 | Average | | | | $ 153.25 |

**FIGURE E-26**   *The Worksheet with Format Changes*

8.   When you are finished, save the worksheet again as WORK3.

     *WARNING:* Although you may change a cell's appearance with the format command, the worksheet still uses the *actual* value within the cell. This can result in numbers that do not exactly add up. For example, if you typed .8 in one cell and then multiplied it by four, the answer 3.2 would appear as expected. However, if you change the format of these cells to display *no decimal places*, the .8 would appear as a 1 and the 3.2 would appear as a 3, thus appearing to show that 1 * 4 = 3.

> **NOTE:** If number signs (#####) fill a cell after you've changed its format or column width, it means that the cell is too *narrow* to show the value. To correct this problem, you must either make the column wider or change the format.

## LESSON 7: COPYING THE CONTENTS OF CELLS

Although you could *type* every formula you need into an appropriate cell in a worksheet, it is much faster and easier to create one formula and then copy it everywhere else. Excel allows you to easily copy the contents of one or more cells to other cells in the worksheet.

     Labels and values, which are constants, will not change when they are copied to other cells. Formulas, on the other hand, will adjust their answers relative to their new location. To prepare for this exercise, complete the following steps:

1.   Open WORK3, which should resemble Figure E-26.

2.   To more clearly see the results of your work, first erase the contents of cells E6, E7, and E8. Use the erase technique you learned earlier: Click cell E6, drag the mouse pointer to cell E8, then press DELETE.

> **NOTE:** Once you have mastered the copy techniques, you need not erase cells before you copy into them, but erasing the cells here allows you to see the result of your actions as you learn the procedure.

     You are now ready to practice the copy command using both the command button approach and a more direct, mouse only, approach.

### Copying from One Cell to Another Cell

Copying the contents of one cell to another is easy. Assume that you want to copy the formula in cell E5 into cell E6 without having to retype the formula all over again. Here's how to do it:

1.   Click the cell whose contents you want to copy (in this example, cell E5).

2.   Click the Copy command button (*Home* tab, *Clipboard* group)—or press CTRL + **C**.

     A blinking rectangle appears around the cell to be copied, and a message in the status bar prompts you to "Select destination ...."

3.   Click cell E6—the cell in which you want the formula to appear.

**4.**   Click the Paste command button (*Home* tab, *Clipboard* group) or press ⏎ to paste the formula into cell E6.

The formula has been copied, and its result appears in the new cell. Note that the answer is not the same in both cells. The formula in E6 calculates the gross pay for Nicole, exactly the same way as the formula in cell E5 calculates Phil's gross pay. The structure of the formula in cell E6 is exactly the same as cell E5, but its references have been adjusted to reflect that it is now one row lower.

## Copying from One Cell to Many Cells

Copying the contents of one cell to a range of cells is a much more powerful command. Assume you want to copy the contents of cell E5 into all the cells in the column down to cell E8. Although you could use the *Copy* and then *Paste* approach, Excel's "fill handle" offers a much easier way to do this.

### Using the Fill Handle to Copy

A much faster copy technique uses the mouse and the "fill handle" of the cell pointer.

**1.**   Click cell E5 to select it.

**2.**   Point to the *fill handle* located at the lower-right corner of the cell pointer, as shown in Figure E-27a. (When correctly positioned, the mouse pointer resembles a small plus sign.)

**3.**   Click and drag the *plus sign* to cell E8, the last cell of the destination range of the copy, as shown in Figure E-27b. The cells E6, E7, and E8 will be highlighted.

**4.**   Release the mouse button and then click anywhere.

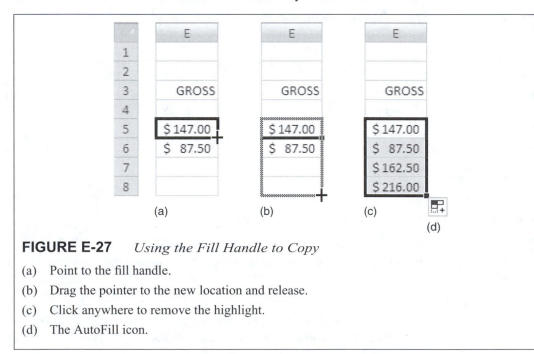

**FIGURE E-27**   *Using the Fill Handle to Copy*

(a)   Point to the fill handle.

(b)   Drag the pointer to the new location and release.

(c)   Click anywhere to remove the highlight.

(d)   The AutoFill icon.

The cell contents have been copied, as in Figure E-27c. Use whichever copy technique you prefer—menu or fill handle.

The formula will copy correctly into each of the three cells in the range E6:E8, with the results adjusted relative to each row.

An "AutoFill" icon (as shown in Figure E-27d) may appear when you copy.

**5.** If the AutoFill icon appears, double-click *any* cell to remove it.

Copying a cell's contents to other cells also copies its formatting. While this is usually an added bonus, you may, at times, have to reformat the copied cells. Try this:

**6.** Identify the range E6:E8 if needed.

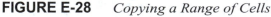

**7.** Click the *Comma* button now to select the proper format.

**8.** Click anywhere to deselect the range.

**9.** Save this worksheet as WORK4.

## Copying a Range of Cells

You can also copy the contents of more than one cell at a time. To do this, you must identify the range prior to invoking the copy command. Practice this technique by copying the contents of the cells in row 5 to row 13. Of course, you can copy a column of cells the same way.

**1.** Click cell A5, the start of the row to copy.

**2.** Click and drag the mouse pointer to cell E5 as shown in Figure E-28a.

**FIGURE E-28**　*Copying a Range of Cells*

(a)  Identify the range to be copied.

(b)  Click at the start of the new location and release.

Now that the range of cells has been specified, you can invoke the copy command as before.

**3.** Click the *Copy* command button (*Home* tab, *Clipboard* group).

The outlining rectangle should now appear around the entire range that will be copied. The message "Select destination …" appears in the status bar.

**4.** Click cell A13 to indicate the start of the destination range.

**5.** Click the Paste command button (or press (CTRL) + **V**).

**NOTE:** You should only identify the *first* cell of the new range. Excel already knows that other cells will be copied, because they were specified in the range before you invoked the copy command.

The contents of the cells in row 5 should be copied to row 13, as shown in Figure E-28b.

**6.** Close this worksheet *without* saving the changes.

## LESSON 8: INSERTING AND DELETING ROWS OR COLUMNS

Spreadsheet programs let you insert new rows or columns anywhere in the worksheet or delete unwanted rows and columns just as easily.

*WARNING:* Deletion should be done with care. Errors will occur if you delete a cell that appears elsewhere in a formula. For example, if you remove the HOURS column from your worksheet, the GROSS column formulas, which depend on the HOURS values, will not work.

### Inserting a Row or Column

**1.** Open WORK4.

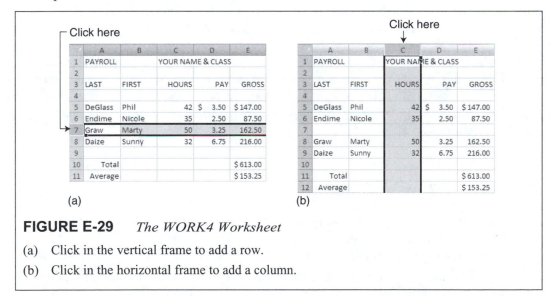

**FIGURE E-29**    *The WORK4 Worksheet*

(a)   Click in the vertical frame to add a row.

(b)   Click in the horizontal frame to add a column.

To *insert a row* above MARTY GRAW (row 7), follow these steps:

**2.** Click the row 7 identifier in the vertical frame (as shown in Figure E-29a).

**3.** Click the *Insert* command button (*Home* tab, *Cells* group). A new row appears.

**NOTE:** When you insert a new row, any function range that includes it will automatically expand to reflect the addition. In this case, the SUM and AVERAGE function ranges have expanded by one row.

Now, *insert a column* to the left of the HOURS column (column C) as follows:

4. Click the C Column identifier in the frame (as shown in Figure E-29b).

5. Click the *Insert* command button. A new column appears.

6. Double-click any cell to remove highlights.

The worksheet should resemble Figure E-30. Note how the rows below row 7 (the inserted row) have moved down one row and the columns to the right of column C (the inserted column) have shifted to the right.

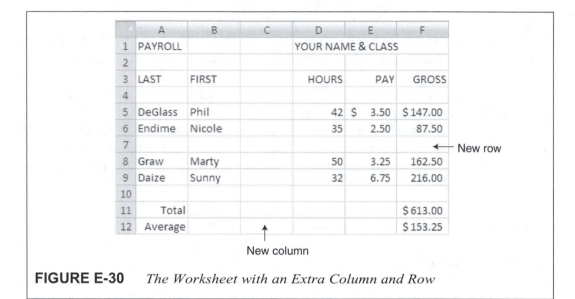

**FIGURE E-30** *The Worksheet with an Extra Column and Row*

**NOTE:** If the last column or row "disappears" off the screen when you insert new ones, it is not lost. There is simply not enough room to show it on your screen. You can always move the pointer or scroll down or right to see it when needed.

## Deleting a Row or Column

You can also delete unwanted rows or columns. Make sure that you are in the correct column or row before you delete it.

To *delete* the blank row above MARTY GRAW (row 7), follow the steps below:

1. Click the row 7 identifier in the frame, as shown in Figure E-31a. The entire row should be highlighted.

2. Click the *Delete* command button (*Home* tab, *Cells* group).

The row is gone. Note how the rows have moved up to take its place.

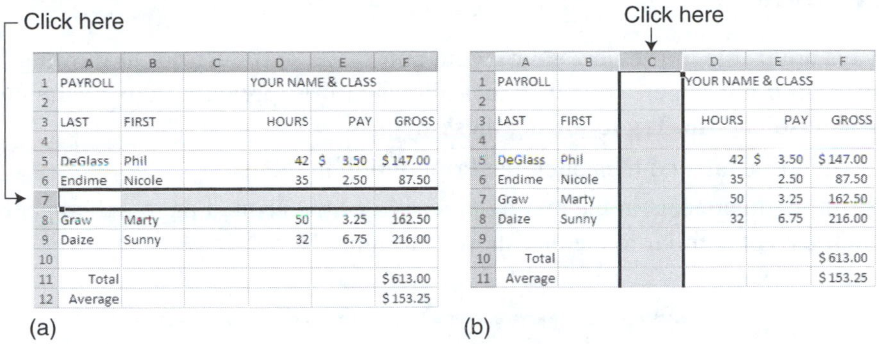

**FIGURE E-31** *Deleting an Entire Row and Column*

(a)   Click the row identifier in the left frame to select the row.

(b)   Click the column identifier in the top frame to select the column.

**NOTE:** If you delete a row (or column) by mistake, click the *Undo* quick access toolbar button to bring it back.

Now, delete the blank column (column C):

**3.** Click the column C identifier in the frame, as shown in Figure E-31b.

**4.** Click the *Delete* command button (*Home* tab, *Cells* group).

The column is no longer there. Columns to its right have been shifted to the left to fill in the space created by deleting column C.

**5.** Do not save this worksheet, but simply close it by clicking the *Microsoft Office Button*, *Close*, *No*.

## LESSON 9: PRINTING A WORKSHEET

Your goal in creating a worksheet is not only to view it on a screen, but to produce printed spreadsheets (called *hardcopies*). Worksheets can be printed in whole or in part. Extremely wide worksheets may be printed in smaller sections that can then be taped together. Depending on your printer, you may also be able to produce hardcopy in compressed print to fit on smaller sheets.

This module presents *basic* worksheet printing. Some changes in type style, size, and other printer characteristics will be demonstrated at the end of the module, but fancier techniques remain for you to investigate on your own.

**1.** Open the WORK4 workbook.

**2.** Make sure your printer is ready: connected to your computer, power on, and has paper.

## Print Preview

It is always advisable to preview your layout and range settings prior to printing. This not only saves time but paper as well. Excel allows you to preview your document on the screen if you so choose. Try following these steps:

**1.** Click the File tab and then click the Print option in the list.

A Print menu appears at the left and a replica of the printed page will appear on your screen on the right, similar to the one shown in Figure E-32a.

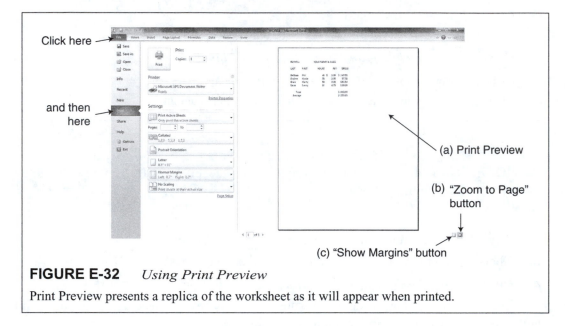

**FIGURE E-32**     *Using Print Preview*

Print Preview presents a replica of the worksheet as it will appear when printed.

**2.** Click the *Zoom to Page* button in the lower right corner to look more closely at the image, as in Figure E-32b.

You can use the scroll bars to move around the screen to examine the proposed output.

**3.** Now, click the "Show Margins" button, as shown in Figure E-32c. Lines appear displaying your margins, as in Figure E-33.

**4.** Click both buttons to remove margins and zoom.

Settings in the Print menu let you set a number of parameters:
- Portion: Active sheets, Entire workbook, or selection
- Specific pages
- Orientation: Landscape or Portrait
- Size of paper
- Margins
- Scaling—percent of full size

**5.** Click the Home tab to end the preview.

Get into the habit of using Print Preview to examine your worksheets before printing. In the long run, you'll save a lot of paper and time.

## Printing a Worksheet

If you do not set any specific range, Excel will automatically print the entire worksheet from the upper-left corner (A1) to the cell in the last row and column that contains an entry. Try this example:

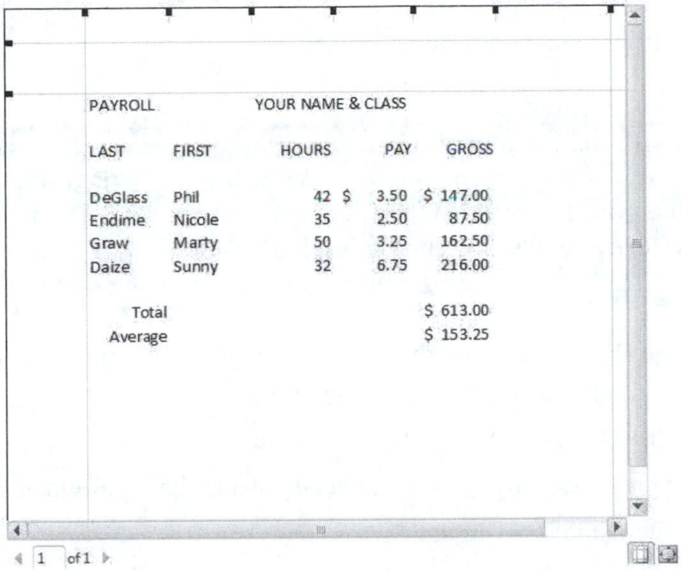

| | | | | |
|---|---|---|---|---|
| PAYROLL | | YOUR NAME & CLASS | | |
| | | | | |
| LAST | FIRST | HOURS | PAY | GROSS |
| | | | | |
| DeGlass | Phil | 42 $ | 3.50 | $ 147.00 |
| Endime | Nicole | 35 | 2.50 | 87.50 |
| Graw | Marty | 50 | 3.25 | 162.50 |
| Daize | Sunny | 32 | 6.75 | 216.00 |
| | | | | |
| Total | | | | $ 613.00 |
| Average | | | | $ 153.25 |

◄ 1 of 1 ►

**FIGURE E-33**    *Print Preview with Margins*

1. Click the File tab and then *Print* to return to the print menu.

2. For now, click the Home tab to end the process. (You'll print later.)

At times, you may want to print a portion of your worksheet, or you may have to re-move a previous range setting that you no longer want. The way to do this is to identify the range of cells you want to print *before* invoking the print command. In this example, you will print the first three columns only—last name, first name, and hours worked. Try this:

3. Identify the desired print area range—A1:C8, as shown in Figure E-34. Click the first cell (A1), drag the mouse pointer to the last cell (C8), and then release the mouse.

4. Click the File tab and then *Print*.

| | A | B | C | D | E |
|---|---|---|---|---|---|
| 1 | PAYROLL | | YOUR NAME & CLASS | | |
| 2 | | | | | |
| 3 | LAST | FIRST | HOURS | PAY | GROSS |
| 4 | | | | | |
| 5 | DeGlass | Phil | 42 | $ 3.50 | $ 147.00 |
| 6 | Endime | Nicole | 35 | 2.50 | 87.50 |
| 7 | Graw | Marty | 50 | 3.25 | 162.50 |
| 8 | Daize | Sunny | 32 | 6.75 | 216.00 |
| 9 | | | | | |
| 10 | Total | | | | $ 613.00 |
| 11 | Average | | | | $ 153.25 |

Print range selected

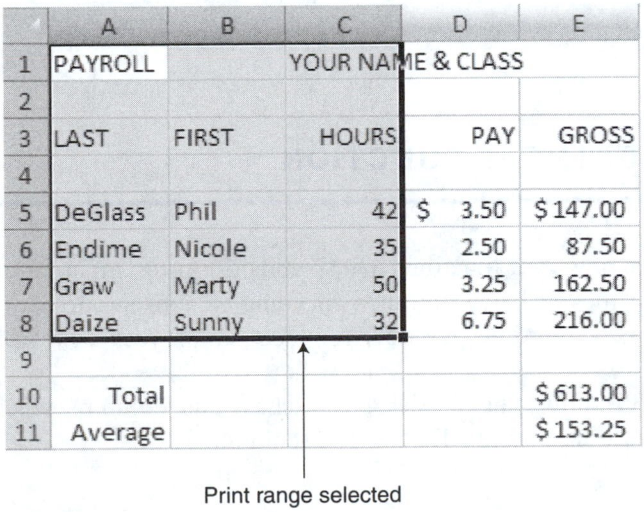

**FIGURE E-34**    *Setting a Print Range*

The selected range (A1:C8) is ready to print.

5.  In the first settings box, click the drop down arrow to access its menu (which currently shows "Print Active Sheets").

6.  Click the "Print Selection" option.

> **NOTE:** If you want to print the entire worksheet, there should be no range specified at all. Simply select the *Print Active Sheets* option in the Print settings before invoking the print command. When in doubt, use Print Preview to see how much of your worksheet will print. Then adjust it as needed.

7.  Examine the *Preview* at the right, which displays the potential hardcopy. Note how only the selected cells will be printed.

8.  Close the Print Preview by clicking the Home tab.

9.  Cancel the print range by clicking any cell outside the highlighted area.

10. Close the file *without* saving it.

**Quick Review #2**

1.  How does your printed worksheet compare to its screen image?
    _____

2.  What range would you specify to print all rows in the worksheet except for the TOTAL and AVERAGE rows? _____

3.  What range would you specify to print only the first names of employees and display their corresponding HOURS, PAY, and GROSS? _____

> **NOTE:** Sometimes worksheets are too wide to fit on regular 8-1/2 inch x 11 inch paper. When that happens, you can adjust some options in the print routine, such as the margin or paper size. Although these situations are beyond the scope of this introduction, you may want to investigate the options in the Page Layout tab of the ribbon.

## LESSON 10: THE IF FUNCTION

One of the more powerful functions in a spreadsheet program automates simple decisions by comparing values or labels and then choosing an appropriate action. For instance, you might want to add overtime pay only for those employees who had worked more than forty hours.

Figure E-35 shows the WORK4 worksheet and columns where you will add the OVERTIME (column F) and ADJ GROSS (column G).

**FIGURE E-35**   *Adjusting Column Headings*

Headings have been added in columns E, F, and G.

First, you'll add new column headings to the worksheet:

**1.** Open the WORK3 worksheet.

**2.** Type **REG** in cell E2, **OVER** in cell F2, and **TIME** in cell F3.

**3.** Type **ADJ** in cell G2 and **GROSS** in cell G3 to finish the headings.

**4.** Right-align the labels in cells E2:G3. (Identify the range and then click the *Right Align* command button.) Your screen should resemble Figure E-35.

## IF Function Logic

You will create an IF function in cells E5 through F8 so Excel can make some decisions. The format is **=IF(test, true, false)**, where a test is first, followed by the two alternatives you want Excel to follow based on the truth of the test. The "true" alternative will be placed in the cell if the test is true. The "false" one will be used if the test turns out to be false.

The test is an equation that relates two values. These values can include cell addresses, formulas, functions, or constants. The values can be compared using such relational operators as $=$, $>$, $<$, $>=$, and $<=$. The actions to be taken can be text, numbers, formulas, or functions as well. For example, here are a few valid IF functions.

| FORMULA | MEANING |
|---|---|
| =IF(A1=5, "Yes", "No") | If the value in cell A1 is 5, display "Yes." If it is not, display "No." |
| =IF(A1>A7,=SUM(A1:A5), 0) | If the value in cell A1 exceeds the value in cell A7, display the total of the range A1:A5. If it is not, display zero. |

**NOTE:** You can also combine two conditions by using the connectors #AND# and #OR#. With an #AND# connector, both conditions must be true for the test to be true; with an #OR# connector, either condition can be true for the test to be true. Examine these examples: =IF(A1=5#AND#A2=6, "Yes", "No"), =IF(A1*5>A7#OR#B2<5, =MAX(A1:A5),0).

## Creating the IF Function

It is now time to make your worksheet more realistic by including overtime pay. In most cases, overtime is calculated as "time and a half." In this example, you will have to change the formula for GROSS to restrict it to regular pay only for the first forty hours. You will also add a new formula to calculate a bonus of *one and one-half times* hourly pay for each extra hour over forty that an employee may have worked.

Thus, the column E, REG GROSS formulas must be changed to say "If the hours worked exceed 40, then multiply only 40 hours times the hourly pay. However, if the hours do not exceed 40, multiply the actual hours worked by the hourly pay." In cell E5, for example, the IF formula would read "=IF(C5>40,40*D5,C5*D5)."

Formulas must also be entered in Column F to calculate the additional overtime pay. Here, you will need to say "If the hours worked exceed 40, then multiply one and one-half times the hourly pay times the extra hours. If not, put a zero in this cell." In cell F5, for example, the IF formula would read: "=IF(C5>40,1.5*D5*(C5-40),0)"

> **NOTE:** Remember the order of operations? The parentheses are needed in "C5-40" to ensure that this subtraction takes place *before* the multiplication.

Here's how to make these changes:

1. Click cell E5 and type **=IF(C5>40,40*D5,C5*D5)** and then press ⏎.

Note that as you type the function, a "tool tip" displays the portion of the IF statement on which you are currently working. It also shows the referenced cells in colored highlights.

2. Copy this formula from cell E5 into the other three cells in column E. (Use the fill handle or click E5, click *Copy*, drag to E8, click *Paste*.)

You can now add the overtime IF formula in column F as follows:

3. Click cell F5 and type **=IF(C5>40,1.5*D5*(C5-40),0)** and then press ⏎.

4. Copy this formula from cell F5 into the other three cells in column F.

5. Click anywhere to cancel the range.

You should now see REGULAR GROSS and OVERTIME *values*, as shown in Figure E-36. If not, go back and correct the formulas. (Your formatting may differ. Do not worry about it for now.)

| | A | B | C | D | E | F | G |
|---|---|---|---|---|---|---|---|
| 1 | PAYROLL | | YOUR NAME & CLASS | | | | |
| 2 | | | | | REG | OVER | ADJ |
| 3 | LAST | FIRST | HOURS | PAY | GROSS | TIME | GROSS |
| 4 | | | | | | | |
| 5 | DeGlass | Phil | 42 | $ 3.50 | 140 | 10.5 | |
| 6 | Endime | Nicole | 35 | 2.50 | 87.5 | 0 | |
| 7 | Graw | Marty | 50 | 3.25 | 130 | 48.75 | |
| 8 | Daize | Sunny | 32 | 6.75 | 216 | 0 | |
| 9 | | | | | | | |
| 10 | Total | | | | $ 573.50 | | |
| 11 | Average | | | | $ 143.38 | | |

**FIGURE E-36**    *Using the IF Function*

Regular gross and overtime are calculated using two sets of IF functions.

Now you can create a formula that will add the regular gross to the overtime pay to calculate the total adjusted gross.

6.  Move to cell G5, type **=E5+F5** and press ⏎. .

7.  Copy the formula in G5 down the column through G8. Check your answers to see that cells G5 and G7 have been increased by the overtime pay.

8.  Now copy the SUM formula that already exists in cell E10 into cells F10 and G10 so that totals appear for the two new columns.

> **NOTE:** An advantage to *copying* is that any format you've set in the old cell will also copy into the new one, saving you the trouble of formatting it later on. Copying also helps you avoid introducing mistakes.

9.  In the same way, copy the AVERAGE formula from E11 into cells F11 and G11 to average the two new columns.

10. The last step is to change the format in columns E, F, and G to match the format in the rest of the worksheet. Use the techniques you learned earlier to change the cells in rows 5, 10, and 11 to currency format with two decimal places (use the $ command button), and the remaining cells to comma format, two decimals (use the comma command button). Your worksheet should resemble Figure E-37.

11. Save the new worksheet as WORK5. (Use Save As.)

| | A | B | C | D | E | F | G |
|---|---|---|---|---|---|---|---|
| 1 | PAYROLL | | YOUR NAME & CLASS | | | | |
| 2 | | | | | REG | OVER | ADJ |
| 3 | LAST | FIRST | HOURS | PAY | GROSS | TIME | GROSS |
| 4 | | | | | | | |
| 5 | DeGlass | Phil | 42 | $ 3.50 | $140.00 | $ 10.50 | $150.50 |
| 6 | Endime | Nicole | 35 | 2.50 | 87.50 | - | 87.50 |
| 7 | Graw | Marty | 50 | 3.25 | 130.00 | 48.75 | 178.75 |
| 8 | Daize | Sunny | 32 | 6.75 | 216.00 | - | 216.00 |
| 9 | | | | | | | |
| 10 | Total | | | | $573.50 | $ 59.25 | $632.75 |
| 11 | Average | | | | $143.38 | $ 14.81 | $158.19 |

**FIGURE E-37**   *The Adjusted Worksheet*
Overtime and adjusted gross are calculated and formatted.

## LESSON 11: FREEZING TITLES AND ABSOLUTE ADDRESSING

As you build larger worksheets, your screen may be unable to display the entire worksheet all at once. The following steps illustrate this point:

1.  Open WORK5 if needed. Press CTRL + HOME to go to cell A1.

2.  Move slowly by pressing the → key until you get to the last column currently on your screen (typically O). So far, so good.

3. Press $\rightarrow$ once more.

As the next column appears on the screen, the last names in column A disappear. They are not really gone, but can no longer be seen in the window area on your screen.

4. Now press $\rightarrow$ to move to the next column.

The first names have vanished as well.

5. Press CTRL + HOME.

## Freezing Titles

Losing sight of the row labels on the left of your worksheet makes data and formula entry more difficult, because you can't easily see which line refers to the data on screen. You can solve this problem by "freezing" the labels in the left columns (the row *titles*) in place. Once frozen, these titles will stay on the screen even when you move the cell pointer. Try the following exercise:

1. Move to cell C5.

The columns to the *left* of this point and the rows above it can now be "frozen" as in Figure E-38a.

2. Click the *View* tab and then *Freeze Panes* (in the *Windows* group).

3. Click the first *Freeze Panes* option in the list to freeze both the row and column titles in place at this point.

A vertical and horizontal line mark the extent of the "frozen" area, as shown in Figure E-38b.

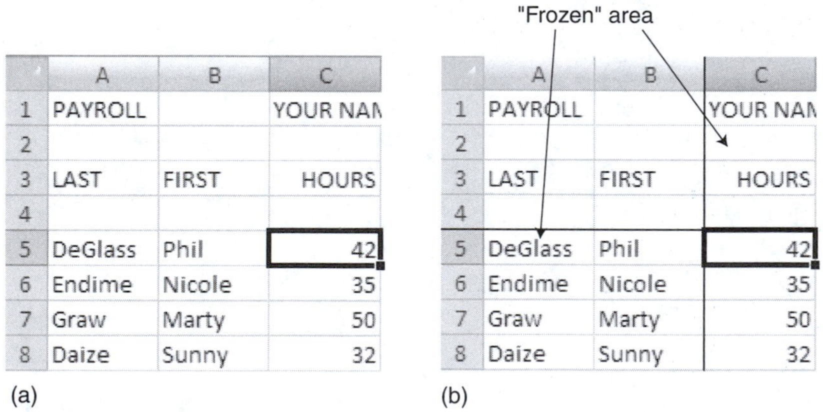

"Frozen" area

|   | A | B | C |
|---|---|---|---|
| 1 | PAYROLL | | YOUR NAM |
| 2 | | | |
| 3 | LAST | FIRST | HOURS |
| 4 | | | |
| 5 | DeGlass | Phil | 42 |
| 6 | Endime | Nicole | 35 |
| 7 | Graw | Marty | 50 |
| 8 | Daize | Sunny | 32 |

(a)

|   | A | B | C |
|---|---|---|---|
| 1 | PAYROLL | | YOUR NAM |
| 2 | | | |
| 3 | LAST | FIRST | HOURS |
| 4 | | | |
| 5 | DeGlass | Phil | 42 |
| 6 | Endime | Nicole | 35 |
| 7 | Graw | Marty | 50 |
| 8 | Daize | Sunny | 32 |

(b)

**FIGURE E-38**    *Freezing Titles*

(a)  Position the pointer in the cell to the right and below the desired "freeze" point.

(b)  Horizontal and vertical lines mark the "frozen" area.

**NOTE:** To freeze columns only, place the cell pointer in row 1; to freeze rows only, place the pointer in column A. To clear the frozen titles, click *Window*, *Unfreeze Panes*.

4. Move to cell R5. Notice how columns A and B stay on the screen!

5.  Press CTRL + HOME . Notice how you return to the first cell *below* and to the *right* of the frozen titles.

6.  Press ↵ , or use the scroll bar, until the cell pointer is in the bottom row on your screen—perhaps 28.

7.  Press ↵ twice more.

Notice how the top titles remain on the screen. You can position the freeze anywhere you want. You may also leave titles frozen or unfrozen as you desire.

## Unfreezing Titles

1.  You do not have to be in any particular cell to unfreeze titles. Simply click the *Freeze Panes* button (*View* tab, *Windows* group) and then the, *Unfreeze Panes* option to unfreeze. Do this now.

2.  Move around the worksheet to see that the columns and rows are no longer frozen.

3.  Close the window when you're done *without* saving the worksheet. (Use the *Microsoft Office Button*, *Close*, *No*.)

## Absolute Addressing

If you type formulas into *every* cell where you need them, you would never have to worry about absolute cell addresses. Yet, as you have seen, it is much more efficient to type just one formula and then copy it to many other cells.

By default, cell references in formulas copy *relative* to the row and column where they appear. For example, if you copy the formula =A1 one row below it, it becomes =A2. If you copy it one column to the right, it becomes =B1. The formula stays relative to its new location. This is called a *relative cell address* and is fine for most copying (gross pay was copied in this way). Of course, constants, such as numbers and text, do not change when they are copied.

But what if you want your copied formulas to refer to the exact same cell as the first formula? In this case, the cell referenced in the formula must stay constant. For this you use an *absolute cell address*. In this simple model, say you want to calculate 7.65 percent (.0765) of the adjusted gross to cover Social Security tax (FICA). Try the following exercise:

1.  Open WORK5.

2.  Move to cell H3. Type **FICA**.

3.  Move to cell I3. Type **NET** and press ↵ .

4.  If needed, right-align the labels in cells H3:I3. (Identify the range and click the Right Align command button.)

5.  Move to cell H2, type **7.65**% and press ↵ .

You are now ready to create formulas that reference cell H2.

## Creating Absolute Cell Addresses

1.  Move to cell H5 and type **=G5*H2** but do not press ↵ . (If you did, retype the formula.)

If you were to copy this formula as is, the cell G5 reference will change relative to each row (which is fine), but the H2 reference will also change. It will become H3, then

H4, and so on. This is wrong! You want the reference to remain H2 so that each formula down the column will multiply the gross pay in that row by the value in cell H2, namely 7.65 percent. To adjust the reference, complete the following steps:

2. Press the [ F4 ] function key ([ F4 ] is the "Absolute" shortcut key) to change this cell reference from relative to absolute. Notice that the formula now reads =G5*$H$2.

The added dollar symbols indicate that the row and column references for H2 are now "absolute" and will remain unchanged when copied. Because there are no dollar symbols attached to the G5 reference, it will remain relative and will change when copied.

3. Press ↵ to complete the formula. Don't worry right now about formatting the cells—they currently use the format of cell G5. The rest is easy.

4. Use any copy method you like to copy the formula in cell H5 into the range H6:H8. (Click cell H5, drag the fill handle to cell H8, and release.)

5. If your results match the values shown in Figure E-39, then the formulas all work correctly. If not, go back and fix them.

| | A | B | C | D | E | F | G | H | I |
|---|---|---|---|---|---|---|---|---|---|
| 1 | PAYROLL | | YOUR NAME & CLASS | | | | | | |
| 2 | | | | | REG | OVER | ADJ | 7.65% | |
| 3 | LAST | FIRST | HOURS | PAY | GROSS | TIME | GROSS | FICA | NET |
| 4 | | | | | | | | | |
| 5 | DeGlass | Phil | 42 | $ 3.50 | $140.00 | $ 10.50 | $150.50 | $ 11.51 | |
| 6 | Endime | Nicole | 35 | 2.50 | 87.50 | - | 87.50 | $ 6.69 | |
| 7 | Graw | Marty | 50 | 3.25 | 130.00 | 48.75 | 178.75 | $ 13.67 | |
| 8 | Daize | Sunny | 32 | 6.75 | 216.00 | - | 216.00 | $ 16.52 | |
| 9 | | | | | | | | | |
| 10 | Total | | | | $573.50 | $ 59.25 | $632.75 | | |
| 11 | Average | | | | $143.38 | $ 14.81 | $158.19 | | |

**FIGURE E-39**    *Copying the Absolute Reference*

The absolute reference to $H$2 has been copied into each of the desired cells.

You can examine the effect of copying the absolute and relative references.

6. Point to each cell in the range H5:H8. As you move down the column, note how the G5 reference changes but H2 does not.

All you need to do now is to add formulas in the NET column and fix up some formatting as follows:

7. Move to cell I5, type **=G5-H5** and press ↵. This will subtract the FICA from the GROSS to calculate the NET payment.

**NOTE:** You could also *point* to each referenced cell instead of typing its address. In this case, you would press ⊜, point to G5, press ⊖, point to H5 and then press ↵.

8. Copy cell I5 into the cell range I6:I8.

9. Copy the SUM function in cell G10 into the range H10:I10.

10. Copy the AVERAGE function in cell G11 into the range H11:I11.

11. Now to fix the cell formats: Set the cells in range H5:I5 to accounting (currency) for-

mat (if needed) and those in H6:I8 to comma format. (Identify the range by dragging the mouse and then click the [$] or [,] command button in the *Home* tab as needed.) You're done. Your worksheet should resemble Figure E-40.

**12.** Save this worksheet as WORK6.

| | A | B | C | D | E | F | G | H | I |
|---|---|---|---|---|---|---|---|---|---|
| 1 | PAYROLL | | YOUR NAME & CLASS | | | | | | |
| 2 | | | | | REG | OVER | ADJ | 7.65% | |
| 3 | LAST | FIRST | HOURS | PAY | GROSS | TIME | GROSS | FICA | NET |
| 4 | | | | | | | | | |
| 5 | DeGlass | Phil | 42 | $ 3.50 | $140.00 | $ 10.50 | $150.50 | $ 11.51 | $138.99 |
| 6 | Endime | Nicole | 35 | 2.50 | 87.50 | - | 87.50 | 6.69 | 80.81 |
| 7 | Graw | Marty | 50 | 3.25 | 130.00 | 48.75 | 178.75 | 13.67 | 165.08 |
| 8 | Daize | Sunny | 32 | 6.75 | 216.00 | - | 216.00 | 16.52 | 199.48 |
| 9 | | | | | | | | | |
| 10 | Total | | | | $573.50 | $ 59.25 | $632.75 | $ 48.41 | $584.34 |
| 11 | Average | | | | $143.38 | $ 14.81 | $158.19 | $ 12.10 | $146.09 |

**FIGURE E-40**    *The Final Worksheet*

**NOTE:** You can change *any* reference by pressing [F4] after typing the reference and before you continue. If you continue to press [F4], all four absolute and mixed cell references will appear in sequence ($A$1, A$1, $A1, and A1). You can stop at the one you want to use. Of course, you can also type each "$" symbol yourself as needed in the formula. In these examples, the "$" before the "A" locks in the column reference, whereas the "$" before the "1" locks in the row reference. Using both locks in the entire reference.

## Tracking and Fixing Errors

There will be times when you will want to locate errors in your worksheet. Here's an easy technique that enables you to see the references in each cell:

**1.** Click to cell G5.

**2.** Press [F2] (the Edit shortcut key).

As shown in Figure E-41, the Insertion Point is placed at the end of the cell formula, ready to edit. The cells that are referenced in the formula are now color-coded for easy identification with their reference in the cell's formula. The corresponding cell is color-coded to match the reference. This allows you to track any mistakes and correct them. For now,

**3.** Press [ESC] to cancel.

| | SUM | ▾ | ✕ ✔ ƒ× | =E5+F5 | | | |
|---|---|---|---|---|---|---|---|
| | A | B | C | D | E | F | G |
| 1 | PAYROLL | | YOUR NAME & CLASS | | | | |
| 2 | | | | | REG | OVER | ADJ |
| 3 | LAST | FIRST | HOURS | PAY | GROSS | TIME | GROSS |
| 4 | | | | | | | |
| 5 | DeGlass | Phil | 42 | $ 3.50 | $140.00 | $ 10.50 | =E5+F5 |
| 6 | Endime | Nicole | 35 | 2.50 | 87.50 | - | 87.50 |
| 7 | Graw | Marty | 50 | 3.25 | 130.00 | 48.75 | 178.75 |
| 8 | Daize | Sunny | 32 | 6.75 | 216.00 | - | 216.00 |

**FIGURE E-41**    *Fixing Errors*

Pressing ⎡F2⎤ in a cell reveals all its cell references with color-coded markings.

## One Last Change

The advantage of putting the 7.65% in a separate cell (H2) will now become clear.

**1.** Click cell H2, type **8%** and press ⏎.

Notice that all the FICA deduction values in the column change to reflect an 8 percent deduction, because they all have formulas that refer to this one cell.

**2.** Close the window *without* saving it.

## LESSON 12: CREATING CHARTS AND SPARKLINES

Excel allows you to generate charts (graphs)—a visual representation of data—directly from worksheet data. In this exercise, you will create the column chart shown in Figure E-42, which compares gross pay and adjusted gross pay for the four employees in the worksheet. In this particular chart, employee first names will appear along the horizontal, or X, axis. Their corresponding regular and adjusted gross salaries will be graphed on the vertical, or Y, axis. Excel will automatically pick the appropriate ranges and layout for the data that will be displayed. You will also create a "sparkline"—a tiny chart placed in a worksheet cell to display data trends.

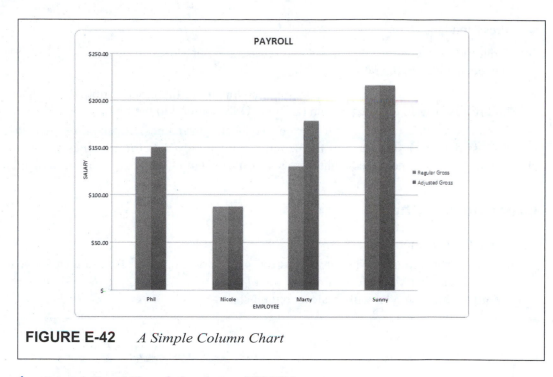

**FIGURE E-42**   *A Simple Column Chart*

1. Launch Excel if needed and open WORK5.

   You first need to specify the data ranges from which Excel will create a chart: These ranges should include the identifying labels and the data that you want to display. In general, you can select one range that contains a set of contiguous columns, or select individual columns if they are not contiguous, as in this example. Using Figure E-43 as a guide, do the following to select the needed columns for this chart:

2. Click cell B5.

3. Drag the mouse pointer to cell B8 and release. The first name column is selected.

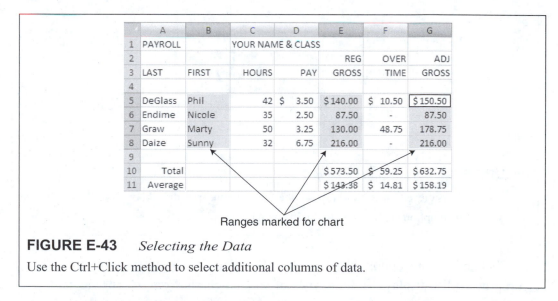

Ranges marked for chart

**FIGURE E-43**   *Selecting the Data*

Use the Ctrl+Click method to select additional columns of data.

If you tried to click another column now, the first selected column would be cancelled. To add a new column but *keep the old one*, the trick is to hold the ⌷CTRL⌷ key while you select each additional column.

4.   Press and hold ⌈CTRL⌋ and click cell E5.

5.   Drag the mouse pointer to cell E8 and release. The first data column (REG GROSS) has been added to the range.

6.   Press and hold ⌈CTRL⌋ and click cell G5 and then drag the mouse pointer to cell G8 and release to add the second data (ADJ GROSS) column to the range.

The three selected ranges identify the desired labels (first names), regular gross, and adjusted gross data. Note that each of the columns contain only data (no headings or totals) and that they are each the same height (four rows). You can now invoke the chart command.

## Creating the Chart

1.   Click the *Insert* tab on the ribbon.

Examine the chart group (as shown in Figure E-44a). You can select from among eleven basic types—the first six appear in the group. (To see more, click the *Other Charts* option.) For this exercise, you will create a column chart:

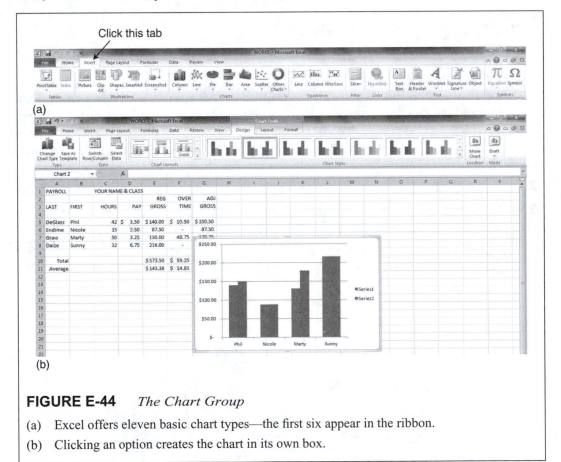

**FIGURE E-44**    *The Chart Group*

(a)   Excel offers eleven basic chart types—the first six appear in the ribbon.

(b)   Clicking an option creates the chart in its own box.

2.   Click the *Column* option.

A drop-down list displays various types of column charts from which you can select. For now,

3.   Click the first option in the 2-D Column group.

Your chart appears in a separate graphic box and a contextual tab ("Design") is added to the ribbon, as shown in Figure E-44b. You can switch the chart type, data, layout, style, and location. We'll try a few to see how it works.

***Chart Layouts.*** Excel offers eleven layouts. In this example, you will apply Layout #9:

4.  Click the *More* button on the right side of the Chart Layout group (as shown in Figure E-45a) to see all eleven layouts (as in Figure E-45b).

5.  Click Layout 9 (3rd row, 3rd column) to apply it.

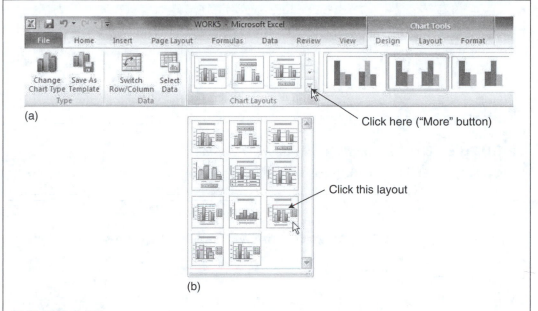

Click here ("More" button)

Click this layout

**FIGURE E-45**   *Applying a Chart Layout*

(a)   Click the *More* button to see Excel's eleven basic chart layouts.

(b)   The chart layouts appear beneath the ribbon.

    The selected chart layout has placeholders in which you can insert identifying titles for the chart and the two data axes. We will use these in a moment.

***Chart Style.*** Excel offers forty-eight styles of varying colors and dimensions. In this example, you will apply Style #3:

6.  Click the *More* button on the right side of the Chart Styles group to see all the available styles.

7.  Click Style #3 to apply it to your chart.

***Chart Location.*** Currently, the chart is an object contained within your worksheet. As such, it will be small and difficult to see clearly. Although charts can be used in this manner, it is better to place them on their own sheets to maximize their size and clarity.

8.  Click the *Move Chart* command button (Design tab, Location group) near the extreme right side of the ribbon.

    A *Move Chart* dialog box appears, as shown in Figure E-46.

9.  Click the *New Sheet* option, then click OK.

    The chart appears maximized on its own sheet with a tab added at the bottom of the worksheet (as in Figure E-47). Now it only remains to add some identifying titles and legend entries. (The goal is to get the chart to look like the sample shown earlier in Figure E-42.)

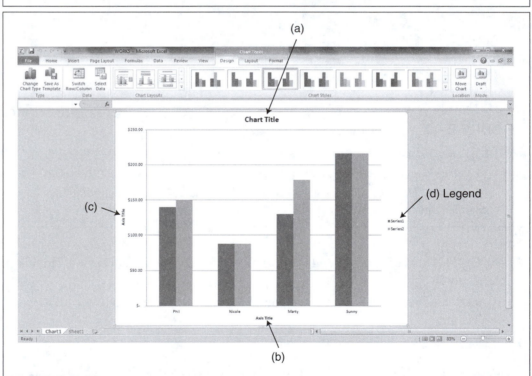

**FIGURE E-46**   *Placing the Chart on its Own Sheet*

Click the "New Sheet" option to place the chart on its own page.

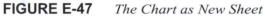

**FIGURE E-47**   *The Chart as New Sheet*

The Chart appears maximized in its own sheet in the workbook.

(a)   Chart Title

(b)   Horizontal Axis Title

(c)   Vertical Axis Title

(d)   Legend

The chart and axes titles can be changed by simply clicking on them and typing new entries:

**10.** Click the "Chart Title" placeholder (at the top of the chart as in Figure E-47a) to select it.

**11.** Click to the left of the "C" in "Chart" to set the insertion point there.

**12.** Delete the text and type **PAYROLL** as the new title.

Now, the axes identifiers:

**13.** Click the horizontal axis title (at the bottom of the chart, as in Figure E-47b) to select it.

**14.** Click to the left of the "A" in "Axis."

**15.** Delete the text, and type **EMPLOYEE**.

**16.** Click the vertical axis title (on the left side of the chart, as in Figure E-47c) to select it.

**17.** Since this text is placed vertically, click *below* the "A" in "Axis."

**18.** Delete the text, and type **SALARY**.

**19.** Click anywhere in the chart.

   The titles are done. Now to complete the legend, which appears at the right of the chart.

> **NOTE:** Legends are useful *only* when there is more than one set of data to identify them to the reader. (When only one set of data appears in a chart, the legend can be deleted—which also creates more space for the chart data.)

   To change the legend identifiers:

**20.** Click the Select Data command button (*Design* tab, *Data* group).

   A Select Data Source dialog box appears, as shown in Figure E-48a.

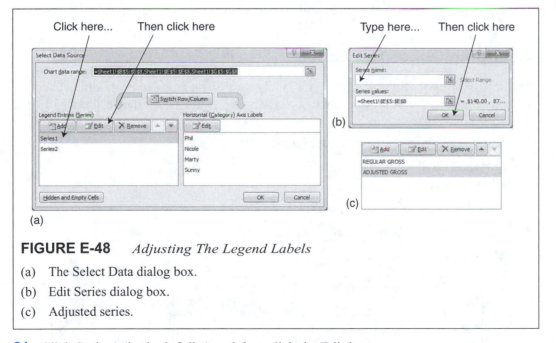

**FIGURE E-48**   *Adjusting The Legend Labels*

(a)   The Select Data dialog box.

(b)   Edit Series dialog box.

(c)   Adjusted series.

**21.** Click Series1 (in the left list) and then click the Edit button.

   An Edit Series dialog box appears, as shown in Figure E-48b.

**22.** Type **REGULAR GROSS** in the Series Name entry box and then click OK.

**23.** Click Series2 (in the left list of the Select Data Source dialog box) and click the *Edit* button just above it.

**24.** Type **ADJUSTED GROSS** in the Series Name entry box and then click OK.

The left side of the dialog box should now resemble Figure E-48c, with both series now correctly identified. (Repeat steps 21-24 if they do not.)

**25.** Click *OK* to accept the changes.

You can also move the legend wherever needed. For example, one last adjustment:

**26.** Click anywhere within the legend—a box appears around it.

**27.** Click any line in the box and drag it slightly to the left, then release the mouse.

Your screen should now match Figure E-42.

> **NOTE:** Charts tend to be easier to understand with fewer data sets. Try to limit the amount of data you display on a chart.

**28.** Save this workbook as WORK5 again.

Both the worksheet and chart are saved as pages within the same WORK5 workbook. If you make changes to the worksheet data, the chart will automatically be adjusted to reflect the new data. It is easy to jump back and forth. Simply click the appropriate sheet tab at the bottom of the workbook window. Try this:

**29.** Click the *Sheet1* tab to switch to the worksheet.

**30.** Click cell C5. Change Phil's hours to **15** and press ⏎.

**31.** Now click the *Chart1* tab to switch back to the chart.

Notice how the new data for Phil has been reflected in the height of the chart bars.

**32.** Repeat steps 29-30 but change Phil's hours back to 42.

## Changing Sheet Tab Labels

The default titles of "Sheet1" or "Chart1" in the worksheet tabs can be modified to convey specific meaning for your workbook. For example, you'll now change the tabs to read "Payroll" and "Salary Chart":

**1.** Right-click the *Sheet1* tab, as in Figure E-49a.

A shortcut menu appears.

**2.** Click the *Rename* option.

**3.** Type **Payroll** to replace its name and press ⏎.

**4.** Right-click the *Chart1* tab and click the *Rename* option.

**5.** Type **Salary Chart** and press ⏎.

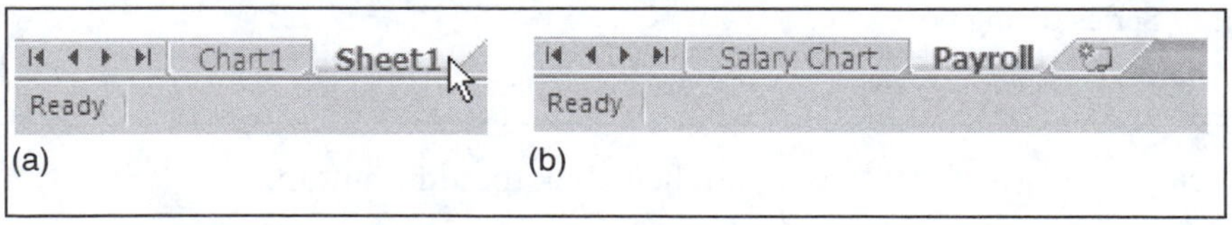

**FIGURE E-49**　　*Changing Sheet Tab Labels*

(a)　Right-click the desired tab to highlight it.

(b)　Click Rename and type the new label.

You can also remove any unwanted sheets in the workbook:

**6.** Right-click the *Sheet2* tab, then click *Delete*. It's gone.

**7.** Right-click the *Sheet3* tab, then click *Delete*.

The bottom of your screen should resemble Figure E-49b.

> **NOTE:** You can always insert an additional worksheet (and corresponding sheet tab) by clicking the *Insert Worksheet* button to the right of the last worksheet tab whenever needed.

**8.** Save the workbook again as WORK5.

## Changing the Chart Type

Once a chart is created, you can easily change its presentation style by invoking the format command. For example:

**1.** If you are in the Payroll worksheet, click the *Salary Chart* tab to switch to the chart.

**2.** Click the *Design* tab if needed and then the *Change Chart Type* command button (in the *Type* Group at the extreme left).

A Change Chart Type dialog box appears. For practice, you'll try changing to a line chart:

**3.** Click the *Line with Markers* subtype, as shown in Figure E-50.

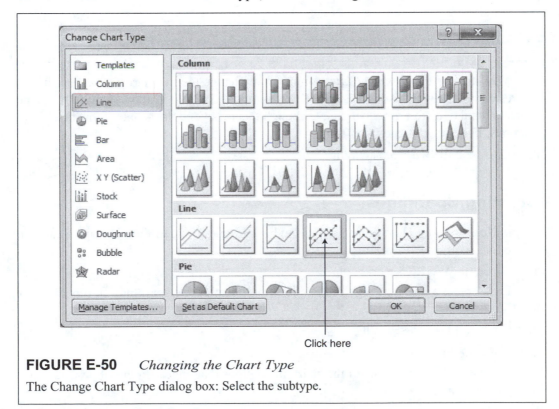

Click here

**FIGURE E-50**    *Changing the Chart Type*

The Change Chart Type dialog box: Select the subtype.

**4.** Click *OK* to select the line chart.

The data are presented as a line chart. Line charts are useful for showing trends over time. However, in this example, the data do not work well as a line chart. A lesson to be learned: You decide what is most appropriate in the presentation of your data. Do not rely on the computer or software to do it for you! Try one more option using the Change command:

**5.** Click the *Change Chart Type* command button (Type group).

**6.** Scroll down to the Bar group, click the *Clustered Bar in 3-D* type (fourth in the row).

**7.** Click *OK*.

Your screen should resemble Figure E-51.

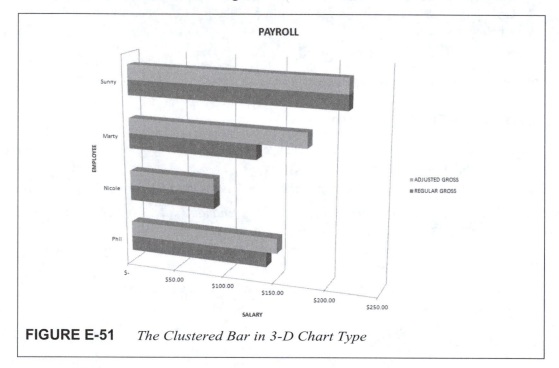

**FIGURE E-51**    *The Clustered Bar in 3-D Chart Type*

You can use the *Change Chart* command to change to any chart type and then view the results to see which style best presents your data. Excel also allows you to mix chart types to display different sets of data (although this is beyond the scope of this brief introduction). Feel free to experiment!

**8.** Close the file *without* saving it.

## Creating Sparklines

A *sparkline* is a tiny chart embedded in the background of a cell that displays a range of cell values in graphic form. It is easy to create:

**1.** Open the WORK5 workbook.

First, select a cell (or range of cells) that will display the sparkline. In this example, use G13.

**2.** Click cell G13 to select it.

**3.** Click the Insert tab.

You can now choose one of the sparkline options that appear in the ribbon, as shown in Figure E-52a:

**4.** Click the Column option (*Insert* tab, *Sparklines* group).

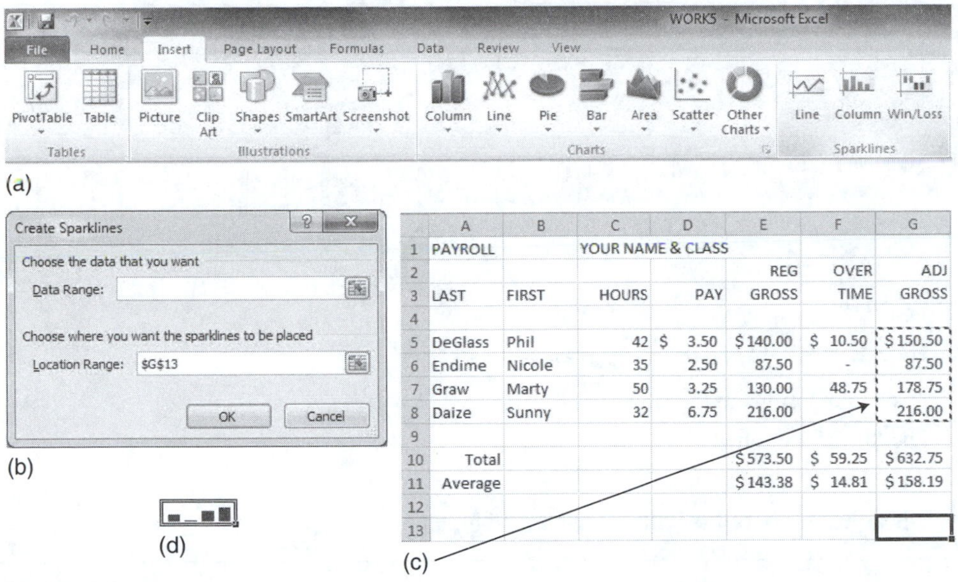

**FIGURE E-52** *Creating a Sparkline*

(a)   Sparkline options appear in the ribbon.

(b)   The Create Sparklines dialog box.

(c)   Select the desired range.

(d)   The sparkline appears in the cell.

A Create Sparklines dialog box appears, as in Figure E-52b. Note the location cell is already listed. In this example, you want to show the data in range G5:G8 in the sparkline. You can simply type the range or drag and drop it as follows:

5.   Click cell G5 and drag the mouse to cell G8, as shown in Figure E-52c. Release the mouse. The dialog box reflects the desired range.

6.   Click OK to accept it.

     A tiny chart, the sparkline, appears in Cell G13, as shown in Figure E-52d.

7.   Click any cell to move away from cell G13.

     Once a sparkline is created, you can adjust its type, style or color easily. Try this:

8.   Click cell G13 to select it.

     Note that the ribbon changes to sparkline tools, as shown in Figure E-53a.

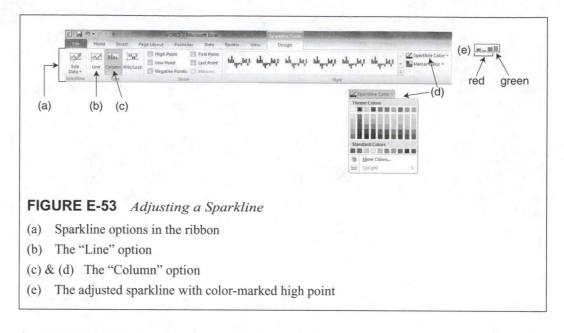

**FIGURE E-53**  *Adjusting a Sparkline*

(a)  Sparkline options in the ribbon

(b)  The "Line" option

(c) & (d)  The "Column" option

(e)  The adjusted sparkline with color-marked high point

1.  Click the "Line" option (*Design* tab, *Style* group) to change to a line chart, as in Figure E-53b.

2.  Now click the "Column" option to change back, as in Figure E-53c.
    You can change the color by clicking a new style or using the sparkline color setting:

3.  Click Sparkline Color (*Design* tab, *Style* group) to open a palette of colors, as shown in Figure E-53d.

4.  Click the red color option.
    One more change:

5.  Click Marker Color, point to High Point, and then click the green color option.

6.  Click anywhere—your sparkline should resemble the one shown in Figure E-53e.

7.  Save this worksheet as WORK5a.

> **NOTE:** Sparklines can be placed in any range of cells as well. In this case, they will appear larger than single-cell sparklines.

## LESSON 13: ENHANCING WORKSHEET APPEARANCE

Although you have created a perfectly fine worksheet, Excel also lets you enhance the images that appear on the screen and printer. You can enlarge the screen image for easier viewing. You can also change colors, sizes, text (font) styles, add cell borders, and add or remove grid lines if desired. This exercise will demonstrate some of the basics to get you started.

1.  If needed, launch Excel.

2.  Open the WORK3 workbook.

## The Zoom Control

The Zoom Control (located at the bottom right) allows you to change the size of the image that is displayed on your screen. You can reduce the zoom to see more of the worksheet area or increase zoom to improve cell readability. The zoom has no effect on the image that is printed. Try this:

1. Press CTRL | HOME to return the pointer to cell A1.

2. Click the Zoom In (+) button in the Zoom control (as shown in Figure E-54a) in the lower-right corner of the window.

   Note how the size of the worksheet display has increased by 10%. (Each click changes the zoom by 10%.)

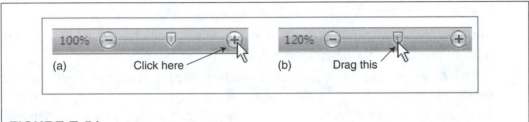

**FIGURE E-54**   *Adjusting the Zoom*

The Zoom control can be used to change the screen magnification.

(a)   Click the Zoom in (+) button to increase magnification in steps of 10%.

(b)   Drag the Zoom slider to any magnification.

3. Click the Zoom in (+) button once more to increase the screen magnification to 120%. You can also use the Zoom slide, as in Figure E-54b.

4. Click and drag the Zoom slider back to 100% and release the mouse. (If this is difficult, just click the Zoom out (-) button to return to 100%.)

> **NOTE:** When you use zoom, only the display changes, not the printed version of the spreadsheet. Use zoom whenever you want to adjust the display to better suit your needs. It will not affect any other command.

## Enhancing the Worksheet

The next set of exercises will show you how to change the type style (or font) of text and then add some borders to produce a worksheet that resembles Figure E-55.

| PAYROLL | | YOUR NAME & CLASS | | |
|---|---|---|---|---|
| **LAST** | **FIRST** | **HOURS** | **PAY** | **GROSS** |
| DeGlass | Phil | 42 | $ 3.50 | $ 147.00 |
| Endime | Nicole | 35 | 2.50 | 87.50 |
| Graw | Marty | 50 | 3.25 | 162.50 |
| Daize | Sunny | 32 | 6.75 | 216.00 |
| Total | | | | $ 613.00 |
| Average | | | | $ 153.25 |

**FIGURE E-55**    *The WORK3 Worksheet with a Few Enhancements*

Assume you want to change the label PAYROLL in cell A1 to a larger type size.

1. Click cell A1 if needed.

2. Click the drop-down arrow to the right of Font Size (second box on the Font group). A list of available sizes appears in a pull-down menu.

3. Click *20* for now. The font in cell A1 has been changed (and the row height has been adjusted accordingly).

To change any type size or style, move to the cell or highlight a range of cells, then click the *Font* drop-down arrow (to change the type style) or the *Font Size* drop-down arrow (to change its size). Here's an easier font change for you to try:

4. Click cell A3.

5. Drag the pointer to cell E3 to highlight the range A3:E3.

6. Click the *Italic* button (in the Font group).

7. Click anywhere to cancel the highlight.

You can also use this technique to add bold or underline to text. Just select the proper command button or style.

## Adding Cell Borders

Excel also allows you to add borders (lines) around individual cells and entire ranges. If you decide to use borders, you can remove the blank rows (row 9 and row 4) because they will no longer be needed to visually separate the data from the headings and summaries. Try the following exercise:

1. Delete row 9. Click the frame border at row 9 and then click the *Delete* button (in the Cells group). It is important to delete row 9 first so that the changing row numbers will not be confusing.

2. Delete row 4 the same way.

3. Identify the range A1:E9. (Click A1 and drag the pointer to E9, then release.)

4. Click the drop-down arrow to the right of the Borders command button (in the *Font* group) as shown in Figure E-56a.

A drop-down menu similar to that shown in Figure E-56b appears on your screen. Each button in this menu represents a different border pattern.

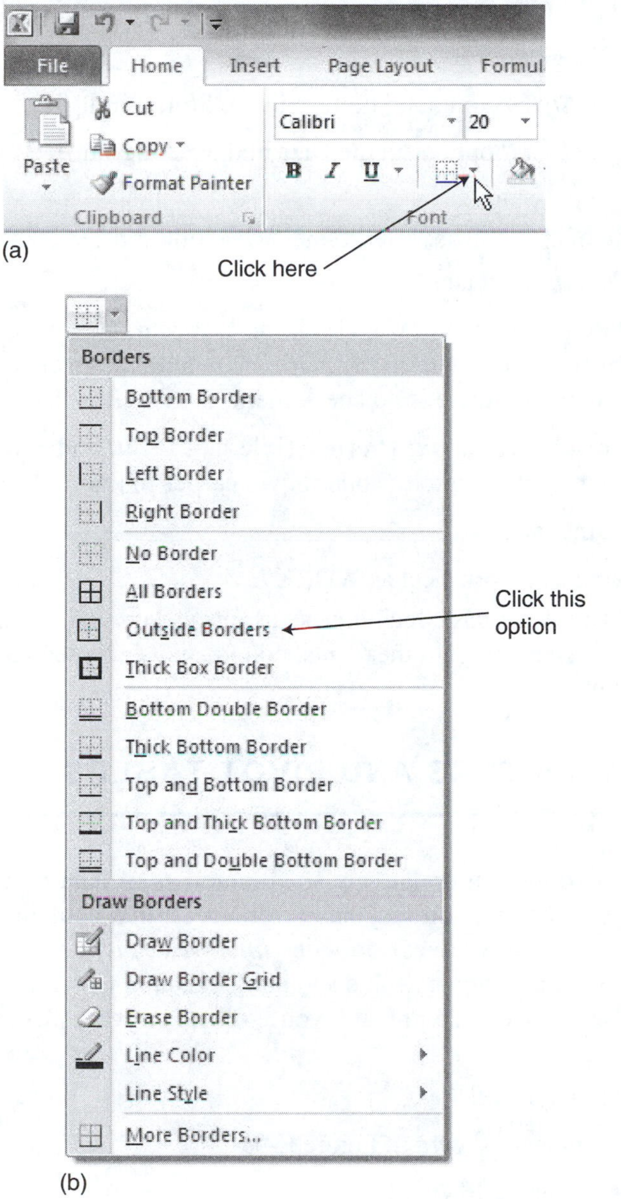

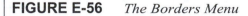

**FIGURE E-56**   *The Borders Menu*

(a)   Click the Borders drop-down button.

(b)   The Borders drop-down menu appears.

**E**

**5.** Click the *Outside Borders* button (seventh icon).

An outside border now appears around the entire range. You will be able to see it if you click or move the pointer out of the range for now.

Now try selecting the border that draws lines around each individual cell as follows:

**6.** Identify the range A3:E7. (Click A3 and drag to E7.)

**7.** Click the drop-down arrow to the right of the Borders command button as before.

**8.** This time, click the *All Borders* button (sixth icon). It's done. You can click or move out of the range to see the effect.

One last change—color. Here, you'll change the colors of the black text on a white background in the column headings to add some interest.

9. Identify the range A3:E3.

10. Click the *Cell Styles* command button (in the Styles group).

11. Click the *Check Cell* option (in the Data and Model group).

12. Click outside the range.

   As a final step, check to see if grid lines will print in the worksheet as follows:

13. Click the *Page Layout* tab.

14. In the Sheet Options group, if a check mark appears next to the *Gridlines Print* option, click it to remove the check mark. This tells the printer that you do not want grid lines printed. (If there is no check mark, do not click it.)

15. To see the results, run *Print Preview* (File tab, *Print*, and *zoom to page* if needed). Compare your worksheet to the one shown earlier in Figure E-55.

16. Click the Home tab.

17. Save the enhanced worksheet as WORK7.

   This small sample of basic techniques has introduced you to some of Excel's powerful features. Feel free to try out other fonts, colors, and screen enhancements as your time and interest permit.

## LESSON 14: FILTERS AND PIVOT TABLES

You have been working with relatively small amounts of data that are easily viewed on one page. At times, though, you may have worksheets that contain hundreds, if not thousands, of rows. Thankfully, Excel provides *filters* and *pivot tables*—two easily-applied features that allow you to organize and summarize data in different ways—without harming the original worksheet.  To prepare, you will need a worksheet with a few entries, as follows:

1. If needed, launch Excel.

2. Create the worksheet shown in Figure E-57.

3. Save it with the name PIVOT1.

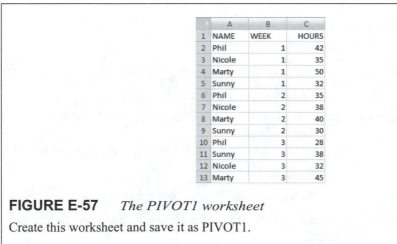

| | A | B | C |
|---|---|---|---|
| 1 | NAME | WEEK | HOURS |
| 2 | Phil | 1 | 42 |
| 3 | Nicole | 1 | 35 |
| 4 | Marty | 1 | 50 |
| 5 | Sunny | 1 | 32 |
| 6 | Phil | 2 | 35 |
| 7 | Nicole | 2 | 38 |
| 8 | Marty | 2 | 40 |
| 9 | Sunny | 2 | 30 |
| 10 | Phil | 3 | 28 |
| 11 | Sunny | 3 | 38 |
| 12 | Nicole | 3 | 32 |
| 13 | Marty | 3 | 45 |

**FIGURE E-57**    *The PIVOT1 worksheet*

Create this worksheet and save it as PIVOT1.

## Filtering

Excel's *filter* feature allows you to focus on certain information by temporarily hiding unwanted data in a worksheet. Once applied, a filter displays only those rows that meet the criteria (conditions) you specify. When you're done, you can easily cancel the filter and return the worksheet to display all of its data. This exercise will introduce Excel's AutoFilter feature. (You can explore more advanced filtering by referring to Excel's help feature in the future.)

**1.** Open the PIVOT1 worksheet if needed. Your screen should resemble Figure E-57.

> **NOTE:** Although you are using only twelve rows of data in this example, the techniques apply to any worksheet with any amount of rows or columns.

**2.** Click the ribbon's *Data* tab and then click the *Filter* button (in the *Sort & Filter* group).

A drop-down arrow appears to the right of each column in your worksheet, as shown in Figure E-58a.

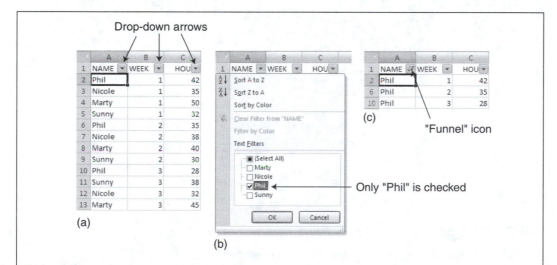

**FIGURE E-58**   *Using Excel's AutoFilter*

(a)  Click the Filter button (Data tab, Sort & Filter group) to create drop-down buttons for each column.

(b)  A Filter drop-down menu appears.

(c)  The filtered worksheet.

Let's say you want to restrict the worksheet to only Phil's information.

**3.** Click the drop-down arrow in Cell A1, the NAME column.

A filter drop-down menu appears, as shown in Figure E-58b. The lower portion of the menu indicates which data are included (with checkmarks). You now simply indicate which data you want to retain. Although you could click every name (except Phil's) to remove the checkmarks, here's an easier way to do this:

**4.** Click the *Select All* option to remove all checkmarks and then click *Phil* (as shown in Figure E-58b). Only Phil's name should display a checkmark.

**5.** Click *OK* to accept this filter.

As shown in Figure E-58c, only those rows that contain Phil's data (the condition you specified) are displayed; all others are hidden. Note, too, that the drop-down button in column A now displays a small "funnel" icon—indicating that this column is now filtered.

To remove the filter:

**6.** Click the drop-down arrow in Cell A1 (the NAME column).

**7.** Click the *Clear Filter from Name* option.

You can also apply filters to restrict *values*. Let's say you wanted to display only those hours that exceed the average worked each week. Try this:

**8.** Click the drop-down arrow in Cell C1, the HOURS column. A filter drop-down menu appears as expected.

**9.** Point to the *Number Filters* option, as shown in Figure E-59a.

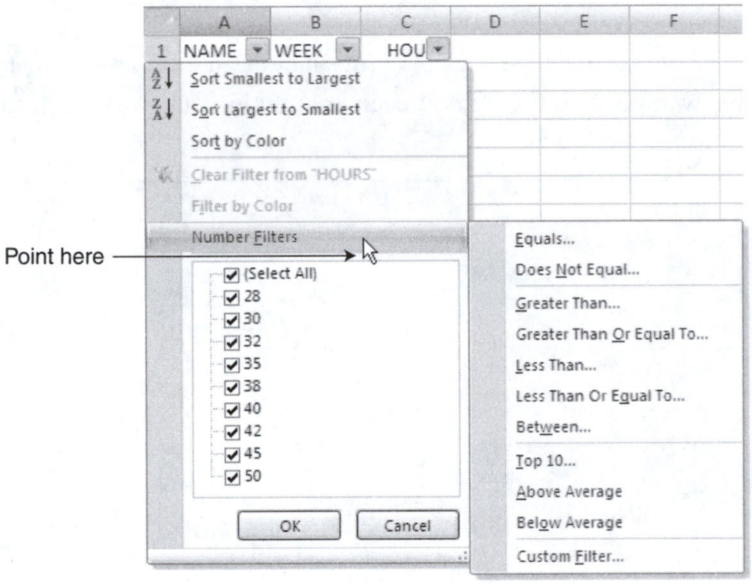

**FIGURE E-59**     *The Numbers Filter Option*

Click the Option button to access a submenu of other options.

**10.** Click the *Above Average…* option in the list.

Note that only those employees whose hours exceed the average of this column are now displayed (and that the HOURS column displays the "funnel" icon. Try one more:

**11.** Click the drop-down arrow in Cell C1 and point to the *Number Filters* option as before.

**12.** Click the *Greater Than Or Equal To…* option in the list.

A Custom Auto Filter dialog box appears. For now, type **35** and click *OK*.

Now the list is filtered to display only those employees whose hours equal or exceed 35. Feel free to explore the other options offered by this menu.

**13.** Clear the Hours filter (click the drop-down arrow in Cell C1 and click the *Clear Filter* option).

**14.** Shut off the AutoFilter feature (click the *Filter* button in the *Sort & Filter* group of the ribbon's *Data* tab).

**15.** Click the *Home* tab to reset the ribbon for now.

## Pivot Tables

Excel's *pivot table* feature—an extension of filtering—allows you to view data in different ways by creating a new sheet that can re-organize and summarize the data without affecting the original. Once invoked, a pivot table can be easily altered ("pivoted") to provide different insights into your data. Here's a brief introduction to its power:

1. Open the PIVOT1 worksheet if needed. Your screen should resemble Figure E-57.

> **NOTE:** Pivot tables can be applied to any amount of rows or columns.

2. Click Cell A2 (any cell within the data range will work).

3. Click the ribbon's *Insert* tab and then click the *Pivot Table* button (leftmost in the *Tables* group).

   A *Create Pivot Table* dialog box appears. For now,

4. Click *OK*.

   A Pivot Table task pane appears, as shown in Figure E-58. The first step is to select the columns to be included in the pivot table. In this example, we will use all three.

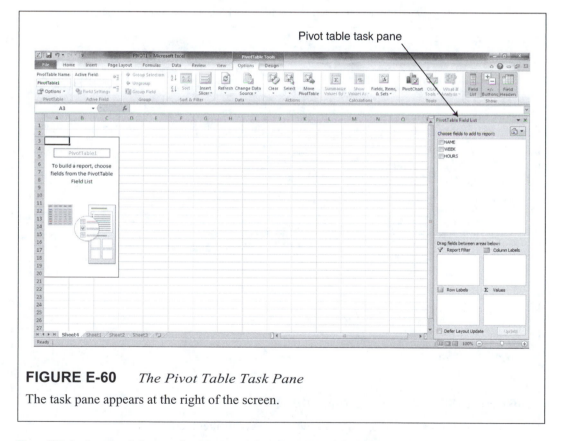

**FIGURE E-60**    *The Pivot Table Task Pane*

The task pane appears at the right of the screen.

5. Click the check boxes for Name, Week, and Hours, as shown in Figure E-61a.

   A pivot table appears, as shown in Figure E-61b. By default, Excel calculates totals (sums) of each value column and places the pivot table on a new sheet in your workbook—in this case, Sheet4. These can easily be changed.

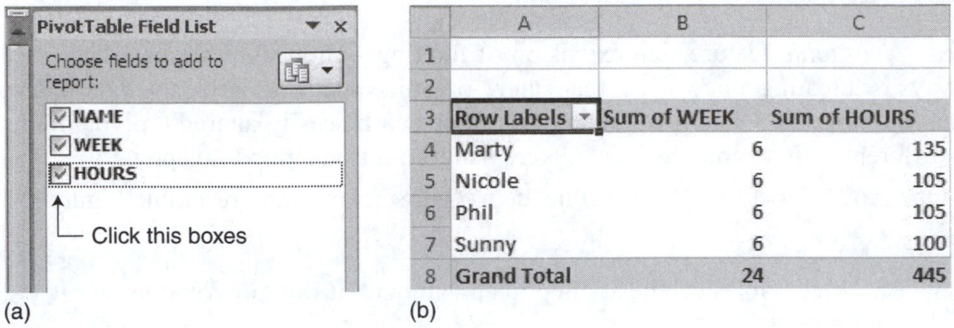

**FIGURE E-61**   *The Initial Pivot Table*

(a)   Click the desired data columns to include in the table.

(b)   The pivot table is created.

*Filtering*: You can apply filtering techniques to a pivot table, just as you did to the original worksheet. For example:

6.   Click in Cell A3 ("Row Labels") to activate its filtering function. The familiar drop-down arrow appears in the cell.

7.   Click its drop-down arrow to access the filter menu, as shown in Figure E-62a.

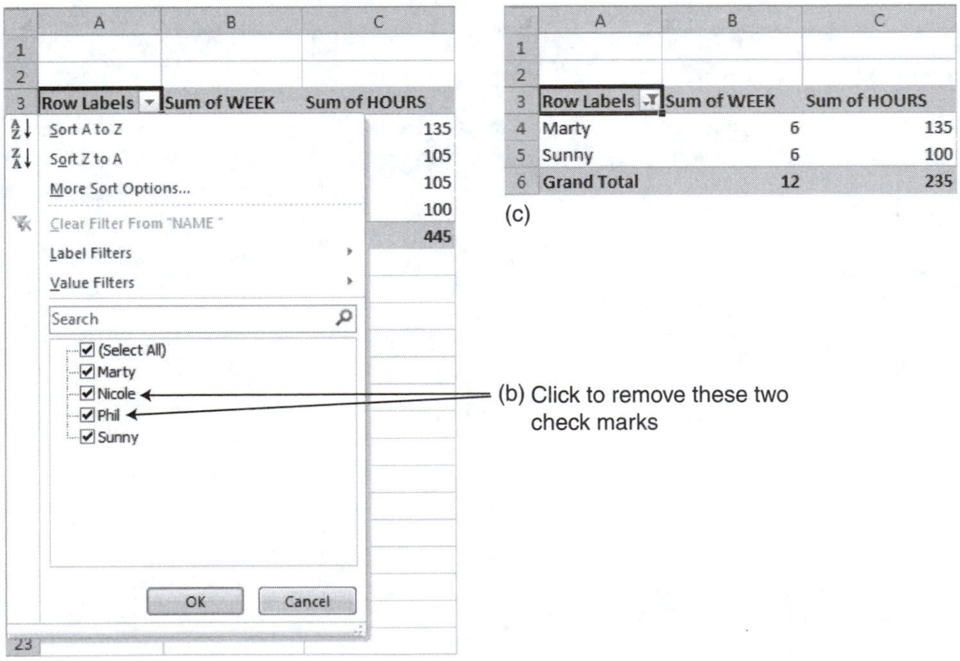

**FIGURE E-62**   *Filtering a Pivot Table*

(a)   Click the cell and its drop-down arrow to access the filter menu.

(b)   Removing checkmarks will filter the pivot table.

(c)   The filtered pivot table.

This menu allows you to sort or filter the NAME label. Let's say you want information only for Marty and Sunny.

8. Click the check boxes for Nicole and Phil to remove them as in Figure E-62b and then click *OK*.

   The table has been filtered, as shown in Figure E-62c.

9. Cancel the filter (click the drop-down arrow in Cell A3 and then click the *Clear Filter from Name* option).

   *Calculations*: You can also change the calculations used to summarize data in the pivot table. For example, let's *count* the WEEK column rather than *sum* it.

10. Double-click Cell B3 (WEEKS) to open its Value Field Settings dialog box, as shown in Figure E-63a. The current calculation is set to "sum."

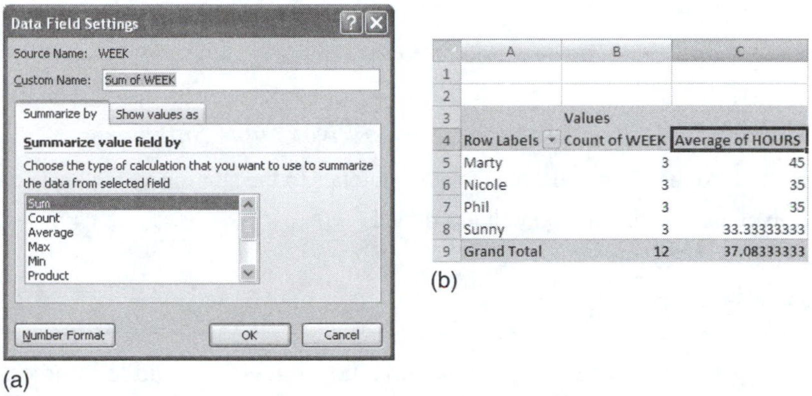

**FIGURE E-63**    *Adjusting Pivot Table Summaries*

(a)    Double-click a cell heading to access its Data Field Settings dialog box.

(b)    The adjusted pivot table.

11. Click the *Count* option in the list and then click *OK*.

    The pivot table now displays a count of the weeks worked. One more change: Let's say you wanted to *average* hours worked rather than total them.

12. Double-click Cell C3 (HOURS) to open its Value Field Settings dialog box.

13. Click the *Average* option and then click *OK*.

    The pivot table now reflects a count of the weeks and an average of the hours, as shown in Figure E-63b.

14. Reset the HOURS summary: double-click Cell C3, click *SUM* and then *OK*.

    *Rearranging*: Pivot tables also allow you to create different views of data without disturbing the original worksheet. In effect, you can "move data around" to see if they present a more meaningful view of the information. If one view isn't helpful, just switch the table around until you find a view that you want to use. It is simply a matter of selecting data fields and dragging them into other areas of the task pane to provide the added detail. For example:

15. Click anywhere within the pivot table.

16. As shown in Figure E-64a, click the HOURS object in the task pane's Field List (extreme right of screen) and drag it just *beneath* the NAMES object in the task pane's Row Labels list.

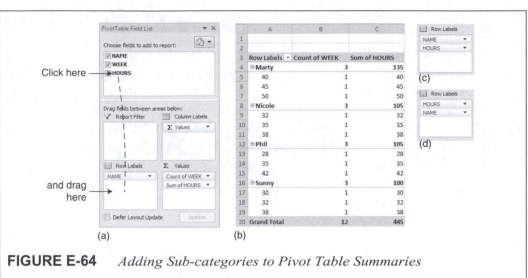

**FIGURE E-64**  *Adding Sub-categories to Pivot Table Summaries*

(a)  Drag fields to the Row Labels list to add subtotals to the summary.

(b)  The pivot table with names and hours added.

(c)  Drag the HOURS object up.

(d)  Drop the object at the top.

Additional detail concerning the weekly hours has been added for each name, as shown in Figure E-64b. Note that the Row Labels list in the task pane (as in Figure E-64a) displays the NAME first, followed by the HOURS they worked each week. You can drag and drop labels to see which pivot table offers the best view of your data. For example, try reversing the order of the NAMES and HOURS data, as follows:

**17.**  As shown in Figure E-64c, click the NAME object in the task pane's Field List and drag it downward just *below* the HOURS object in the Row Labels list and then drop it there (as in Figure E-64d).

As shown in Figure E-65, the adjusted pivot table now shows each set of hours *first*, followed by those employees who matched this number in specific weeks. This pivot table may not be as helpful in understanding the data as the previous one. The moral of the story—you can "pivot" the table and sub-total it anyway you want, but you are still responsible for deciding which view works best.

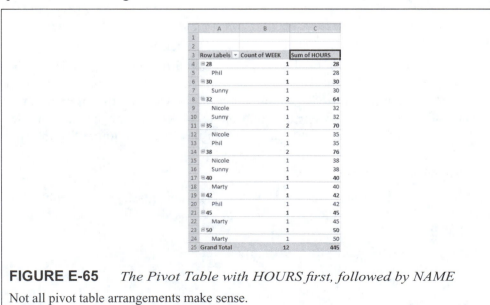

**FIGURE E-65**  *The Pivot Table with HOURS first, followed by NAME*

Not all pivot table arrangements make sense.

To remove a particular view, click *Undo* in the Quick Access Toolbar, or just drag and drop the undesired label out of the Row Labels box entirely. For now,

**18.** Drag the HOURS object back beneath the NAMES object in the Row Labels box. The pivot table returns to its former state.

One last adjustment:

**19.** Click the *Options* tab.

**20.** Examine the Show group in the ribbon (as shown in Figure E-66).

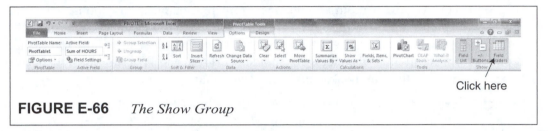

Click here

**FIGURE E-66**   *The Show Group*

**21.** Click the *Field Headers* option to hide this feature. Note that the column headings are simplified.

**22.** Save this workbook (which includes the original data and this pivot table) as PIVOT2.

Feel free to experiment with filters and pivot tables (and their options) to become better acquainted with other ways to present worksheet data.

**23.** If desired, exit from Excel.

You're done! Go on to the projects to see how well you've learned basic spreadsheet techniques.

## SPREADSHEET PROJECTS

Complete these projects to see how well you've mastered basic spreadsheet techniques. For each one, type your name in cell A1, your class in cell A2, the project number in cell F1, and the date in cell F2. Do not change column widths for these four labels, but allow the longer labels to spill over into the next cell.

**Project 1**  *Class Grades I:* Create a class report with headings and columns of proper width for STUDENT NAME, TEST 1, TEST 2, TEST 3, and AVERAGE. Type six names into the worksheet, with three test scores each. Have the spreadsheet automatically calculate and display in the AVERAGE column the average of the three scores for each student. Format all numbers to show no decimals. Save the workbook as SHEET1 and print it.

**Project 2**  *Class Grades II:* Open SHEET1. Add four names to the list of six and three test scores for each new name. Copy the average formula so that all students show averages. Create a class average row along the bottom. Have the worksheet calculate and display the average for each test column and an overall average in the average column. Format the average *column* (not *row*) to show one decimal. Save the workbook as SHEET2 and print it.

**Project 3**  *Class Grades III:* Open SHEET2. Delete the second student row. Create a bar chart that displays each student's name and overall average. Add titles. Label the sheet tabs appropriately. Save the workbook as SHEET3. Print the chart only.

**Project 4** *Expense Report I:* Create a six-month expense report as follows:

| EXPENSE | JAN | FEB | MAR | APR | MAY | JUN | TOTAL | AVG |
|---------|-----|-----|-----|-----|-----|-----|-------|-----|
| RENT | 400 | 400 | 400 | 420 | 420 | 420 | | |
| PHONE | 68 | 75 | 50 | 48 | 55 | 65 | | |
| FOOD | 125 | 145 | 175 | 170 | 150 | 120 | | |
| CLOTHES | 200 | 75 | 150 | 50 | 75 | 100 | | |
| MISC | 120 | 50 | 65 | 100 | 125 | 60 | | |

Add a TOTAL row beneath all columns. Format all numbers to comma, zero decimals. Add formulas for TOTAL (in the TOTAL column and row) and AVERAGE (in the AVG column) to calculate results. Change column widths as needed to fit the spreadsheet on one screen. Right-align the labels for month, TOTAL, and AVG to place them over their numbers. Save the workbook as SHEET4 and print it.

**Project 5** *Expense Report II:* Open SHEET4. Between RENT and PHONE, insert a row labeled UTILITIES. Enter monthly values of 40, 56, 52, 80, 60, 85. Type (or copy) formulas for the row's total and average. Change the format to currency, zero decimals in the RENT and bottom TOTAL rows. (All other rows remain comma, zero decimals.) Add six *column* sparklines in Column J, one to the right of each expense (change colors as desired) to display month data. Save the workbook as SHEET5 and print it.

**Project 6** *Expense Report III:* Open SHEET5. Skip a row under TOTAL and add a row labeled INCOME with 1000 entered for each month. Add a row beneath it labeled SAVINGS. Create formulas that will appear under each month's income to show how much money remains for savings after expenses are subtracted from income. Create formulas for row totals and averages. Save the workbook as SHEET6 and print it.

**Project 7** *Interest Table:* Create a spreadsheet to calculate how much a deposit of $1,000 would be worth if left in a bank for ten years at 6.5 percent annual interest. Show principal and interest for each year as follows:

Annual Interest Rate:      .065

| YEAR | PRINCIPAL | INTEREST |
|------|-----------|----------|
| 1 | $1,000.00 | (a) |
| 2 | (b) | |

At the bottom of the PRINCIPAL column, create a *line* sparkline to show its growth.

**NOTE:** Note that the interest in cell (a) is the principal to its left times the absolute reference to the cell that contains .065. The new principal in cell (b) is the old principal plus the interest in the row above it. Copy these formulas in the remaining cells as needed. Save the workbook as SHEET7 and print it.

**Project 8** *Advertising Report:* Create an Advertising versus Sales report, as shown below. Set the value format to show dollar signs but no cents.

| | lst Qtr | 2nd Qtr | 3rd Qtr | 4th Qtr | Total |
|---|---------|---------|---------|---------|-------|
| Sales | $5,214 | $6,807 | $7,546 | $12,264 | (e) |
| Advertising | $ 450 | $ 500 | $ 600 | $ 1,250 | (f) |
| Advertising as a % of Sales: | (a) | (b) | (c) | (d) | |

In the cells marked (a) through (d), create formulas that will calculate the percentage of sales represented by advertising, and present the results with two decimals. In cells (e) and (f), create formulas for total sales and advertising. Save the workbook as SHEET8 and print it.

**Project 9** *Inventory I:* Create an inventory value sheet with proper column widths and value formats as follows:

**SHOW-BIZ NOVELTY COMPANY INVENTORY AS OF 4/25/07**

| ITEM | QUANTITY | UNIT PRICE | VALUE |
| --- | --- | --- | --- |
| BALLOON | 1,735 | $0.11 | (a) |
| CARD | 26 | 1.25 | (b) |
| FUNNY FORK | 336 | .79 | (c) |
| OOPS EGG | 605 | 1.35 | (d) |
| CLOWN NOSE | 1,122 | .90 | (e) |
| TOTAL VALUE: | | | (f) |

Create formulas in cells (a) through (e) to multiply the quantity by the unit price to calculate the value. Format the BALLOON and TOTAL VALUE cells in the VALUE column to show dollars and cents, and the four remaining cells, comma and two decimals only. Create a formula to total these values in cell (f). Save the file as SHEET9 and print it.

**Project 10** *Inventory II:* Open SHEET9. Add a fifth column titled REORDER. Use an IF statement to print the word "ORDER" if quantity is below 500 units, or a dash if 500 or above. (Hint: Use the text "Order" and "-" in the true and false locations in the IF function.) Save the workbook as SHEET10 and print it.

**Project 11** *Retail Discount:* Create a spreadsheet that will calculate all discounted prices shown below. Use absolute and relative references to the discount percentages. (**NOTE:** One mixed reference in cell C4 could be copied through the range.) Report all numbers to two decimal places. Show dollar signs on the top row of numbers only. Save the workbook as SHEET11 and print it.

| | | PRICE WITH DISCOUNT OF: | | |
| --- | --- | --- | --- | --- |
| ITEM | PRICE | 10% | 15% | 20% |
| Belt | $35.00 | | | |
| Jacket | 150.00 | | | |
| Pants | 90.00 | | | |
| Shirt | 25.00 | | | |
| Suit | 425.00 | | | |

**Project 12** *Grade Point Average I:* Create a spreadsheet that lists all the courses you've taken by semester. Include columns for course numbers and titles, credits, and final grades. Then have the spreadsheet calculate your college grade point average on the bottom. You may add columns as needed for "quality points" or other intermediate calculations. Use your college handbook as a guide to the steps in calculating your GPA. Save the file as SHEET12 and print it.

**Project 13** *Grade Point Average II:* Using SHEET12, filter the worksheet so that only courses in which you received a "B" are displayed. Print the filtered worksheet and save as SHEET13a. Remove the filter. Create a pivot table that presents all courses in GRADE ORDER. Save the file as SHEET13b and print only the pivot table.

**Project 14** *Projected vs. Actual Expenses:* Create the spreadsheet below that compares projected and actual expenses by calculating a percent difference between the two. Calculate totals for the first two columns and an overall percent difference. Format to match the spreadsheet below. Percents should show one decimal place. Save the file as SHEET14 and print it.

### PROJECTED VS. ACTUAL COMPARISON

| ITEM | PROJECTED EXPENSE | ACTUAL EXPENSE | PERCENT DIFFERENCE |
|------|-------------------|----------------|--------------------|
| RENT | $4,000 | $4,000.00 | |
| ELECTRICITY | 2,400 | 3,245.15 | |
| SUPPLIES | 7,500 | 7,230.95 | |
| INSURANCE | 2,000 | 2,150.00 | |
| CONSULTANTS | 3,000 | 2,500.00 | |
| TOTAL: | | | |

**Project 15** *Accounting Example:* Using material from an accounting course, create a balance sheet, trial balance, or income statement. Include a copy of the original. Print and save the file as SHEET15.

## CONTINUING ON YOUR OWN—THINGS TO CONSIDER

This module presented basic spreadsheet concepts. However, other advanced techniques can greatly expand your use of spreadsheets. Remember, you can't harm the program or computer by experimenting. You might want to refer to other manuals or documentation to look into these topics:

1. Using vertical and horizontal look-up tables.

2. Sorting and extracting data.

3. Using range names.

4. Developing macro commands.

5. Protecting cells and using passwords.

6. Using manual recalculation.

7. Extracting data to another worksheet or database.

8. Hiding columns for security or to suppress printing.

9. Using additional features to enhance worksheet appearance.

## COMMAND SUMMARY—EXCEL 2010

**NOTE:** The Ribbon command button is shown in BOLD CAPS followed by its location in parentheses—Tab (in italics) and Group—as in "**BOLD** (*Home*, Font)."

| | |
|---|---|
| ABSOLUTE REFERENCE: | Press F4 to add $ to cell reference as needed |
| ADD A ROW OR COLUMN: | See INSERT |
| AVERAGE: | =AVERAGE(X1:X2) (X1=first, X2=last cell) |
| BEGIN EXCEL: | Double-click desktop icon, or click *Start*, *All Programs*, Excel |
| CLEAR SCREEN: | *MS Office Button*, *Close*, *No* (if needed) |
| COLUMN WIDTH: | (In column) **Format** (*Home*, Cells), *Width*, # ⏎ |
| COPY ONE CELL: | (In cell) **Copy** (*Home*, Clipboard), show new range, ⏎ |
| COPY A RANGE: | Select range, **Copy** (*Home*, Clipboard), move to start new range, ⏎ |
| CREATE A CHART: | (Select data) Any **Chart** type (*Insert*, Chart), continue |
| DELETE ROW/COLUMN: | (In row/column *frame*) **Delete** (*Home*, Cells) |
| ERASE A CELL: | (In cell) ⌊DELETE⌋ |
| ERASE WORKBOOK: | *MS Office Button*, *Close*, *No* (Erases current screen only) |
| EXIT EXCEL: | *MS Office Button*, *Exit Excel* |
| FILTER: | **Filter** (*Data*, Sort & Filter), click column drop-down arrow |
| FORMAT: | (Select range) then any **FORMAT** button (*Home*, Number)—*Comma* for commas or fixed numbers or *Accounting* for currency (dollars) |
| IF: | =IF(test, t, f) where test = condition, t = result if true, f = result if false |
| INSERT ROW/COLUMN: | (In row/column *frame*) **Insert** (*Home*, Cells) |
| LAUNCH EXCEL: | See Begin Excel |
| TEXT POSITIONING: | Select cells, any **ALIGNMENT** button (*Home*, Number) |
| OPEN A WORKBOOK: | *MS Office Button*, *Open* or *New* (for new workbook) |
| PIVOT TABLE: | **Pivot Table** (*Insert*, Tables) |
| PRINT: | *MS Office Button*, *Print*, *OK* |
| QUIT EXCEL: | See Exit Excel |
| SAVE A WORKBOOK: | *MS Office button*, *Save* (or *Save As*), type filename, ⏎ |
| SELECT A RANGE: | Point to first cell, drag to last cell |
| SUM (OR TOTAL): | =SUM(X1:X2) where X1=first cell, X2=last cell |
| TITLES: | To Freeze: Move one cell to the right and below titles to be frozen, then **FREEZE PANES** (*View*, Window), then *Freeze* Panes |
| | To Unfreeze: **FREEZE PANES** (*View*, Window), then *Unfreeze* Panes |
| UNDO: | **Undo** Quick Access toolbar button |

**E**

# DATABASE MODULE

## ACCESS 2010

**A**

## LESSON 1: LAUNCHING ACCESS

This module examines some basic techniques in Microsoft Office 2010's database management system—Access. A database is like a large electronic filing cabinet. It contains data that you have chosen to gather about employees, clients, inventory, or other items. Access lets you design sophisticated filing systems and reports that make record keeping easy, and provides an extensive menu system that lets you create files, edit and update their data, and develop reports. You can also ask questions (queries) concerning any data in the database.

Access offers many powerful commands, but you'll examine only the basic ones to get started. Once you've mastered the basics of Access, you may want to examine its many other features.

The startup instructions for your computer were presented in the introductory module. Refer back to the appropriate instructions as needed to remind you how to start your computer system.

1.  If needed, start Windows.

2.  If appropriate for your system, make sure that a formatted diskette—on which you'll save your work—is in drive A (this is unnecessary if you are using a flash drive or a folder on your hard disk or network).

The easiest way to launch a program is to use a desktop or taskbar icon (if one exists).

**3.** If your desktop (or taskbar) displays an Access icon, double-click it now and continue with the next section—the Access Program Window.

If there is no icon, or if you prefer, you can always launch Access through the Start menu. Try this approach, using Figure A-1 as a reference:

**4.** Click the Start button to access the Windows menu.

**5.** Point to *All Programs* to access its menu.

**6.** If the Microsoft Access menu item appears in the next menu, skip to step 8.

**7.** Point to the menu item that contains Microsoft Access. This is often Microsoft Office. If a different menu item contains Access, write its title here for future reference: _____.

**8.** Click the Microsoft Access menu item to launch it, as in Figure A-1.

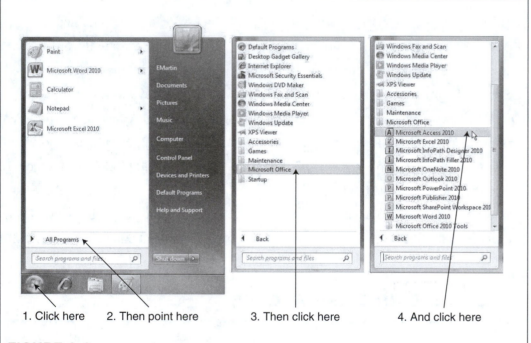

1. Click here      2. Then point here          3. Then click here          4. And click here

**FIGURE A-1**    *Launching Access*

To launch Access, click Start, Programs, and then the Access menu item to launch Access (your list may differ).

## The Access Program Window

A "Getting Started in Access" program window now appears, similar to Figure A-2. Examine this screen for a moment.

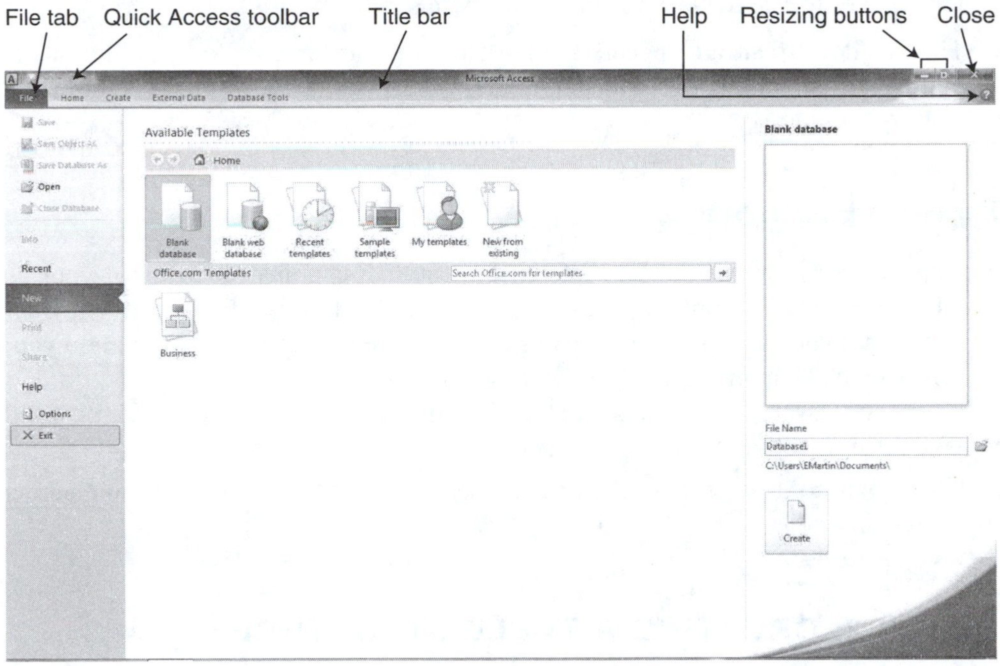

**FIGURE A-2**    *The Getting Started Access Program Window*

a.    **Title bar:** The screen's top line displays the typical window items: a title bar displaying Microsoft Access in the center with two resizing buttons and a close button at the right. If you are not sure of the functions of these items, review the introductory module.

**NOTE:**  If the window is not full size, maximize it now by clicking the maximize button in the upper-right corner of the screen.

b.    **File tab:** The purple tab in the upper-left corner is the File tab. Clicking it opens a file menu with commands for saving, printing, closing a file, and exiting the program. It also provides access to many Access options settings.

c.    **Quick Access Toolbar:** Access's Quick Access toolbar ("QAT")—just above the File tab—contains often-used command buttons such as save, undo, and redo. You can customize this toolbar to include any other commands you wish to add.

d.    **Available Templates:** The middle portion (pane) of the window lists database *templates* that are available online. Templates contain professionally-prepared database components that can be modified to your particular needs. In the future, you may want to explore these, but for now, you will create your own database to learn the techniques.

e.    **New Database Button:** The Blank Database button allows you to create a new database "from scratch." You'll use this in a moment.

f.    **Open Recent Database:** The right pane may list previously-used database files. If the one you want to open is listed, you could simply click it to open it for use. Although this works well on a single-user computer—where files tend to be available—

it may not work in a lab or public setting where many users create their databases on removable storage devices. (Feel free to try this in the future.)

g. The Windows **taskbar** appears at the bottom of the screen. You can click its Start button to launch other programs or Windows features, as you have seen in the introductory module.

## The Help Feature

Access provides an extensive Help reference menu that can answer many of your questions. To invoke the Help menu, click the *Help* command button in the left list. Once in the Help menu, you can select the index or other feature to locate the information you desire. To close the Help menu, click the Help window's close button.

Note that Lesson 2 will take some time to complete. Do not continue for now unless you have the time to finish the entire lesson.

1. If you want to exit for now, click the Close button ("X") in the upper-right corner of the window.

## LESSON 2: CREATING A TABLE STRUCTURE

In Access, data are grouped into a database hierarchy of fields, records, and tables. A *field* contains an individual piece of data and is identified by a unique field name, such as "STUDENT ID NUMBER." Related fields are grouped together to form a *record* that typically contains the data relevant to one particular person or thing, such as data about one student. Groups of records form a *table*. A school might have a student table that contains all the biographical data (name, address, phone number, etc.) for all its students. A set of tables and related objects, in turn, comprises one *database*. A school's database, for example, may include separate tables for student biographical data, student grades, alumni, employee payroll, inventory, and all the reports related to them.

Because this is your first use of a database, you must start by opening a new database and then designing its first table *structure*, or layout, of the data you want to place into each record. In general, you can design as many table structures as you want or need in a database. For this example, you will create a database called COMPANY and then enter the structure for one table named SALES, as shown in Table A-1.

| Field Name | Data Type | Size | Description |
| --- | --- | --- | --- |
| ID | Text | 3 | Customer ID Number |
| LAST | Text | 15 | Customer's Last Name |
| FIRST | Text | 10 | Customer's First Name |
| PHONE | Text | 14 | Phone: (999) 999-9999 |
| AMOUNT | Currency | Auto | Amount of Invoice |
| INVDATE | Date/Time | Auto | Date of Invoice |
| PAID | Currency | Auto | Amount Paid |

**TABLE A-1**     *The Structure for the SALES Table*

> **NOTE:** In an actual office environment, you might also include fields for Company, Address, Items Purchased, Payment Dates, Terms, and so on. In general, field names should be short and remind you of the data being stored in that field. For example, the last name field might be called LAST, LASTNAME, LNAME, or something similar.

1.  If needed, launch Access by following the steps in Lesson 1.

2.  Click the *Blank database* button in the left center of the window.

    A Blank Database pane appears on the right side of the window, as shown in Figure A-3.

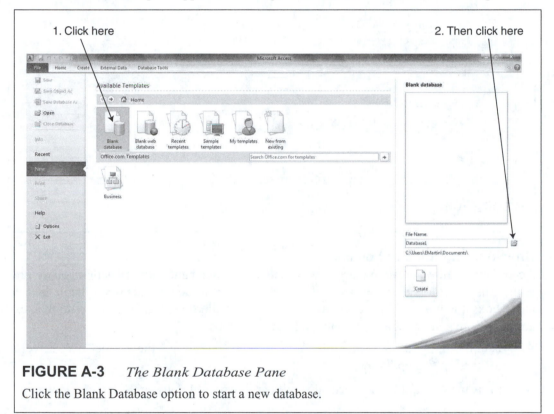

**FIGURE A-3**    *The Blank Database Pane*

Click the Blank Database option to start a new database.

3.  Click the *Browse* icon to the right of the filename.

    A File New Database dialog box appears, as shown in Figure A-4. *Dialog boxes* allow the computer to "talk" to you. You can make changes in the items, accept what's there, or cancel the command.

A

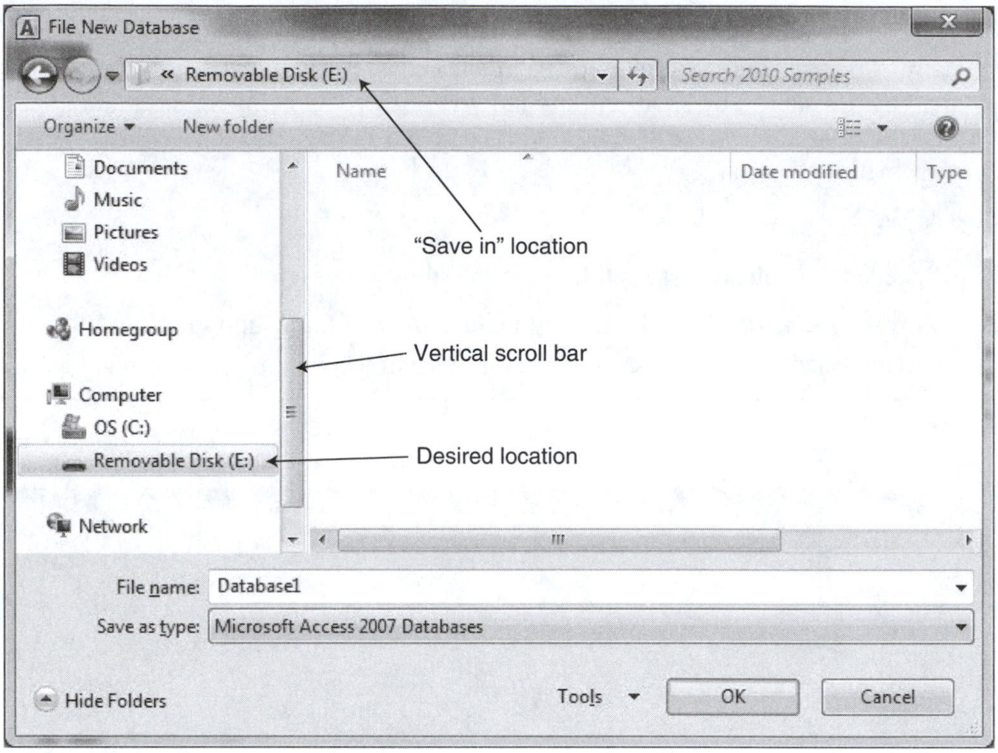

**FIGURE A-4**    *The File New Database Dialog Box*

### Checking the Save in Location

Access must know where to place new files that you create and older files that you've previously used. Although you can specify a location every time you identify a file in the File name box, it is wiser to inform Access where to find all your needed files. To do this, examine the *Save in* box and complete the following steps:

4. Examine the entry shown in the *Save in* box. If it shows the correct disk drive or folder, skip to step 7 now.

5. If it is incorrect, drag the vertical scroll bar down until you see the desired location.

6. Click the *3-1/2 Floppy (A:)* drive (or find the flash drive or folder you want to use).

> **NOTE:** Get into the habit of checking the *Save in* box when you start Access. Once it is correct, you need not check it again. If you are using a LAN, it is likely that the correct location has already been set for you.

You can now name the database:

7. Click in the *File name* entry box and delete its contents.

8. Type **Company**.

9. Click the *OK* button to continue.

The filename ("Company.accdb") appears in the File Name entry box; its location (path) appears beneath it. (Since 2007, Access adds the "accdb" extension to identify the file, in this case as an Access 2010 database.)

**10.** Click the *Create* button beneath the filename.

The Access window now reflects the as yet empty database, as shown in Figure A-5. The database file serves as a container for all the various objects—such as tables, forms, and reports—that you will place in it.

Take a moment to examine the additional components of this window:

**a.** **Ribbon:** Beneath the title bar is the heart of Access's menu system—the ribbon (the four-line band across the top of the window). The *ribbon* is divided into core tasks, each represented by a *tab*, which is subdivided into *groups*, and *command buttons* that can be clicked by mouse to perform needed tasks. The command buttons remain in view and are always available for immediate use. (By default, the Home tab—as shown in Figure A-5—appears when you open a database, since it is the one you will use most often.) Access's ribbon includes seven "standard" tabs. At times, based on your actions, "contextual" tools will be added as temporary tabs (shown in a different color accent). When you finish your task, the contextual tab will disappear from the ribbon.

**NOTE:** Although you can leave any ribbon tab active, it is a good idea to click the "Home" tab when you are finished using a set of commands, so it is always available.

**b.** **Database Objects Pane:** The left window pane contains all the objects—such as tables, forms, and reports—associated with the current database. At the moment, only a single table appears.

**c.** **Active Objects Window:** The central portion of the window displays any objects that are currently active. Each is identified with its own tab at the top of the pane, such as "Table1" in Figure A-5. (You can right-click this tab to access a menu to save or close the object as needed.)

**d.** **Status bar:** The status bar appears at the bottom of the screen (currently displaying "Datasheet View" at the left). It displays important messages about your database, including explanations and the status of various objects.

**e.** **View selector:** To the right of the status bar are two small command buttons that allow you to change how the workbook appears on your screen. The Access views (at present) include: datasheet and design view. Others will be added to the selector as needed.

**A**

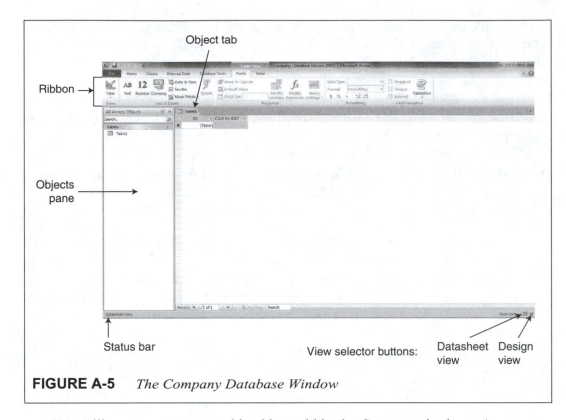

**FIGURE A-5**    *The Company Database Window*

You will now create a new table object within the Company database. Access provides a number of ways to do this. You can import data from another source or simply name desired fields and have Access format them as you enter data. A more direct approach (and the one you will use here) is to create the table yourself. Since this must be done in Design view, do the following:

**11.** Click the *Design* view button (at the extreme lower-right corner). If you are not sure which button is correct, point to it with the mouse and wait. A "tool tip" box will appear identifying the button.

A Save As dialog box appears, as shown in Figure A-6a.

**12.** Type **SALES** (as shown in Figure A-6b) and click OK to accept it.

| (a) | (b) |
|---|---|

**FIGURE A-6**    *Saving a Table*

The Save As dialog box enables you to specify a table name.

(a)    The dialog box.

(b)    Adding the desired table name.

An empty table window appears as in Figure A-7. The tab titleshows that the table is currently called SALES

The top section (or pane) of the window awaits entries for field name, data type, and description. The bottom pane lets you adjust size and set limits, or checks, on the data that the program will accept (as you will soon see). The insertion point is now waiting for you to define a field name. A triangle pointer also indicates the current field line.

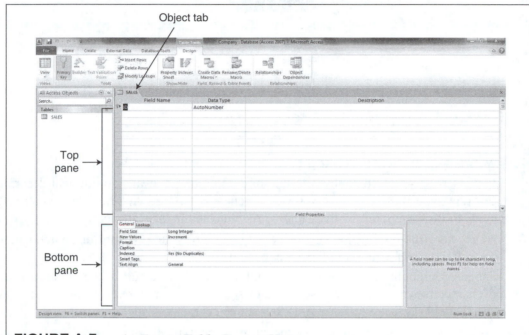

**FIGURE A-7**    *An Empty Table Design View*

**NOTE:**  Access saves changes as you enter them. For this reason, if you are using a diskette or flash drive to store your data, never remove it until the database you are using has been closed (or Access has been exited).

## Filling in the Table Structure

Now you need to fill in a row for each field in your table. First, a field name:

1.  Using Table A-1 as a guide, type **ID** and press ⏎. The insertion point moves to the *Data Type* column. (Field names can contain up to sixty-four characters.)

    You can choose from among eleven data types in Access. The ones of interest at the moment are text, number, currency, and date/time. *Text* fields can contain any combination of up to 255 characters (letters, numbers, or special symbols). *Number* fields contain numbers on which you intend to perform math. *Currency* fields are number fields with special formatting: They typically display two decimals, a currency symbol, and commas (when needed). *Date/Time* fields contain any valid date (and time if desired) from the year 100 to 9999.

    There are a number of ways you can set the desired data type. You can simply type its first letter ("T" for "Text," "N" for "Number," and so on) and then press the ⏎ key to accept it. If you'd rather select the field type from a list, you can click the drop-down arrow at the right of the *Data Type* field to open a data type list as shown in Figure A-8 and then click on the desired type. You'll try both techniques here.

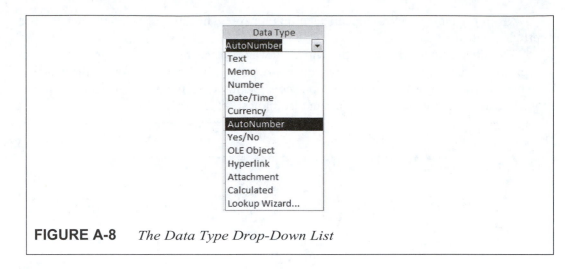

**FIGURE A-8**   *The Data Type Drop-Down List*

2.   We want the ID field to be a text field, so type *T* (for text) and then press ⏎.

The insertion point now moves to the third column and awaits an optional description. For now, you'll skip it. Since you want to change the suggested field size, you must now move to the lower pane on the window. As indicated in the status bar:

3.   Press ⎡F6⎤ (the F6 function key located at the top of your keyboard) to switch panes or click the *Field Size* box in the lower pane list.

The insertion point now moves to the Field Size box. By default, all text fields are set to 255 characters wide—an immense waste of space for our purposes. In this case, you want the ID field (as listed in Table A-1) to be three characters wide.

4.   ⎡BACKSPACE⎤ if needed to remove the current size, type **3** and press ⏎ as shown in Figure A-9.

5.   Because this is the only change you want to make, click the first row of the Description column in the top pane (to the right of the *Text* entry).

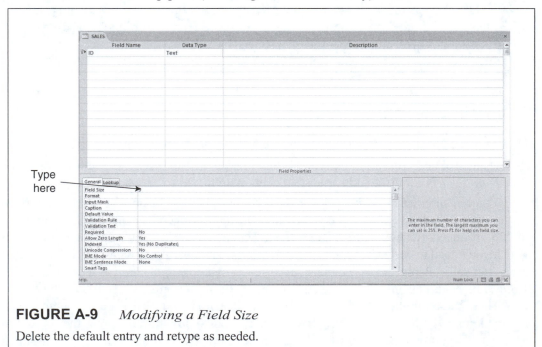

**FIGURE A-9**   *Modifying a Field Size*
Delete the default entry and retype as needed.

**NOTE:** If you make a mistake, use the arrow keys (→, ↓, ←, ↑) or F6 as needed to change location and correct it.

6.    For the first field description, type **Customer ID Number** and press ↵ to continue.

7.    Now, create the next three text fields (LAST, FIRST, and PHONE) with the same technique. Using Table A-1 as a guide, type each *Field Name* ↵ F6 *Size* ↵ click the top pane and type the *Description* ↵ until the insertion point is on the fifth field line, as shown in Figure A-10. Make sure that you enter each field size appropriately.

8.    For Field 5, type the field name **AMOUNT** and press ↵.

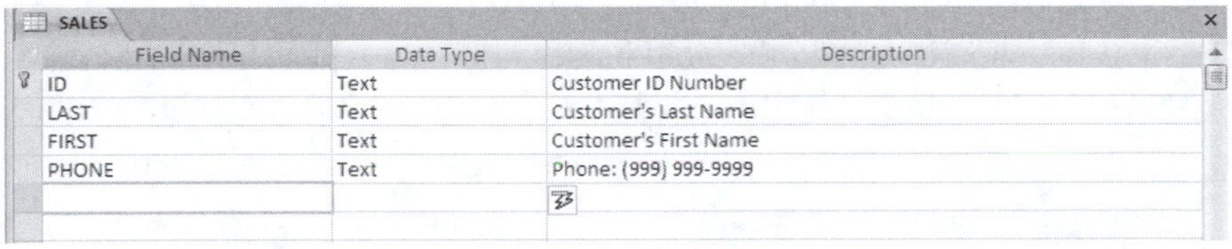

| Field Name | Data Type | Description |
|---|---|---|
| ID | Text | Customer ID Number |
| LAST | Text | Customer's Last Name |
| FIRST | Text | Customer's First Name |
| PHONE | Text | Phone: (999) 999-9999 |

**FIGURE A-10**    *A Partially Completed Structure*

Field names, data types, descriptions, and sizes (not shown) have been entered for the first four fields.

You must now set the field type to *Currency*. Of course, you could simply type the C mnemonic, but try the list approach, as follows:

9.    Click the drop-down arrow in the *Data Type* column to open the list as you've seen in Figure A-8.

10.    Click the *Currency* choice and then press ↵.

Currency is automatically defined to include a $ symbol and two decimal places.

**NOTE:** The size of numeric and date fields (as you will see) is automatically set by Access. There is no need (or opportunity) to set the field size as you did with text fields.

11.    Type **Amount of Invoice** in the Description column and press ↵ to complete the AMOUNT column.

12.    For Field 6, type **INVDATE** and press ↵.

13.    To set a field type, press D for *Date/Time* and press ↵. or select it from the list as you learned in steps 9–10.

You must now select an appropriate date format, as follows:

14.    Press F6 to switch to the lower pane.

15.    Click the drop-down arrow at the extreme right of the Format row.

A set of date/time format options appears, as shown in Figure A-11.

| | |
|---|---|
| General Date | 6/19/2007 5:34:23 PM |
| Long Date | Tuesday, June 19, 2007 |
| Medium Date | 19-Jun-07 |
| Short Date | 6/19/2007 |
| Long Time | 5:34:23 PM |
| Medium Time | 5:34 PM |
| Short Time | 17:34 |

**FIGURE A-11**   *Date/Time Format Options*

**16.** Click the *Short Date* option in the list.

**17.** Now, click the Description column in the appropriate row, type **Date of Invoice** and press ⏎ to complete the Invdate field.

**18.** Enter the PAID currency field by typing **PAID** ⏎ **C** ⏎ **Amount Paid** ⏎.

The field list should contain the field names and data types shown in Figure A-12. If not, use the arrow keys to scroll (if needed) and then go back and change as necessary.

| Field Name | Data Type | Description |
|---|---|---|
| ID | Text | Customer ID Number |
| LAST | Text | Customer's Last Name |
| FIRST | Text | Customer's First Name |
| PHONE | Text | Phone: (999) 999-9999 |
| AMOUNT | Currency | Amount of Invoice |
| INVDATE | Date/Time | Date of Invoice |
| PAID | Currency | Amount Paid |

**FIGURE A-12**   *The Completed Table Field List*

## Validity Checks

While you're in this window, you can practice using the Access validity checks, which let you control the range and appearance of data. Although these checks are optional, they help keep data consistent by eliminating many common entry errors. Validity checks include:

- *Input Mask:* a format that standardizes data appearance.
- *Default Value:* a value that is used automatically if no data are entered in this field.
- *Validation Rule:* sets lower and/or upper limits for acceptable field data.
- *Required:* Access will not accept the record unless this field contains data.

It is a good idea to use validity checks whenever possible—simply identify the field and then specify the validity check. For example, let's say you want to ensure that the LAST field is entered in each record.

### Setting a Required Field

**1.** Click the LAST name field.

**2.** Click the *Required* field box in the bottom pane.

**3.** Click the *Required* row's drop-down arrow to access the choice list.

**4.** Click *Yes*.

**5.** Click any field in the upper pane (or press F6).

## Setting a Validation Rule

Let's say the AMOUNT field data should not exceed $5,000. You can specify this using the *validation rule* validity check as follows:

**6.** Click the *AMOUNT* field name in the upper pane.

**7.** Click the *Validation Rule* entry line in the lower pane.

**8.** Type **<=5000** to indicate "less than or equal to 5000."

When you set a validity check, you should also provide a message that will appear when the rule specified by the check is broken. Do this as follows:

**9.** Click the *Validation Text* row (just beneath the Validation Rule).

**10.** Type **AMOUNT cannot exceed $5,000**. Your screen should resemble Figure A-13. Change it if it does not.

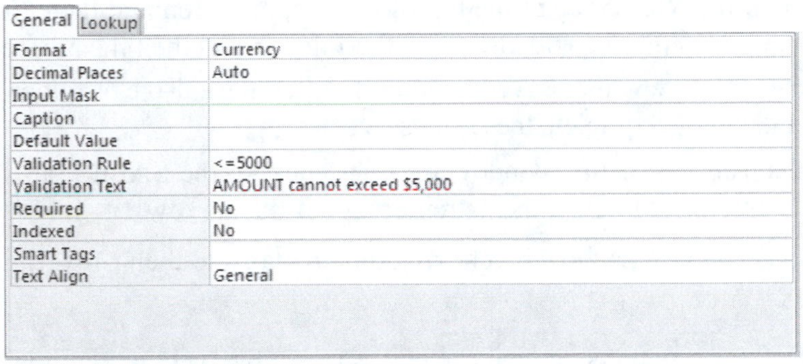

| General | Lookup |
|---|---|
| Format | Currency |
| Decimal Places | Auto |
| Input Mask | |
| Caption | |
| Default Value | |
| Validation Rule | <=5000 |
| Validation Text | AMOUNT cannot exceed $5,000 |
| Required | No |
| Indexed | No |
| Smart Tags | |
| Text Align | General |

**FIGURE A-13**    *Setting a Validation Rule*

The Validation Rule and Text rows have been entered.

**11.** Return to the upper pane (as you did in step 5).

## Setting an Input Mask

Suppose you want the phone data to be entered in a consistent format. You can do this by specifying an input "mask" or picture for the data. A mask is simply a pattern into which data will be placed.

**12.** Click the *PHONE* field in the upper pane.

**13.** Click the *Input Mask* entry line in the lower pane.

**14.** Type **(999) 999-9999** to indicate that data will automatically include parentheses and a hyphen as shown.

**NOTE:** You may want to read the Access Help screens on "Input Mask properties" to see a list of all possible mask symbols and their uses.

**15.** Press ⏎ to accept the input mask.

Access will insert some additional formatting characters into the mask. Do not be concerned.

**16.** Click anywhere within the upper pane.

**NOTE:** To see if a validity check has been set for a given field or to change it, simply click or highlight the desired field and then review the settings on the bottom pane of the window.

In the future, you might also want to set a default value to be used for *all* records. To do this, simply identify the field, select *Default*, type the desired value, and press the ⏎key.

## Saving the Table Structure

When you've finished creating a table structure, you must save it for future use. Complete the following steps to save the table:

1.   Right-click the *SALES* tab at the top of the design screen and then click Save in the list that appears. (You could also click the File tab and then the *Save* option.)
     The table structure will be saved on your diskette, flash drive or folder. Now, to close the table and database, complete these steps:

2.   Close the Table Structure window by right-clicking the SALES tab and then *Close* (or click its *Close* button at the extreme right of the tab row).

3.   Close the Database window by clicking the File tab and then *Close database*.

**NOTE:** If you want to stop, you can exit Access now by clicking the File tab and then the *Exit* option (or by simply clicking the program  Close button) or you can go on to the next lesson.

## LESSON 3: ENTERING DATA AND EXITING

Now that you've created a database and table structure, your next task is to enter data for individual records into the table.

1.   If you've exited from Access, launch it now (if needed, review Lesson 1).
     You must now open the Company database and its subordinate SALES table for use. You can select the appropriate commands from the File tab or use the "Recent Database" option in the File list. Both are listed in steps 2 and 3 next—use the one you prefer.

2.   Click the "Recent" option in the File list.

3.   If the *Recent Database* pane displays the correct "Company" database, simply click *Company* now. Go to step 8.

4.   If the "Company" database does not appear in the pane, click the *Open* option in the left list.

**NOTE:** If you're not sure which button to use, point to the button for a moment with your mouse and wait. The button's title appears below it in a "tool tip" box. Once you confirm that the button is correct, click it.

An Open dialog box appears as in Figure A-14.

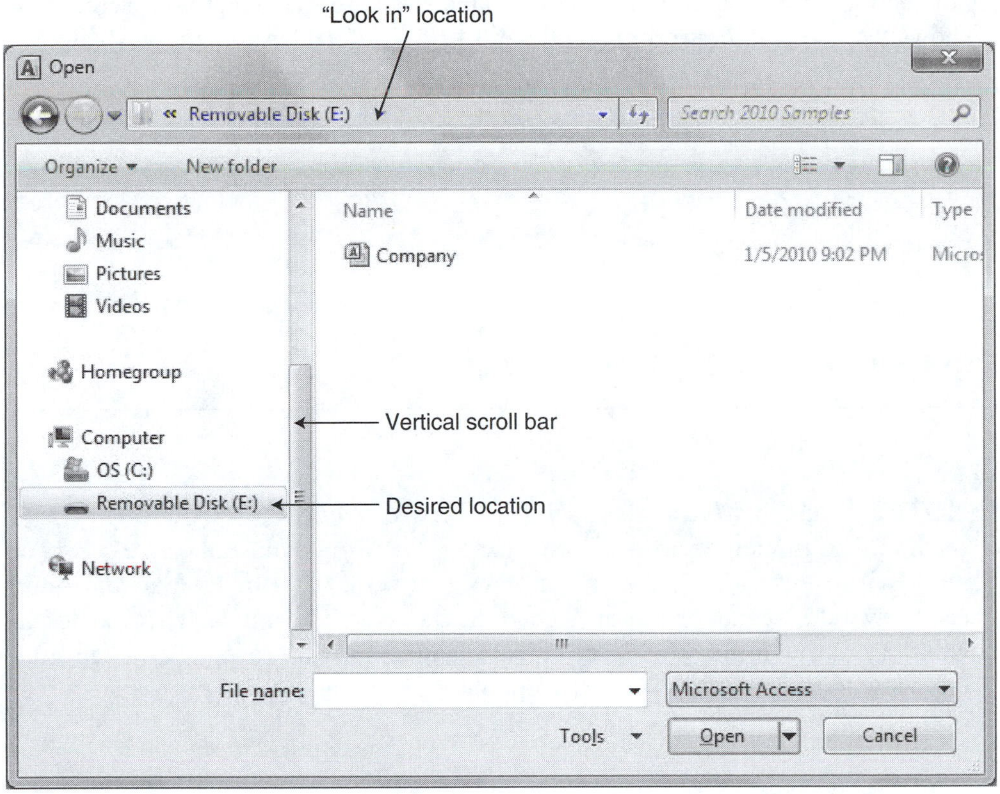

**FIGURE A-14**    *Opening a Database*

The Open dialog box lists available database files—other files may be displayed.

5.  Check the entry in the *Look in* box. If it is not the appropriate folder, change it now (use the vertical scroll bar and click the desired location).

6.  Click the desired database—*Company*—to highlight it.

7.  Click *Open*.

8.  If a Security Alert appears on the screen, check with your instructor as to the proper procedure. Typically, click the *Enable Content* button.

9.  Examine the object list for the Company database, which appears in the left pane, as shown in Figure A-15. Each item in the pane is an object associated with the Company database file. (As you create each, it will appear in the list.)

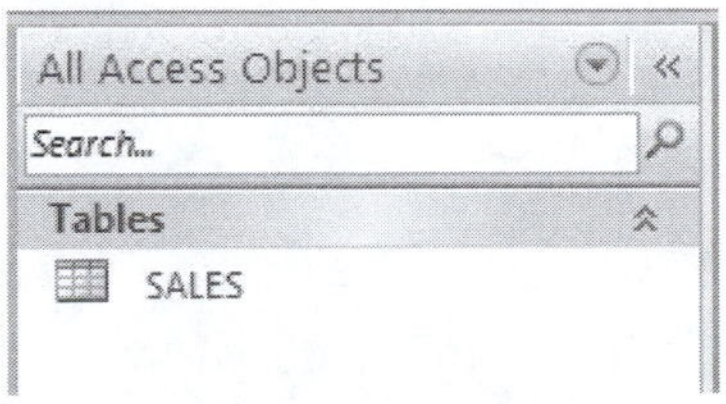

**FIGURE A-15**    *The Database Object List*

The SALES table appears in the object list.

**10.** Double-click the *SALES* table to open it.

An empty table appears, as shown in Figure A-16. The column sequence and headings match the fields you specified in your table structure. Note that your screen's status bar shows that you will be working on Record 1 of 1—all tables contain one blank record.

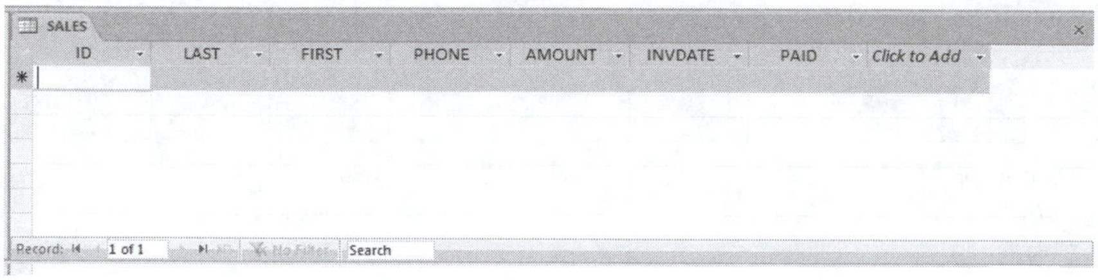

**FIGURE A-16**    *The Empty SALES Table*

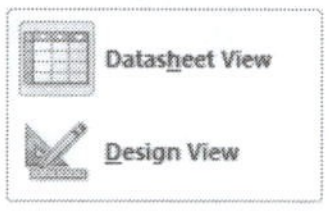

**NOTE:** You can view a table in *Design* view or *Datasheet* view. As you have seen, in Design view you work with a table's *structure*—you can create, view, or modify it in this view. In Datasheet view, you work with the table's *data*—and can view, add, delete, or edit as needed. In Datasheet view, data are presented in column and row format (fields are columns and records are rows). To switch from one view to the other, click the appropriate *View* button in the lower-right corner of the window.

**11.** You may want to type everything in capital letters as it is shown in this manual. If so, press the [ CAPS LOCK ] key now.

Table A-2 contains the data you will enter for the first six records that you want to place in your SALES table. For instance, the first record shows Lionel Twain, whose ID is 005, PHONE is (213) 555–1234, AMOUNT is 234.65, and DATE is 10/7/10. Note that there is no value listed for the PAID field, which will come later in the module.

| ID | LAST | FIRST | PHONE | AMOUNT | INVDATE |
|----|------|-------|-------|--------|---------|
| 005 | TWAIN | LIONEL | (213) 555-1234 | $234.65 | 10/7/10 |
| 008 | PARKER | CARR | (212) 555-9876 | $1,256.80 | 7/6/10 |
| 034 | KERCHIEF | HANK | (212) 555-1023 | $130.95 | 4/25/10 |
| 037 | TYME | JUSTIN | (718) 555-0982 | $450.00 | 11/1/10 |
| 046 | BEACH | SANDY | (817) 555-1122 | $534.12 | 9/8/10 |
| 086 | ROSKOPE | MIKE | (213) 555-1458 | $1,045.35 | 2/17/10 |

**TABLE A-2**    *Data for the First Six Records*

## Entering Data into a Table

An insertion point appears in the first column, showing where your entry will be placed. An asterisk pointer in the left margin shows the new record. The status bar displays the field definition you entered earlier as a prompt for data entry—in this example, "Customer ID Number." Entering data into the table couldn't be easier. Simply type the data and then press ⏎. If the entry exceeds a specified field width (or violates a validity check), Access will not let you enter it. An error message will appear in a window advising you of the mistake and expecting you to take some corrective action. Otherwise, the entry will be accepted and the insertion point will move to the next field.

> **NOTE:** To fix an error, use an arrow key or backspace to move to the error, re-type it, and press ⏎ to accept the correction. You can also use [TAB] and [SHIFT] + [TAB] to move among the field columns.

Refer to Table A-2 as you work to see what data you must enter into each record. You will also get a chance to see how the validity checks help with data entry. The first item is an ID of 005.

**1.** To place 005 into the first record, type **005** and press ⏎.

The value is accepted, and the insertion point moves to the next column.

**2.** Type **TWAIN** and press ⏎.

The insertion point moves again. Remember, the LAST name field is required. Access will not let you proceed unless you enter a last name.

**3.** Next, type **LIONEL** and press ⏎.

The insertion point moves to the PHONE column. Because you created an input mask for this field, you need only type its numerals. The parentheses and hyphen will be added automatically. Try the following steps:

**4.** Type **213** with *no* parentheses.

Note that the parentheses are automatically added to your data. Now continue with the remaining digits as follows:

**5.** Type **5551234** and press ⏎. Do *not* type any hyphen.

The input mask automatically adds the hyphen in the proper position. You're now in the AMOUNT column. Recall that you set a maximum limit for this field. To see how this validity rule works, enter a number that exceeds $5,000 as follows:

**6.** Type **8000** and press ⏎.

Note that the insertion point does not move and the error message you created earlier appears, as shown in Figure A-17.

**A**

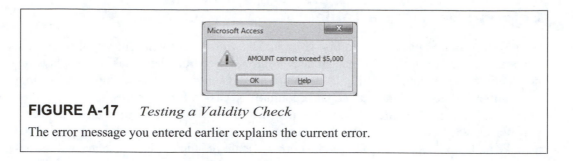

**FIGURE A-17**    *Testing a Validity Check*

The error message you entered earlier explains the current error.

You cannot proceed until the error is corrected. To do this, you must acknowledge the error, erase the entry, and then retype it as follows:

**7.** Click the *OK* button to acknowledge the message and remove the dialog box from the screen.

**8.** Press ⎡BACKSPACE⎤ four times to erase the incorrect entry.

**9.** Type the correct entry of **234.65** (decimal point but no dollar sign) and press ⎡↵⎤.
   The entry is now accepted, and the insertion point now moves to the next field.

**10.** Type **10/7/10** in the DATE field and press ⎡↵⎤.

> **NOTE:** If the typed date is invalid (the month is not between 1 and 12 or the day exceeds the allowable number for the month), Access' built-in validity check will not accept it. To correct this, click the *OK* button, press ⎡BACKSPACE⎤ and then re-enter the date.

**11.** Press ⎡↵⎤ to skip the PAID field for now.

Because PAID is the last field, Access takes you to a new blank row and awaits the second record. The asterisk pointer shows you the new record location.

**12.** Using Table A-2 as a guide, enter the remaining records (one to a row), typing all data as you did for TWAIN. Remember, type phone number digits *only*. When you finish the last record (ROSKOPE), the pointer should show the next record as shown in Figure A-18.

| SALES | | | | | | |
| ID | LAST | FIRST | PHONE | AMOUNT | INVDATE | PAID |
| --- | --- | --- | --- | --- | --- | --- |
| 005 | TWAIN | LIONEL | (213) 555-1234 | $234.65 | 10/7/2010 | |
| 008 | PARKER | CARR | (212) 555-9876 | $1,256.80 | 7/6/2010 | |
| 034 | KERCHIEF | HANK | (212) 555-1023 | $130.95 | 4/25/2010 | |
| 037 | TYME | JUSTIN | (718) 555-0982 | $450.00 | 11/1/2010 | |
| 046 | BEACH | SANDY | (817) 555-1122 | $534.12 | 9/8/2010 | |
| 086 | ROSKOPE | MIKE | (213) 555-1458 | $1,045.35 | 2/17/2010 | |

**FIGURE A-18**    *The SALES Table with Six Records Entered*

Although you can leave the table on the screen, it is wiser to clean up by closing windows when you no longer need them.

 **13.** Close the datasheet window for the SALES table by clicking its Close button (on the extreme right of the tab row) or by right-clicking the SALES table tab and clicking Close.

Records are saved when you move the insertion point to another column or row. In addition, when you close a table's window, all its records are saved to your diskette, flash drive, or folder.

**14.** You can also close the main Company database window now by clicking the File tab and then the *Close* option.

## Exiting Access

Leaving Access is easy. However, be sure you *always* leave the program by following the steps listed below. Otherwise, you may find that your tables have not been closed correctly.

**1.** Click the File tab and then *Exit* or click the Access Close button. (If you are using a diskette or flash drive, *never* remove it while you are exiting Access.)

You will return to the Windows desktop. You could now shut down Windows using your routine procedure, if you wish to stop for now.

### Quick Review #1

**1.** List the step-by-step procedure for launching the Access program.

_____

**2.** How can you tell which table is in use?

_____

**3.** What does setting the *Look in* entry accomplish?

_____

**4.** What happens to data entry if you omit a required field?

_____

**5.** Why is it important to close a database properly?

_____

## LESSON 4: ADDING NEW RECORDS

Adding new records to an existing table is almost identical to entering the original set. Practice adding records as follows:

**1.** If your computer is off, follow the Access launch procedure in Lesson 1. If appropriate, make sure your diskette or flash drive is properly placed before launching Access.

**2.** Open the Company database. (Click "Recent" and then *Company* in the "Recent Database" pane or use the File tab, Open procedure.)

**3.** Open the SALES table. (Double-click *SALES* in the object list.)

Your screen should appear in Datasheet view, displaying a table that contains all six records. The asterisk "New Record" symbol (*) should appear in the bottom row indicating that the table is available for editing.

You must now position the record pointer at the end of the table so that you can add more records. In a small table, you can simply press ⌜PGDN⌝ or ⌜↓⌝ to move to the desired record. In a larger table, however, you should learn to use the record location menu, as follows:

4.  Click the *New (Blank) Record* button on the status bar to move there immediately. The status bar shows that Access will add a seventh record to the table.

5.  Using the data in Table A-3, enter the data for the four new records, as you did before. Remember to press ⌜↵⌝ to skip the PAID field and go on to the next record. You can use ⌜←⌝ to return to a previous field.

| ID | LAST | FIRST | PHONE | AMOUNT | INVDATE |
|----|------|-------|-------|--------|---------|
| 113 | DEDOGG | PAT | (203) 555-0101 | $123.00 | 5/16/10 |
| 660 | FEGIVIN | ALICE | (213) 555-6464 | $1,443.50 | 3/17/10 |
| 754 | DEDOGG | FEE | (212) 555-0099 | $211.90 | 4/6/10 |
| 123 | VALE | NOAH | (516) 555-0705 | $550.00 | 1/22/10 |

**TABLE A-3**   *Records to Be Added to the SALES Table*

6.  After you've entered the VALE record, add one more record using an ID of 111, your own last and first names, any phone number, an amount of 100, and any date. Press ⌜↵⌝ to skip the PAID field.

    Your screen should resemble Figure A-19, which displays the completed table. Your name will appear in the final record (as mine does in the example).

| ID | LAST | FIRST | PHONE | AMOUNT | INVDATE | PAID |
|----|------|-------|-------|--------|---------|------|
| 005 | TWAIN | LIONEL | (213) 555-1234 | $234.65 | 10/7/2010 | |
| 008 | PARKER | CARR | (212) 555-9876 | $1,256.80 | 7/6/2010 | |
| 034 | KERCHIEF | HANK | (212) 555-1023 | $130.95 | 4/25/2010 | |
| 037 | TYME | JUSTIN | (718) 555-0982 | $450.00 | 11/1/2010 | |
| 046 | BEACH | SANDY | (817) 555-1122 | $534.12 | 9/8/2010 | |
| 086 | ROSKOPE | MIKE | (213) 555-1458 | $1,045.35 | 2/17/2010 | |
| 113 | DEDOGG | PAT | (203) 555-0101 | $123.00 | 5/16/2010 | |
| 660 | FEGIVIN | ALICE | (213) 555-6464 | $1,443.50 | 3/17/2010 | |
| 754 | DEDOGG | FEE | (212) 555-0099 | $211.90 | 4/6/2010 | |
| 123 | VALE | NOAH | (516) 555-0705 | $550.00 | 1/22/2010 | |
| 111 | MARTIN | EDWARD | (718) 555-0000 | $100.00 | 1/1/2010 | |

**FIGURE A-19**   *The Complete SALES Table*

7.  Close the table (right-click the SALES tab and click Close or click the *Close button* to the extreme right of the tab).

8.  If you want to stop for now, close the database. Otherwise, continue to the next section.

## LESSON 5: EDITING RECORDS

There are times when records must be edited to correct errors or reflect changes that have occurred since the time they were entered (updated). To practice the edit technique, you will now update the PAID field to show payments that have been made since the records were originally entered.

**NOTE:** The edit procedure can change the data in any field as needed. Use it to correct any typing errors you may have made.

1.  If needed, launch Access following the procedure in Lesson 1.

2.  Open the Company database and its SALES table.

    You must position the pointer at the proper record for editing. In this case, you want to edit the first record. If the pointer is already on record 1, do nothing. Otherwise, position the pointer as follows:

3.  Click the *First Record* button on the status bar.

    The pointer should now indicate the first record.

**NOTE:** You can also press `PGUP`, `PGDN`, `↑`, or `↓` to move to any record from your current location in the table.

You can now change any data on the screen. Use the mouse or arrow keys to move the insertion point to the item, type the new information (using `BACKSPACE` or `DELETE` to erase any characters you do not need), and press `↵`. Use the edit technique to update the PAID field to reflect the amounts listed in Table A-4.

| REC | LAST | FIRST | Change PAID to: |
|---|---|---|---|
| 1 | TWAIN | LIONEL | $200.00 |
| 2 | PARKER | CARR | $1,000.00 |
| 3 | KERCHIEF | HANK | $130.95 |
| 4 | TYME | JUSTIN | $450.00 |
| 5 | BEACH | SANDY | $500.00 |
| 6 | ROSKOPE | MIKE | $1,045.35 |

**TABLE A-4**   *Data to Be Updated in the PAID Field*

4.  Move to the PAID field with `→`. (Keep an eye on the FIRST name or status bar record number to be sure that you're editing the correct record.)

5.  Look up the PAID value for record 1 in Table A-4. In this case, it's 200, so type **200** and, this time, press `↓`.

**NOTE:** Pressing `↓` keeps your insertion point in the same field column. You could press the `↵` key, but that would move you to the next field or, if you are at the end of a record, to the start of the next record.

6.  Repeat this process to change the PAID field for the next two records only (PARKER and KERCHIEF).

    Use the arrow keys to move from one record to another.

7.  When you arrive at record 4 (JUSTIN TYME), stop.

    You are going to try another entry technique with the remaining records. Access allows you to view or edit records either as a complete datasheet (as you have been doing) or as individual forms. In Datasheet view, records appear in separate rows. In Form view, each record is given its own screen. It doesn't matter which view you use, and you can switch between them whenever you want. Try the following exercise:

8.  Click the *Create* tab in the ribbon.

    Your ribbon should now resemble Figure A-20.

9.  Click the *Form* command button (in the Forms group) as shown in Figure A-20.

Click here    Then click here

**FIGURE A-20**    *Access Ribbon's Create Tab*

As shown in Figure A-21a, a form displaying the data for a single record will appear in a window on the screen.

10. Click the *View* drop-down button (at the extreme left of the ribbon) and then Form View.

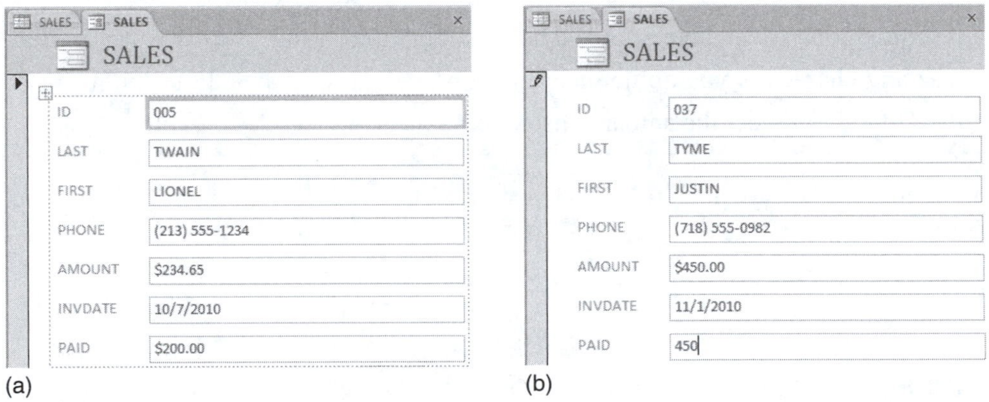

**FIGURE A-21**    *Entering Data into a Form*

(a)    A record displayed as a form.

(b)    The new data has been entered in the PAID field for TYME's record.

The highlighted bar shows the current entry position, as shown in Figure A-21a. Now continue to enter the remaining data as follows:

11. Move to Tyme's record. (Press PGDN three times or click Next on the status bar.)

12. Click the PAID field to move the highlight to it.

13. Type **450** as in Figure A-21b, and press ↵.

**NOTE:**  The data in the PAID field is updated, and the next record appears.

14. Click the next PAID field (or click ↓ to move to it).

15. Type **500** and press ↵.

16. Click the PAID field for ROSKOPE and enter his data (**1045.35**) in the same manner.

Now that you're done, you can save this form so that it will be available to you in the future, or simply re-create it each time it is needed. In actual use, you will want to save customized forms with the following procedure. To save the form:

17. Click the File tab and then Save.

A Save As dialog box appears to save the new form.

18. Type **SALES1** and then click *OK* to save the form with this name.

19. Close the *Form* window (click its Close button).

   You should now be back in the Datasheet (table) view again. Examine the table, noting the added data now displayed in the PAID field. You may have to press the arrow keys to move to the PAID field column. Now that you're done, clear the entire desktop as follows:

20. Close the table (click its Close button or right-click the SALES tab and click Close).

21. Close the Database (File tab, *Close*). You can exit Access for now or continue.


## LESSON 6: VIEWING TABLE DATA

What good are tables, records, and data unless you can view them on the screen in a useful format? At times, you will want to move around a table to see specific data or to view your data in a format different from the one you used to enter them.

   Access allows you to adjust the on-screen appearance of your data by offering options to change justification, type style, size, and color. Although you are encouraged to examine these options, they are beyond the scope of this brief manual.

   In this section, you'll practice moving around a datasheet table and adjusting some characteristics (properties) of its component parts (objects). To prepare to do this, complete the following steps:

1. Launch Access and open the Company database.

2. Open the SALES table.

   Although there are only eleven records in the SALES table, you can practice techniques applicable to moving around tables of any size.


### Status Bar Movements

As you have seen, the status bar offers mouse shortcuts that allow you to reposition the pointer at various records within the table. Refer to Figure A-22, which displays the appropriate buttons, as you try some of these quick table movements.

1. Click the *Last Record* button to position the highlight at the last record in your table.

2. Click the *First Record* button to move to the first record.

3. Click the *Next* button to move down one record (or press ↓).

4. Click the *Previous* button to move up one record (or press ↑).

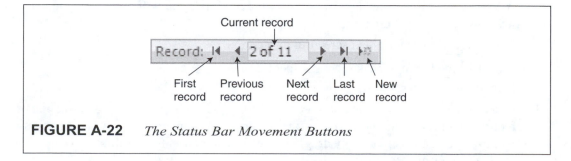

**FIGURE A-22**    *The Status Bar Movement Buttons*

## Techniques with Larger Tables

Although you can maximize any table window to see more of its contents, there will be times when your table will contain more fields or records than the screen can display at any given time. The PgDn and PgUp keys are useful when this situation occurs. PgUp moves the pointer a full screen of records upward, whereas PgDn moves a full screen of records down the list. You can also use the vertical or horizontal scroll bars (as in any window) to view additional records as needed. To see this more clearly, you will now resize the table to simulate a window that cannot show all records or fields, as follows:

1. Click the *Restore Down* button on the program window (second button at the upper-right).

2. Point to the bottom frame of the table window, just below the status bar. Click and drag the frame upward so that only about six records are displayed, as in Figure A-23. Then, release the mouse button.

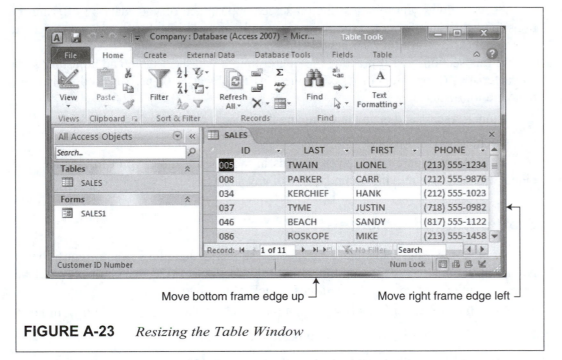

Move bottom frame edge up ⌐          Move right frame edge left ⌐

**FIGURE A-23**    *Resizing the Table Window*

3. Now drag the right frame of the table window to the left until the AMOUNT field is no longer visible (as in Figure A-23). Release the mouse button.

A Vertical scroll bar now appears in the window. First, you will practice some vertical moves by following these steps:

4. Press PgDn to see the next screenful of records.

5. Press PgUp to move back up one screenful.

Now try using the scroll bar:

6. Click the *down arrow* at the bottom of the vertical scroll bar to scroll down the list of records; then click the *up arrow* at the top to scroll upward. (Of course, as in any window, you can also move by dragging the vertical box in the scroll bar.)

Now, try the following horizontal move:

7. Press → to scroll right through the columns until you see the PAID field.

Note that the ID and LAST fields have disappeared. Don't worry; they are still part of the table, but are just not visible in the window at the moment. This is a typical problem in tables with a large number of fields—you may not be able to view all of the fields you need at the same time. Fortunately, there are two ways to fix this: Use field freeze or reposition the fields. You'll look at both techniques now.

### Field Freeze

Freezing a field column means marking it so it remains on the screen as you scroll horizontally through a table. You can freeze one or more fields at the left of a table and then move to view others at the right. You do this by invoking the freeze command at the desired position. Here's how:

1. Press ⬅ until you are in the leftmost column, which displays the ID field.

2. Point to the ID field name at the top of the column, so that the mouse pointer changes to a downward arrow, as shown in Figure A-24a.

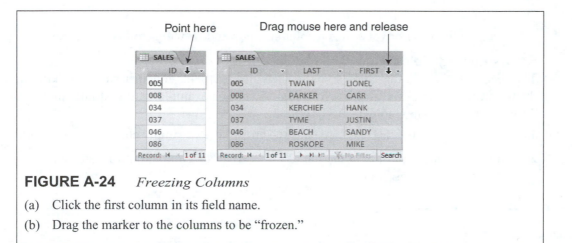

**FIGURE A-24**    *Freezing Columns*

(a)   Click the first column in its field name.

(b)   Drag the marker to the columns to be "frozen."

3. Click and then drag the new pointer to the right until it points to the FIRST name column, as in Figure A-24b. The ID, LAST, and FIRST fields should appear highlighted. Release the mouse button.

4. Right-click at the top of the "FIRST" column to open a shortcut menu.

5. Click the *Freeze Fields* option in the list. The three field columns are now "frozen."

6. Scroll right (press ➡) to see the PAID field.

As shown in Figure A-25, the column freeze keeps the three columns in place, allowing you to view other fields as needed. You can set the freeze at any column, including as many (or as few) fields as you want.

To shut off the field freeze, complete the following steps:

7. Right-click at the top of the "FIRST" column and then click *Unfreeze All Fields* in the list.

| ID | LAST | FIRST | PAID |
|---|---|---|---|
| 005 | TWAIN | LIONEL | $200.00 |
| 008 | PARKER | CARR | $1,000.00 |
| 034 | KERCHIEF | HANK | $130.95 |
| 037 | TYME | JUSTIN | $450.00 |
| 046 | BEACH | SANDY | $500.00 |
| 086 | ROSKOPE | MIKE | $1,045.35 |



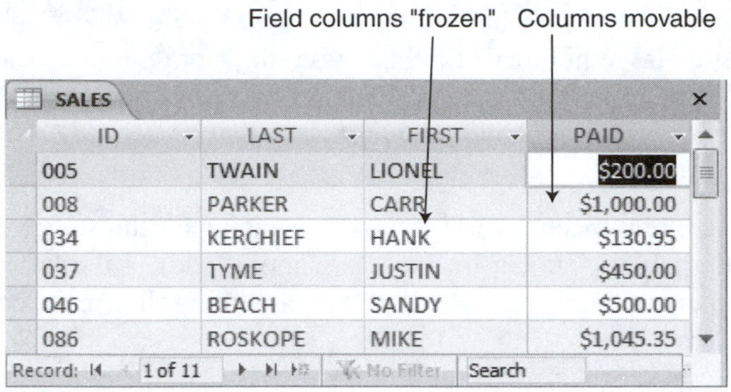

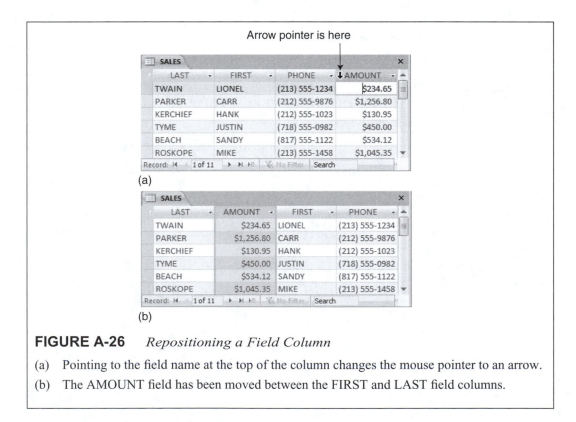

**FIGURE A-25** *Using Column Freeze*

As you scroll, the "frozen" fields remain on the screen.

Because there are now no frozen columns, the window will scroll normally again.

## Repositioning Fields

The second technique that allows you to view desired fields together simply repositions them on the screen exactly where you want them. For example, you will now move the AMOUNT column next to the LAST column.

1. Move to the AMOUNT column. (Use the arrow keys or simply click it if it is visible.)
2. Move the mouse pointer to the top of the AMOUNT column until its shape changes to a small arrow, as in Figure A-26a.

| LAST | FIRST | PHONE | AMOUNT |
|---|---|---|---|
| TWAIN | LIONEL | (213) 555-1234 | $234.65 |
| PARKER | CARR | (212) 555-9876 | $1,256.80 |
| KERCHIEF | HANK | (212) 555-1023 | $130.95 |
| TYME | JUSTIN | (718) 555-0982 | $450.00 |
| BEACH | SANDY | (817) 555-1122 | $534.12 |
| ROSKOPE | MIKE | (213) 555-1458 | $1,045.35 |



| LAST | AMOUNT | FIRST | PHONE |
|---|---|---|---|
| TWAIN | $234.65 | LIONEL | (213) 555-1234 |
| PARKER | $1,256.80 | CARR | (212) 555-9876 |
| KERCHIEF | $130.95 | HANK | (212) 555-1023 |
| TYME | $450.00 | JUSTIN | (718) 555-0982 |
| BEACH | $534.12 | SANDY | (817) 555-1122 |
| ROSKOPE | $1,045.35 | MIKE | (213) 555-1458 |



**FIGURE A-26** *Repositioning a Field Column*

(a) Pointing to the field name at the top of the column changes the mouse pointer to an arrow.

(b) The AMOUNT field has been moved between the FIRST and LAST field columns.

3. Click the mouse button. Note that the AMOUNT column is highlighted.

4.  Now, point to the AMOUNT field name (in the top row). Then, click and drag the pointer left, until it is to the left of the FIRST name field. The screen will automatically scroll as you move.

5.  Release the mouse button.

    As shown in Figure A-26b, the AMOUNT field will now appear to the left of the FIRST name field.

> **NOTE:** You can reposition fields as often as you want. The changes will not affect the table's operation and will not be saved, unless you accept them when you close the window.

Practice using the status bar, arrow keys, scroll bars, field column freeze, and field repositioning. When you have mastered these techniques, close the table as follows:

6.  Maximize the window. (Click its Maximize button.)

7.  Close the table. (Right-click the SALES tab and click Close.)

    Because you have changed the table's properties, a dialog box will ask if you want to save the changed layout.

8.  Click the *No* button to leave the table in its original format, prior to the changes you made.

## Adjusting Column Width

At times, your columns will be too wide for your data. Although this is not harmful, you may want to automatically adjust them to save space and more easily view the data on the screen. Try this:

1.  Open the SALES table for use. (Double-click the SALES:Table object.)

2.  As shown in Figure A-27a, point to the right side of the ID column frame. (When positioned correctly, the mouse pointer changes to a horizontal line with two arrows.)

3.  Double-click this place in the frame.

    The width of the column is automatically adjusted to fit the largest data in the column (in this case, three characters), as shown in Figure A-27b.

4.  Repeat this procedure on the six remaining columns, so that your screen resembles Figure A-27c.

5.  Right-click the SALES tab and then click *Save* to save these changes.

6.  Close the table.

A

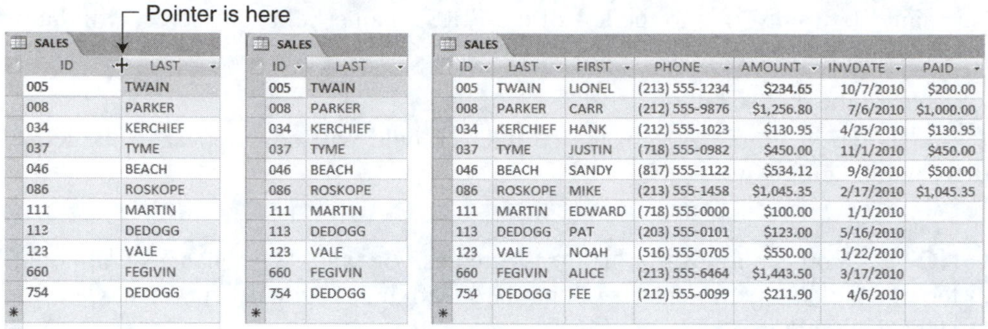

Pointer is here

| SALES | |
|---|---|
| ID | LAST |
| 005 | TWAIN |
| 008 | PARKER |
| 034 | KERCHIEF |
| 037 | TYME |
| 046 | BEACH |
| 086 | ROSKOPE |
| 111 | MARTIN |
| 113 | DEDOGG |
| 123 | VALE |
| 660 | FEGIVIN |
| 754 | DEDOGG |

| SALES | |
|---|---|
| ID | LAST |
| 005 | TWAIN |
| 008 | PARKER |
| 034 | KERCHIEF |
| 037 | TYME |
| 046 | BEACH |
| 086 | ROSKOPE |
| 111 | MARTIN |
| 113 | DEDOGG |
| 123 | VALE |
| 660 | FEGIVIN |
| 754 | DEDOGG |

| SALES | | | | | | |
|---|---|---|---|---|---|---|
| ID | LAST | FIRST | PHONE | AMOUNT | INVDATE | PAID |
| 005 | TWAIN | LIONEL | (213) 555-1234 | $234.65 | 10/7/2010 | $200.00 |
| 008 | PARKER | CARR | (212) 555-9876 | $1,256.80 | 7/6/2010 | $1,000.00 |
| 034 | KERCHIEF | HANK | (212) 555-1023 | $130.95 | 4/25/2010 | $130.95 |
| 037 | TYME | JUSTIN | (718) 555-0982 | $450.00 | 11/1/2010 | $450.00 |
| 046 | BEACH | SANDY | (817) 555-1122 | $534.12 | 9/8/2010 | $500.00 |
| 086 | ROSKOPE | MIKE | (213) 555-1458 | $1,045.35 | 2/17/2010 | $1,045.35 |
| 111 | MARTIN | EDWARD | (718) 555-0000 | $100.00 | 1/1/2010 | |
| 113 | DEDOGG | PAT | (203) 555-0101 | $123.00 | 5/16/2010 | |
| 123 | VALE | NOAH | (516) 555-0705 | $550.00 | 1/22/2010 | |
| 660 | FEGIVIN | ALICE | (213) 555-6464 | $1,443.50 | 3/17/2010 | |
| 754 | DEDOGG | FEE | (212) 555-0099 | $211.90 | 4/6/2010 | |

(a)          (b)          (c)

**FIGURE A-27**   *Adjusting Column Widths*

(a)   Point to the right edge of the column identifier.

(b)   Double-click to adjust the width.

(c)   All widths have been adjusted.

## Printing a Table

Tables are easy to print. Although you will learn how to generate a formal report of table data later in this module, the following technique shows you how to print the table for immediate use.

1. Open the SALES table for use.

    It is always a good idea to preview your printing before actually sending it to paper. This avoids wasted paper and time. Try this:

2. Click the File tab, click the *Print* option, and then click *Print Preview* in the list that appears on the right.

    A small screen image of your data appears as it will look when printed.

3. Click the *Zoom In* button (the "+" at the extreme right of the status bar) four times to set a 90% zoom.

    The image enlarges to resemble Figure A-28.

4. You could scroll around this image to examine it if desired. For now,

5. Click the *Close Print Preview* button in the ribbon to close Print Preview.

    When you want to print the data:

6. Make sure your printer is ready.

7. Click the File tab and then *Print*.

8. Click the Print option in the list that appears.

    A Print dialog box appears. This box allows you to specify the number of copies and pages that will be printed. You could print one copy of the table by clicking OK. But for now, continue as follows:

9. Click *Cancel*.

| ID | LAST | FIRST | PHONE | AMOUNT | INVDATE | PAID |
|---|---|---|---|---|---|---|
| 005 | TWAIN | LIONEL | (213) 555-1234 | $234.65 | 10/7/2010 | $200.00 |
| 008 | PARKER | CARR | (212) 555-9876 | $1,256.80 | 7/6/2010 | $1,000.00 |
| 034 | KERCHIEF | HANK | (212) 555-1023 | $130.95 | 4/25/2010 | $130.95 |
| 037 | TYME | JUSTIN | (718) 555-0982 | $450.00 | 11/1/2010 | $450.00 |
| 046 | BEACH | SANDY | (817) 555-1122 | $534.12 | 9/8/2010 | $500.00 |
| 086 | ROSKOPE | MIKE | (213) 555-1458 | $1,045.35 | 2/17/2010 | $1,045.35 |
| 111 | MARTIN | EDWARD | (718) 555-0000 | $100.00 | 1/1/2010 | |
| 113 | DEDOGG | PAT | (203) 555-0101 | $123.00 | 5/16/2010 | |
| 123 | VALE | NOAH | (516) 555-0705 | $550.00 | 1/22/2010 | |
| 660 | FEGIVIN | ALICE | (213) 555-6464 | $1,443.50 | 3/17/2010 | |
| 754 | DEDOGG | FEE | (212) 555-0099 | $211.90 | 4/6/2010 | |

*(SALES — 1/6/2010)*

**FIGURE A-28**    *The Printed Version (and Preview) of the SALES Table*

## Viewing the Table Structure

At times, you may want to review the exact arrangement of your table: its field names, types, sizes, and validity checks. This is useful when you are considering modifying its structure (adding or deleting fields) or preparing reports.

To view a table structure on the screen, complete the following steps:

1.  Open the Company database and SALES table for use if needed.

2.  Click the *Design View* button (right edge of status bar).

The table structure window appears on the screen (as you've seen in Figure A-12), displaying your field list. You can move the pointer down through the listed fields to examine their individual validity checks.

3.  When you are finished, close the table.

4.  Close the main database as well.

> **NOTE:** RESTRUCTURING THE TABLE—To *restructure* the table itself, move the insertion point to the appropriate field. You can change field names, type, or size. To add new fields, move to the row where you want the new field to appear and press ( INSERT ); then fill in the new information. To delete an old field, right-click its row and click *Delete Row*. When you finish making changes, close the window and then accept the changes as desired.

## LESSON 7: THE QUERY COMMAND

One of the advantages of a database program is its ability to search through a table to select those records that meet certain criteria. At times, you will want to see only specific records—for example, those with phone numbers in the 213 area code or records with a last name of SMITH. Other times, you will want to view only selected fields.

In these instances, you can create a *query* that will allow you to designate specific criteria to be used when searching for records to be viewed. Queries are questions you ask of a table. You can use queries temporarily and then discard them, or save as many queries as you want, and then open each one for use whenever you need it. Assume you want to create a query that will include only those records whose AMOUNT field exceeds $500.

## Creating a Query

**1.** Launch Access if needed and open the Company database.

**2.** Click the *Create* tab in the ribbon.

**3.** Click the *Query Design* command button (*Macros and Code* group).

A Show Table dialog box appears. Here you must indicate the table name that the query will use in developing its answer. Although you can type field names directly, specifying a table name will make it easier to select fields as you need them.

**4.** Click the *SALES* table if needed to highlight it.

**5.** Click the *Add* button to add this table to the query.

**6.** Now click its close button to remove this dialog box from the screen.

A Query window appears, as in Figure A-29. A table box with field names appears at the upper left. Empty field columns appear at the bottom of the window. These columns control what fields will appear in the final result and how records will be selected.

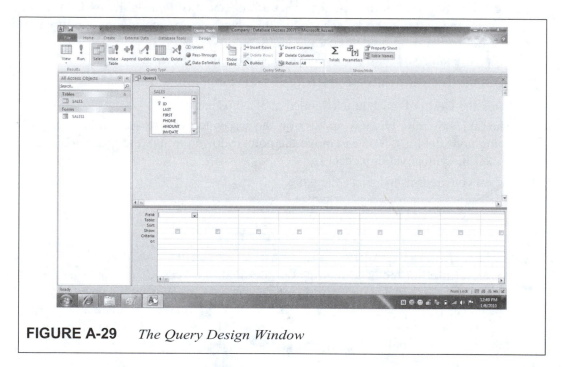

**FIGURE A-29**     *The Query Design Window*

Access uses a Query-by-Example or QBE technique. In QBE, you move to a field column, select a field, and then type an example of what you are seeking. You can also type a search condition (criterion) that explains the acceptable data limits. When the query is run, Access finds the records that meet your search pattern. Although you can create very sophisticated searches, you will examine only the basic ones here.

### Selecting Fields

If you want all fields to appear in the query's answer, you need only double-click the asterisk in the SALES table list. In this example, however, you will learn how to select individual fields, to control the fields (and order) that will be used in response to the query. In this query, you'll include ID, FIRST, LAST, and AMOUNT. Here's an easy way to do this:

**1.** Point to the ID field in the SALES table list as shown in Figure A-30a.

**2.** Double-click the *ID* field.

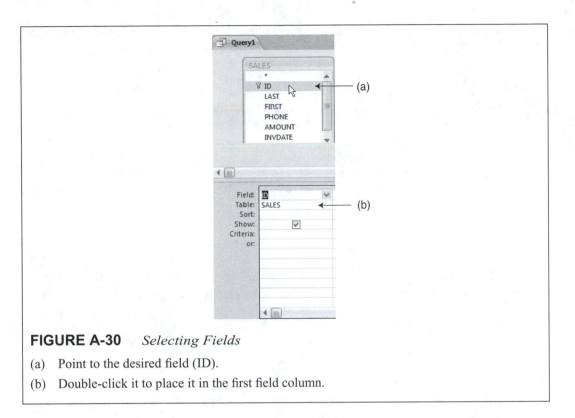

**FIGURE A-30**   *Selecting Fields*

(a)   Point to the desired field (ID).

(b)   Double-click it to place it in the first field column.

The field is copied into the first field column, as shown in Figure A-30b. Note that a check mark appears in the Show box, indicating that this field will be displayed.

**3.**   Double-click *FIRST* in the *SALES* table list to place it into the second column.

**4.**   Double-click *LAST* in the *SALES* table list to place it into the third column.

**5.**   Double-click *AMOUNT* in the *SALES* table list to place it in the fourth column.
The bottom portion of your screen should resemble Figure A-31a.

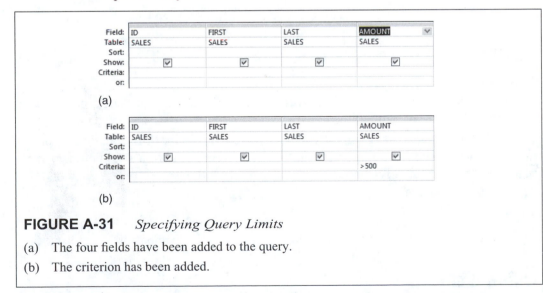

**FIGURE A-31**   *Specifying Query Limits*

(a)   The four fields have been added to the query.

(b)   The criterion has been added.

**NOTE:**   You can add fields in any order in a query—they need not match the order of the table.

To specify query limits for one (or more) fields, you can simply move to the appropriate field column, and type in an example or a search condition, as you will see next.

> **NOTE:** If you do not specify at least one search criterion, all records will be included.

For example, to restrict the query search to all records whose AMOUNT field exceeds $500, complete the following steps:

**6.** Click the *Criteria* row of the AMOUNT column.

**7.** Type **>500** and press ⏎ as in Figure A-31b.

> **NOTE:** You can use many different relational operators to set conditions. These include operators such as: = (equal to), > (greater than), < (less than), <> or NOT (not equal to), <= (less than or equal to), >= (greater than or equal to), and LIKE (pattern match).

**8.** You can now click the *Run* command button (*Results* group).

As shown in Figure A-32, a Query table appears on the screen displaying those records with AMOUNTs greater than 500. This list, known as a *dynaset* (short for dynamic set), is the response to a query. If you save the query, you can use it and its dynaset in the future.

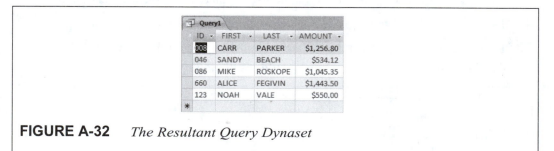

| ID | FIRST | LAST | AMOUNT |
|----|-------|------|--------|
| 008 | CARR | PARKER | $1,256.80 |
| 046 | SANDY | BEACH | $534.12 |
| 086 | MIKE | ROSKOPE | $1,045.35 |
| 660 | ALICE | FEGIVIN | $1,443.50 |
| 123 | NOAH | VALE | $550.00 |

**FIGURE A-32**  *The Resultant Query Dynaset*

**9.** Close the Query table (right-click its tab and then click *Close*, or click the Close button at the extreme right of the tab row).

A dialog box appears, asking if you want to save the query. Most queries are one-of-a-kind in nature and need not be saved. However, you can save a specific query if you plan to use it again. In this example, save the query as follows:

**10.** Click the *Yes* button.

**11.** In the *Query Name* entry box that appears, type **SALES Q1** and click *OK*.

The query is saved for future use and will appear in the Database's object list.

## Using a Query

Whenever you want to search for certain records, you need only invoke the specific query you want, and then view or use the dynaset it generates. Only the records that match the query condition will be included. Here's an example:

1. Open the Company database if needed.

2. Double-click the *SALES Q1* object.

   The dynaset response to the query you created earlier returns to the screen.

**NOTE:** You can switch between query design and datasheet by clicking the *View* drop-down arrow and then the view selector buttons as needed.

When you no longer need a search condition, you can close the query table and then open the table from which it was generated. When you open the original table, all the records will reappear, as follows:

3. Close the query table.

4. Open the SALES table (double-click *SALES:Table*). Note that all the records are still in the database.

5. Close the table.

## Editing a Query

You can edit queries as your needs change. For example, you will now change the SALES Q1 query to show FIRST, LAST, and PHONE fields only for AMOUNTs that are $1,000 or less.

1. Open the SALES Q1 query in design view from the Company database dialog box. (Double-click *SALES Q1*, then click the *View* drop-down arrow in the ribbon and then the *Design View* selector button.)

   The Query Design window reappears. Unlike a blank query screen, a retrieved query retains whatever settings were placed in it when it was last saved.

### Changing a Criterion

2. Click in the criteria row of the AMOUNT column (where it currently shows >500).

3. DELETE the >500, type <=**1000** and then press ↵.

   Of course, you can assign any condition to the appropriate columns in the future.

### Changing Fields in the Query Table

You can also add or remove fields to control which will be included when the query dynaset is generated. First, you will remove the ID column. Here's how:

4. Select the desired column (namely, ID) by pointing to the bar above the field row, as shown in Figure A-33a.

   As you have seen earlier, the mouse pointer changes to a down arrow.

A

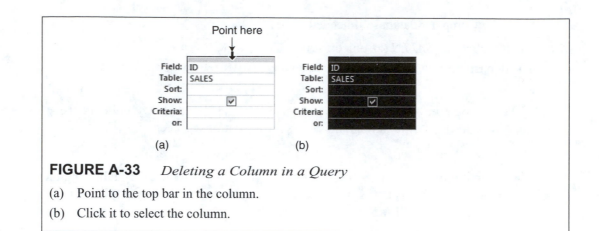

**FIGURE A-33**    *Deleting a Column in a Query*

(a)   Point to the top bar in the column.

(b)   Click it to select the column.

**5.**   Click the mouse to highlight the column, as in Figure A-33b.

**6.**   Press DELETE.

The column disappears, showing that this field will no longer be included in the dynaset. (Remember, this does not change the original data—it just removes this column from the display.)

You can also add fields to be displayed in the dynaset. For example, to add the PHONE field in the third column, do the following:

**7.**   Click the *Field* row in the third column—it currently contains AMOUNT.

**8.**   Click the *Insert Columns* command button in the ribbon (*Query Setup* group) to insert a new field column.

You can now select a field to display here.

**9.**   Access the field list for this column by clicking the drop-down arrow in the Field row, as shown in Figure A-34a.

**10.**   Click the *PHONE* field, as shown in Figure A-34b.

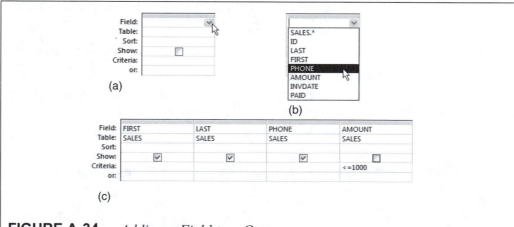

**FIGURE A-34**    *Adding a Field to a Query*

(a)   Click the Field row drop-down arrow.

(b)   Click the PHONE option in the list.

(c)   The completed field list: only fields with checkmarks in the Show box will appear in the dynaset.

**NOTE:** If you were to double-click the *PHONE* field in the SALES table list, Access would place it in the next available column at the right. Steps 7–10 are only necessary when you want to place a field somewhere other than at the end.

One more change. Let's say you did not want to display the AMOUNT in the dynaset even though it will be used to select records. You can easily control which fields are displayed through the Show box in each column.

**11.** Click the *check mark* in the Show box of the AMOUNT column to remove the check from the box.

The check marks in the Show boxes now indicate that only the fields FIRST, LAST, and PHONE will be included, as in Figure A-34c. If your screen is different, change it now to match.

**12.** Run the query (click the *Run* command) to generate the dynaset shown in Figure A-35.

This query yields the FIRST, LAST, and PHONE for records in which AMOUNT is less than or equal to $1,000.

| SALES Q1 | | |
|---|---|---|
| FIRST ▾ | LAST ▾ | PHONE ▾ |
| LIONEL | TWAIN | (213) 555-1234 |
| HANK | KERCHIEF | (212) 555-1023 |
| JUSTIN | TYME | (718) 555-0982 |
| SANDY | BEACH | (817) 555-1122 |
| PAT | DEDOGG | (203) 555-0101 |
| FEE | DEDOGG | (212) 555-0099 |
| NOAH | VALE | (516) 555-0705 |
| Your name appears here | | (718) 555-0000 |
| * | | |

**FIGURE A-35**    *The Query Dynaset with Restricted Fields*

As expected, only three fields are listed in the dynaset.

**13.** When you are finished looking at the dynaset, close it.

A dialog box will appear, asking if you want to save the modified query.

**14.** Click *Yes* to save the modified query as SALES Q1.

The query will be saved again for future use. You can create or modify as many queries as you like. You can give each new query a different name, or use an existing name to replace an old query with the new one.

A

### Creating Multiple Criteria

You can also create multiple criteria that allow you to ask more than one question in the query. For example, if you type two criteria on the same row in different fields (as in Figure A-36a) or in the same field, separated by an "and" (as in Figure A-36b), both criteria must be met for the records to be included in the resulting table. This is called an AND connector, because both the first criterion *and* the second criterion must be met. If you type criteria on separate lines (Figure A-36c), either one can be met to include records. This is called an OR connector, because either the first criterion *or* the second must be met, but not necessarily both.

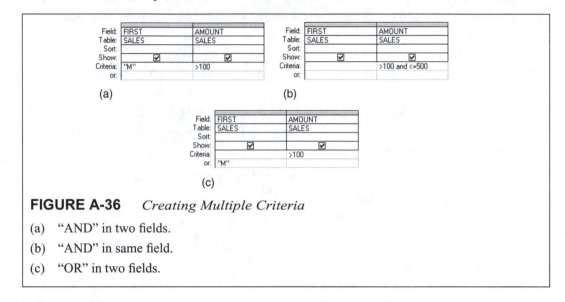

**FIGURE A-36**     *Creating Multiple Criteria*

(a)   "AND" in two fields.

(b)   "AND" in same field.

(c)   "OR" in two fields.

**Access Practice Sheet**

Your Name:_____

Class: _____ Date: _____

For questions 1 through 4, fill in an appropriate field name, type, and width in the blanks on the right. Be sure to correctly identify the type of data (number, date, or alphanumeric). Then, in the last blank, write a sample of how you might expect the data to appear. Your example should reflect the characteristics you defined. Use the sample as a guide:

| FIELD | NAME | TYPE | SIZE | EXAMPLE |
|-------|------|------|------|---------|
| Sample: First Name | FIRST | Text | 10 | EDWARD |
| 1. Phone number | _____ | _____ | ____ | _____ |
| 2. Date of birth | _____ | _____ | ____ | _____ |
| 3. Social Security # | _____ | _____ | ____ | _____ |
| 4. Amount owed | _____ | _____ | ____ | _____ |

5. How are currency fields different from number fields?
   _____

6. What commands can you invoke to tell Access to begin the procedure to ADD new records?
   _____

7. How does Access indicate the field in which you are currently typing?
   _____

8. What condition should be placed in the PAID column of a query design to find records whose PAID field equals zero? _____

A

## LESSON 8: DELETING RECORDS

At times, you will want to delete records from your table. Deleting records is easy, but can have dire consequences. Once you delete a record, it is gone forever. So, be careful! First, you will practice deleting record 3 for HANK KERCHIEF.

### Deleting One Record at a Time

1. Launch Access, open the Company database, and open the SALES table for use.

2. Select the third record (ID 034) by clicking the row's leftmost column (left of the ID field) as shown in Figure A-37.

Click here

| ID | LAST | FIRST | PHONE | AMOUNT | INVDATE | PAID | Click to Add |
|---|---|---|---|---|---|---|---|
| 005 | TWAIN | LIONEL | (213) 555-1234 | $234.65 | 10/7/2010 | $200.00 | |
| 008 | PARKER | CARR | (212) 555-9876 | $1,256.80 | 7/6/2010 | $1,000.00 | |
| 034 | KERCHIEF | HANK | (212) 555-1023 | $130.95 | 4/25/2010 | $130.95 | |
| 037 | TYME | JUSTIN | (718) 555-0982 | $450.00 | 11/1/2010 | $450.00 | |
| 046 | BEACH | SANDY | (817) 555-1122 | $534.12 | 9/8/2010 | $500.00 | |
| 086 | ROSKOPE | MIKE | (213) 555-1458 | $1,045.35 | 2/17/2010 | $1,045.35 | |

**FIGURE A-37**   *Selecting a Row*
Click the row's leftmost column (in the border) to select it.

Make sure that you have identified the correct record, because the next step will re-move the record from the table *permanently*. You should look at the status bar to verify the record number and visually check the pointer at the left of the record. The entire row will be highlighted. If you marked the wrong row, click anywhere within the table (or press an arrow key) and then select the correct record.

3. Press DELETE.
   A warning message appears. At this point, you could cancel the delete or accept it.

4. Click the Yes button.
   The record is gone! It is no longer included in the list. Note that the records beneath it have been moved up and renumbered to reflect the change. The status bar also shows that only ten records remain.

5. Close the table.

### Deleting a Group of Records

Using a more powerful query technique, you can delete those records that match certain criteria. For example, you might delete all records with AMOUNTs greater than $600, or those records whose area code is 212. This procedure requires careful thought, for *every record that matches your criteria* will be deleted. Try the following technique:

1. Open a new query (Click *Create* tab, *Query Design* button) and add the SALES table for use with the query, then close the "Show Table" dialog box. (Review the tech-nique in Lesson 7 if needed.)
   A blank Query window appears. You can now specify the conditions that will select the records to be deleted.

**2.** Click the *Delete* button (in the *Query Type* group of the ribbon).

As shown in Figure A-38a, the labels in the bottom screen have changed somewhat from the typical query.

**NOTE:** If a security warning appears below the ribbon, click *Options, Enable the Content, OK,* and then repeat from Step 1.

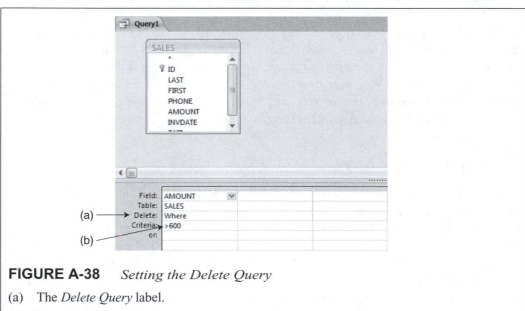

**FIGURE A-38**    *Setting the Delete Query*

(a)    The *Delete Query* label.

(b)    Type the desired criteria.

Now assign the criteria as you would in any query, by following these steps:

**3.** Place the AMOUNT field in the first column (double-click it in the SALES list—double-clicking from the table places the selected field in the next available column).

**4.** Click the *Criteria* row in the same column.

**5.** Type **>600** and press ⏎ as in Figure A-38b. This assigns the criterion that will be used to find the records.

**WARNING!** If you do not specify at least one search criterion, *all records* will be deleted.

It is always wise to check the results of a delete query *before* you actually invoke it. (You can actually use this technique to see the results of any query.) To do this:

**6.** Click the *Datasheet View* button (in the *Results* group in the ribbon). Note that three records will be deleted as expected.

**7.** Click the *Design View* button (in the *Results* group) to return to the Delete Query window.

**8.** Now, run the query (by clicking the *Design* tab in the ribbon if needed and then the *Run* command button.

A warning appears noting that three rows (records) will be removed. You could cancel the procedure to retain the records, but for this exercise, delete the records as follows:

**9.** Click *Yes* and then close the query window *without* saving it.

10. Open the SALES table and note that there are now only seven records in it (three have been marked "Deleted").

11. Click the *Refresh All* button (in the *Results* group).

12. Close the table.

## LESSON 9: SORTING RECORDS

Access allows you to rearrange records into other sequences without having to retype data. An easy way to do this is to sort the data in a table. The sort command can temporarily rearrange the records in a table, or it can copy the sorted records into a completely new table. This is useful if you want to retain the original order of the data. You can sort a table as often as you like. Before you sort, however, let's examine another technique for arranging records that you encountered briefly in Lesson 2—the primary key.

### Using a Primary Key

Much of Access's power comes from its ability to locate and combine data from one table or from many separate tables. To do this more efficiently, each table should include a primary key—a field (or set of fields) that uniquely identifies each record in the table (and rearranges the records in this order). There are three types of primary keys: autonumber, single-field, and multiple-field. An autonumber primary key is an additional field added by Access that will automatically enter a sequential number each time you add a new record. Using an autonumber primary key keeps the records in the order that they were entered. If you have a field in your table that contains unique values (such as ID), you may want to designate it as the primary key instead. For example, to use the ID field as the primary key, do the following:

1. If needed, launch Access and open the SALES table.

2. Click the *Design View* command button (*Views* group).
   Using Figure A-39a as a guide:

3. Click the extreme left margin of the ID field to select the row.
   Examine the left column. If a "key" icon appears, the ID field is already set as the primary key.

4. If there is no key icon, click the *Primary Key* command button to designate the ID field as the primary key.
   A key icon appears in the left margin of the ID field row, as shown in Figure A-39a.

5. Save the table (right-click the *Sales* tab and click *Save*).

6. To see the effect, click the *Datasheet View* command button (*Home* tab, *Views* group) to return to the table.
   Note that the records are now arranged in ID order, as shown in Figure A-39b. To deactivate a primary key, do the following:

7. Repeat steps 2–5 to remove the key icon from the left margin of the ID field.

"Key" icon

| Field Name | Data Type | |
|---|---|---|
| ID | Text | Customer ID Number |
| LAST | Text | Customer's Last Name |
| FIRST | Text | Customer's First Name |
| PHONE | Text | Phone: (999) 999-9999 |
| AMOUNT | Currency | Amount of Invoice |
| INVDATE | Date/Time | Date of Invoice |
| PAID | Currency | Amount Paid |

(a)

| ID ▾ | LAST ▾ | FIRST ▾ | PHONE ▾ | AMOUNT ▾ | INVDATE ▾ | PAID ▾ | Click to Add ▾ |
|---|---|---|---|---|---|---|---|
| 005 | TWAIN | LIONEL | (213) 555-1234 | $234.65 | 10/7/2010 | $200.00 | |
| 037 | TYME | JUSTIN | (718) 555-0982 | $450.00 | 11/1/2010 | $450.00 | |
| 046 | BEACH | SANDY | (817) 555-1122 | $534.12 | 9/8/2010 | $500.00 | |
| 111 | MARTIN | EDWARD | (718) 555-0000 | $100.00 | 1/1/2010 | | |
| 113 | DEDOGG | PAT | (203) 555-0101 | $123.00 | 5/16/2010 | | |
| 123 | VALE | NOAH | (516) 555-0705 | $550.00 | 1/22/2010 | | |
| 754 | DEDOGG | FEE | (212) 555-0099 | $211.90 | 4/6/2010 | | |

(b)

**FIGURE A-39**    *Rearranging Records*

(a)   Setting a primary key.

(b)   Table sorted on ID field.

**NOTE:** In this table, the LAST field would not be appropriate to be used as a primary key, because it is not unique—there are records with the same last name. If table records have no identical LAST names, you could use the field as a primary key.

## Sorting with One Field

The easiest sort to create is one based on a single field. Unlike a primary key, a sorted field need not contain unique values. In this example, you will sort records by the AMOUNT field.

1.   If needed, launch Access and open the SALES table in Datasheet view.

2.   Click the first (topmost) data cell in AMOUNT field, as shown in Figure A-40a.

3.   Click the *Ascending* command button (*Sort & Filter* group).          A↓ Ascending

The records now appear in ascending (increasing) order by AMOUNT. You can se-lect any single field in this manner and reorganize the table, as shown in Figure A-40b.

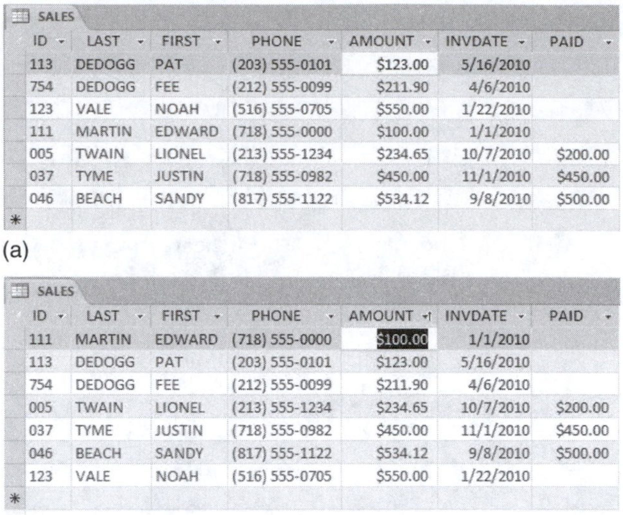

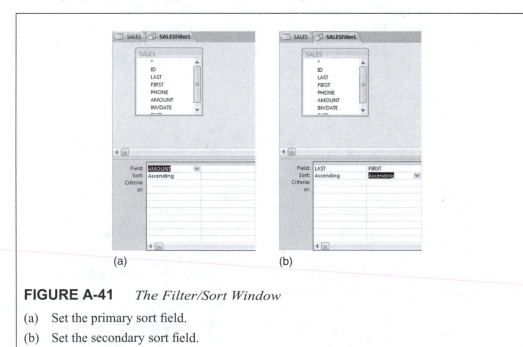

**FIGURE A-40**   *Sorting With One Field*

(a)   Click the topmost record in the desired column.

(b)   The table has been sorted on the AMOUNT field.

## Sorting with Multiple Fields

You can also sort on any combination of fields. This technique uses a *filter*, much like a query, that specifies all the fields and orders for the sort. In this example, you will sort on LAST and FIRST name fields.

**1.**   In the SALES table, click the *Advanced* command button (*Sort & Filter* group) and then the *Advanced Filter/Sort* option in the list that appears.

A query-like screen appears, as shown in Figure A-41.

**FIGURE A-41**   *The Filter/Sort Window*

(a)   Set the primary sort field.

(b)   Set the secondary sort field.

In much the same way that you use a query, you can now select fields and specify the sort orders. Using Figure A-41a as a guide, do the following:

**2.** In the first column, select the LAST name field. (Click the drop-down arrow in the first field column and then click LAST.)

The order in which you select fields determines their precedence in the sort: The first selected field will be sorted first and so on.

**3.** In the second row of the same column, select Ascending order if needed. (Click the cell, then its drop-down arrow, and then click *Ascending*.)

> **NOTE:** You can change the order from ASCENDING (normal) to DESCENDING (reverse) order by selecting Descending from the list.

**4.** Click in the Field row of the second column, select the FIRST name field, and then select Ascending order in the Sort row (as you did in step 3), as shown in Figure A-41b.

The column order will sort the table by LAST name first, and then by FIRST name, for those records whose LAST names are identical.

**5.** To sort the table, click the *Toggle Filter* command button (*Sort and Filter* group).

The sorted SALES table will appear as in Figure A-42. The records have been rearranged as you specified. Note that the records are in LAST name order. Where LAST name is identical (as in DeDogg), the records are further sorted by FIRST name. You can sort on as many fields as you want.

| ID | LAST | FIRST | PHONE | AMOUNT | INVDATE | PAID |
|----|------|-------|-------|--------|---------|------|
| 046 | BEACH | SANDY | (817) 555-1122 | $534.12 | 9/8/2010 | $500.00 |
| 754 | DEDOGG | FEE | (212) 555-0099 | $211.90 | 4/6/2010 | |
| 113 | DEDOGG | PAT | (203) 555-0101 | $123.00 | 5/16/2010 | |
| 111 | MARTIN | EDWARD | (718) 555-0000 | $100.00 | 1/1/2010 | |
| 005 | TWAIN | LIONEL | (213) 555-1234 | $234.65 | 10/7/2010 | $200.00 |
| 037 | TYME | JUSTIN | (718) 555-0982 | $450.00 | 11/1/2010 | $450.00 |
| 123 | VALE | NOAH | (516) 555-0705 | $550.00 | 1/22/2010 | |

**FIGURE A-42**    *The Sorted Table*

> **NOTE:** To return to the original (or natural) order, you can click the *Clear All Sorts* command button, which cancels the sort. If the original record order must be maintained, you might also create a number field in the original table structure (before sorting) and then type an order number for each record that shows its position in the sequence (such as 1,2,3, and so on). Then, no matter how many times you sort the table, you can return to the original order simply by sorting on the order number field. (You could also create an autonumber field to keep track of the original order.)

**6.** Save the table and then close it.

**7.** You can exit Access for now or continue.

> **NOTE:** You can also specify sort order directly in a query so that when a query is used, the records appear in the desired order automatically.

## LESSON 10: FINDING RECORDS

At times, you will want to quickly find a specific record to view its contents or edit it. In a small table, such as SALES, you can simply use the arrow keys or the view techniques you have learned to find data quickly. However, in large tables that contain hundreds or thousands of records, you will need a more efficient method. The Find command serves this purpose. The Find command lets you search by any field and quickly move to the first record that matches your search.

For example, to find a record with a FIRST name of PAT, complete the following steps:

**1.**  If needed, open the SALES table.

The *Find* technique consists of moving to the column that you want to search, invoking the command, and setting the search criterion.

**2.**  Click in the top row of the column for FIRST name.

**3.**  Click the *Find* button (*Find* group).

A Find and Replace dialog box appears as in Figure A-43.

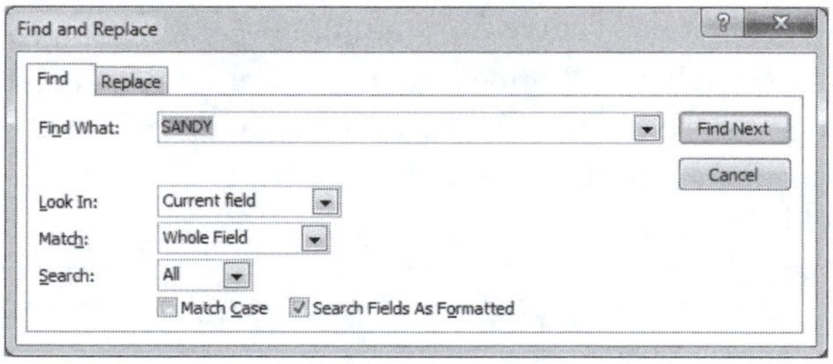

**FIGURE A-43**   *The Find Dialog Box*

Examine the screen for a moment. You can simply type the desired search for an exact match, or click the drop-down arrow in the Match entry box to use some of the additional Match settings in the dialog box as follows:

- Any Part of Field—looks for matches anywhere within the field data.

- Whole Field—matches text exactly with no wildcards used. You'll learn more about wildcards in a moment.

- Start of Field—looks for matches starting with the leftmost character of the field data.

- You can also click the *Match Case* check box, which instructs Access to search for text that matches capitalization exactly as you typed it. Otherwise, any text that matches (regardless of capitalization) will be included.

**4.**  If the dialog box covers your data, you might want to click its title bar and drag it down slightly so that you may see the effects of these exercises.

To practice finding records, try the following:

**5.**  Type **PAT** in the *Find What* entry box and click *Find Next*.

The highlight moves to the first record whose FIRST name is PAT. The find merely locates the record. You can close the Find dialog box and then use any technique to edit the record. You might also press the arrow keys to move to other records as well.

**6.**  Close the Find box (click its close button).

NOTE: You could click the *Find Next* button to move to the next record that matches the condition. You can also use the arrow keys to move to another field and enter a new search condition.

## Using Wildcards

A wildcard is a symbol that extends your search capabilities by allowing Access to ignore certain characters in the search. Access's basic wildcards are listed in Table A-5.

| Symbol | Example | will find | Matches any: |
|---|---|---|---|
| * | *an | man, woman | number of characters |
| ? | w?ll | wall, well, will | single character |
| # | 4#6 | 456, 406, 416 | single digit |
| [ ] | w[ae]ll | wall & well | single character in the list |
| ! | w![ae]ll | will | single character NOT in the list |
| - | w[a-c]ll | wall | single character in the range |

**TABLE A-5**    *Access's Wildcards*

You could use the wildcards "?" or "*" in the search condition to look for partial text strings. The "?" symbol stands for one character, whereas the asterisk (*) represents any number of characters. For example, *M** would find a field that starts with an M followed by any number of characters; *\*M\** would find a field with an M anywhere in it. Similarly, *??M* would find a field in which M was the third character, and so on.

NOTE: The asterisk (*) wildcard can be placed only in the first and/or last position of a search condition.

Try some of the following search examples to see how the techniques work.
To find an ID of 754:

1. Click the top row of the ID field.

2. Invoke the *Find* command as before.

3. Type **754** and click *Find Next*.

To find a PHONE within the 718 area code:

1. Click the top row of the PHONE field.

2. In the Find dialog box (still open) type **(718)*** and click *Find Next*.

3. Click *Find Next* again.

4. If a "Finished" notice appears, click *OK* to acknowledge.

5. Close the box.

6. Close the table without saving. You can exit Access or continue.

## Quick Review #2

What will *these* searches do? Try them and see.

1. In the LAST column, S* _____

2. In the PHONE column, *12* _____

3. In the PAID column, [!45]* _____

4. In the DATE column, */7* _____

## LESSON 11: CREATING A REPORT TEMPLATE

An important reason for using a computer database is the ease with which reports can be created on a screen or a printer. These reports are often designed on paper first to be certain that they fit not only decision-making needs but physical paper or screen size as well.

For practice, you'll create a report displaying each record's ID number, last and first names, invoice date, amount owed, and money paid. You'll also list all records in alphabetical order by last name. Figure A-44 shows how this report might look.

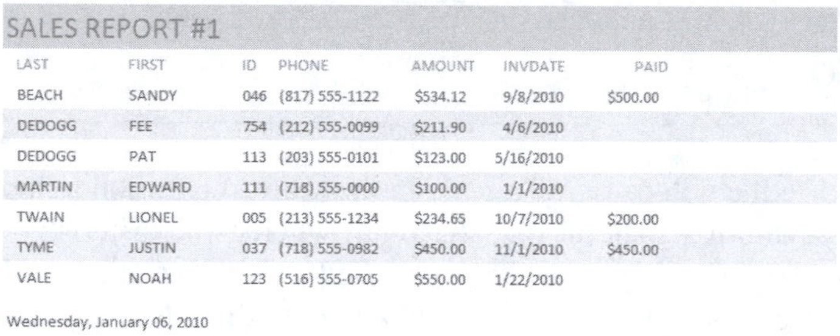

SALES REPORT #1

| LAST | FIRST | ID | PHONE | AMOUNT | INVDATE | PAID |
|------|-------|-----|----------------|---------|----------|---------|
| BEACH | SANDY | 046 | (817) 555-1122 | $534.12 | 9/8/2010 | $500.00 |
| DEDOGG | FEE | 754 | (212) 555-0099 | $211.90 | 4/6/2010 | |
| DEDOGG | PAT | 113 | (203) 555-0101 | $123.00 | 5/16/2010 | |
| MARTIN | EDWARD | 111 | (718) 555-0000 | $100.00 | 1/1/2010 | |
| TWAIN | LIONEL | 005 | (213) 555-1234 | $234.65 | 10/7/2010 | $200.00 |
| TYME | JUSTIN | 037 | (718) 555-0982 | $450.00 | 11/1/2010 | $450.00 |
| VALE | NOAH | 123 | (516) 555-0705 | $550.00 | 1/22/2010 | |

Wednesday, January 06, 2010

**FIGURE A-44**    *The Basic SALES Report*

### Creating a Report Template

1. Launch Access if needed and open the Company database.

2. Click the *Create* tab in the ribbon.

Although you could build a report from scratch, it is much easier to let Access lead you through the process by using its Report Wizard.

3. Click the *Report Wizard* command button (*Reports* group).

The Report Wizard, as shown in Figure A-45, now lets you select the fields you want, in the order you want them to appear, by simply selecting the individual fields you want to use.

> **NOTE:** If you enter the name of a query here, the report will include only those records that satisfy the query's conditions.

4. Click *LAST* in the Available Fields list to select it.

5. Click the ( **>** ) button in the center to move the LAST field to the field order list at the right as in Figure A-46a.

6. Now, select and move the FIRST field, using the same procedure as described in steps 4–5.

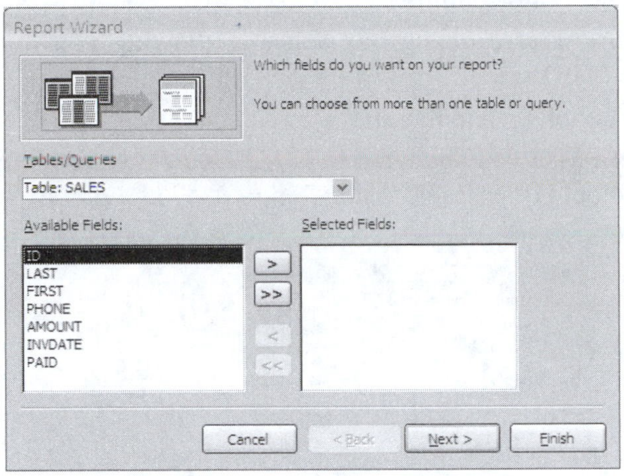

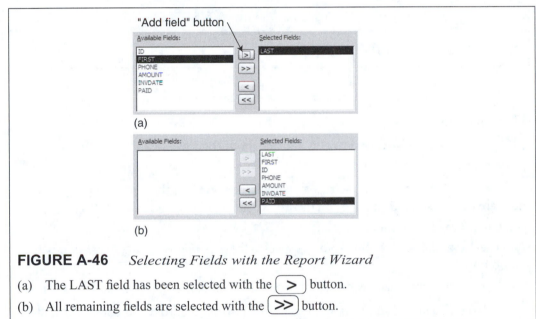

**FIGURE A-45**   *The Initial Report Wizard Dialog Box*

**FIGURE A-46**   *Selecting Fields with the Report Wizard*

(a)   The LAST field has been selected with the ⟨ > ⟩ button.

(b)   All remaining fields are selected with the ⟨ >> ⟩ button.

You could continue to select individual fields in the order you would want them to appear. In this example, the remaining fields can also be selected with one command, as follows:

**7.** Click the ⟨ >> ⟩ (double arrow) button in the center to transfer the remaining fields to the report list in their current order.

All fields have now been selected and appear in the field order list, as shown in Figure A-46b.

**NOTE:** If you make a mistake, use the ⟨ < ⟩ or ⟨ << ⟩ buttons to transfer fields back to the available list and repeat the selection process.

8.  Click the *Next* button to continue.

The next Report Wizard dialog box appears, allowing you to specify a grouping (classification) level. For now,

9.  Click the *Next* button to skip this step.

Next, the wizard asks you about a sort order. You could name up to four fields and indicate a sort direction. For example, using Figure A-47 as a guide:

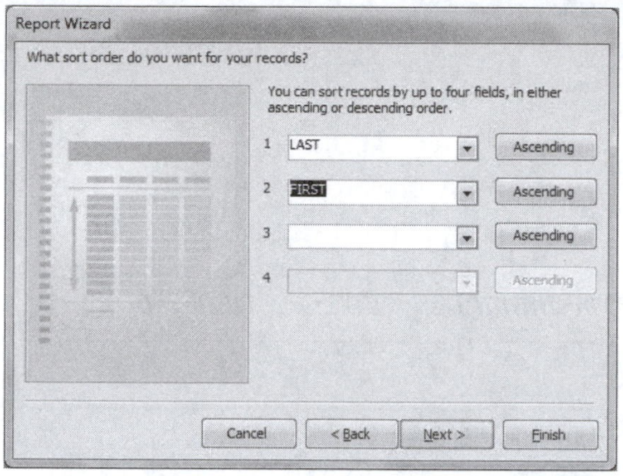

**FIGURE A-47**    *Setting Sort Fields*

10.  Click the #1 drop-down arrow to indicate the first sort.

11.  Click *LAST*.

12.  Click the #2 drop-down arrow to indicate the second sort.

13.  Click *FIRST*.

You have indicated that the records should be sorted on the LAST name field and, if there are duplicate LAST names, on the FIRST name field.

14.  Click *Next* to continue.

The Next dialog box allows you to specify the general layout and page orientation of your report.

- Columnar reports display one record per page with fields arranged one below the other.

- Tabular reports present data in the traditional rows (records) and columns (fields).

- Justified reports present data in a form.

- Landscape orientation places data across the length of a page, whereas portrait orientation displays data across its width.

15.  Click the *Tabular* report button if it is not already selected.

16.  Click *Portrait* orientation if it is not already set.

17.  Click *Next* to continue.

You now can type an appropriate title that will appear at the top of the report.

18.  Click the title box and type **SALES REPORT #1**.

19.  Click the *Finish* button to end the Report Wizard process.

Access creates the report according to your specifications and displays it in a Print Preview window, as in Figure A-48. Fields appear in the order they were selected.

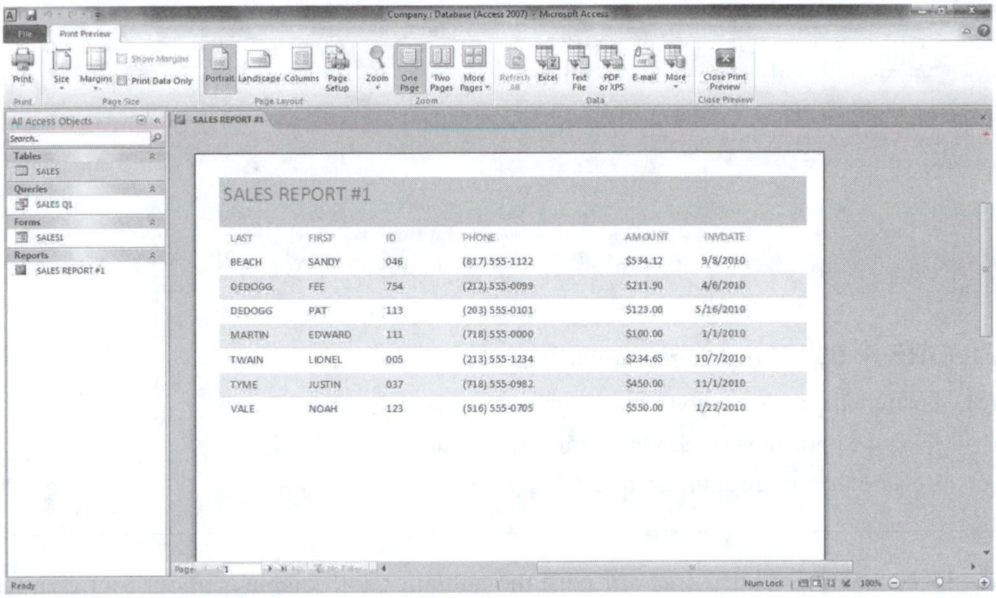

**FIGURE A-48**　　*The Print Preview Window*

The columns are not exactly as we want them in the final report (especially the ID and Phone columns), so we can alter the design to better present the data as follows:

**20.** Click the *Layout View* button (status bar in the lower-right corner of the window).

A layout window should appear, as shown in Figure A-49. (Your screen may show a Property Sheet pane.)

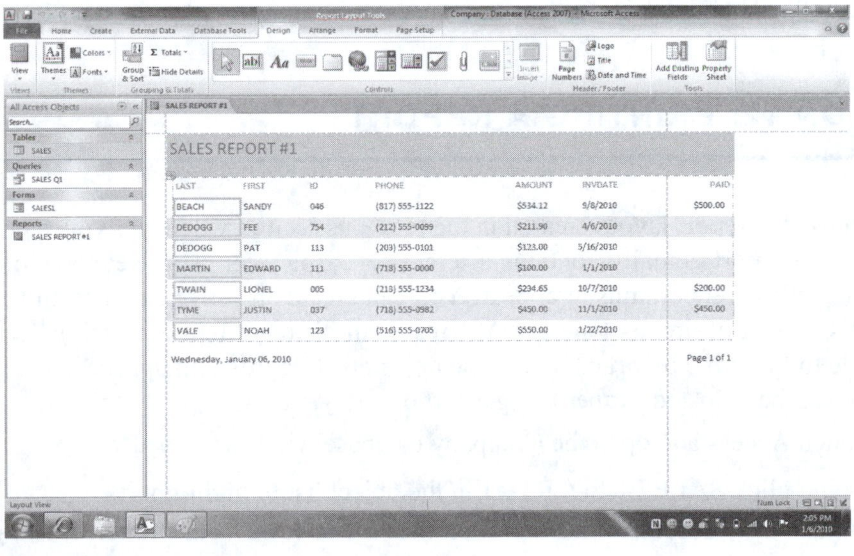

**FIGURE A-49**　　*The Report Layout Window*

First fix the ID column width:

**21.** Click the ID column to select it.

**22.** Point to the right side of the ID column (just to the left of "PHONE") until the pointer appears as a double-pointed arrow, as in Figure A-50a.

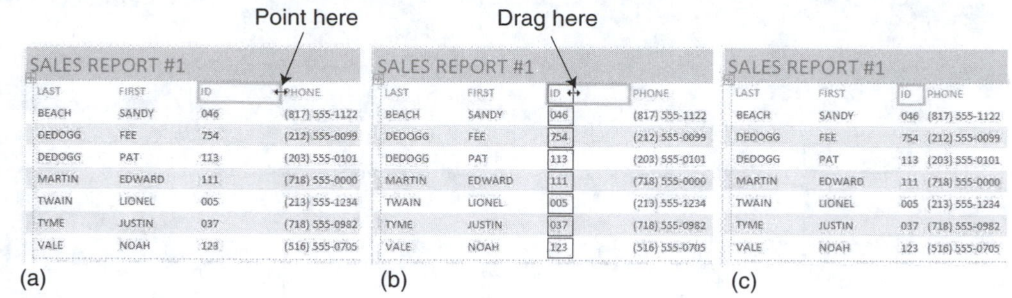

**FIGURE A-50**   *Adjusting Column Width*

(a)   Position the mouse pointer at the right side of the column.

(b)   Drag the pointer as needed to narrow the column.

(c)   Release the mouse at the desired column width.

**23.** To reduce the width, drag *left* until the column width displays about four characters as in Figure A-50b (the three ID digits followed by a small space—this need not be exact). Your screen should now resemble Figure A-50c

**24.** In a similar fashion, reduce the AMOUNT, INVDATE and PAID columns. Your screen should resemble Figure A-44. Adjust the columns if it does not.

To save and close the adjusted report:

**25.** Right-click the report's tab and click *Close*.

A dialog box appears.

**26.** Click *Yes* to save the report.

**27.** Close the database window and exit Access, or continue on to the next lesson.

## LESSON 12: PRINTING A REPORT

You can use the report layout created in the previous section whenever you want to print a report. Each report actually contains a template—a picture, or a skeleton—of how you want your titles and columns to appear. You can create and save as many of these report templates as you desire, as long as you give them different names. Each uses an associated table to fill in the report contents when it prints. Records will appear in their specified order, or can be adjusted further using a sort or query.

**1.** Launch Access and open the Company database window if needed.

**2.** Double-click SALES REPORT #1 in the object list to highlight it.

You can now generate your report on the screen or on your printer. It is a good idea to generate a screen version of a report first. This way, you can check for errors or adjustments without wasting paper.

**3.** Click the *Print Preview* button on the status bar to generate a screen preview of the report.

The report on your screen should resemble Figure A-44. You can use the scroll bars to examine all of its parts. Notice that the date is automatically supplied at the bottom of the page. All your records (including the record containing your name) should appear in alphabetical order.

4.  If you *do not* want to generate the report on the printer, skip to Step 7 now.

5.  To print, click the *Print* command button in the ribbon, or press CTRL + **P**.

6.  Make sure your printer is connected, then click *OK*.

7.  Close the window.

## Creating Reports with Selected Records

You can also use a report layout to select records from a table just as you did with the Query command earlier. Although you can use (or create) any query, here you will create a new query to restrict the report to those records whose AMOUNT field exceeds $400.00. Follow these steps to create a report using selected records:

1.  Open the SALES table.

2.  Click the *Create* tab and then the *Query Design* button (*Macros and Code* group).

3.  Click *Add* in the Show Table dialog box and then close the box.

    As expected, a blank query form appears.

4.  In the leftmost column, click the drop-down arrow and then click *SALES.** from the drop-down list to include all fields in the query.

    Only the fields that appear both in the query and the report template will appear in the report. Therefore, it is best to include all fields in a query that will be used with a report. The easiest way to do this is to click the *SALES.** option to immediately select all fields. (You could also double-click the *SALES.** option in the SALES table list.)

5.  Click in the second field column and use the drop-down arrow to select the AMOUNT field.

6.  Remove the check mark from the Show checkbox. (It has already been selected by clicking the *SALES.** option earlier.)

7.  Click the Criteria row, type **> 400** and press ↵. Your screen should resemble Figure A-51. Change it if it does not.

| Field: | SALES.* | AMOUNT |
|---|---|---|
| Table: | SALES | SALES |
| Sort: | | |
| Show: | ☑ | ☐ |
| Criteria: | | >400 |

**FIGURE A-51**    *Setting the New Criterion*

8.  Right-click the *Query1* tab (located just below the ribbon) and then click *Save*.

9.  Type **SALES Q2** for the query name and click *OK*.

10. Close the query window (right-click its tab and click *Close*).

    Your query can now be used with the report template to generate a report that includes only those records whose AMOUNT exceeds $400. To do this, you must first tell the report to use the SALES Q2 query instead of the entire SALES table. This can be done as follows:

**11.** Double-click the SALES REPORT #1 object in the left pane to open it.

**12.** Click the *Design View* button (in the status bar).

**13.** Click the *Property Sheet* button (Tools group) to open the task bar.
A Property Sheet pane appears as shown in Figure A-52a.

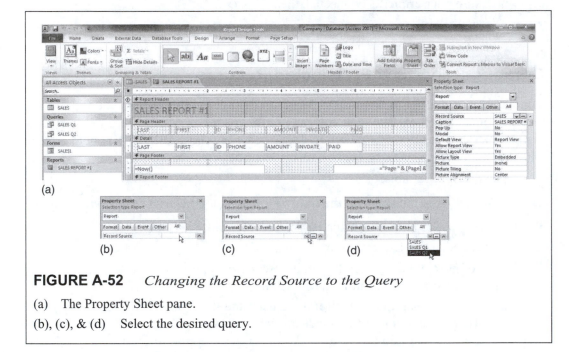

**FIGURE A-52**    *Changing the Record Source to the Query*

(a)    The Property Sheet pane.

(b), (c), & (d)    Select the desired query.

**14.** Click the Record Source box, as shown in Figure A-52b.

**15.** Click the drop-down arrow next to Record Source as shown in Figure A-52c.

**16.** Click the *SALES Q2* query file, as shown in Figure A-52d.

**17.** Close the Property Sheet pane to see the entire report.
You can now view the effects of the query and sort order as follows:

**18.** Click the *Print Preview* button (status bar) to see the report. (Of course, you could also print it out if desired, but here we're saving paper.)

Your screen should resemble Figure A-53. Note that these records are the ones that satisfy the query's criterion of AMOUNT>400 and appear in alphabetical order by LAST and FIRST name. Not every record in the SALES table appears in the report. Report templates can be used with any table to display *all* the data that the table contains. When used with a query, a report will contain *only* those records that satisfied the query's conditions.

**19.** Close all windows, but *do not* save the report.

SALES REPORT #1

| LAST | FIRST | ID | PHONE | AMOUNT | INVDATE | PAID |
|------|-------|-----|-------|--------|---------|------|
| BEACH | SANDY | 046 | (817) 555-1122 | $534.12 | 9/8/2010 | $500.00 |
| TYME | JUSTIN | 037 | (718) 555-0982 | $450.00 | 11/1/2010 | $450.00 |
| VALE | NOAH | 123 | (516) 555-0705 | $550.00 | 1/22/2010 | |

**FIGURE A-53**    *A Preview of the Report with Selected Records*

## LESSON 13: MODIFYING A REPORT TEMPLATE

So far, so good. But what if you make a mistake on the report layout? Or what if you want to move or delete a column, or decide to show totals? The nice thing about report templates is that they can be modified at any time. You will examine some basic Access report modifications. (Of course, you could always create a new report with the Report Wizard if the changes are extensive.)

### Copying a Report Template

Although you could modify the SALES REPORT #1 report directly, it is wiser to copy the report and then modify the new one without changing the original. This would leave you with two separate reports. Try this for practice, as follows:

1.  Open the Company database, if needed.

2.  Right-click the SALES REPORT #1 report in the left object pane.

3.  Click *Copy*.

4.  Right-click anywhere in the left pane and then click *Paste*.

    A Paste As dialog box appears as in Figure A-54. You can now assign a new name to the report that will be copied.

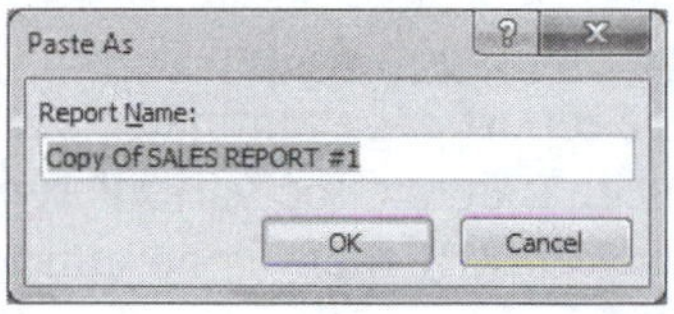

**FIGURE A-54**    *Copying SALES REPORT #1 into SALES REPORT #2*

5.  Delete the current entry and type the new report name, **SALES REPORT #2**.

6.  Click the *OK* button.

    The SALES REPORT #1 report is copied into SALES REPORT #2, and you return to the database window for further work.

### Modifying a Report

Using SALES REPORT #2, you will now learn how to make a few report modifications. These changes include changing a report title, editing a column heading, deleting and moving data columns, and adding some summary statistics. Ultimately, your report will look like Figure A-55.

A

ACCESS PRACTICE REPORT #2
Prepared by Your Name

| LAST | FIRST | AMOUNT | INVDATE | PAID |
|------|-------|--------|---------|------|
| BEACH | SANDY | $534.12 | 9/8/2010 | $500.00 |
| DEDOGG | FEE | $211.90 | 4/6/2010 | |
| DEDOGG | PAT | $123.00 | 5/16/2010 | |
| MARTIN | EDWARD | $100.00 | 1/1/2010 | |
| TWAIN | LIONEL | $234.65 | 10/7/2010 | $200.00 |
| TYME | JUSTIN | $450.00 | 11/1/2010 | $450.00 |
| VALE | NOAH | $550.00 | 1/22/2010 | |
| | Totals | $2,203.67 | | $1,150.00 |

**FIGURE A-55**   *The Modified Report with Totals*

**NOTE:** You do not have to complete this entire section before stopping. If you want to exit after completing a procedure, save the Report (right-click its tab and use Save). You can then invoke the report design sequence and continue.

1. Double-click the SALES REPORT #2 object.

2. Click the *Design View* selector button (status bar).

The Report Design window will appear again, this time with SALES REPORT #2 in the tab. First, a few words about the report design view.

The design view shows the report page template "skeleton" or format. This format is divided into *bands*, or sections, that define the various report components. Each band has a border and an entry area beneath it. If there is no entry area showing, then the band is considered closed. Here are descriptions of the main bands:

- The **Report Header** band shows text that will appear at the beginning of the report, such as the report title. A report footer band appears at the bottom of the design, containing text that will appear at the end of the report, such as summary totals or averages.

- The **Page Header** band shows text that will appear at the top of each page, such as the field column headings. Access provides a heading for each column using the appropriate field name from the table. Note that numeric data (which includes currency) are right-aligned in those columns. A page footer band appears near the bottom of the design. Access has automatically placed a date and page number counter here.

- The **Detail** band shows the position and contents of each row of data. Access has set aside a column for each table field, in the order you specified in the Report Wizard. Lines are drawn to show where data will appear in each column. When the report is generated, each record's data will appear on a separate line in neat columns.

Other bands may be added for groups, subtotals, and other features. You may want to compare the design to the finished report.

You can now adjust any report parameters you want. A few examples of basic parameters you can adjust follow:

## Modifying the Report Heading

Access uses the heading you specified in the Report Wizard create procedure. However, you can modify the heading in the design itself to include a more descriptive title, as follows:

1. Click the *Sales Report #1* title located at the top left of the report header band, as shown in Figure A-56. A rectangular box should now surround the object, indicating that it has been selected. If not, click it again.

2. Press (DELETE) to remove this object from the report header.

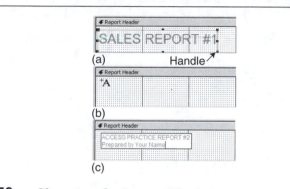

**FIGURE A-56**  *Changing the Report Heading*

(a)  Click the title to select it.

(b)  Delete the object and use the label tool to enter a new heading.

(c)  The completed title.

You can now add text to create a new title.

3. Click the *Label* command button in the *Controls* group.

4. As shown in Figure A-56b, move the mouse pointer (which now resembles "+A") to the left edge of the report header.

5. While pointing at this position, click the mouse to create a label object. An "I" pointer will appear at that spot.

Now you can enter your new heading, as follows:

6. Type **ACCESS PRACTICE REPORT #2**.

7. Press (CTRL) + (↵) to create a new line. The pointer moves to the next line. Note, too, that the header band automatically expands to accept a second title line.

8. Type **Prepared by** then press (SPACE) and type your name.

The title in the report header should resemble Figure A-56c. If not, delete the title and repeat steps 3–8. Let's say you want to center the title as well. Try the following:

9. Click any blank area in the report header to end the label procedure.

10. Point to any line in the title that you just typed and click the mouse to open the object. A box appears around the title, as in Figure A-57a.

11. Point to the square handle in the center of the right edge of the object box as shown in Figure A-57b. The mouse pointer will change to a horizontal double-pointed arrow. (Make sure that the pointer does not appear as a diagonal arrow or a hand. Point again if needed.)

12. Now, drag the edge of the object box to the right, until it aligns with the right edge of the report (just over the end of the PAID field in the Page Header band) as shown in Figure A-57c.

13. Click the Format tab in the ribbon and then *Center* command button (*Font* group). The lines in the box are now centered. That's enough title changes for this simple report.

**A**

**14.** This is a good place to save your work. Right-click the SALES REPORT #2 tab and then click *Save*.

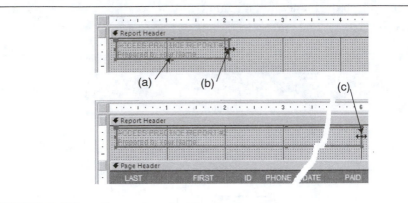

**FIGURE A-57**    *Centering the Heading*

(a)    Select the object.

(b)    Click the center handle at its right edge.

(c)    Drag the edge to the right edge of the report.

## Changing a Column Heading in the Page Header

To change a column heading, you need only select the appropriate heading and then make the adjustment. Let's say you wanted to change the LAST column heading to read LAST NAME. Here's how to do it:

**1.** Click the LAST name column heading in the Page Header band to select it and then click it once more to open its text box, as shown in Figure A-58a. (Do not double-click.)

**2.** Move the pointer after the "T" in "LAST."

**3.** Press SPACE and then type NAME as shown in Figure A-58b.

**4.** Click outside the text box to deselect it.

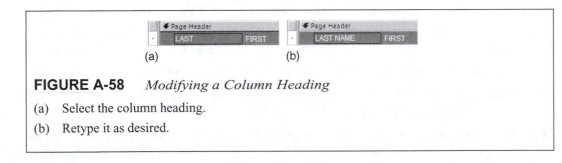

**FIGURE A-58**    *Modifying a Column Heading*

(a)    Select the column heading.

(b)    Retype it as desired.

## Deleting a Column

To delete a column, you simply identify it in the "Arrange" tab and then press the DELETE key. The trick here is making certain that you have removed all references to the column in other parts of the report—not just the column titles.

1. Click the "Arrange" tab in the ribbon.

2. Select the PHONE column heading in the Page Header band by clicking it.

3. Click the Select column button (*Rows and Columns* group).

4. Press [DELETE] to remove the column.

   The PHONE field name beneath it in the Detail band also disappears and the remaining columns automatically shift left to fill the empty space.

5. Now, delete the ID column using the same technique.

   Your screen should resemble Figure A-59. If not, delete the objects as needed.

6. Save the SALES REPORT #2 again.

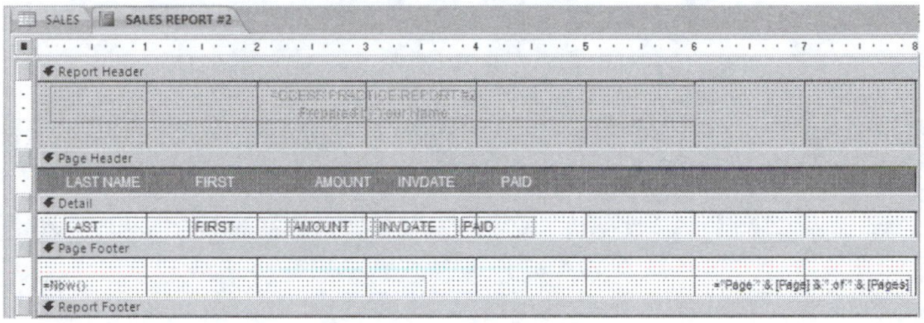

**FIGURE A-59**    *The Report with Repositioned Columns*

The FIRST, AMOUNT, and DATE columns have moved in the Page Header and Detail bands.

## Adding Summary Statistics

At times, you may want to calculate and display summary statistics (such as totals, averages, or counts) in your report. Access does not automatically include numeric totals when you create a report using the Report Wizard, but you can add summary statistics to any report. In this example, perform these steps:

1. Open the SALES REPORT #2 in Design view if needed.

2. Click the Design tab in the ribbon and then the Text Box command button (*Controls* group).

   Your goal is to place a holder for the AMOUNT total directly beneath its corresponding data holder in the detail band.

3. Position the pointer cross hair so that it is aligned with the first tick of the left ruler and directly beneath the 2 1/4-inch marker on the top ruler, in the Report Footer band as shown in Figure A-60a.

4. Click and drag the pointer just past the tick mark to the 3-inch marker and down approximately two tick marks, as shown in Figure A-60b. Then release the mouse.

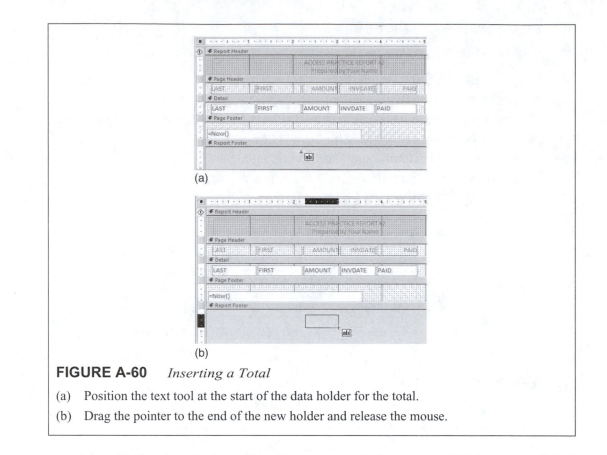

**FIGURE A-60**    *Inserting a Total*

(a)    Position the text tool at the start of the data holder for the total.

(b)    Drag the pointer to the end of the new holder and release the mouse.

A text label and an "unbound" text box appear. At the moment, this box is not linked to any particular value. You can now specify the properties of this new box by completing the following steps:

**5.**    Click the *Properties Sheet* command button (*Tools* group) to open the taskbar.

A Text Box properties box appears, in this example, *Text40* appears as shown in Figure A-61a. (Your text number may differ from the figure—it doesn't matter.) Using Figure A-61b as a guide, complete the following steps:

**6.**    Click the *All* tab if needed.

**7.**    Click the *Name* row, delete its contents, type **TOTAL_AMT** and press ↵.

**8.**    In the Control Source row, type **=SUM([AMOUNT])** and press ↵. Be sure to type the equal sign, parentheses, and brackets as shown.

| Property Sheet ✕ | | Property Sheet ✕ | |
|---|---|---|---|
| Selection type: Text Box | | Selection type: Text Box | |
| Text40 ▼ | | TOTAL_AMT ▼ | |
| Format Data Event Other **All** | | Format Data Event Other **All** | |
| Name | Text40 | Name | TOTAL_AMT |
| Control Source | | Control Source | =Sum([AMOUNT |
| Format | | Format | Currency |
| Decimal Places | Auto | Decimal Places | 2 |
| Visible | Yes | Visible | Yes ▼ |
| (a) | | (b) | |

**FIGURE A-61**    *Adding Total Properties*

(a)    The default Text Box settings.

(b)    The new settings.

This formula tells Access to sum the AMOUNT field.

9.  In the Format row, type **C** for currency format and press ⏎.

10. In the Decimal Places row, type **2** and press ⏎.

11. Close the properties pane.

12. Repeat steps 3–11 to place another text box directly under the PAID column in the same row as the TOTAL_AMT box you just added. Assign a name of **TOTAL_PAID** and the formula **=SUM([PAID])**.

The Report Footer band should now display four boxes (with some overlap) as shown in Figure A-62. Using this figure as a guide, finish the report footer as follows:

13. Click the *Text42* box (near its right side to stay away from the overlap), as shown in Figure A-62a, and then press ⌈DELETE⌉ to remove this box. (Your text number may differ—simply delete whatever text box appears in the *right* box as shown.)

14. Click the *Text40* box, as shown in Figure A-62b. (Again, your number may differ, but use the *left* box.)

15. Click the box again. Then press ⌈BACKSPACE⌉ to remove the text label and type **Totals:**

16. Your report footer layout should resemble Figure A-62c.

17. Save the report design (right-click the report's tab and click Save).

> **NOTE:** If one of the totals displays a set of pound signs (#######) when viewed, then the object box is too narrow to adequately display the data. Simply return to the design view, click the right side of the object box and drag it slightly wider.

18. Preview the report to see the effects of your changes—compare this to Figure A-55.

19. Close all open boxes and windows. You can now exit Access.

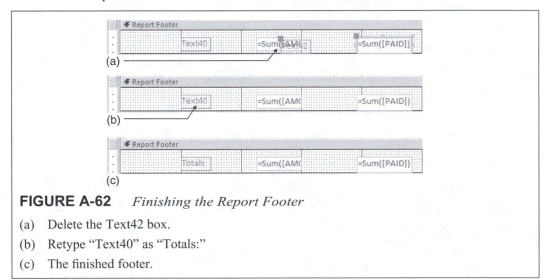

**FIGURE A-62**    *Finishing the Report Footer*

(a)   Delete the Text42 box.

(b)   Retype "Text40" as "Totals:"

(c)   The finished footer.

You are now finished with this module, but you have only scratched the surface of Access commands in this brief introduction. Although you should now understand the basics of database management, there are many other techniques with graphics, calculated fields, customized forms, and multiple tables that you might explore on your own to learn the true power of relational databases. For now, try the projects to see how well you've learned the basics of Access.

## DATABASE MANAGEMENT PROJECTS

Complete these projects to see how well you've mastered basic database techniques in Access. You may want to write the project number, your name, and date on each printout to identify it. Before you begin, you must create a new database named PROJECTS into which you will place the tables and other objects you create.

**Project 1** *Creating a Table with Records*

a. Open the PROJECTS database you just created and create a table called SOFT-WARE with the following structure:

| FIELD NAME | TYPE | WIDTH |
|---|---|---|
| VOLUME | Number, no decimals | |
| DISK | Text | 40 |
| TYPE | Text | 2 |
| FILE | Text | 4 |

b. Using the table in step a, enter the following records and then print the table. Make sure to type your name for the DISK field in the first record.

| VOL DISK | TYPE | FILE |
|---|---|---|
| 1 <YOUR NAME> | ID | XXXX |
| 2 WORDPERFECT 6.0 | WP | PROG |
| 3 WORDPERFECT 7.0 | WP | PROG |
| 4 WORD 98 | WP | PROG |
| 5 WORD 2002 | WP | DATA |
| 6 EXCEL | SS | PROG |
| 7 ACCESS 2002 | DB | PROG |
| 8 LETTERS 1 | WP | DATA |
| 9 LETTERS 2 | WP | DATA |
| 10 BUDGET 2003 | SS | DATA |

**Project 2** *Editing and appending:* Using the SOFTWARE table you created in Project 1, do the following:

a. Edit record 6 so that the DISK field will show EXCEL 2002 instead of EXCEL.

b. Modify the FILE data in record 5 to read PROG instead of DATA.

c. Add these new records:

| VOL DISK | TYPE | FILE |
|---|---|---|
| 11 APPROACH | DB | PROG |
| 12 LOTUS 1-2-3 | SS | PROG |
| 13 LETTERS 3 | WP | DATA |
| 14 BUDGET 2002 | SS | DATA |
| 15 BUDGET 2001 | SS | DATA |
| 16 WINDOWS 98 | SH | PROG |
| 17 RECORD SET 1 | DB | DATA |
| 18 RECORD SET 2 | DB | DATA |

d. After all records have been added and edited, print the table.

**Project 3** *Deleting Records:* Using the SOFTWARE table from Project 2, do the following:

a.  Delete these two records individually from the table: WORDPERFECT 6.0 and RECORD SET 2. Do not use a query.

b.  Print the table to show that these have been deleted.

**Project 4** *Selecting records:* Using the SOFTWARE table from Project 3, and the appropriate query, create and then print the dynasets that do the following:

a.  List those records that show the word DATA in the FILE field.

b.  List only the VOL and DISK fields for all records.

c.  List only the DISK and FILE fields for those records that show WP in the TYPE field.

**Project 5** *Sorting the records:* Using the SOFTWARE table from Project 4, do the following:

a.  Sort the table into alphabetical order by the DISK field. Print the table.

b.  Sort the table by TYPE and DISK fields. (Use the advanced filter/sort.) Print the table.

**Project 6** *Creating a Report:* Using the SOFTWARE table from Project 5, do the following:

a.  Create a report that will display the following title and four columns of data, as follows:

LISTING OF DISKS PREPARED BY (type your name here)

| **VOLUME** | **DISK** | **TYPE** | **FILE** |
|---|---|---|---|
| XXX | XXXXXXXXXXXXXXXXXXXXX | XX | XXXX |

b.  Save this report as SOFTRPT1 and then print it.

**Project 7** *Modifying the Report:* Using the SOFTRPT1 report template you created in Project 6, do the following:

a.  COPY the SOFTRPT1 report template into SOFTRPT2 to create a second report template.

b.  Modify the new report template SOFTRPT2 to change the title, remove the VOLUME column, change the heading of the DISK column to CONTENTS, and move the FILE column as shown below:

NEW LISTING OF DISKS PREPARED BY (type your name here)

| **FILE** | **CONTENTS** | **TYPE** |
|---|---|---|
| XXXX | XXXXXXXXXXXXXXXXXXXXXXXXX | XX |

c.  Save this report template and print the report.

**Project 8** *Putting It All Together:* Using the SOFTWARE table and the appropriate query, print the following reports using the SOFTRPT1 report template:

a.  Only those records that contain the label DATA. (Hint: The FILE field must have the word DATA in it.)

b.  Only those records that relate to word processing. (Hint: The TYPE field must show WP.)

c.  Only those records whose DISK contents start with the word BUDGET.

**A**

**Project 9** *Creating a Payroll Table:*

a.  In the PROJECTS database you created earlier, create a table called PAYROLL with the following structure:

| FIELD NAME | TYPE | WIDTH |
|---|---|---|
| LAST | Text | 15 |
| FIRST | Text | 10 |
| DEPT | Text | 5 |
| HOURS | Number, no decimals | |
| RATE | Currency | |

b.  Using the structure in Project 9a, add the following records to the table. Make sure that you type your own name for the LAST and FIRST name fields in the first record.

| LAST | FIRST | DEPT | HOURS | RATE |
|---|---|---|---|---|
| \<Your Name> | \<Your Name> | ACCTG | 45 | 10.00 |
| EMPLENTY | BILL | ACCTG | 32 | 9.50 |
| SINDEMAIL | CHUCK | PAYRL | 50 | 11.25 |
| THEMALL | SUE | LEGAL | 30 | 8.50 |
| LITTLE | KAREN | SALES | 55 | 15.00 |

c.  After completing the entry of the five records, print all the records.

**Project 10** *More Editing and Adding:* Using the PAYROLL table created in Project 9, do the following:

a.  Change BILL's RATE from 9.50 to 9.75.

b.  Change KAREN's HOURS from 55 to 52.

c.  Add three more records using data from your own imagination.

d.  After records are added and edited, print all the records.

**Project 11** *Sorting the Records:* Using the PAYROLL table, do the following:

a.  Sort the table into alphabetical order by LAST and FIRST names; then print all records.

b.  Sort the records by the RATE field. Print all records.

**Project 12** *Creating a Report:* Using the PAYROLL table, do the following:

a.  Create a report template named PAYRPT1 that will display the following title and columns of data.

PAYROLL REPORT PREPARED BY (type your name here)

| LAST NAME | FIRST | DEPT | HOURS | RATE |
|---|---|---|---|---|
| XXXXXXXXXXXXXXX | XXXXXXXXXX | XXXXX | XXX | XX.XX |

b.  YOU MAY SKIP THIS STEP. For extra credit, add a column called PAY to the right of the RATE column that will calculate the gross pay (HOURS * RATE). This skill was not covered in the manual.

c.  Save this report template, and then print the report for all the records.

**Project 13** *Modifying the Report:* Using the PAYRPT1 report template you created in Project 12, do the following:

a.   COPY the PAYRPT1 report template to PAYRPT2 to create another report template.

b.   Modify the new report template, PAYRPT2, to remove the DEPT column.

c.   Save this report template, and print the report.

**Project 14** *Putting It All Together:* Using the PAYROLL table and the appropriate query, use the PAYRPT1 report template to print the following reports:

a.   Only those personnel in the ACCTG department.

b.   Only those personnel whose HOURS exceed 40.

**Project 15** *On Your Own:* Design your own table (called MUSIC) to manage a music collection. Include fields for TITLE, ARTIST, RECORD COMPANY, TYPE (LP, CD, TAPE, and so on), and any other fields you might desire.

a.   In the PROJECTS database, create the table structure and add ten or more sample records.

b.   List the records to the printer.

c.   Sort the table by title and list it to the printer.

## CONTINUING ON YOUR OWN—THINGS TO CONSIDER

This module presented all the basic database management concepts that should be sufficient for most uses. However, there are other topics beyond the scope of this manual that will greatly expand your abilities and applications of database management programs. Feel free to refer to the *Help* screens that are offered in Access and to any documentation that is available to you.

Remember, you cannot harm the program or the computer by experimenting. You might want to look into these topics:

1.   Relational and logical operators.

2.   Creating customized entry and search screens.

3.   Combining search conditions.

4.   Creating calculated fields in a table, a query, and a report.

5.   Importing from, and exporting to, spreadsheets and word processing programs.

6.   Creating true relationships between tables.

7.   Merging graphics into the program.

8.   Merging records from another table.

9.   Writing command programs to automate database functions.

10.  Creating report templates with groups and subtotals.

**A**

## COMMAND SUMMARY—ACCESS 2010

**NOTE:** Ribbon command button is shown in BOLD CAPS followed by its location in parentheses—Tab (in italics) and Group—as in "**BOLD** (*Home*, Font)."

| | |
|---|---|
| ADD A NEW RECORD: | Open table, move to bottom, type data |
| | To end: right-click table tab, Close |
| CLOSE A WINDOW: | Click the window's close button, or right-click its tab, *Close* |
| CREATE A DATABASE: | *Blank database* button in center pane, Browse in right pane, check *Save in* drive, name, *OK* |
| CREATE A QUERY: | See QUERY |
| CREATE A REPORT: | Open database, *Create tab*, **REPORT WIZARD** (*Create*, Reports) |
| CREATE A TABLE: | Open database, *Create tab*, *Design View* button, type name, *OK* |
| DELETE A RECORD: | Open table, click leftmost column of row, DELETE , *Yes* |
| EDIT A RECORD: | Open table, move to record, edit the record |
| EXIT ACCESS: | **MS OFFICE** button, *Exit Access* |
| FIND A RECORD: | Open table, click in top of row, **Find** (*Home*, Find) |
| HELP WINDOW: | **HELP**, follow screen |
| LAUNCH ACCESS: | Start Windows, find and click Access icon |
| MODIFY A REPORT: | Open database, double-click report object, **DESIGN VIEW** |
| OPEN A TABLE: | Open database, double-click table object |
| PRINT A TABLE: | Open table, **MS OFFICE** button, *Print*, *OK* |
| QUERY: | Create: in database, **QUERY DESIGN** (*Create*, Other), select table, *Add*, *Close*, then select desired fields and criteria |
| | Use: Open database, double-click query object |
| QUIT ACCESS: | See Exit |
| REPORT GENERATION: | Open database, double-click report object, then: to see on screen, click **MS OFFICE** button, point to *Print*, click *Preview*; to print, open report, click **MS OFFICE** button, click *Print*, *OK* |
| SORT RECORDS: | Open table, click topmost cell in field, **ASCENDING** or **DESCENDING** (*Home*, Sort & Filter) |
| VALIDITY CHECK: | In table structure, highlight field, then enter desired validity check |

# PRESENTATION GRAPHICS MODULE

## POWERPOINT 2010

## LESSON 1: LAUNCHING POWERPOINT

This module introduces you to the basics of Microsoft Office 2010's presentation graphics program, PowerPoint. A presentation graphics program enables you to combine text, graphics, and visual special effects into a professional-looking presentation designed for individuals, small conferences, or large audiences. With a few simple commands, you can prepare material for overhead transparencies, color slides, outline notes, handouts, or on-screen graphics. You can also prepare screen presentations with many of the graphic "tricks" used by professionals—fades, dissolves, and wipes. PowerPoint includes color-coordinated templates, clip art, outlining functions, and layout programs that simplify the most complicated effects. Once you master the basic techniques presented in this module, you may want to explore the many advanced features of PowerPoint by invoking the Help screens offered in the program.

Remember to watch your screen as you invoke commands. Examine the effect of each mouse action or keystroke before you continue to the next. In this way, you will understand each command.

P

As you saw in the Introductory module, your computer needs special startup programs. Refer back to the appropriate instruction as needed to remind you how to start your computer system.

1. If needed, start Windows.

2. If appropriate for your system, make sure that a formatted diskette—on which you'll save your work—is in drive A (this is unnecessary if you are using a flash drive or folder on your hard disk or network).

    The easiest way to launch a program is to use a desktop or taskbar icon (if one exists).

3. If your desktop displays a PowerPoint icon, double-click it now and continue after step 8.

    If there is no icon, or if you prefer, you can always launch PowerPoint through the Start menu. Try this approach, using Figure P-1 as a guide:

4. Click the *Start* button to access the Windows menu.

5. Point to the *All Programs* item to access its menu.

6. If Microsoft PowerPoint appears in this menu, skip to step 8.

7. Point to the menu item that contains Microsoft PowerPoint. This may be a menu item entitled "Microsoft Office." If a different item contains PowerPoint, write its title here for future reference: _____.

8. Click the Microsoft PowerPoint menu item to launch it, as shown in Figure P-1.

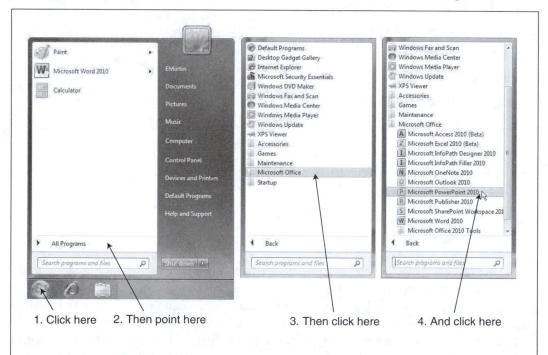

1. Click here    2. Then point here          3. Then click here    4. And click here

**FIGURE P-1**   *Launching PowerPoint*

To launch PowerPoint, click Start, All Programs, and then the PowerPoint menu item to launch PowerPoint (your list may differ).

Your screen should now contain copyright information. After a few moments, a PowerPoint window appears.

9. Maximize the PowerPoint window if it is not at its full-screen size.

## The PowerPoint Window

You should now see the PowerPoint window, as shown in Figure P-2. As in other Microsoft Office programs, this window contains the program and a document window through which you can see the materials develop as you work on them.

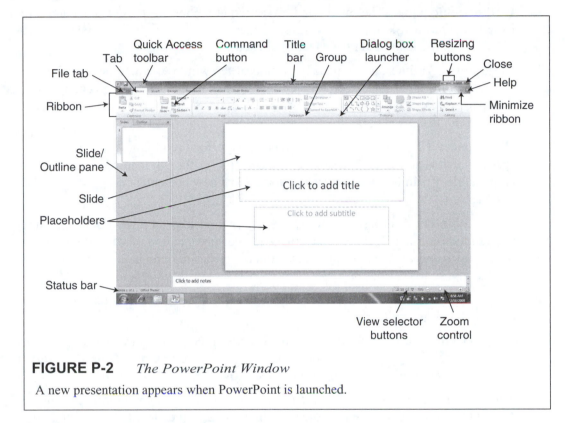

**FIGURE P-2**    *The PowerPoint Window*

A new presentation appears when PowerPoint is launched.

The next few paragraphs identify the important parts of the PowerPoint window. Locate each on your own screen as you read about it. Many items may already be familiar to you, since they are common to all Windows screens. These items will remain on the screen as you type and will provide you with useful information about your document. Examine the screen from the top-left corner to the bottom right.

a.   **Title bar:** At the top of the screen is PowerPoint's title bar. As in all windows, the identifying title appears in the center ("Presentation 1 – Microsoft PowerPoint"); the resizing and close buttons are at the right.

b.   **File tab:** The red tab in the upper-left corner is the File tab. Clicking it opens a file menu with commands for saving, printing, closing a file, and exiting the program. It also provides access to many PowerPoint options settings.

c.   **Quick Access Toolbar:** PowerPoint's Quick Access toolbar ("QAT")—just above the File tab—contains often-used command buttons such as save, undo, and redo. You can customize this toolbar to include any other commands you wish to add.

d.   **Ribbon:** Beneath the title bar is the heart of PowerPoint's menu system—the ribbon. The *ribbon* is a collection of *tabs*, *groups*, and *command buttons* that can be clicked by mouse to perform needed tasks. (More on this shortly.) Clicking the *Minimize Ribbon* button (or [CTRL] + [F1]) will reduce the ribbon display only tabs.

**P**

> **NOTE:**  The title bar, File tab, quick access toolbar, and ribbon are standard features found in every Microsoft Office 2010 program.

e.  **Outline/Slide pane:**  The small window section at the left of the screen (if active) is called the Outline/Slide pane. It displays either an outline or slide sequence of your presentation (depending on which tab is clicked).

f.  **Task pane:**  At times, a task pane (a portion of the window) will appear on the right side to provide additional information or commands when needed. You can leave the task pane open or close it by clicking its Close button to maximize the workspace. (There is no task pane currently displayed.)

g.  **Workspace:** The remainder of the screen, except for the bottom line, is the workspace, which is now available for your presentation. Although it currently displays an empty slide, it will be filled later when you build a new presentation or open an existing one.

h.  **Mouse pointer:** A mouse pointer, currently shaped like an arrow, appears somewhere on the screen. The pointer displays the current location of your mouse on the screen. As in other Windows programs, other symbols may replace the arrow as you use the mouse for various purposes.

i.  **Status bar:** The line at the bottom of the window is the status bar. It displays important messages as you work.

j.  **View selector:** To the right of the status bar are three small command buttons that allow you to change how the workbook appears on your screen. The PowerPoint views include: normal, slide sorter, and slide show.

k.  **Zoom:** The right-most section of the status bar contains a zoom control (currently at 100%) that allows you to change the magnification of screen text from 10% to 500%. You can drag the center indicator to any magnification you wish, or click the [+] and [–] icons to change the magnification in steps of 10.

l.  **Taskbar:** The Windows taskbar appears at the bottom of the screen.

Additional features and buttons will appear when you open a presentation window. We'll discuss these in a moment.

## Getting On-Screen Help

PowerPoint offers a Help feature that provides easy access to information about the program and its commands. To get on-screen help at any time,

1.  Click the *Help* button, located at the extreme right of the ribbon (or press F1).

    A PowerPoint Help dialog box and question area will appear. You can type keywords of interest. Try the following example:

2.  Type **ribbon** and press ⏎ (or click the *Search* button).

    A list of options appears. You could pick one topic by clicking it, but for now,

3.  Click the dialog box's Close button.

> **NOTE:**  If you want to stop for now, exit PowerPoint by clicking the *File tab* and then clicking *Exit*.

**Quick Review #1**

**1.** List the steps needed to launch PowerPoint on your computer.

_____

**2.** Which tab appears on the ribbon when you first launch PowerPoint?

_____

**3.** What can be placed in PowerPoint's workspace?

_____

**4.** Where would you look to find a presentation's name?

_____


## LESSON 2: CREATING AND SAVING A NEW PRESENTATION

**NOTE:** Be sure to complete this entire lesson before stopping so you'll know how to save your work and exit properly.

PowerPoint enables you to create presentations in a series of *slides*, or pages, which can effectively communicate your ideas to your audience. In this exercise, you create the first slide of a presentation about PowerPoint itself. To prepare for this exercise,

**1.** If needed, launch PowerPoint again and obtain a blank work screen. (Follow steps 1–9 in Lesson 1.)

Each time you launch PowerPoint, a blank title slide will automatically appear in the window. It is a good idea to begin each presentation with a title slide that identifies the topic. You can begin to work with this slide immediately.

You can create a completely blank presentation (with no color or design) or (once you get used to the program) one based on a design template that controls the color scheme, font styles and sizes, background graphics, and general layout of the overall design. Selecting no design leaves the screen in plain black-and-white mode until you change it. When you launch PowerPoint, it assumes you want to create a blank presentation. That's fine for now.

To help learn PowerPoint, you will now create a brief presentation about this book—*Discovering Microsoft Office 2010*. The techniques you learn here can then be applied to presentations of any length that you may care to develop. The first step is to create the first (or title) slide as shown later in Figure P-3.

Your screen is currently in "Normal" view, as shown in Figure P-2. The *Normal* view splits the window into three sections, or *panes*—a slide/outline pane at the left, the presentation at the right, and a section for notes at the bottom. You will learn more about these views later.

P

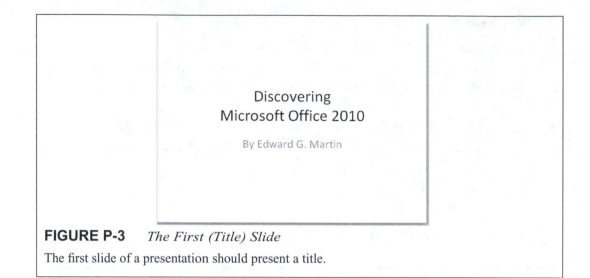

**FIGURE P-3**     *The First (Title) Slide*

The first slide of a presentation should present a title.

The window presents the title slide layout with two placeholders—one for a title, and one for a sub-title. Using Figure P-3 as a guide, you need only click each placeholder to open it and then enter the desired text to complete the basic slide as follows:

**2.** Type **Discovering**

> **NOTE:** PowerPoint will automatically open the title placeholder when you begin typing. (If you do not use a placeholder, it will remain blank when the slide is displayed.)

**3.** Press ⏎ to move to the next line.

**4.** Type **Microsoft Office 2010** but do *not* press the Enter key (or you'll create an unwanted third line).

Note that the text is automatically centered with an appropriately large font size (Calibri, 44 point, as shown in the Font group of the ribbon). Now for the subtitle:

> **NOTE:** If you make an error, press the BACKSPACE key to delete the characters, or use the arrow keys to move to the error, then delete and retype as needed.

**5.** Click anywhere within the subtitle placeholder.

**6.** Type **By Edward G. Martin** but do *not* press the Enter key.

**7.** Click anywhere outside the placeholder box to close the placeholder.

The text for the title slide is complete. Note that the style, size, color and layout is selected by the program. (You can always change them later.) Your slide should look like Figure P-3. If it does not, click within the placeholder again, delete the error, and retype. Then, click outside the placeholder. (A small copy of your slide appears in the left slide pane.) One more change:

**8.** Click the *Outline* tab at the extreme left of the screen (in the slide/outline pane, just about an inch beneath the Home tab).

Note that an outline of your slide now appears in the left pane of your window.

## Saving the Presentation

The slide that appears on your screen is now in your computer's primary memory (RAM), but is not yet saved on your diskette, flash drive, or folder. Unless you save the presentation, it will be lost when you exit from PowerPoint. As in other Microsoft Office programs, it is a simple process to save your work:

1. Click the red File tab and then *Save* to begin the save process.

> **NOTE:** Command buttons are shown in the margin where appropriate. To see a command button's function, point to it with the mouse and wait a moment. Its title will appear in a small box (called a "tool tip") beneath it.

   Because this is the first time you are saving this presentation, a Save dialog box automatically appears, as shown in Figure P-4.

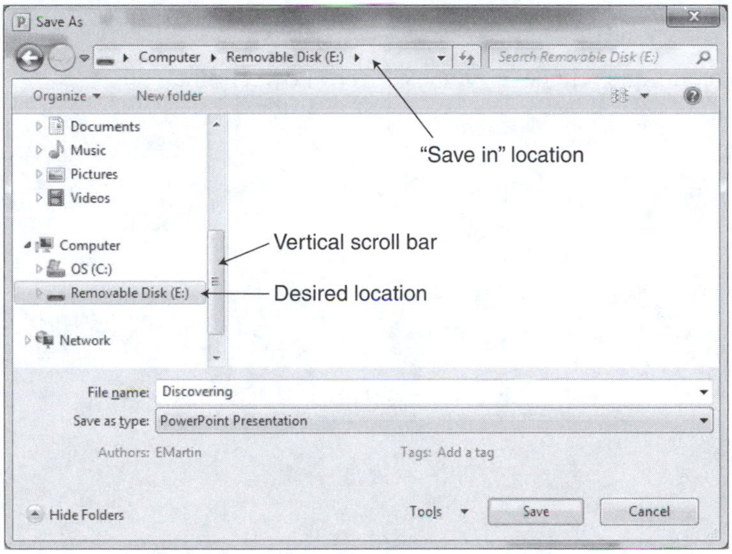

**FIGURE P-4**    *The Save As Dialog Box*

2. Check the *Save in* entry. If it is correct, choose 3-1/2 Floppy (A:) or the appropriate folder, continue with step 3. If the entry is not correct, change it as follows:

   a. Drag the vertical scroll bar down on the left side to see the desired drive or folder.

   b. Click the desired disk drive or folder.

   c. Click the *File name* box.

   Note that PowerPoint has listed the first word of the slide, "Discovering," as the suggested filename for now. It is easily changed:

3. Type **OFFICE1** and then click the *Save* button.

> **NOTE:** Although your list may not display it, PowerPoint automatically adds a .PPTX extension to the file to identify it as a PowerPoint 2010 presentation. (Earlier versions of PowerPoint—prior to 2007—used a .PPT extension.)

**P**

If you are using drive A, its indicator light should glow briefly as the file is saved to your diskette. You will then return to PowerPoint and may continue.

## Exiting PowerPoint

When you finish working in PowerPoint, you will want to exit from it. If you have already saved your presentation, you will simply return to Windows. However, if you've made any changes to your presentation since last saving it, PowerPoint will ask you if you want to save the changes before actually exiting.

1.  Click the File tab and then *Exit* (at the bottom of the list) to begin the Exit command.

2.  If you are asked to save changes, click *No*. You should now be returned to Windows.

> **NOTE:** In routine use, you may want to save your changes by selecting Yes. However, in this example, you have already saved your presentation, and there is no reason to go through the save procedure again.

Use this technique whenever you exit from PowerPoint.

**PowerPoint Practice Sheet—Screen Exercises**

Your Name: _____

Class: _____ Date: _____

1. Name two ways that you can enter text into a title placeholder:

   (a) _____     (b) _____

2. Fill in the names of the items shown in the screen below.

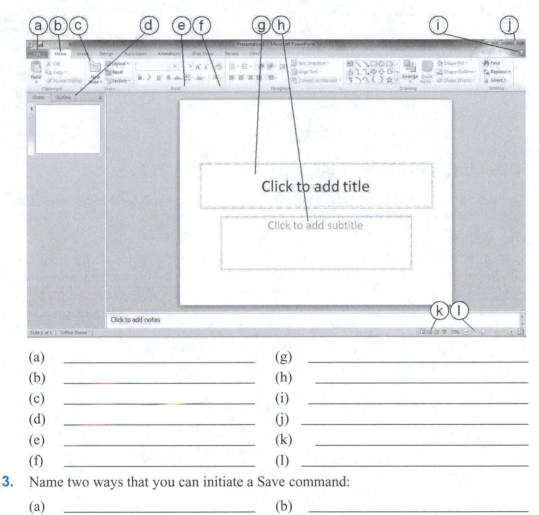

   (a) _____     (g) _____
   (b) _____     (h) _____
   (c) _____     (i) _____
   (d) _____     (j) _____
   (e) _____     (k) _____
   (f) _____     (l) _____

3. Name two ways that you can initiate a Save command:

   (a) _____     (b) _____

4. Click the *New Slide* drop-down button (*Home* tab, *Slides* group). View the nine available layouts. List them here:

   (a) _____     (d) _____     (g) _____
   (b) _____     (e) _____     (h) _____
   (c) _____     (f) _____     (i) _____

   Then, close the dialog box.

**P**

## LESSON 3: OPENING AN EXISTING PRESENTATION

Once you have saved a presentation to your diskette, flash drive, or folder, it is available for viewing, modification, or printing. To prepare for these exercises, complete the following steps:

1.  Follow the procedure in Lesson 1 to launch PowerPoint if necessary.

2.  Close the current presentation (click the File tab and then *Close*).

> **NOTE:** It is always a good idea to work with one presentation at a time. Before opening a presentation (or creating a new one), make sure that all others have been closed.

### Opening a Presentation

Opening a presentation retrieves the file from your diskette (or folder) and copies it into a window. Open the OFFICE1 presentation as follows:

1.  Click the File tab.

    A list of recently-opened PowerPoint presentations may appear on the right side of the file menu, as shown in Figure P-5). In the future, if one of these files is the one you want to open, just click it. For now, though, you will try the traditional open procedure:

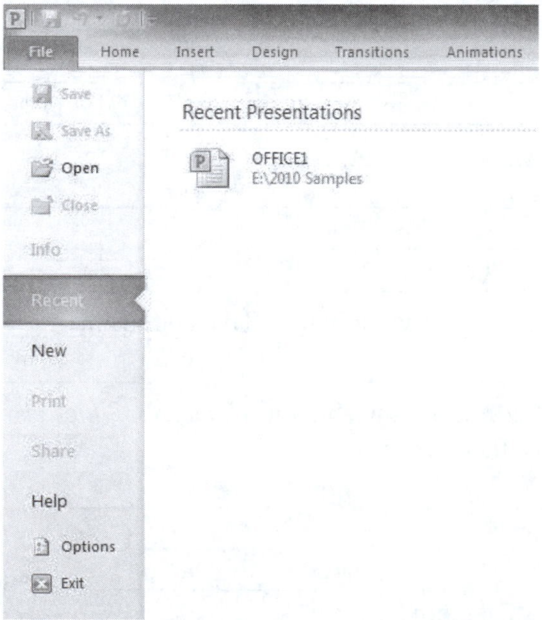

**FIGURE P-5**    *The File menu*

Recently-opened presentations may appear in the right side of the menu.

2.  Click *Open*.

    An Open dialog box waits for you to type or select a filename, as shown in Figure P-6.

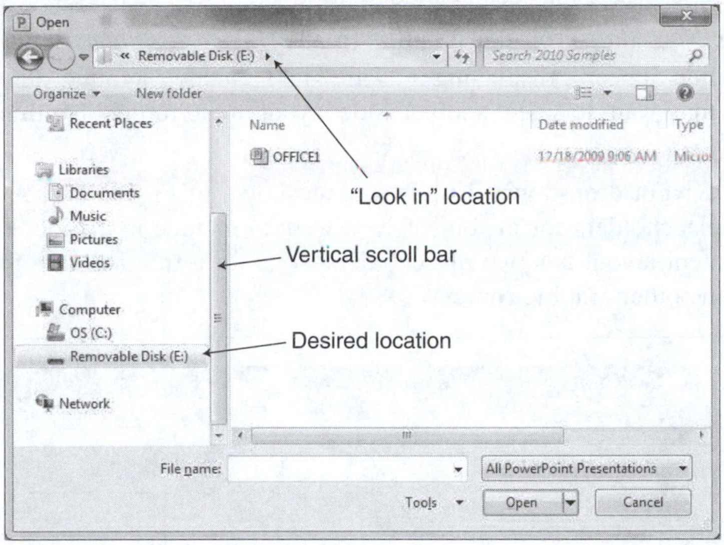

**FIGURE P-6**    *The Open Dialog Box*

3.  Scroll down the left side to the desired drive or folder.

4.  If it is not already highlighted, click *OFFICE1* in the list to highlight it.

    Note that a preview of the title slide may be displayed at the right for easy identification. (Do not be concerned if your screen does not display this preview for now.)

5.  Click the *Open* button (at the bottom) to open the OFFICE1 presentation for use.

6.  If your presentation window is not at maximum size, click the maximize button at the upper-right corner of its window. (It is easier to work in a maximized window.)

    Note that the maximized window shares its title bar with the program window, which reads "OFFICE 1 – Microsoft PowerPoint."

7.  If necessary, click the *Outline* tab in the left pane to display the outline view.

## Adding Additional Slides

The remaining two slides of the presentation, as shown in Figure P-7, can now be created with a procedure similar to that used for the title slide.

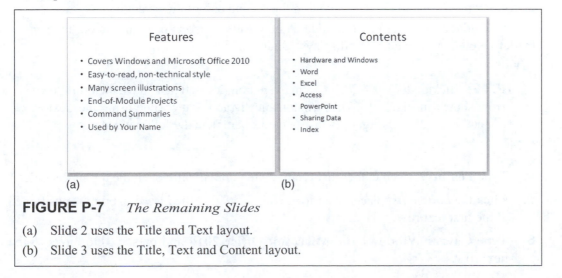

(a)                                                    (b)

**FIGURE P-7**    *The Remaining Slides*

(a)   Slide 2 uses the Title and Text layout.

(b)   Slide 3 uses the Title, Text and Content layout.

For example, create the second slide by following these steps:

1. Click the *New Slide* drop-down button (in the *Home* tab, *Slides* group).

A new slide appears, displaying a "Title and Content" layout. Although this is fine for now, you may want to select another slide layout in the future. Try this:

2. Click the *Layout* button (*Home* tab, *Slides* group).

A Slide Layout drop-down list appears, as shown in Figure P-8. A layout contains one or more placeholders for the objects you want to include in a slide. For example, the Title and Content layout has two placeholders—one for a title and one for a bulleted list of text (or some other graphic content).

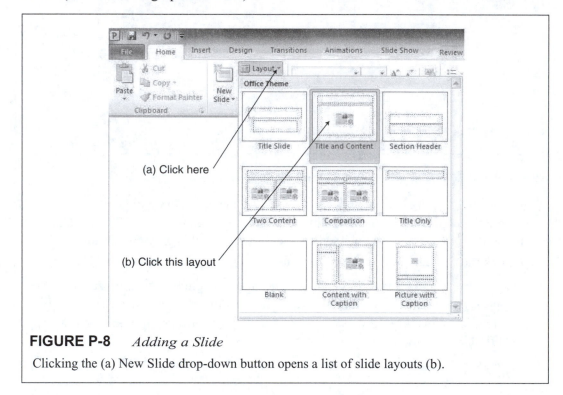

**FIGURE P-8**    *Adding a Slide*

Clicking the (a) New Slide drop-down button opens a list of slide layouts (b).

The Slide Layout list displays nine slide layouts. You can select the one you want to use for a particular slide. (Of course, you can always change a slide's layout later.) Note that the current layout is highlighted. For now,

3. Click the *Title* and *Content* layout in the second column to select it.

Its layout appears in the new slide. A new slide 2 also appears in the outline pane at the left. Note that the status bar displays "Slide 2 of 2."

**NOTE:** Clicking the *New Slide* command button (located just above the drop-down arrow shown in Figure P-8a) will automatically add a new slide using the Text & Content layout. Using Figure P-7a as a guide, complete the following steps:

4. Type **Features**. (Remember that typing will automatically open the top placeholder.)

5. Click the *bottom list* placeholder to open it. Note that the insertion point is positioned at the first text row.

6. Type **Covers Windows and Microsoft Office 2010** and press ⏎ to move to the next row.

The next text bullet appears.

7. Type **Easy-to-read**, **non-technical style** and press ⏎.

8. Type **Many screen illustrations** and press ⏎.

9. Type **End-of-Module Projects** and press ⏎.

10. Type **Command Summaries** and press ⏎.

11. Type **Used by** [SPACE] and then type your name, but *do not* press the Enter key. (If you did, press [BACKSPACE] to erase it.)

12. Click anywhere outside the placeholder box.

    Now create the third slide using the same procedure:

13. Click the *New Slide* drop-down button (*Home* tab, *Slides* group).

14. Click the *Layout* button.

15. This time, click the *Two Content* layout option.

    Using Figure P-7b as a guide, complete the slide as follows:

16. Type **Contents** (which is automatically placed into the top placeholder).

17. Click the *left list* placeholder to open it.

18. Type **Hardware and Windows** and press ⏎.

19. Type **Word** and press ⏎.

20. Type **Excel** and press ⏎.

21. Type **Access** and press ⏎.

22. Type **PowerPoint** and press ⏎.

23. Type **Sharing Data** and press ⏎.

> **NOTE:** In future presentations, if you wanted to create subheadings (lower-level bullets), you could press the [TAB] key and then continue typing. To return to an upper-level bullet, press [SHIFT] + [TAB].

24. Type **Index** but *do not* press the Enter key.

25. Click anywhere outside the placeholder box.

26. Click the File tab and then *Save* to save the OFFICE1 presentation again.

    You have now completed the basic text entry. (You will add a graphic image to Slide 3 in Lesson 5.) Of course, you could edit the text by viewing any slide with [PgDn] or [PgUp], clicking the placeholder, and then editing the text.

## LESSON 4: VIEWING THE PRESENTATION

Now that you have created the basic slide layout and text, you can begin to explore the various view modes offered by PowerPoint. To prepare for this, begin with the following steps:

1. If needed, launch PowerPoint and open the OFFICE1 presentation.

2. Click "Slides" in the left slides/outline pane to reset it.

**3.**    Press PgUp to move to the title slide (Slide 1 of 3) if you are not already there.

PowerPoint offers six presentation view modes that allow you to review and modify your presentation: *Normal view, Reading view, Outline view, Slide Sorter view, Notes Page view,* and *Slide Show.* (There are also Master views that will not be discussed here.) Each view presents a different look at your presentation. The following set of exercises will introduce you to each of these views.

## Normal View

PowerPoint's Normal view is often used for creating and editing slides. You are probably using it right now. As you have seen, Normal view presents one slide on the screen at a time—in the right pane of the window. Normal view actually presents three views on the screen—namely, Outline, slide, and Notes Page—all in their own section (or *pane*). Your screen should now display the title slide, as shown in Figure P-9. You will also see a vertical scroll bar along the right edge of the window. This bar lets you use a mouse to view different slides in the presentation. You can click either arrow to move the screen incrementally in the desired direction. You can also drag the elevator button on the scroll bar to scroll quickly among the slides. In addition, two slide buttons appear at the bottom of the vertical scroll bar (as shown in the margin). By clicking either button, you can move forward or backward through your slides, one at a time.

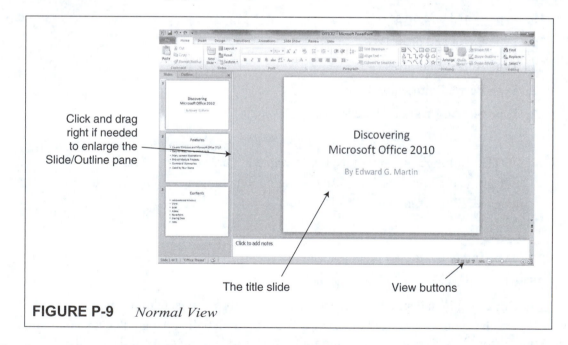

**FIGURE P-9**    *Normal View*

**1.**    If your screen is not in Normal view, click the Normal View button (in the lower-right corner) to switch to it.

**2.**    If slides are not easily read, you can click the frame, as in Figure P-9, and drag right as needed.

Note that the slide number (in this example, Slide 1 of 3) is displayed at the lower left in the status bar and that the first slide in the left pane is highlighted. Each time you press the PgDn or PgUp key (or click the Next or Previous slide button), the next slide in your presentation is shown. Here's an example:

**3.**    Press PgDn to see the second slide.

Note that the slide counter in the status bar now shows Slide 2 of 3.

**4.**  Press ⃞PgDn⃞ again to see the third slide.

**5.**  Press ⃞PgUp⃞ twice to return to the first slide (or drag the scroll bar).

While in Normal view, you can type or edit text, change the layout, or add graphics and shapes.

## The Outline View

Now, examine the left pane of the window, which can display the sequence of your presentation as a series of small, individual slides or a text outline. You can switch between them by clicking the appropriate tab. For example,

**1.**  Click the *Outline* tab in the left pane to switch to Outline view, as shown in Figure P-10a.

As shown in Figure P-10b, an outline of your entire presentation appears in the expanded left pane of the Normal window. The Outline view allows you to work on your presentation through its text outline. Each slide is identified by its number at the left of the outline. A slide icon identifies the start of each new slide. The slide's title appears as a major heading (in a larger font) with the remaining contents shown as subheadings. Note that bulleted lists are displayed as well. A vertical insertion point indicates the current text.

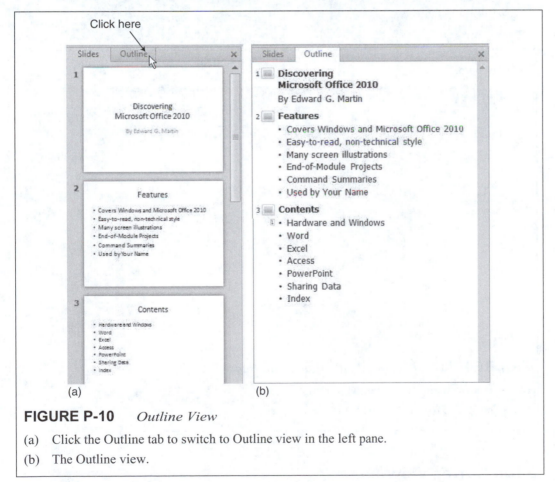

**FIGURE P-10**  *Outline View*

(a)  Click the Outline tab to switch to Outline view in the left pane.

(b)  The Outline view.

**2.**  Click the "D" in "Discovering" in Slide 1 of the outline to move there.

You can now scroll through your entire outline, or print it, to examine the sequence, organization, and content of your presentation. Try this:

3.   Press the down arrow or use the scroll bar, to move down through your outline.

In the Outline view, you can also add or delete text or change the order of slides (by moving blocks of text).

4.   Return to Slide 1. (Click its title.)

You can also switch this pane to display individual slides:

5.   Click the *Slides* tab button to switch the left pane to Slide view.

The left pane now displays the sequence of your slides as individual slide images, as shown in Figure P-10a. You can leave the left pane in either view as desired, or close it if not needed. Try this:

6.   Click the Outline/Slide pane close button, as shown in Figure P-11a.

This maximizes the slide view, as shown in Figure P-11b. Whenever you want to re-open the Outline/Slide pane, do this:

7.   Click the *View* tab on the ribbon.

8.   Click the Normal command button (in the *Presentation Views* group).

> **NOTE:** Clicking the View selector button in the status bar will not return the Slide/Outline pane to the screen. This must be done by following steps 7 and 8, through the ribbon.

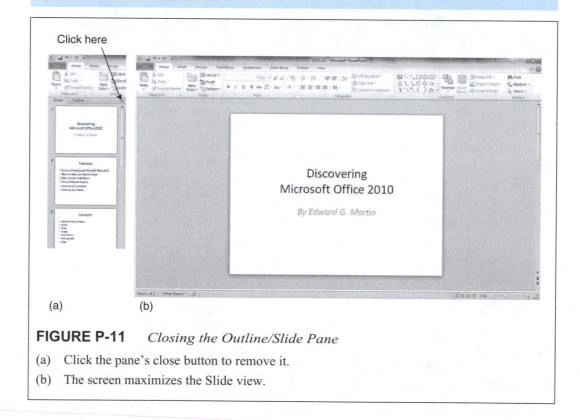

**FIGURE P-11**   *Closing the Outline/Slide Pane*

(a)   Click the pane's close button to remove it.

(b)   The screen maximizes the Slide view.

## Slide Sorter View

1.   To switch to Slide Sorter view, click its button, second on the view toolbar, or click the *Slide Sorter* command button (*View* tab, *Presentation Views* group) in the ribbon.

As shown in Figure P-12, the Slide Sorter view appears on your screen. The Slide Sorter presents a miniature view of all the slides in your presentation as if you had placed them on a table in the order that you want them to appear.

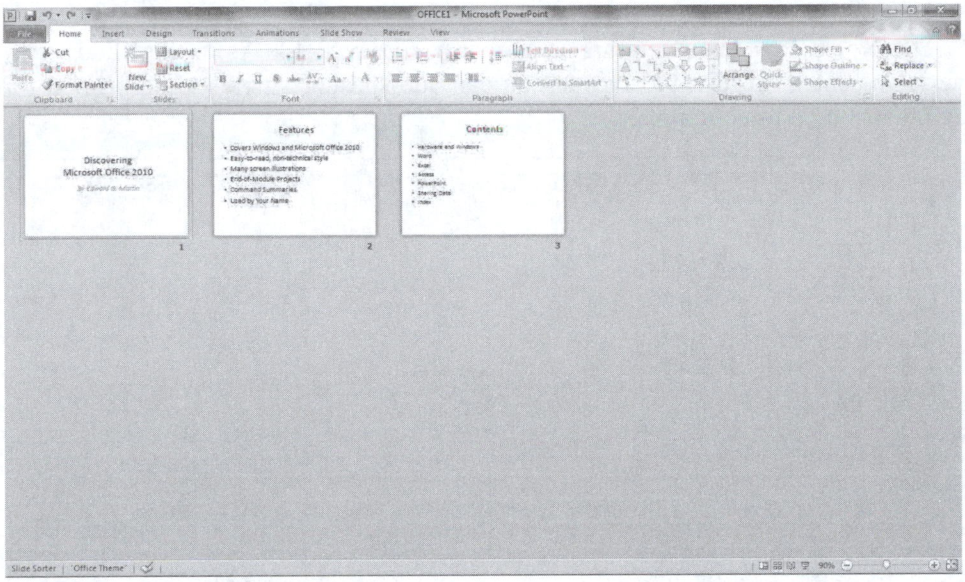

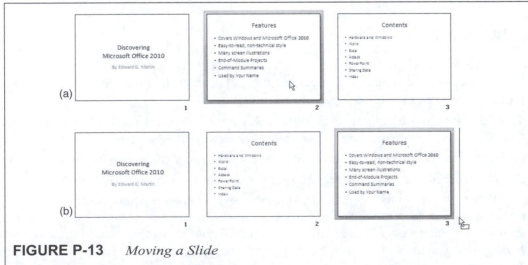

**FIGURE P-12**  *Slide Sorter View*

Note that each slide is identified by a number beneath its lower-right corner and that the status bar indicates the active view. The Slide Sorter lets you review the flow of your presentation, rather than each individual slide. You can change the slide order or add transition effects (as you will see). For example, to switch the second and third slides by mouse, try the following:

2.  Click the second slide to highlight it, as shown in Figure P-13a.

3.  Click and drag the slide past the third slide (a vertical line will show you your position, as in Figure P-13b) and release.

4.  Repeat steps 2–3 to place the slides back in their original order.

**FIGURE P-13**  *Moving a Slide*

(a)  Click the slide to select it.

(b)  Drag it to its new position and release the mouse.

## Notes Page View

**1.** To switch to Notes Page view, click the *View* tab on the ribbon, and then the *Notes Page* command button in the *Presentation Views* group. (Since it is not used that often, there is no view button on the status bar for Notes Page).

The Notes Page view appears as shown in Figure P-14. As in the Slide view, each slide is presented on its own screen. You can add speaker's notes to be printed for your use or distributed to your audience.

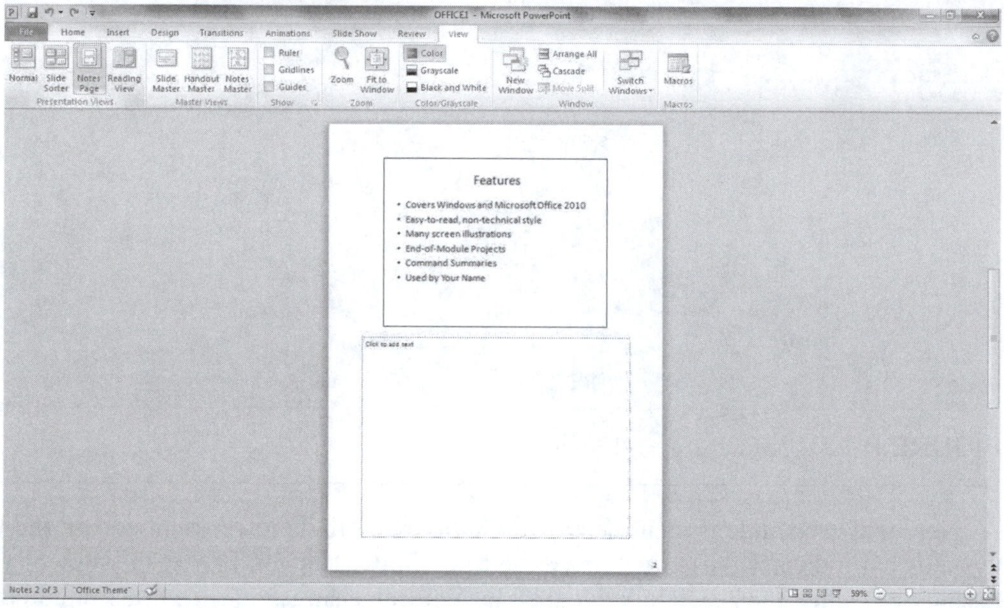

**FIGURE P-14**    *Notes Page View*

To do this, you would simply click the placeholder at the bottom of the screen, type the notes, and then click outside the box. For now, continue with these steps:

**2.** Press `PGDN` to move to the next slide.

**3.** Press `PGUP` as needed to return to the title slide.

## Slide Show

Slide Show is a full-screen presentation of each slide that allows you to review the final impact of your sequencing, organization, and content. It is the view that you use to present your work to your audience.

**1.** To switch to Slide Show, click the fourth view button on the status bar, or click the *Slide Show* command button (*View* tab, *Presentation Views* group).

Your first slide appears on the screen. Here's an example of moving through the show:

**2.** Click the mouse to see the second slide. (You could also press `↵` or `PGDN`.)

While you are in the Slide Show, you can move the mouse pointer to draw the attention of your audience to various screen items. You can also press `CTRL` + **P** to change the mouse pointer into a "pen" with which you can hold down the mouse button to temporarily draw on the slide for emphasis. To continue to the next slide, press `CTRL` + **A** to change the mouse pointer back. Then, click the mouse to move to the next slide.

> **NOTE:** Using the pen does not change the original slide. When you exit from the slide, you can choose to keep or discard any lines you may have drawn.

3.  Click the mouse (or press ⏎) to see the third slide.
    You can move through your entire presentation by clicking the mouse or pressing ⏎ or PGDN. You can press PGUP or BACKSPACE to return to a previous slide.

4.  Click the mouse once more. Note that an End of Slide Show screen appears.

5.  Now click the mouse one last time.
    A dialog box appears, asking you to keep or discard your annotations.

6.  Click *Discard* to erase your annotations and return to the PowerPoint window.

7.  Return to Normal view and click the *Home* tab.

> **NOTE:** You can press ESC to end the slide show at any time.

**Quick Review #2**

1.  What is a slide layout? _____

2.  How do you add an additional slide to a presentation?
    _____

3.  Name the five view modes.
    _____

4.  Identify the steps needed to open a presentation.
    _____

5.  What is a placeholder? _____

## LESSON 5: ENHANCING WITH TEXT AND GRAPHICS

Once text has been entered, you can edit the presentation in much the same way as you do in a word processor. You can insert and delete text, adjust the layout, change fonts, and add graphics. The following exercises demonstrate the fundamental techniques. Use them as needed in the future. To prepare, start with these steps:

1.  If needed, launch PowerPoint and open the OFFICE1 presentation.

2.  Switch to Normal view, close the left pane, and move to the title slide if you are not there.

> **NOTE:** As you have seen, closing unneeded task panes maximizes the slide work area, making it easier to work on your slides.

P

## Inserting Text

Inserting text is simply a matter of positioning the insertion point and then typing. You can insert text in the Normal or Outline views. Try inserting the word "Suite" as follows:

**1.** In the title slide, click to the immediate left of the "2" in "2010" on the second line of the title, as shown in Figure P-15a. A rectangular highlight will mark the open placeholder.

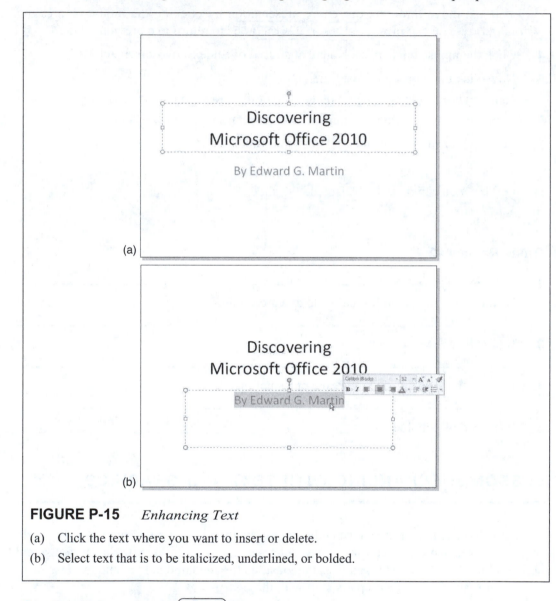

**FIGURE P-15** *Enhancing Text*

(a)   Click the text where you want to insert or delete.

(b)   Select text that is to be italicized, underlined, or bolded.

**2.** Type **Suite** and press (SPACE).

**3.** To end the insert, click outside the placeholder.

## Deleting Text

Deleting text is just as easy. Let's say you now want to delete the word "Suite" from the title slide.

**1.** In the title slide, click to the immediate left of the "S" in the word "Suite."

**2.** Press DELETE six times until Suite and the space after it have been removed.

**3.** To end the delete, click outside the placeholder.

## Changing Fonts

The default font styles or sizes can be modified as needed. You simply identify the text and invoke the command. For example, to italicize the subtitle "By Edward G. Martin," perform the following steps:

**1.** In the title slide, click the "B" in "By" and drag the mouse pointer to the space after the "n" in "Martin." The entire line should be highlighted, as shown in Figure P-15b.

As you point, a small "toolbox" containing command buttons for the most common font changes appears. For now, ignore it.

**2.** Click the *Italic* command button (*Home* tab, *Font* group or in the toolbox that appears on the screen).

> **NOTE:** If you make a mistake when changing fonts, click the *Undo* toolbar button. Then, try again.

**3.** Click outside the placeholder to end.

You can use a similar technique to bold, underline, shadow, or change the text color, font, or size as desired.

**4.** Save the modified presentation again as OFFICE1.

## Enhancing the Presentation with Graphic Images

Until now, you have used text and layout alone to present your work. Often, you will want to enhance the text with graphic images (or "objects") that can be added to the slides. A number of the slide layouts provide preset locations for adding graphics. You can also insert, position, and resize graphics however you want to better suit your needs.

PowerPoint offers two methods for adding graphics to your presentations; you can select images (called *clip art*) from Microsoft's Clip Art Gallery, or you can draw your own using PowerPoint's drawing tools. (Later, you will learn to add any image file to a slide.) These brief exercises will demonstrate the basics of both techniques. First, you will add clip art to the placeholder in Slide 3.

### Adding Clip Art Images to a Slide Placeholder

Let's say you want to add a clip art graphic image in the placeholder of the third slide. Try the following:

**1.** In OFFICE1, switch to Normal view if you are not already there, and close the left pane if necessary.

2.  Press [ PGDN ] twice (or scroll) to move to Slide 3.

3.  Examine the right placeholder for a moment (as shown in the margin).

    By clicking one of the six icons shown, you can add a table, chart, clip art, picture, SmartArt graphic, or media clip. Let's add a clip art graphic image into the placeholder of the third slide.

4.  Click the Clip Art icon located on the upper-right corner of the placeholder, as shown in Figure P-16. A Clip Art task pane appears on the right side of the window, as shown in Figure P-17.

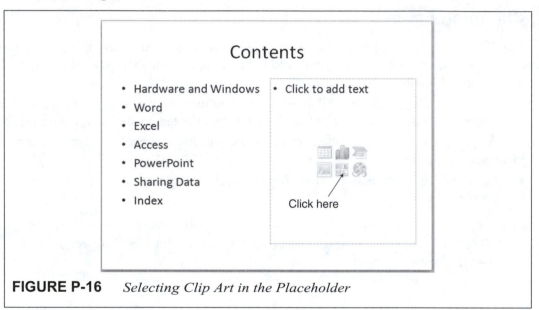

**FIGURE P-16**     *Selecting Clip Art in the Placeholder*

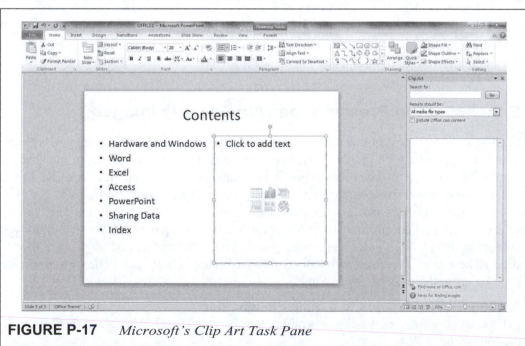

**FIGURE P-17**     *Microsoft's Clip Art Task Pane*

    Let's say you want to use the computer image as shown in the left margin. To locate the image easily, use the search feature as follows:

5.  Click the *Search* for entry box.

**6.** Type **computers** and then click the *Go* button.

A set of selected images that match your search word appears on the screen (your choices may differ).

**7.** Point to the desired image (typically in the first row, first column of the images).

The descriptive keywords "business, computers, computing" should appear in a tool tip. Make sure that you find the correct image before proceeding. (If your software does not contain this image, use any image of your choice.)

**8.** Click the image to select it.

The image appears in a placeholder, as shown in Figure P18. You will learn to change its size in a moment. Note, too, that a Picture Tools Format tab has been added to the ribbon. For now:

**9.** Click outside the image to deselect the placeholder.

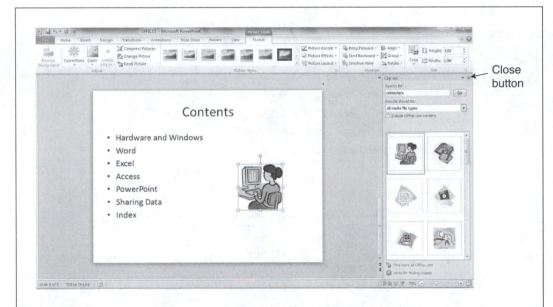

Close button

**FIGURE P-18**    *Inserting Clip Art*

The clip art image has been inserted into the placeholder, automatically positioned within the center of the placeholder.

**10.** Click the Clip Art task pane's Close button (as shown in Figure P-18) to close it.

**11.** Save the presentation as OFFICE2.

## Adding Clip Art Images Without a Placeholder

You can also insert clip art directly into a slide without using a placeholder. Try this:

**1.** Open the OFFICE2 presentation if necessary.

**2.** Move to Slide 2.

**3.** Click the *Insert* tab on the ribbon.

**4.** Click the *Clip Art* command button (*Illustrations* group).

The Clip Art task pane reappears. In this example, you will locate and then and select the "Book" clip art as shown in the margin.

**5.** Click the *Search for* box and delete the current entry.

6.  Type **book** and click the *Go* button.

7.  Now, click the book image to select it. (If this image is not available, choose any other image.)

8.  Close the task pane.

9.  If the clip art appeared on the right side of the slide, click the Undo Quick Access toolbar button to cancel the layout.

The clip art graphic is now centered in your slide as shown in Figure P-19a. The edges and corners of the graphic frame are marked with small squares and circles, known as *handles*. These handles can be used to change the size of the graphic, as you will see shortly. (The green handle that appears above the image can be dragged left or right to rotate an image if desired.)

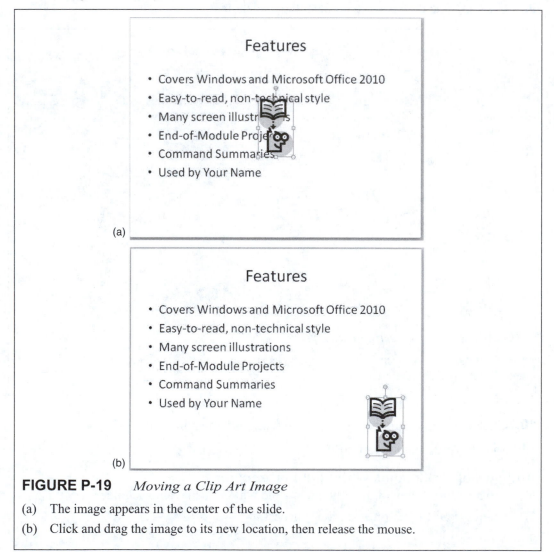

**FIGURE P-19**     *Moving a Clip Art Image*

(a)   The image appears in the center of the slide.

(b)   Click and drag the image to its new location, then release the mouse.

You can now practice repositioning the graphic. To move the image to the lower-right corner, as shown in Figure P-19b, perform the following steps:

10. Point to any spot *within* the graphic image, then click and hold down the left mouse button. Your mouse pointer should resemble a plus sign with four arrows.

11. Drag the pointer (and image) to the lower-right and release the mouse, as shown in Figure P-19b.

**NOTE:** You can also press the arrow keys to move the graphic to the desired position.

To resize the graphic, as shown in Figure P-20, complete the following steps:

**12.** Point to the upper-left corner handle of the graphic image, as shown in Figure P-20a. (Your pointer will change to a diagonal double-pointed arrow when correctly placed.)

**13.** Click and drag the handle toward the upper left (away from the center of the image) until the image size, as shown by a dotted rectangle, expands to approximately the same size as that shown in Figure P-20b (this need not be exact). Then release the mouse.

**14.** If the size is not correct, drag the upper-left handle toward or away from the image center as needed to adjust it and then release the mouse.

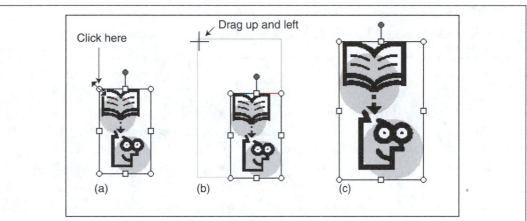

**FIGURE P-20**    *Resizing the Graphic Image*

The image can be resized by dragging a corner frame handle as needed.

(a)  Click a corner handle.

(b)  Drag away from the image's center.

(c)  The resized image.

**NOTE:** Dragging a corner handle (circle) to resize an image maintains the image's proportions and keeps the image looking correct. Using an edge handle (square) only changes the height or width you have selected and will alter the appearance of the image.

**15.** Click anywhere in the slide, away from the text areas, to deselect the image.

**16.** Now move to Slide 3, drag the image slightly to the right and enlarge the image to resemble that shown in Figure P-21. (Hint: Drag its upper-left corner handle away from the center and then drag its lower-right as needed. You may also need to reposition the graphic.)

**17.** Save the presentation again as OFFICE2.

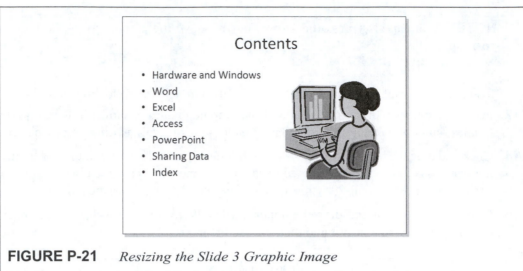

**FIGURE P-21**     *Resizing the Slide 3 Graphic Image*

This image can also be resized by dragging corner frame handles as needed.

**NOTE:** Many different graphic images can be used in a PowerPoint slide—not just clip art. If you have access to the Internet, for example, you can visit a website, right-click a desired image, and save it on your diskette, flash drive, or folder in JPEG or BMP format. Once an image is saved, you can insert the image into a slide. You will try this in the last lesson of this module.

## Drawing Images on a Slide

You can also draw images with PowerPoint's *Insert* tab. For example, to add a shape at the upper-right of Slide 2, try the following:

1.   In the OFFICE2 presentation, move to Slide 2.

It is helpful, when positioning graphics, to invoke a ruler to assist with their placement. To do this:

2.   Click the *View* tab and then the *Ruler* checkbox to invoke rulers on the screen.

3.   Now click the *Insert* tab on the ribbon.

Examine the ribbon and ruler in Figure P-22a. Each command button invokes a different tool that can be applied to the slide.

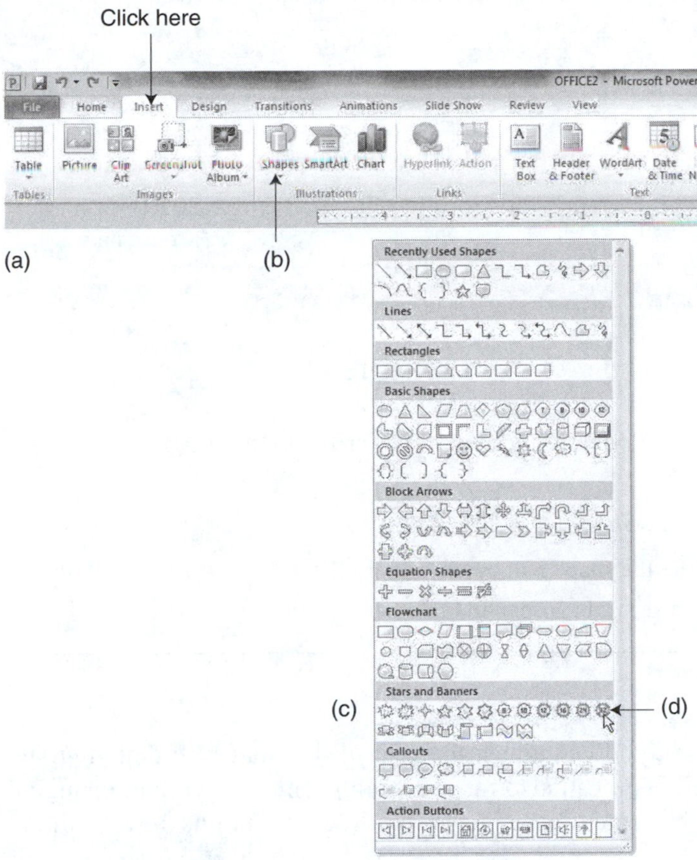

**FIGURE P-22**    *The Insert Ribbon Tab*

(a)   The Insert ribbon and ruler appear.

(b)   Click the *Shapes drop-down* button.

(c)   The Shapes list.

(d)   Click this 32-point star shape.

3.   Click the Shapes drop-down button in the Illustrations group, as shown in Figure P-22b.

A Shapes down-down list appears, as shown in Figure P-22c. You can now select any shape that you want to place on the screen. In this example, continue with the following steps:

4.   Click the *32-Point Star* shape (see Figure P-22d).

5.   Now, as shown in Figure P-23a, point to the upper-right corner of the slide, approximately 2.5 inches to the right and 3.5 inches above center (as shown by the lines in each respective ruler). Note that the arrow pointer has changed to a cross-hair for easier placement.

6.   Using Figure P-23b as a guide, click and drag the pointer right and down, so that it is approximately 4 inches to the right and 2 inches above center. Then release the mouse.

P

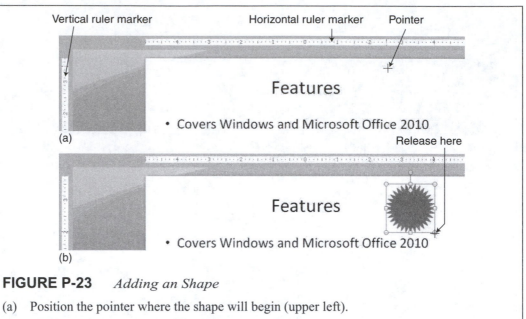

**FIGURE P-23**   *Adding an Shape*

(a)   Position the pointer where the shape will begin (upper left).

(b)   Drag the pointer to the lower-right corner and release.

> **NOTE:** As with clip art, you can adjust the size of the image by dragging any corner handle as needed. You can also move the entire image, without changing its size, by pointing to the center of the image and dragging it to its new location.

**7.**   Click anywhere outside the graphic to deselect it.

### Adding Text to a Graphic Image

You might also want to add some text to the shape you have drawn. Complete the following steps:

**1.**   Click the *Insert* tab on the ribbon.

**2.**   Click the *Text box* command button (*Text* group).

**3.**   Now, click within the shape where the text will be placed.

**4.**   Type **2010**.

**5.**   Click outside the seal to deselect it. The text has been centered within the shape.

One more change to explore:

**6.**   Double-click the shape to select it. Note that a *Format* tab appears in the ribbon, as shown in Figure P-24a.

**7.**   Click the *More* button in the *Shape Styles* group (as in Figure P-24b) to see all the available styles (Figure P-24c).

**8.**   Click *Intense Effect – Orange, Accent 6* (as in Figure P-24d).

**9.**   Click outside the shape to de-select it.

**10.**   Save the presentation again as OFFICE2.

> **NOTE:** To remove a graphic from a slide, click it and then press ⌐DELETE⌐.

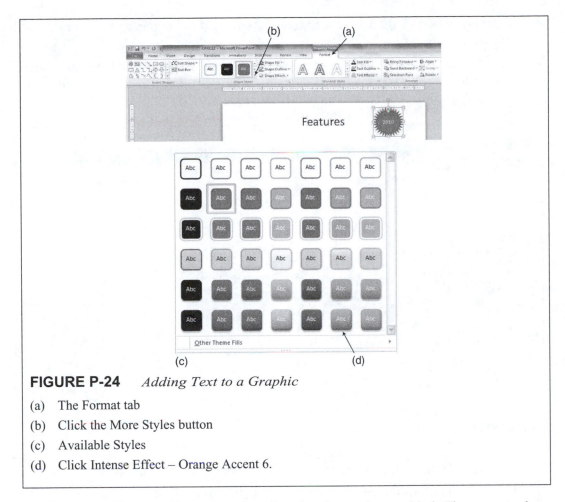

**FIGURE P-24**   *Adding Text to a Graphic*

(a)   The Format tab

(b)   Click the More Styles button

(c)   Available Styles

(d)   Click Intense Effect – Orange Accent 6.

You may also want to explore the other drawing tools provided. There are tools to copy graphic objects, rotate them, or change their color.

## LESSON 6: PRINTING THE PRESENTATION

You can use Slide Show to display your presentation to an audience, but you may also want to print handouts, overheads, or notes to distribute. To prepare, start with these steps:

1.   Launch PowerPoint if needed, open OFFICE2, and move to Slide 1.

2.   Click the File tab and then *Print*.

A Print screen appears as shown in Figure P-25. (Note that the printer listed on your screen will differ from the one in the figure.) Examine the screen for a moment:

• The Printer box identifies the current printer and allows you to adjust its properties. If the printer is not correct for your system, click the drop-down arrow to its right and then click the correct printer.

Examine the "Settings" portion of the screen:

• The *Slides* drop-down list lets you specify what part of the presentation will print: *All* slides, only the *Current Slide*, a partial *Selection*, or a custom range of *Slides*.

• The *Layout* drop-down list lets you select full-page slides, handouts (with 1, 2, 3, 4, 6, or 9 slides per page), notes pages, or your outline.

**P**

- The *Copies* box at the top of the screen lets you set the number of copies that will print (typically, 1).

- The *Color/Grayscale* option at the bottom enables you to print black and white, grayscale, or color versions of color slides. (The *Pure Black and White* option often improves the image produced on non-color printers.)

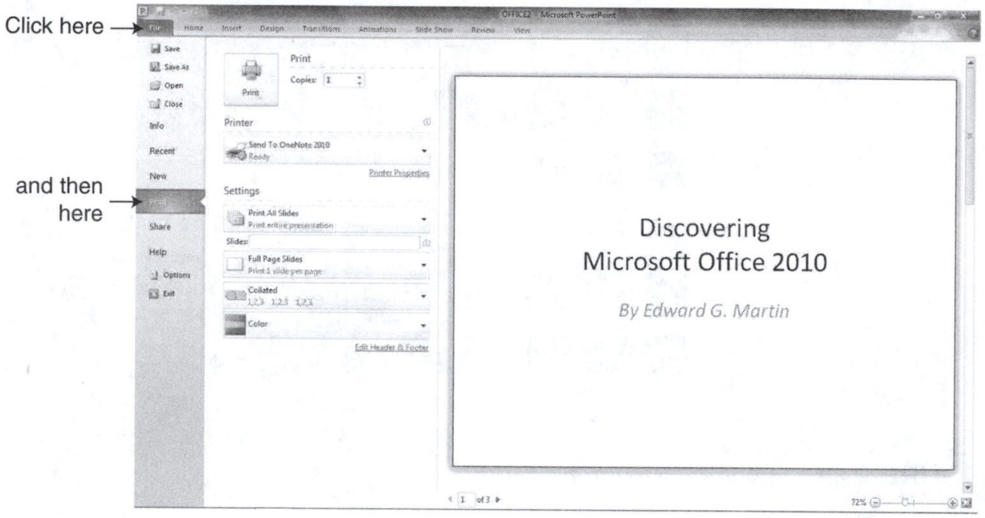

**FIGURE P-25**     *The Print Screen*

For example, to print only the second slide, perform the following steps:

**3.** Click the *Slides* option button (which currently displays "Print All Slides").

**4.** Click the "Custom Range" option.

**5.** Delete any current entry in the box, and then type **2** in the "Slides" entry line.

**6.** Click outside the box.

**NOTE:** You may specify any range of slides. For example:

| | | |
|---|---|---|
| 2 | = | print slide 2 only |
| 2,4 | = | print slides 2 and 4 |
| 2-6 | = | print all slides between slides 2 and 6 |
| 2- | = | print slides from slide 2 to the end |
| -3 | = | print slides from the start to slide 3 |

It is a good idea to preview your slide on the screen before wasting paper. Power-Point's Preview feature lets you do this. As shown in Figure P-26a, a preview appears. You can scroll to see other slides as needed.

If you wanted to print your slide, you could now click the *Print* button to send the image to the printer. But for now:

**7.** Click the *Home* tab to close the Print screen.

Let's try one more example. To print your presentation as a three-slide handout, do the following:

**8.** Click the File tab and then *Print*.

**9.** Click the *Print Layout* drop-down arrow (currently shows "Full Page Slides").

**10.** In the *Handouts* section, click the "3 Slides" option.

**11.** Click the *Slides* drop-down arrow (currently shows "Custom Range").

**12.** Click "Print All Slides" to ensure that all slides will be printed.

**13.** Your screen should resemble Figure P-26b. Change it if it does not.

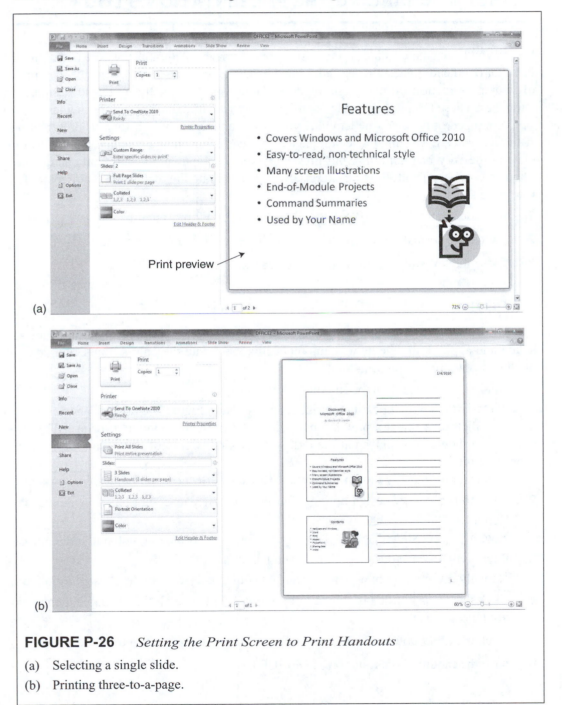

**FIGURE P-26**     *Setting the Print Screen to Print Handouts*

(a)   Selecting a single slide.

(b)   Printing three-to-a-page.

Note that the preview displays the resulting page.

> **NOTE:** Before you print, examine the Preview to be sure that the settings in the Print screen are correct *before* invoking the final Print command.

**14.** For now, click the *Home* tab to close the *Print* screen.

## LESSON 7: CHANGING THE PRESENTATION'S LOOK

So far, you have created slides using basic text and images. Although they are useful in this form for overhead transparencies and printed handouts, you can greatly enhance the impact of your presentation by using one of PowerPoint's professionally produced designs, or templates. These templates provide coordinated layouts, formats, and color schemes.

You need only select the template you desire and then apply it to your presentation. Although you are learning the technique near the end of this module, you can apply a template at the very beginning of your presentation's development as well, and change it as often as you like. The following exercise will demonstrate the technique. To prepare, follow these steps:

**1.** If needed, launch PowerPoint and open the OFFICE2 presentation.

**2.** Switch to Normal view and move to the first slide if you are not there.

**3.** Close the left slide/outline pane if necessary.

### Using a Design Theme

A design theme lets you choose the overall style or "look" of your presentation. Once selected and applied, the theme will automatically coordinate the colors, fonts, and layouts in all slides within the presentation.

**1.** Click the *Design* tab in the ribbon.

A Design tab will appear in the ribbon, as shown in Figure P-27a. The Themes group of this tab lets you select a professionally-designed presentation theme for use. The current design theme is displayed at the left, with the first twelve of forty other designs appearing in the row.

You can point to any design theme icon to see its effect on your slides. For example,

**2.** Point to the *Angles* design option—fourth icon. (If you do not have the Angles design, pick another design.)

Note how your slide displays changes in color, background, layout, and font choices.

**3.** Point to the *Aspect* design option (seventh icon).

A totally different set of options appears on your slide. Now, apply a design as follows:

**4.** Click the *More* button (as shown in Figure P-27b) to see all the available themes (as in Figure P-27c).

**5.** Click the *Oriel* option (fourth icon in the third row) to apply it to the slide.

**6.** Save the modified presentation as OFFICE3.

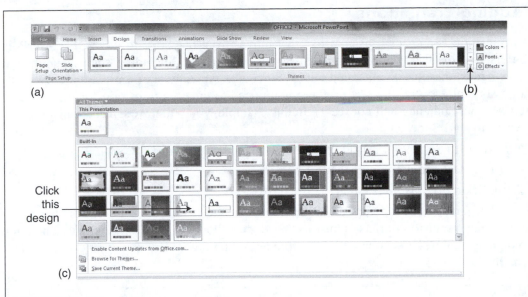

**FIGURE P-27**    *The Design Tab*

(a)    Click the Design tab to access its features in the ribbon.

(b)    Click the *More* button to see all available designs.

(c)    The designs.

> **NOTE:** When you save a presentation, the new file will retain whatever design changes you have made.

7.    Run the Slide Show and press ⌈PGDN⌉ to see the changes in each of the three slides.

> **NOTE:** When you change a design, you may have to adjust the size or position of graphics you have placed in slides so that they do not conflict with other objects. Clip art that has been put in placeholders will automatically be adjusted to conform.

## LESSON 8: ADDING TRANSITIONS AND BUILDS TO THE SLIDE SHOW

By default, Slide Show presents slides in sequence by abruptly replacing one slide with another. However, PowerPoint lets you apply professional transitions and builds to add special visual effects that enhance your presentation. The following exercises let you explore the basics of these enhancements. These steps will help you prepare:

1.    Launch PowerPoint and open the OFFICE3 presentation.

2.    Click the *View* tab and then the *Normal* command button (in the *Presentation Views* group) to reset the left slide/outline pane.

**P**

## Adding Transitions

A transition is a special visual effect that moves from one slide to the next. PowerPoint offers five basic transitions from which you can choose, including such techniques as cuts, fades, dissolves, splits, and wipes. Since you typically start a presentation with the title slide already on the screen, there is no need to create a transition for the title slide (since your audience will not see it). In this example, you will now select a transition with which to start Slide 2.

**1.** Move to Slide 2 ( PgDn  or just click it in the left pane).

To select a transition, do the following:

**2.** Click the *Transitions* tab in the ribbon.

The Transitions tab appears in the ribbon, as shown in Figure P-28. This tab allows you to set a transition effect, adjust its speed, and choose manual or automatic operation. You can also preview your settings before accepting them. The transition group displays the first ten of 35 choices.

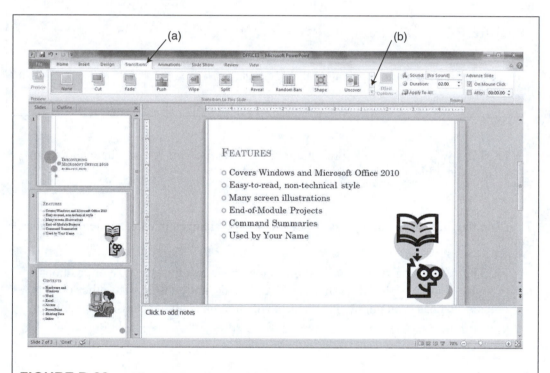

**FIGURE P-28**    *The Transitions Ribbon Tab*

(a)   The Transitions ribbon provides access to slide transitions.

(b)   Click the center down arrow of the Transition group to see additional options.

**3.** Click the center down arrow (as shown in Figure P-28b) to move to row 2.

**NOTE:** Clicking the *More* button in the *Transition to this Slide* group displays all fifty-eight options, but obscures the screen so that the transition cannot be clearly previewed. It is better to use the down-arrow to view a row at a time when previews are desired.

4.  Point to the ninth option icon ("Glitter") and watch the screen as the effect is previewed. You could continue to change rows and click/view other options, but for now,

5.  Click the "Glitter" icon (row 2, icon 9) to apply it to Slide 2.

Glitter

### Changing the Transition Speed (Duration)

6.  Click the *Duration* box.

7.  Click the down arrow to set a speed of 2.00.

Note the effect in the slide. You can set any transition speed you desire by setting the appropriate number in the speed box. If you examine the other speeds, be sure to set 2.00 before continuing.

> **NOTE:** If your computer can produce sound, you could click the Transition Sound drop-down box and select a transitional sound as well. You would then hear it sampled through your speakers.

8.  Click the *Preview* button at the extreme left of the ribbon to preview the changes.

> **NOTE:** The *Apply to All* command button will apply the selected transition to all slides in the presentation. This may be desirable in the future, but for this exercise, you need to apply the transition to each slide separately.

9.  Examine the slide pane at the far left of the window. Note that a small star icon appears under the "2" of the second slide, showing that a transition has been set.

Now for Slide 3. Continue with the following steps:

10. Move to Slide 3.

11. Using the *Transition* tab, set the transition effect to *Ripple* (seventh icon, second row).

12. Do *not* change the duration (currently 1.39).

13. Click the *Home* tab.

14. Save the presentation as OFFICE4.

15. Move to Slide 1 and run *Slide Show* to see the transition effects.

## Using Builds

A *build* (also known as a "progressive disclosure") is another visual special effect. Unlike a transition, which affects how you to move to a new slide, a build is used *within* a slide's text list to display each item one at a time. A build allows you to focus your audience's attention on each single item in the list, revealing the next one only when your presentation is ready for it. You will now select some build effects for the last two slides.

1.  If needed, launch PowerPoint, open OFFICE4, switch and move to Slide 2 as needed.

To select a build for Slide 2, complete the following steps:

2.  Close the left slide/outline pane to see your complete slide.

3.  Click within the text list in the middle of the slide to select its placeholder.

P

**4.** Click the *Animations* tab in the ribbon.

A Custom Animation ribbon appears, as shown in Figure P-29.

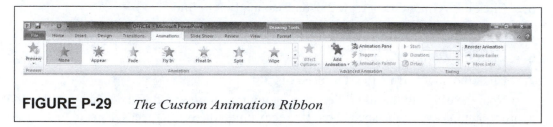

**FIGURE P-29**    *The Custom Animation Ribbon*

This ribbon allows you to select a build effect for any part of your slide. You can also indicate whether you want the previous text row to be dimmed when the new row is revealed. (Dimming a previous row further focuses your audience's attention on the new point that is revealed on the slide.)

## Setting a Build Effect

You can now adjust the build to disclose each item with a special effect. Examine the *Animation* group in the ribbon as in Figure P-29.

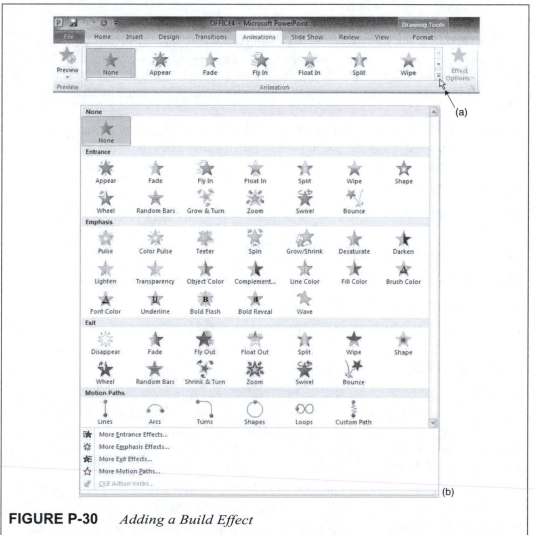

**FIGURE P-30**    *Adding a Build Effect*

Click the More button (a) to see available options (b).

The first seven effects (of 51 possible effects) appear.

**5.**   Click the *More* button (as in Figure P-30a) to see all the options.

A list of four categories of effects will appear, as shown in Figure P-30b, namely, Entrance, Emphasis, Exit, and Motion Paths. You can scroll through them to find the one you want.

**6.**   In the Entrance option, click the *Fly In* option (third).

The main effect appears on the slide. Once you select the main effect, you can adjust its direction using a follow-up drop-down list.

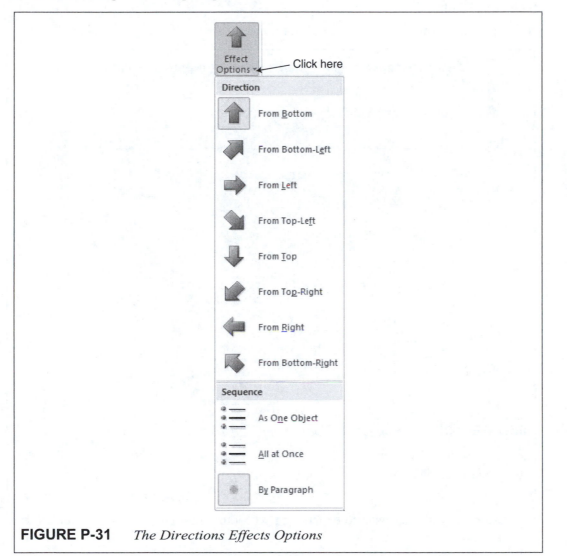

**FIGURE P-31**     *The Directions Effects Options*

**7.**   Click the Effect Options drop-down button to access its list, as in Figure P-31.

**8.**   Click the *From Left* option.

The screen demonstrates your direction choice.

**9.**   Click the Animation Duration arrow up to set the duration to 1.00.

**10.**  Click the *Preview* button.

The effect is demonstrated on the slide. There are literally thousands of combinations of effects, speeds, and directions. You can experiment with many of the effects that PowerPoint offers. Here's one more to consider:

P

## Dimming Previous Bullets

By default, each text row that is "disclosed" (revealed) remains on the screen after it appears. However, you can also dim the previous bullet so that the new one will be colored differently. This way, each new item can be emphasized as you reveal it. To do this, continue with these steps:

**11.** Click the Show Additional Effects button, as shown in Figure P-32a.

A Fly-In dialog box appears, as shown in Figure P-32b.

**12.** Click the *After Animation* drop-down arrow to access its list. (It currently reads "Don't Dim.")

**13.** Click the orange color box (the fifth) to select it.

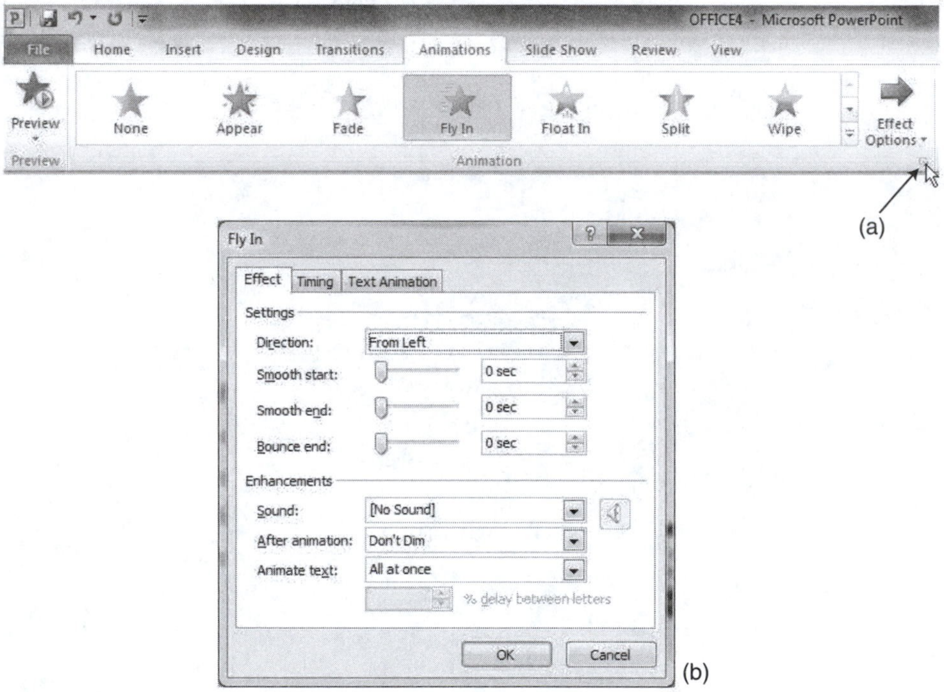

**FIGURE P-32**   *Adding Additional Effects*

(a)   Access the Effect options.

(b)   The Effects dialog box.

Later on, you may want to experiment with other dim colors to see the effect they will have on your presentation.

**14.** Click the *OK* button to accept it. The screen will preview the slide build.

**15.** Using the same techniques, move to Slide 3 and select the *Split* build effect, *without* any dim. (Here's how: PgDn, click the text, *Split*.)

**16.** Save the presentation again as OFFICE4.

## Running the Presentation Show

You can now view your handiwork in creating the transitions and builds by running the Slide Show. Remember that you will control the speed of the presentation by clicking the mouse. You can also press ⏎ or PGDN to see each change.

**1.** Move to the first slide in the OFFICE4 presentation.

Now, watch your screen carefully as you perform the next few steps of the exercise.

**2.** Invoke the *Slide Show*.

As expected, the first title slide appears on the screen. The title slide is typically started before your audience enters the room and remains on the screen until you are ready to begin. You would then greet your audience, give some introductory remarks, and get ready to move to the first content slide of your presentation (Slide 2). To move to the next slide:

**3.** Click the mouse to continue (or press ⏎ or PGDN).

The Dissolve transition changes the screen from the title slide to the second. As shown in Figure P-33a, only the title is displayed. The bulleted items do not yet appear. This is due to the build effect that you specified for this slide. Each bullet will only appear as you move ahead in the presentation.

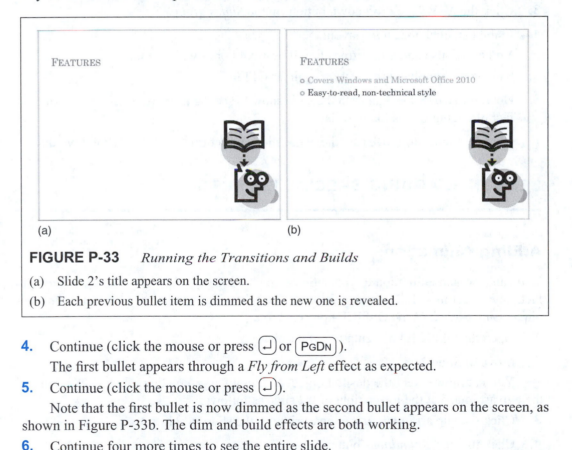

(a)                                        (b)

**FIGURE P-33**    *Running the Transitions and Builds*

(a)    Slide 2's title appears on the screen.

(b)    Each previous bullet item is dimmed as the new one is revealed.

**4.** Continue (click the mouse or press ⏎ or PGDN).

The first bullet appears through a *Fly from Left* effect as expected.

**5.** Continue (click the mouse or press ⏎).

Note that the first bullet is now dimmed as the second bullet appears on the screen, as shown in Figure P-33b. The dim and build effects are both working.

**6.** Continue four more times to see the entire slide.

**NOTE:**   While you are in the show, you can press **P** or the PGUP key to move backward through the presentation.

**7.** Now continue to the third slide (click the mouse or press ⏎).

Note the effect of the transition. Again, your build instructions ensure that only the title appears.

8. Click five more times.

Note that each bullet appears with a *Split* effect. Note, too, that the points remain on the screen without dimming.

9. Continue to move through the list until the show ends and you return to the presentation window.

## Finishing the Show

Notice that when you completed the last slide, the show simply displayed a black slide with an "End of Slide Show" message. Although this is fine, it is not the most professional effect you can achieve. One of PowerPoint's tips suggests that you end the show by placing a blank slide as the last one. This way, the words disappear, but the template remains to neatly end the presentation. To do this, follow these steps:

1. Move to Slide 3.

2. Click the *Home* tab if needed.

3. Click the *New Slide* drop-down button (in the *Slides* group).

4. In the list, click the *Blank* layout.

You could also add a final transition if desired. For now, leave it as is.

5. Save your complete presentation again as OFFICE4.

6. Now, move to Slide 3 and run the slide show to see the more professional-looking effect of ending with a blank slide.

7. Click as needed to move past the blank slide and return to the PowerPoint window.

## LESSON 9: ADDING SPECIAL EFFECTS

## Adding Animation

You can also add animation to your title or graphic images to provide further interest. In fact, any object in a slide can be animated. The following exercise demonstrates the technique using Slide 2 of the OFFICE4 presentation.

1. Open the OFFICE4 presentation, if necessary.

2. Move to Slide 2.

You can now select the desired object and apply an animation effect. Let's animate the clip art image at the lower-right of the slide as follows:

3. Click the clip art image at the lower-right of the slide to select it.

4. Click the *Add Animations* button.

5. Click the *More Entrance Effects* option (near the bottom of the list). An "Add Entrance Effect" dialog box appears.

6. Scroll down to the Exciting category and click the *Spiral In* option.

7. Click *OK*.

8. Your screen should resemble that shown in Figure P-34. Correct it if it does not.

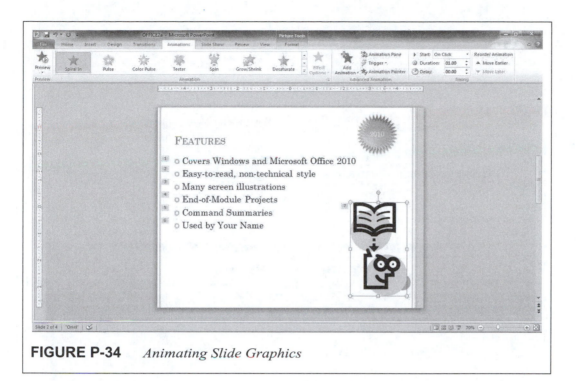

**FIGURE P-34**    *Animating Slide Graphics*

9.   To see the effect, click the *Preview* button (left side of ribbon).
     Try one more:

10.  Click the *32-Point Star* in the upper-right corner of the slide to select it.

11.  Click the *Add Animation* button.

12.  In the *Entrance* list, click the *Swivel* option.

> **NOTE:** Once you use an effect, it will appear in the list of effects in the future.

13.  If desired, click the *Preview* button.

You have now animated the two graphic objects in the slide. Any slide object (including the title) may be animated in a similar manner. You may want to examine some of the other animation effects in the future.

### Setting Order and Timing

Once you have animated the desired objects, you may also want to adjust the order in which they will appear, and whether they will appear automatically or upon a mouse click. The order of animated objects is indicated by the number to the left of each object in the slide. For example, as shown in Figure P-34b, the graphic images will appear in the seventh and eighth position of the sequence. You can now adjust the list as desired by simply clicking an object and then clicking the appropriate move key (up or down) to change its position in the list. Let's say you wanted the graphic objects to appear first and second in the slide, before the text list. Try this:

14.  Click the *32-Point Star* (object number 8) to select it, as shown in Figure P-35a.

**P**

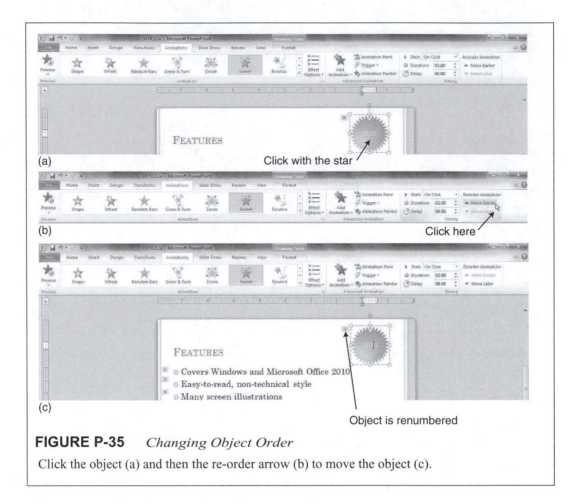

**FIGURE P-35**     *Changing Object Order*

Click the object (a) and then the re-order arrow (b) to move the object (c).

**15.** Click the *Move Earlier* re-order arrow, as shown in Figure P-35b twice, until the object is renumbered as object number 1 (as shown in Figure P-35c).

The star image will now be the first animated object to appear in the slide during Slide Show. Now, let's repeat the procedure to move the other graphic image up the list so that it appears second:

**16.** Click the new object number 8 (Picture 1) to select it.

**17.** Click the *Move Earlier* re-order arrow once to renumber it to number 2 in the list.

Both graphic images will now appear on the slide in the first and second sequence.

**18.** Click the first object (32-Point Star) to select it again.

**19.** Examine the "Start" option box, near the right of the ribbon (as shown in Figure P-36a).

Note that it displays the phrase "On click." This indicates that the graphic image will appear on the slide only after you click the mouse. You can change the object's setting so that it will appear on the screen automatically:

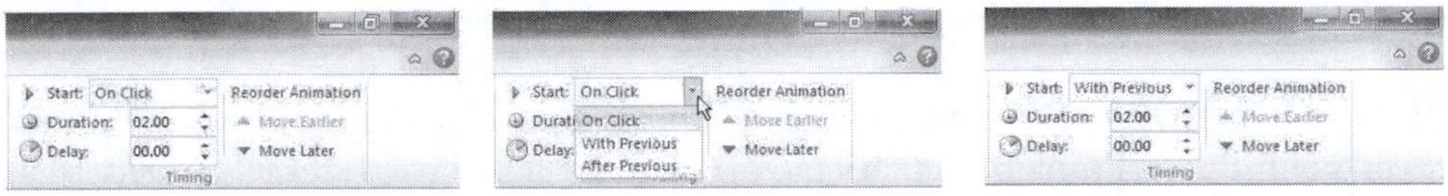

**FIGURE P-36**   *Setting Manual and Automatic Options*

(a)   Start option box.

(b)   Drop-down options.

(c)   Setting changed.

**20.** Using Figure P-36b as a guide, with the object still highlighted, click the Start option's drop-down arrow to open its menu.

**21.** Click the *With Previous* option.

As shown in Figure P-36c, the setting has been changed. The With Previous setting will cause the image to appear immediately when the slide opens. Since the object will appear immediately, note, too, that the object number has been set to "0." You can now change the setting for the second image as well (now identified as object #1):

**22.** Click *Picture1* in the list to select it.

**23.** With the object highlighted, click its Start option's drop-down arrow to open its menu.

**24.** Click the *After Previous* option.

This will tell PowerPoint to display the second image automatically, immediately after the first image has appeared.

> **NOTE:** If you had clicked the With Previous option, both graphics would appear at the same time on the screen. You can also change the "Delay" setting to increase the "wait" time. You may want to use this effect in the future.

**25.** Click the *Preview* button to see how the graphics appear automatically on the screen in animated form.

**26.** Click the *Home* tab.

**27.** Move to Slide 1.

**28.** Resave the presentation as OFFICE4.

P

## LESSON 10: GETTING IMAGES FROM THE WORLD WIDE WEB

If you have access to the Internet, you can capture images from the World Wide Web to place in your PowerPoint presentations. (If you do not have Internet access, just read through this section for future use.) The process is to visit a desired Web page using a Web browser—a program for accessing the Internet—and then "capture" an image for use. If you know the exact address of the Web page you wish to visit, you can go there directly or use an Internet search engine (such as Google or Yahoo) to locate an appropriate Web site. Once you learn the technique, feel free to surf the Web using a Web browser (such as Microsoft Internet Explorer, Netscape Navigator, Mozilla Firefox, or Opera) and then copy any images you may find there. Try this:

1.  Launch any Internet browser. (Internet Explorer is used as an example but any browser can be used.)

    You could search the Internet and locate a desired Web page, or type the address of the Internet Web page you want to open. Each Web page in the World Wide Web is identified by a unique address, known as a Uniform Resource Locator, or URL for short. Each URL is divided into three parts: a protocol, a domain (the computer where the page is located), and a path (folder and filename), as shown in the sample URL in Figure P-37.

**FIGURE P-37**    *A Sample URL*

Components of a typical Uniform Resource Locator.

Try this exercise to add an image from Wiley's Web page on the Internet to your OFFICE4 title slide:

2.  Click the *Address* entry line in the Internet browser and delete any current listing.

    You can now type the URL for Wiley, as follows:

3.  Type **http://www.wiley.com** and press ⏎.

4.  If a Dial-Up Connection dialog box appears, click *Connect* to continue.

    The desired Web site is loaded, and your screen should resemble Figure P-38 (the images and locations may differ slightly). You can now copy the desired image.

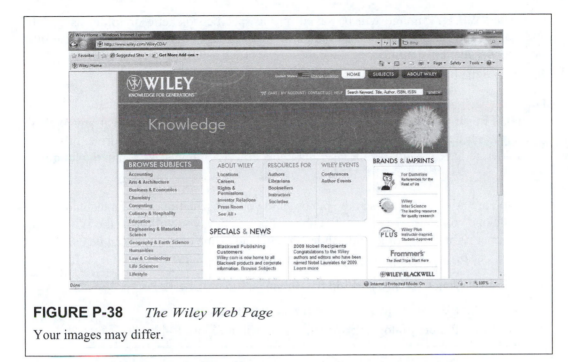

**FIGURE P-38**    *The Wiley Web Page*

Your images may differ.

5.   Locate, and then right-click the image of the Wiley logo, as shown in Figure P-39.

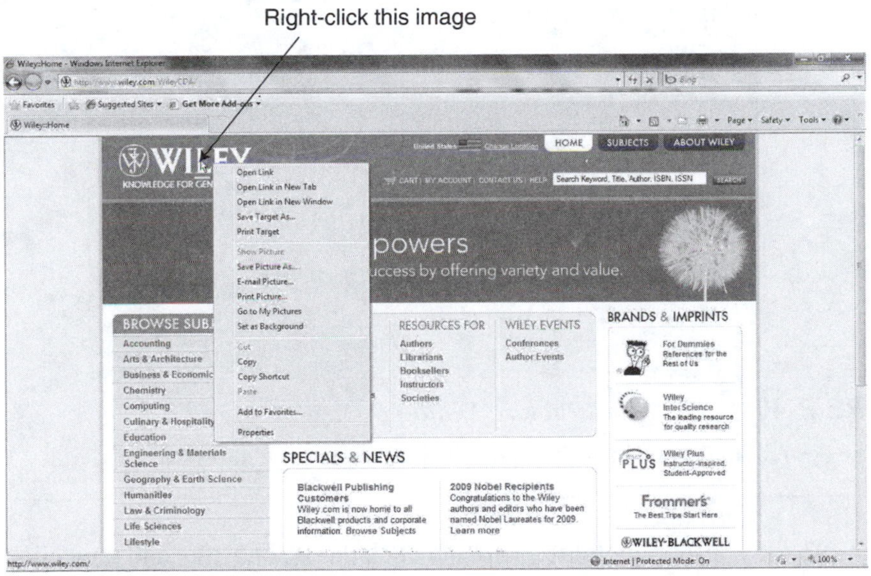

**FIGURE P-39**    *Selecting an Image from the World Wide Web*

After locating the correct Web page, right-click the desired image to open its shortcut menu.

6.   Click *Save Picture As* (or *Save Image As* depending on your browser) in the shortcut menu that appears.

7.   Select the appropriate Save in path for your system and then *Save* the file with the name "Wiley."

P

The "WILEY" image will be saved on the specified diskette or folder as a "GIF" file—a standard image format used on the Internet. (Images that you copy from the Internet may be saved in a number of standard formats such as GIF, JPEG, or BMP.)

**8.** Close the browser software window.

> **NOTE:** If you are familiar with your browser software, you can visit any Web page you desire, right-click an image, save it on your diskette, flash drive, or in a folder, to have it available for inserting into a PowerPoint presentation in the future.

You are now ready to insert the picture into your presentation, using a technique similar to the one you learned earlier with clip art. For practice, you will place the Wiley image in the upper right corner of the title slide (although any slide or position can be used).

**9.** Launch *PowerPoint* and open the OFFICE4 presentation.

**10.** In Slide 1, click the *Insert* tab in the ribbon.

**11.** Click the *Picture* command button (in the *Images* group).

An Insert Picture dialog box appears, as shown in Figure P-40.

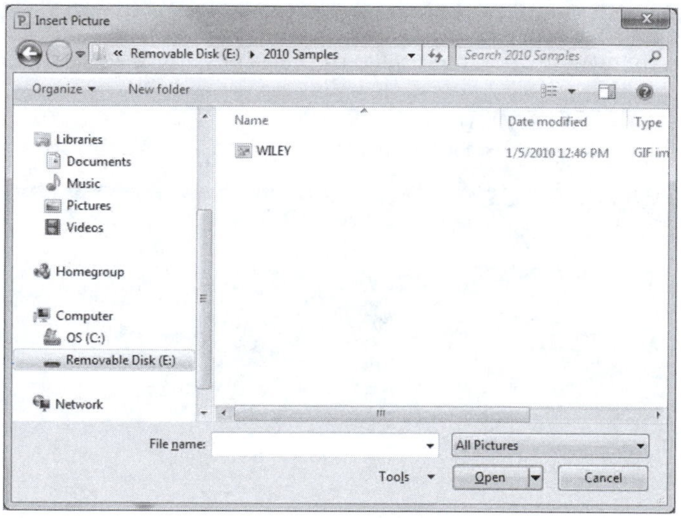

**FIGURE P-40**    *The Insert Picture Dialog Box*

Click the desired image and then click Insert to place the image into your slide.

**12.** Move to the appropriate folder, find and click the *WILEY* file, and then click *Insert*. The Wiley graphic appears near the center of the slide.

**13.** Resize the image slightly larger (this need not be exact) and then drag it to the upper-right corner of the slide, as shown in Figure P-41.

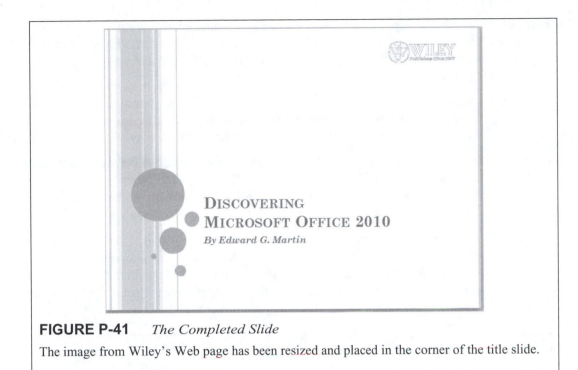

**FIGURE P-41**    *The Completed Slide*

The image from Wiley's Web page has been resized and placed in the corner of the title slide.

**14.** Resave the presentation as OFFICE4.

**15.** Run the Slide Show from the title slide to see the effect.

**16.** Close the OFFICE4 window when you are finished.

**17.** If you wish to stop, exit PowerPoint.

You have now completed this module. Try the Presentation Graphics projects to see if you can apply the basic techniques of the PowerPoint presentation program. Feel free to explore the many templates and effects that PowerPoint has to offer.

## PRESENTATION GRAPHICS PROJECTS

Complete these projects to see how well you've mastered basic presentation and graphic techniques in PowerPoint. You may want to write the project number, your name, and date on each printout to identify it.

**Project 1** *Module Overview I:* Using an appropriate layout and design of your choice, create a presentation that summarizes the module's first paragraph on page P-1. Create a title slide, and then include two more "bullet" list (Title and Content) slides: one entitled "Purpose" with a placeholder for a graphic, and the other entitled "Enhancements." Save the presentation as SHOW1. Print the three slides on one page, and then print a copy of the outline.

**Project 2** *Module Overview II:* Open the SHOW1 presentation that you created in Project 1. Change the design to another style. Add a clip art graphic to the Purpose slide, and add your own art from the Internet in the Enhancements slide. Save as SHOW2. Print the second and third slides only.

**P**

**Project 3** *Résumé I:* On a blank form, create a text-only presentation about yourself. Using this "video résumé," create a title and three additional slides that present information concerning your education, employment, and other skills and personal data. Save the presentation as SHOW3. Print an outline of your presentation.

**Project 4** *Résumé II:* Open SHOW3. Apply an appropriate color template for your presentation. Add clip art (or any graphics of your choice) to the education and personal slides to enhance them. Save as SHOW4 and print these two slides only.

**Project 5** *Résumé III:* Open SHOW4. Create interesting transitions between each slide. Add build effects on the slide with bulleted lists that will allow you to present each point separately. Animate the graphics of any slide. Save as SHOW5. Print two slides to a page and then, next to each slide, write in the transition, build, and animation effects you have chosen.

**Project 6** *Article:* Select an article from a recent newspaper or magazine. Using appropriate templates and effects, create a title slide that identifies the article, author, publication, date, and page number. Then create a presentation of no less than two additional slides that summarize the content of the article. Save as SHOW6 and print the slides. Attach the original (or photocopy) of the article to your project.

**Project 7** *Movie Presentation:* Using appropriate designs, art, and special effects, create an advertisement for a recent (or classic) movie of your choice. Your presentation should identify the movie, main actors, and studio, and provide a short synopsis of the plot. Save as SHOW7 and print the slides, three to a page. If you base your presentation on a printed advertisement, include the copy of the advertisement. (If you have Internet access, you may want to download appropriate graphics.)

**Project 8** *Television Ad:* Create a presentation about one of your favorite television programs (present or past). Select an appropriate design and clip art to complement the text. Identify the show's title, main characters, actors, channel, day, and time, and give a brief synopsis of the program. Save as SHOW8 and print slides six to a page.

**Project 9** *Travel Brochure:* Create a video travel brochure using appropriate templates, art, and effects that will highlight points of interest in your town, city, or state. Identify yourself as the contact person for more information. Save as SHOW9 and print the slides, three to a page.

**Project 10** *Party Invitation:* Create a one-page presentation to invite people to a celebration. Identify the reason to celebrate (holiday, anniversary, achievement, and so on), and the date, time, and place. Add clip art as needed. Save as SHOW10 and print the page.

## CONTINUING ON YOUR OWN—THINGS TO CONSIDER

This module has presented all the basic presentation graphics functions sufficient for almost every purpose. However, there are other topics beyond the scope of this module that will expand your presentation skills. You have gained enough experience and confidence to continue on your own using the reference manual that came with your program or the on-screen Help menus. Good luck! Here are some topics you might like to explore:

1.  Inserting date, time, or page numbers on each slide (headers and footers).
2.  Adding tables and charts to a slide.
3.  Incorporating graph data.
4.  Drawing ovals, arcs, and rotating graphics.
5.  Creating hidden slides.
6.  Creating branching slide presentations.
7.  Using the Spellcheck program.
8.  Changing tab settings and line spacing.
9.  Rehearsing and timing your presentation.
10. Automating the presentation.
11. Changing outline levels of bullets.
12. Adding SmartArt and WordArt.
13. Adding movies and media clips.
14. Modifying backgrounds.
15. Adjusting master slides.

**P**

## COMMAND SUMMARY—POWERPOINT 2010

**NOTE:** Ribbon command button is shown in BOLD CAPS followed by its location in parentheses—Tab (in italics) and Group—as in "**BOLD** (*Home*, Font)."

| | |
|---|---|
| ADD A NEW SLIDE: | **NEW SLIDE drop-down button** (*Home*, Slides) |
| ALIGN TEXT: | Select text, any **ALIGN** button (*Home*, Paragraph) |
| ANIMATE GRAPHIC: | **Custom Animation** (*Animations* tab) |
| APPLY INTERNET GRAPHIC: | In browser at a Website, right-click image, save as JPEG or BMP. |
| | In PowerPoint slide, **PICTURE** (*Insert*, Illustration), find and click the image file name, *Insert*. |
| APPLY A DESIGN THEME: | Any **THEME** (*Design*, Themes) |
| BEGIN POWERPOINT: | Double-click the PowerPoint icon or Start, *All Programs,* locate and click icon. |
| BUILD: | In slide, click placeholder, **CUSTOM ANIMATION** (*Animations*, Animation). |
| CANCEL A COMMAND: | ESC , click outside menu, or select Cancel |
| CLIP ART: | Add: **CLIPART** (*Insert*, Illustrations) |
| | Move: Click and drag image to new location |
| | Resize: Click corner handle and drag to size |
| CLOSE PRESENTATION: | *MS Office button*, *Close*, then *No* if needed |
| CREATE A PRESENTATION: | *MS Office button*, *New* |
| CUT TEXT or ART: | Select and DELETE |
| DELETE TEXT: | In placeholder, BACKSPACE erases to the left of insertion point; DELETE erases to the right. |
| DRAWING: | Click **SHAPE** drop-down (*Insert*, Illustrations) |
| EXIT POWERPOINT: | *MS Office button*, *Exit* or the Close button |
| FONT: | Any **FONT** button (*Home*, Font) |
| HELP: | **HELP** to start |
| INSERT TEXT: | Click placeholder or TAB ↵ ; type text and then click outside or TAB . |
| LAUNCH POWERPOINT: | See BEGIN POWERPOINT. |
| MOVE PLACEHOLDER: | Drag as needed or TAB to placeholder; use arrow keys to reposition, then ↵. |
| OPEN A FILE: | *MS Office button*, *Open*, highlight name, *OK* |
| PRINT: | *MS Office button*, *Print*, select option, and then *Print* |
| RULER: | *Ruler* check box in *View* tab |
| RUN SLIDE SHOW: | Click the *Slide Show* view selector button in status bar. |

| | |
|---|---|
| SAVE A PRESENTATION: | *MS Office Button*, *Save* or *Save As*, type name ⏎. |
| SCREEN (VIEW) MODES: | Any **VIEW SELECTOR** (*View*, Presentation Views) or status bar. |
| SPELLER: | `F7` |
| TRANSITIONS: | Any **TRANSITION** button, (*Animations*, Transition), set effect, set speed, *OK*. |

# APPENDIX

## SHARING DATA AMONG PROGRAMS

Microsoft Office is a *suite* program. That is, it is a collection of full-featured programs with similar commands that can work together as one program. You can transfer data from one application to another or work with more than one application at a time. This appendix will briefly introduce some of the basic techniques for sharing data among the applications you have learned. You are encouraged to explore other techniques on your own.

## SHARING DATA

There are four basic methods for sharing data among applications: moving, copying, embedding, and linking. As you have seen, *moving* deletes data in one location and transfers it to another location; *copying* duplicates data in another location without harming the original. *Embedding* is similar to copying except that it involves two or more applications. For example, you might embed part of an Excel worksheet into a Word document.

    *Linking* differs from the other methods because it not only copies data but also creates a *dynamic* connection between the original program (called the "source") and the new program (the "destination"). Whenever the source data are changed, the data in the linked destination are also automatically updated. For example, if you link an Excel worksheet with a Word document, any changes you make to the worksheet in the future will also appear in the Word document.

### Moving and Copying

As you have seen in earlier modules, you can move or copy data. Here's another technique using the mouse to "drag and drop" selected data to a new location. To move a sentence in Word, for example, you would do the following:

- First, identify the block. (Point to the start of the text, click and hold the mouse button, then move to the end of the desired block.) Then release the mouse button.

- Next, to move the block, point anywhere within the highlighted block, click and hold the mouse button, then drag the mouse to the new location and release. (To copy, press CTRL as you click and hold the mouse button.)

## Object Linking and Embedding

A block of data that you share betweens applications is known as an object. Objects are shared by either linking or embedding them. Your decision to link or embed an object depends on a number of factors, including the resultant file size (embedded files are larger), the need to update the object in the future, and the availability of the source document once the transfer is made. The following exercises will provide some insight into the basic techniques for both linking and embedding.

## LINKING AN OBJECT

You can link any Office object from one application to another. In this exercise you will link part of your WORK3 Excel worksheet to your SAMPLE2 Word document. To do this, follow these steps:

> **NOTE:** If needed, refer back to the appropriate module to review the method used to accomplish each of the following tasks:

1.   Start Windows.

2.   If appropriate, make sure your diskette is in the appropriate drive (or flash drive is available).

   When creating a link, start with the source document. In this case, the WORK3 worksheet in Excel.

3.   Launch Excel and open the WORK3 worksheet (from your diskette, flash drive, or folder).

4.   Identify the block (in this case, A3:E8) to be linked. (Click *cell A3* and then drag the mouse to *cell E8*.)

5.   Click the *Copy* command button (*Home* tab, *Clipboard* group) or press CTRL + **C**.

   The block of cells (the "object") has been copied into the Windows clipboard and is now available for linking.

6.   Launch Word and open the destination *document*—SAMPLE2.

7.   Move past the first paragraph, and press ↵ to enter a blank line.

8.   Click the *Paste* drop-down arrow (*Home* tab, *Clipboard* group).

9.   Click the *Paste Special* option in the list that appears. A Paste Special dialog box appears, as shown in Figure S-1.

10.   Click *Paste Link* to establish a linked object.

11.   If it is not already highlighted, click the *Microsoft Excel Worksheet Object* option in the list.

12.   Click *OK*.

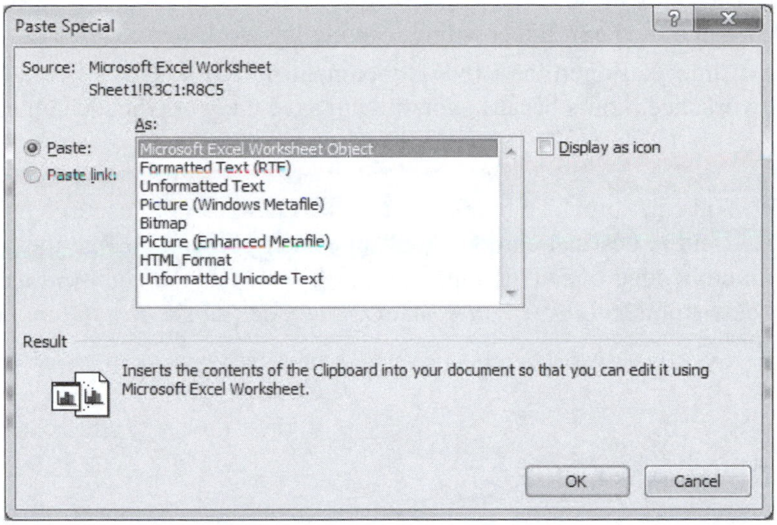

**FIGURE S-1**   *The Paste Special Dialog Box*

The selected portion of worksheet WORK3, which is still in Excel, appears within the Word document where the insertion point was positioned, as in Figure S-2. (Your column widths may differ.)

Using a word processor like Word 2010 is not as hard as it seemed to be before I began to use this manual. I am typing already and can't wait to try out every one of the other functions. As I type, the words appear on my screen. This is pretty easy. Soon I will learn how to save this document on a disk or flash drive. I hope I can learn how to use the program effectively.

| LAST | FIRST | HOURS | PAY | GROSS |
|------|-------|-------|-----|-------|
| DeGlass | Phil | 42 | $ 3.50 | $ 147.00 |
| Endime | Nicole | 35 | 2.50 | 87.50 |
| Graw | Marty | 50 | 3.25 | 162.50 |
| Daize | Sunny | 32 | 6.75 | 216.00 |

**FIGURE S-2**   *The Linked Object*

The worksheet from the Excel source has been linked into the Word destination document.

The object in Word is now linked to the original worksheet so that any changes you make in Excel will be reflected here as well. To see this, continue as follows:

13. Switch back to Excel (click the Excel button on the Windows taskbar or double-click the worksheet in Word).

14. Change Phil's hours in cell C5 to **50** and then press ⏎.

15. Switch back to *Word* (click the Word button on the Windows taskbar).

16. Point within the worksheet. Right-click it and then click the *Update Link* option.

    The linked object in Word has been updated to show the change in the block data.

**NOTE:** Word or Excel need not be active for this change to occur. The Word document would be updated the next time you opened it for use.

**17.** Save the amended Word document as LINK1.

**18.** Exit Word and then exit Excel without saving the worksheet.

The next time you open the LINK1 document in Word, Phil's hours should reflect the original worksheet hours because you did not save the worksheet changes in Excel.

> **NOTE:** You can "break" a link so that future changes in the source file will not be updated in the destination document. In effect, you can change the linked object to an embedded one. To do this in Word, for example, right-click the object (worksheet). Point to *Linked Worksheet Object*, click *Links*, *Break Link*, *OK*.

## EMBEDDING AN OBJECT

When you *embed* an object into an application, you are simply copying the data from one program into the new location. There is no dynamic link established between the two programs. The procedure is almost identical to the one for linking, as shown in the following example. When embedding an object, you must first create it or identify it. In this case, you will use the same block in the WORK3 worksheet.

> **NOTE:** Unlike copying, embedding does retain some connection to the source program that created the object. If you double-click on an embedded object, you will open the program from which it came for editing purposes.

**1.** Follow steps 1–7 in the previous exercise to identify the object.

**2.** Now that you are in Word, click the Paste command button (*Home* tab, *Clipboard* group).

The selected portion of worksheet WORK3 has been copied into the Word document. However, unlike a linked object, changes you may make in the original Excel worksheet will not affect this Word document. An embedded object is like a photograph that you take from one program and paste it into another. The photograph will not change in the future, even if the original object does.

**3.** Exit Word without saving the new document.

**4.** Exit Excel without saving the worksheet.

## MAIL MERGE

Another way to share information among programs is to use mail merge. *Mail merge* lets you combine data with a form letter (or other document) to create customized letters, labels, or other forms. Most often, you will take data from a database or worksheet, and have all (or some) of it automatically copied into a Word document. Although some initial work is required to set up a mail merge, it will save you many hours of typing individual letters or labels in the future.

The mail merge process involves five steps:

- Identify a *main document* that will be used for all the letters, forms, or labels.

- Link the main document to a *data source* which contains the data to be added.

- Modify the *list of recipients* (those for whom you want a letter generated).

- Add text and *mail merge fields* (data placeholders) to the main document.

- Preview and complete the *merge*.

To show you the technique, this exercise will merge data from an Excel worksheet into a Word form letter.

1. Start Windows if needed. If appropriate, make sure your diskette (or flash drive) is in the appropriate drive.

If an Excel worksheet is used as the data source, it must first be adjusted so that it can be understood by the mail merge. Your goal is to make the worksheet look like Figure S-3—that is, field names must appear in the top row, followed by the data rows. Each row contains the data for one record. To accomplish this, perform the following steps:

2. Launch Excel and open the WORK3 worksheet.

3. Delete rows 11, 10, 2, and 1 in this order. (Remember? Click in the frame identifier of the row, then click the *Delete* command button—*Home* tab, *Cells* group.)

**NOTE:** Deleting the rows in reverse order eliminates any confusion as rows are renumbered.

| | A | B | C | D | E |
|---|---|---|---|---|---|
| 1 | LAST | FIRST | HOURS | PAY | GROSS |
| 2 | | | | | |
| 3 | DeGlass | Phil | 42 | $ 3.50 | $ 147.00 |
| 4 | Endime | Nicole | 35 | 2.50 | 87.50 |
| 5 | Graw | Marty | 50 | 3.25 | 162.50 |
| 6 | Daize | Sunny | 32 | 6.75 | 216.00 |

**FIGURE S-3**    *The Excel Merge1 Data Source*

Modify the WORK3 worksheet to match this screen.

4. Save this worksheet as MERGE1 and then exit from Excel. The data source is now prepared for use in the merge.

5. Launch Word.

6. Click the *Mailings* tab, and then the *Start Mail Merge* command button (*Start Mail Merge* group).

At this point, a drop-down menu appears, as shown in Figure S-4.

**Step 1—Identify the Main Document:** Select the type of document you want to create (in this case, a letter).

7. If not already selected, click the Letters option in the menu.

**Step 2—Link to a Data Source:**

8. Click *Select Recipients* (*Start Mail Merge* group).

**FIGURE S-4**     *The Mail Merge Drop-Down Menu*

Here, you indicate the location of the data source (in this case, the MERGE1 worksheet you just created.)

9.  Click the *Use existing list* option in the menu.

A Select Data Source dialog box appears. This box works just like an Open dialog box. You simply identify the diskette, flash drive, or folder that contains your data file. Try this:

10. If the Look in entry is not correct, scroll down the left side and select the flash drive or folder where you saved the MERGE1 worksheet.

11. Click the MERGE1 file to select it.

12. Click the *Open* button.

The program recognizes your file as an Excel worksheet. Since this file has three sheets, you must now tell Mail Merge to use only the first sheet for the data.

13. In the Select Table dialog box that appears, click the Sheet 1$ option and then click *OK*.

### Step 3—Refine the List:

14. Click the *Edit Recipient List* command button.

A Mail Merge Recipients dialog box appears, as shown in Figure S-5. This box lets you specify which records you want to include in the mail merge. In the future, you could restrict the data by selecting various criteria in the top row (such as only specific zip codes, or amounts that exceed a specific value). You could also click individual rows to remove their checkmark, thus omitting that row from the mail merge. In this exercise, you do not want to empty rows of data to produce letters, so,

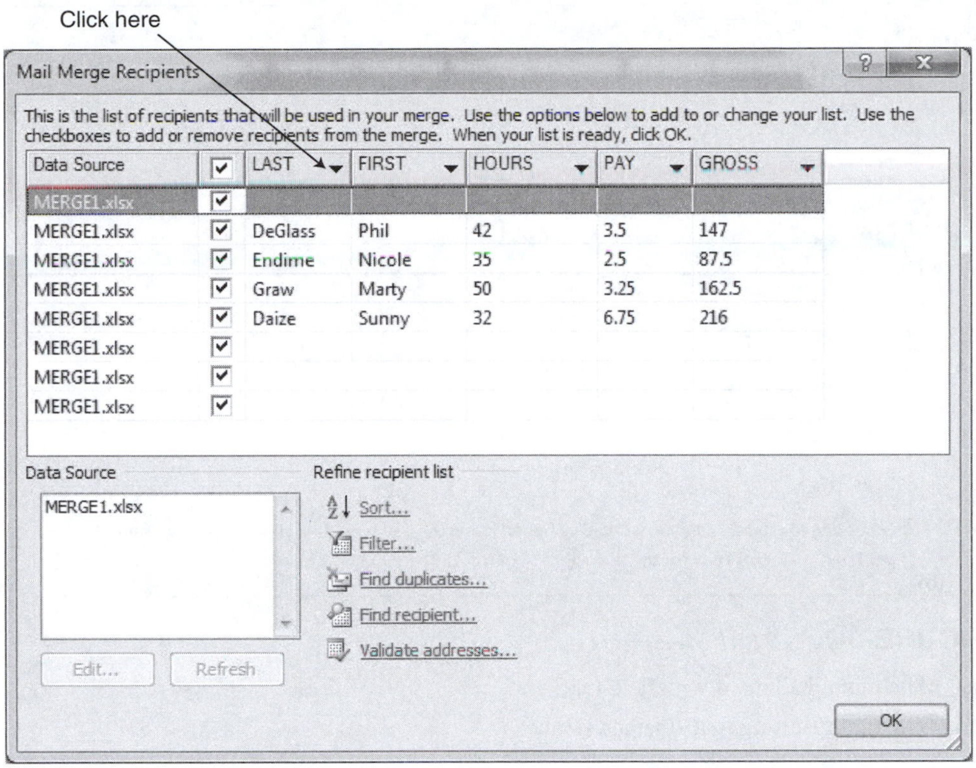

Click here

**Mail Merge Recipients**                                    ? X

This is the list of recipients that will be used in your merge. Use the options below to add to or change your list. Use the checkboxes to add or remove recipients from the merge. When your list is ready, click OK.

| Data Source | ☑ | LAST ▾ | FIRST ▾ | HOURS ▾ | PAY ▾ | GROSS ▾ |
|---|---|---|---|---|---|---|
| MERGE1.xlsx | ☑ | | | | | |
| MERGE1.xlsx | ☑ | DeGlass | Phil | 42 | 3.5 | 147 |
| MERGE1.xlsx | ☑ | Endime | Nicole | 35 | 2.5 | 87.5 |
| MERGE1.xlsx | ☑ | Graw | Marty | 50 | 3.25 | 162.5 |
| MERGE1.xlsx | ☑ | Daize | Sunny | 32 | 6.75 | 216 |
| MERGE1.xlsx | ☑ | | | | | |
| MERGE1.xlsx | ☑ | | | | | |
| MERGE1.xlsx | ☑ | | | | | |

Data Source

MERGE1.xlsx

Refine recipient list

↕ Sort...

🔽 Filter...

🔁 Find duplicates...

🔍 Find recipient...

✔ Validate addresses...

Edit...    Refresh

OK

**FIGURE S-5**    *The Mail Merge Recipients Dialog Box*

15. Click the drop-down arrow at the top of the first column (labeled "LAST"), as shown in Figure S-5.

16. Click the "(*Nonblanks*)" option.

The "Nonblanks" option tells mail merge to include only those records that have an entry in this column (LAST name). It will ignore any row that is blank. Note that now only the four employee rows (those with nonblank names) remain in the list.

17. Click *OK* to accept the list as is.

**Step 4—Add text and merge fields to the main document.** You are now ready to create your form letter.

18. Examine the ribbon at the top of the window (as shown in Figure S-6).

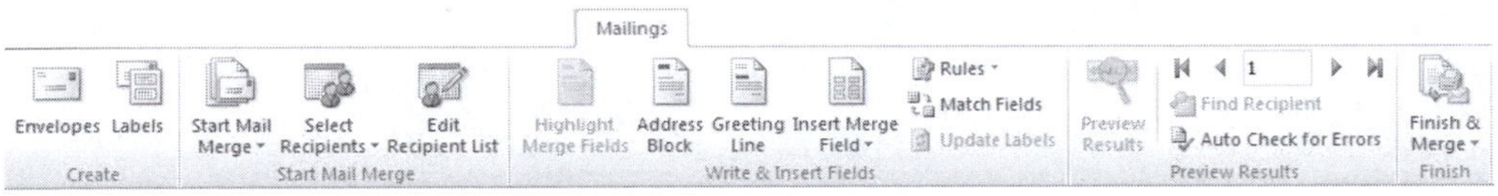

| Mailings |
|---|

Envelopes Labels | Start Mail Merge ▾  Select Recipients ▾  Edit Recipient List | Highlight Merge Fields  Address Block  Greeting Line  Insert Merge Field ▾  Rules ▾  Match Fields  Update Labels | Preview Results  Find Recipient  Auto Check for Errors | Finish & Merge ▾

Create | Start Mail Merge | Write & Insert Fields | Preview Results | Finish

**FIGURE S-6**    *The Merge Ribbon*

Let's assume that you want to create a short notice as in Figure S-7 for each record (row) in the MERGE1 worksheet.

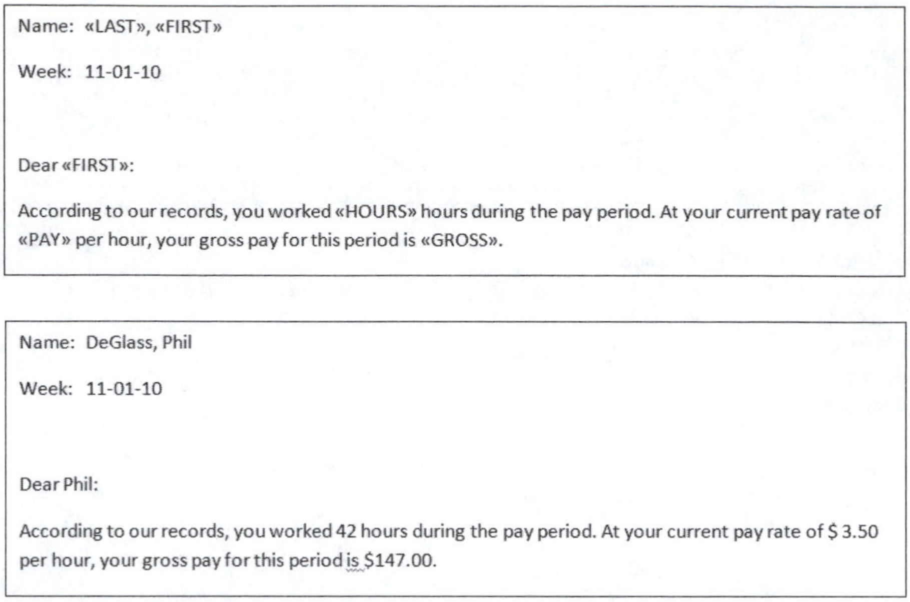

Name:  «LAST», «FIRST»

Week:  11-01-10

Dear «FIRST»:

According to our records, you worked «HOURS» hours during the pay period. At your current pay rate of «PAY» per hour, your gross pay for this period is «GROSS».

(a)

Name:  DeGlass, Phil

Week:  11-01-10

Dear Phil:

According to our records, you worked 42 hours during the pay period. At your current pay rate of $ 3.50 per hour, your gross pay for this period is $147.00.

(b)

**FIGURE S-7**    *Mail Merge*

(a)   The main document with field markers.

(b)   The first resulting mail-merged notice.

To do this, you will create a form, as shown in Figure S-7a, that tells Word where to place the data from each desired field. Using Figure S-7a as a guide, do the following:

**19.** Type **Name**: and then press TAB.

**20.** Click the *Insert Merge Field* command drop-down button (*Write & Insert Fields* group) as in Figure S-8a to place a field marker in the document.

A drop-down list appears, as shown in Figure S-8b, listing the five available worksheet fields, namely, LAST, FIRST, HOURS, PAY, and GROSS. To insert a field into your document, you simply click the desired field, click Insert, and then close the dialog box, as follows:

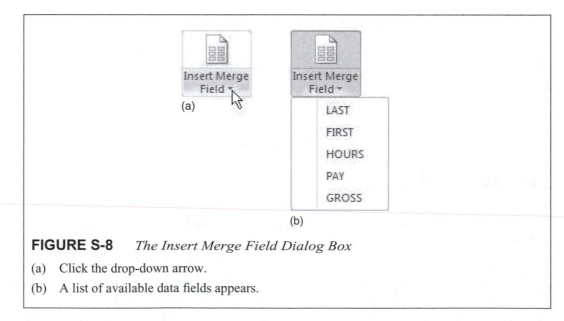

**FIGURE S-8**    *The Insert Merge Field Dialog Box*

(a)   Click the drop-down arrow.

(b)   A list of available data fields appears.

**21.** Click LAST.

A field marker for the LAST field appears on the screen, indicating that "LAST" data will be placed here when the form is merged.

**22.** You want a comma and space to follow the last name, so type a comma (,) and then press [SPACE].

**23.** Click the *Insert Merge Field* drop-down arrow to insert a field marker for FIRST.

**24.** Press [↵] to move to the next line.

> **NOTE:** To remove an incorrect field marker from the document, click the left arrows of the field marker (<<), drag the mouse past the right arrows (>>) to select the entire marker, and then press the [DELETE] key.

**25.** Type **Week:** and then press [TAB].

**26.** For now, type any date, such as *11-01-10*, and then press [↵] twice to move down two lines in the document.

Since it is text, this date will appear unchanged on all the forms that are created.

**27.** Type **Dear** and press [SPACE].

**28.** Insert a merge field marker for FIRST, then type a colon (:) and press [↵].

**29.** Type **According to our records, you worked** and press [SPACE].

**30.** Insert a merge field marker for HOURS and press [SPACE].

**31.** Now type **hours during this pay period. At your current pay rate of**

**32.** Press [SPACE] and then insert a merge field marker for PAY.

**33.** Press [SPACE] and type **per hour, your gross pay for this period is**

**34.** Press [SPACE] and then insert a field marker for GROSS.

**35.** Type a period (.) to end the sentence and press [↵].

This brief document is almost finished, except for one last step. In this particular example, you want the numeric data for PAY and GROSS to appear as currency (money) with dollar signs and two decimal places. Unfortunately, mail merge does not copy formatting. You must, therefore, add a "numeric picture switch" that provides Word with an example of how the number should appear. (There are many switches that you can add to mail merge markers to change their format. Feel free to explore these using Word's help feature in the future.) For now, here's the basic technique:

**36.** Press [ALT] + [F9] (press and hold the Alt key, press the F9 function key and then release both) to display field codes.

Your screen now displays the word "MERGEFIELD" before each field name. To add a switch to change the PAY format:

**37.** Click just after the word PAY, as shown in Figure S-9a.

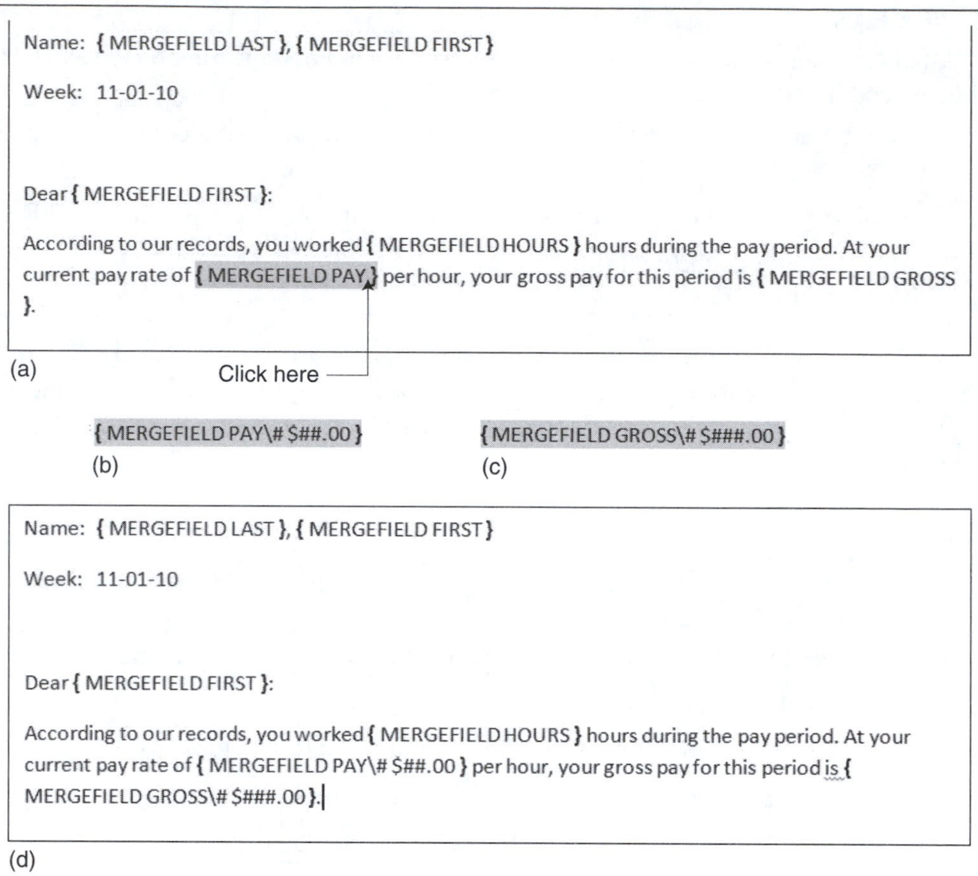

Name: { MERGEFIELD LAST }, { MERGEFIELD FIRST }

Week:  11-01-10

Dear { MERGEFIELD FIRST }:

According to our records, you worked { MERGEFIELD HOURS } hours during the pay period. At your current pay rate of { MERGEFIELD PAY } per hour, your gross pay for this period is { MERGEFIELD GROSS }.

(a)                    Click here

{ MERGEFIELD PAY\# $##.00 }          { MERGEFIELD GROSS\# $###.00 }
(b)                                  (c)

Name: { MERGEFIELD LAST }, { MERGEFIELD FIRST }

Week:  11-01-10

Dear { MERGEFIELD FIRST }:

According to our records, you worked { MERGEFIELD HOURS } hours during the pay period. At your current pay rate of { MERGEFIELD PAY\# $##.00 } per hour, your gross pay for this period is { MERGEFIELD GROSS\# $###.00 }.

(d)

**FIGURE S-9**   *ADDING A FORMAT "SWITCH"*

(a)   Click after the field name.
(b)   Type \# followed by the desired format.
(c)   Type the GROSS format.
(d)   Field markers have been placed.

**38.** Type **\# $##.00**

Your screen should resemble Figure S-9b. The "\#" tells mail merge that a numeric switch is being added to this field. The "$" symbol and decimal point show where these symbols will appear. The number sign ("#") and zero ("0") symbols are numeric place-holders. A zero means that a digit (0-9) must appear in that spot; a "#" sign means that a digit should only appear there if the value is large enough. For example, the format of $##.00 will include a dollar sign and decimal point, and leaves space for a four-digit value (up to 99.99) to be displayed. The # symbols will allow a digit to appear here only if the data value is large enough. Using two zeroes after the decimal point require that two decimal places must appear. For example, using this format, .5 would appear as $.50; 3.4 would look like $3.40, and 82.56 would appear as $82.56. Note that all the values have a dollar sign and 2 decimal places, even though they do not have the same number of digits to the left of the decimal. (Using the format $00.00 would produce strange looking values, such as $00.50 and $03.40 for example.)

**NOTE:** You can place as many "#" symbols and zeroes as you desire to fit your expected data. For example, the format of $#,###.00 would allow for numbers up to 9,999.99 and also include a comma only if the number is 1,000 or greater.

Now for the GROSS. This number is typically going to be larger than the PAY. Here, you want to leave space for a value that probably exceeds 100, but will never be greater than 1,000. You will leave an extra placeholder as follows:

**39.** Click just after the word GROSS.

**40.** Type \# **$###.00** as shown in Figure S-9c.

**41.** Now click outside the field marker to deselect it. The field markers for PAY and GROSS should resemble those in Figure S-9d. Fix them if they do not.

**42.** Press ⎡ALT⎤ + ⎡F9⎤ to close the field codes display. Your document now simply shows the field marker names and their position in the document. Compare your screen to Figure S-8a.

You can now see how the final pages will appear by viewing the merged data before you actually invoke the merge command, as follows:

**43.** Click the *Preview Results* command button (*Preview Results* group). The first record's data should replace the field markers, as shown in Figure S-7b.

**44.** To see how other letters will appear when merged, click the *Next Record* arrow key in the *Preview Results* group to move forward through your list of recipients. Click the *Previous Record* arrow key to move back. Try it. Note how the data change for each record.

Once you are satisfied with the appearance of the document, you could print the entire merge by clicking the *Print* option or create and save the merged document by clicking the *Finish & Merge* command button (*Finish* group). Clicking this option allows you to edit the letters further before actually printing and saves the results of your work. Finish with the following step:

**45.** Click the *Finish & Merge* command button (*Finish* group) in the menu.

**46.** In the list that appears, click the *Edit Individual Documents* (Merge to New Docs) option.

A Merge to New Document dialog box appears.

**47.** Click *OK*.

A new document ("Letters1") is created with four pages—one letter for each employee selected in the data source. You could now move through the entire document, edit it as desired, save it, print it, or do anything else as you would with any Word document. For now,

**48.** Close this document without saving it.

**49.** Click the *Preview Results* button to shut it off.

**50.** Now, save the form letter as MERGE.

**51.** Close the document.

## Mail Merge in the Future

Once a mail merge document and data source have been created and linked, the hard work is done. Whenever you want to generate these form letters in the future, you could go into the data source (in this case, the Excel MERGE1 worksheet), edit the data (add more employees or change their data), and then simply bring up the merge document in Word. Refer to Figure S-6 to locate each of the buttons mentioned. Try this to see the effect:

1. Open the MERGE document in Word.

2. If a dialog box appears, click *Yes*.

3. Click the *Mailings* tab.

4. Click the *Edit Recipient List* button (*Start Mail Merge* group).

5. In the dialog box that appears, click the "LAST" column drop-down arrow, and then click the (Nonblanks) option.

6. Click *OK*.

7. To see your data, click the *Preview Results* command button and then click the *Next Record* or *Previous Record* toolbar buttons to move through the data.

8. To actually merge the data, click the *Finish & Merge* command button. Get the idea?

9. Close all documents without saving.

A final note: This brief introduction has presented some basic data-sharing techniques. You are encouraged to explore the use of linked and embedded objects, mail merge, and other data conversions that will help you exchange data with programs outside Microsoft Office.

# INDEX